Critical Security Studies

An introduction, 2nd edition

Columba Peoples and Nick Vaughan-Williams

Routledge
Taylor & Francis Group

LONDON AND NEW YORK

First published 2015
by Routledge
2 Park Square, Milton Park, Abingdon, Oxon OX14 4RN

and by Routledge
711 Third Avenue, New York, NY 10017

Routledge is an imprint of the Taylor & Francis Group, an informa business

British Library Cataloguing-in-Publication Data
A catalogue record for this book is available from the British Library

Library of Congress Cataloging-in-Publication Data
Peoples, Columba, author.
Critical security studies : an introduction / Columba Peoples and Nick Vaughan-Williams. – Second edition.
pages cm
Includes bibliographical references and index.
1. Security, International. 2. National security. I. Vaughan-Williams, Nick, author. II. Title.
JZ5599.P46 2015
355'.033–dc23
2014007901

ISBN: 978-0-415-84183-2 (hbk)
ISBN: 978-0-415-84184-9 (pbk)
ISBN: 978-0-203-76423-7 (ebk)

Typeset in Times by
FiSH Books Ltd, Enfield

Critical Security Studies

Critical Security Studies introduces students to the sub-field through a detailed yet accessible survey of evolving approaches and key issues. This second edition contains two new chapters and has been fully revised and updated.

Written in an accessible and clear manner, *Critical Security Studies*:

- offers a comprehensive and up-to-date introduction to critical security studies
- locates critical security studies within the broader context of social and political theory
- evaluates fundamental theoretical positions within critical security studies in application to key issues.

The book is divided into two main parts. The first part, 'Approaches', surveys the newly extended and contested theoretical terrain of critical security studies: Critical Theory, feminism and gender theory, postcolonialism, poststructuralism and securitisation theory. The second part, 'Issues', then illustrates these various theoretical approaches against the backdrop of a diverse range of issues in contemporary security practices, from environmental, human and homeland security to border security, technology and warfare, and the war against terrorism. This edition also includes new chapters on constructivist theories (Part I) and health (Part II).

The historical and geographical scope of the book is deliberately broad and readers are introduced to a number of key illustrative case studies. Each of the chapters in Part II concretely illustrate one or more of the approaches discussed in Part I, with clear internal referencing allowing the text to act as a holistic learning tool for students.

This book is essential reading for upper-level students of critical security studies, and an important resource for students of international/global security, political theory and international relations.

Columba Peoples is Senior Lecturer in International Relations in the School of Sociology, Politics and International Studies, University of Bristol, UK.

Nick Vaughan-Williams is Reader in International Security in the Department of Politics and International Studies, University of Warwick, UK.

Contents

List of illustrations

Figures

Tables

Boxes

Acknowledgements

The authors would like to acknowledge the following people for their help and support in the genesis, writing and production of this book. At Aberystwyth University, Columba's interest in the subject was originally sparked by Richard Wyn Jones and Mike Williams through their teaching and subsequent supervision. On-going conversations and critical engagements with both ever since have provided a constant source of encouragement for this project. Nick's time co-teaching Critical Security Studies with Ken Booth, also in Aberystwyth, was rewarding and instrumental in developing his interest in the field. Nick would also like to pay tribute to the undergraduate and postgraduate students who have taken his modules at the University of Exeter and the University of Warwick for many inspirational discussions. Likewise Columba would like to acknowledge the invaluable input and feedback received from undergraduate students over the years on his Critical Security Studies module at the University of Bristol. Our ideas for the book benefited from the thoughtful and supportive comments of nine anonymous reviewers on proposals for both editions; their advice proved immensely useful during the writing process. We are grateful to João Nunes for discussing the new chapter on health with us at an early stage in its development; and to Cian O' Driscoll and contributors to the Glasgow Global Security Network seminar on 'The Past and Future of Critical Security Studies' for their feedback on the project as a whole. Thanks are due to Drew Ellis, Martin Millard and Mary Weir at Bristol for their help in providing the illustrations used in the text. We would also like to thank the staff at Routledge, particularly Andrew Humphrys and Hannah Ferguson, for their assistance in producing the book. Finally, Nick would like to thank Madeleine and Helena, and Columba would like to thank Julie and Cillian and Darragh for all their support.

Preface to the second edition

Since the publication of the first edition of *Critical Security Studies: An Introduction* in 2010, the field of critical security studies has expanded rapidly. The approaches and issues identified in the first edition of the text remain key reference points. But as befiting an area of study that is in large part characterised by its intellectual vitality, new work has applied, extended and critiqued those approaches; and developments in the issue-areas covered in the first edition attest not only to their continuing salience, but also the need to examine those issues afresh. This second edition has been revised and fully updated to reflect the evolution of the theoretical approaches and issues covered in the text. Each of the chapters from the first edition, whilst retaining the core of the material and arguments, has been extended accordingly. As well as being updated throughout, substantive new additions to this second edition include discussions of: historical materialism as a potentially distinctive way of envisaging the contribution of Critical Theory to the study of security; the (re)turn to materiality, understood in a different sense, within poststructuralist and international political sociology approaches; the study of security narratives and militarised masculinity within feminist and gender approaches; the concepts of risk and resilience, particularly in the context of homeland security and the war against terrorism; and the privatisation of security as a seemingly ever-intensifying aspect of warfare in the information age. The publication of this new edition has also allowed for greater attention to 'constructivist theories' in Part I of the text. Previously covered briefly in the Introduction to the first edition, the addition of this new chapter allows readers to consider at length both the general significance of social construction in relation to critical security studies and the plurality of constructivist theories of security. In Part II the addition of another new chapter on health reflects both the extent to which global health issues are increasingly viewed through the lens of security and the way in which critical scholarship in this area now provokes us also to consider the 'medicalisation' of security discourse and practices in contemporary global politics. As is exemplified by these new chapters, what remains distinctive about the book as a whole is that it challenges and encourages readers to delve deeper into the political-theoretical roots and normative agendas of critical approaches to the study of security, and to explore different avenues for issue-based research drawn from those approaches. With new and updated text boxes to enhance understanding of key concepts, thinkers and debates, revised questions for discussion, and a refreshed guide to further reading, the second edition of *Critical Security Studies: An Introduction* aims to continue to support teaching and learning in this vibrant sub-discipline.

Introduction

Mapping critical security studies and travelling without maps

Abstract

This introductory chapter situates the text within the existing literature and field of international security, aiming in particular to identify the meaning(s) of the term 'critical security studies'. We begin with an overview and evaluation of three dominant ways in which the field of security studies has previously been mapped and how critical security studies is usually placed within these mappings: an intellectual map; a temporal map (or timeline); and a spatial map. Assessing the merits and disadvantages of each mapping, the introduction then outlines the chapter structure and pedagogical features of the book as a whole.

This book aims to introduce readers to the burgeoning field of critical security studies. Readers are likely to be wondering what security is and what it means to adopt a critical stance in the study of it. The fact that there is no universally agreed answer to each of these questions, however, immediately flags both the complexity and vibrancy of this area of research. For a start, the use of the prefix 'critical' is particularly vexed. It is difficult to imagine any approach to the study of security, or any other area of intellectual inquiry, that would claim to be 'uncritical'. Reference to 'critical' work is therefore a rhetorical device that must be recognised, understood and interrogated as such. There is no singular definition of what it means to be critical in security studies – and any rigid definition of the term critical security studies will tell you more about the position from which that definition is attempted than anything else. Rather, there is an array of different perspectives that has become associated with this term. Among these perspectives there are crisscrossing lines of convergence and divergence over the object, method and implications of being 'critical'. In this book we do not wish to get too caught up in the trap of imposing what we think critical security studies *is* or *ought* to be. This seems to us to be neither possible, given the radically different starting points taken by various critical approaches, nor necessarily desirable in light of the plurality of intellectual approaches these different starting points give rise to. Instead, this introduction is driven by claims made about 'criticality' in the literature that we survey, and by examining the way different approaches critically assess contemporary issues. In other words, we take the boundaries of 'critical' security studies to be defined by those who frame their work using this label. By consequence this text provides an overview of multiple critical studies *of* security issues and practices rather than an attempt to present a homogeneous or monolithic area of research, and in doing so recognises that there are internal boundaries (and boundary disputes) between these various approaches as well.

As indicated above, the term 'critical' can be used in various ways and evades easy definition. However, the concept of security is in many ways no less contested. The once dominant association of the concept of security with military threats, and with the protection of the state – or 'national security', the study of which has in turn provided the original foundation for disciplinary security studies – is no longer unquestioned. Indeed, it would be overly simplistic to think that such an understanding of the concept of security was ever completely taken for granted. Arnold Wolfers, one of the founding fathers of the realist approach to security that tends towards this 'traditional' definition of security, acknowledged early on that national security itself is, at best, 'an ambiguous symbol' (Wolfers 1952) that can be defined in multiple ways. The precise definition of what it means to be secure, the causes of insecurity, and who or what the concept of security should apply to, have long been debated. Some have even been led to conclude that security is an 'essentially contested concept' (Baldwin 1997: 10): a concept that is identifiable primarily by the lack of shared agreement over its meaning. It is this space for ambiguity and contestation that in turn opens the way (and some would say creates a necessity for) critical approaches to security. The concept of security is itself contested, yet it also remains central to our understanding of the world and has powerful effects when applied to particular issues (Huysmans 1998a). On this basis alone, therefore, the study of security remains a particularly appropriate site for the application of critical approaches.

Leaving aside for the moment the particular ways in which different approaches to security define (or are defined) as 'critical', it is worth noting that the derivation of the term from the Greek *kritikos* refers to an 'ability to make judgements', from *krinein*, meaning to 'separate', 'discriminate', 'decide' (Williams 1976: 74–76). This, it could be argued, is a minimally shared commonality between different critical approaches to security: they are all constantly involved in judgements about what security means, and in deciding and discriminating what the objects and objectives of security studies should be. Moreover, and crucially, critical approaches to security recognise these tasks as central to their intellectual activity. They all, in different ways, refute the idea that security has a constant or definitively settled meaning and content that can be taken for granted. In their landmark 1997 edited volume, *Critical Security Studies: Concepts and Cases*, Keith Krause and Michael C. Williams proposed a broad and flexible understanding of the term critical security studies that also follows from this point:

> Our appending of the term critical to security studies is meant to imply more an orientation toward the discipline [of security studies] than a precise theoretical label. [. . .] If the objective (or at least the outcome) of much scholarship in security studies has been to render the question and problem of security apolitical and largely static, critical theory takes the question of change as its foundation, in both an explanatory and an evaluative sense.
>
> (Krause and Williams 1997: xii)

It is in this vein – one that reads critical security studies as an 'orientation' rather than in terms of a 'precise theoretical label' – that we want to situate this introductory text. The Krause-Williams volume remains a pioneering collection of important theoretical and empirical interventions that have helped shape critical security studies as a pluralistic field. By now, however, there have been several major developments since the publication of that text that demand contemporary coverage and assessment. The period since 1997, for example, has witnessed the development of various theoretical innovations that are covered in the proceeding chapters. In terms of emerging issues, the field has seen increasing scholarly attention given to areas formerly marginalised in the study of security, such as environmental degradation, aid and development, health, migration and international terrorism, among others. There have also been fresh appraisals of the nature and value of critical security studies, its relationship with international relations (IR), 'mainstream' security studies and other disciplines, and how best to characterise the field and its component parts.

In this context an updated assessment of critical approaches to security, taking into consideration the mushrooming of such enterprises since the mid- to late-1990s, seems both necessary and timely. Of course, there are other introductions to critical security studies available, varying from chapter-length considerations (Mutimer 2010) to book-length treatments, which consider different methodologies (Salter and Mutlu 2013; Shepherd 2013b) and the field in relation to IR theory (Fierke 2007) and security studies as a whole (Buzan and Hansen 2009; Collins 2010; Sheehan 2005; Williams 2008). This volume is distinctive, however, in that we take as our running focus the political-theoretical underpinnings of such critical approaches to security. By locating seemingly different perspectives within the wider terrain of political theory (and social theory more broadly), we want to suggest that more sophisticated – and layered – appreciations of critical security studies might emerge. Critical approaches to security do not, after all, exist in a vacuum, and by analysing how various theoretical currents have flowed through and shaped each of these theoretical enterprises we hope to demonstrate the way in which critical security studies can be thought of as comprising a continuum of approaches that in many respects defy straightforward categorisation. As an initial step towards this updated assessment, we first review some of the most prominent ways of representing – or mapping – the field of critical security studies.

Mapping the field of critical security studies

What is at stake in mapping the field of critical security studies? The 'map' metaphor has been popular in surveys of critical approaches to security (Buzan and Hansen 2009; Smith 2000; Wyn Jones 1996). Maps of this sort can of course be incredibly helpful, especially when there is an absence of familiarity with the subject matter. They provide an overview of a terrain of study and a sense of certainty about where things are in relation to each other. When reflecting on the maps used to navigate critical approaches to security as they have developed over recent decades it is possible to identify three dominant narratives. The first is an intellectual narrative based on the negative definition of critical approaches to security against more 'traditional' perspectives. The second is a range of temporal narratives used to make claims about the trajectory of the development of critical security studies in relation to historical events and discourses about the 'beginnings' and 'endings' of different periods. The third concerns a set of spatial narratives that emphasises the emergence of different 'schools of thought', each anchored by a geographical referent point (Aberystwyth, Copenhagen and Paris).

Part of the aim of this introduction is to flesh out these dominant narratives in order to provide an acquaintance with some of the chief efforts that have been made to understand and define the emergence of a field of critical security studies. As with any emerging area of study, critical security studies is also marked by the development and use of a distinctive lexicon that is worth noting at this point. Though these three mappings have different emphases, it is possible to identify a series of key concepts, outlined below, which are shared across these mappings and are also frequently referred to later in the text.

From 'traditional' to 'critical'

One of the dominant intellectual narratives used to map the emergence of critical security studies involves the invocation of 'traditional' approaches to security against which more

---

Box I.1 Key concepts in critical security studies

Referent object: An entity that is taken as the focus for analysis in security studies (e.g. the state, the human, the ecosystem); or, put differently, 'that which is to be secured'.

Traditional approaches/traditional security studies: A shorthand, most commonly used by writers in or sympathetic to critical security studies, which refers to realist, liberal, peace studies and strategic studies perspectives in the study of security that prioritise the state as the referent object of security, and focus primarily on military threats to the security of the state (sometimes also known as a 'state-centric' approach).

Broadening: The broadening of the security agenda relates to the move away from a narrow focus on the military sector to analysis of issues in other sectors (e.g. environmental, economic, political and societal spheres).

Deepening: The deepening of theoretical approaches relates to the idea that the state is not the only referent object of security.

Normative: A normative position is one that explicitly takes a stance on what *should* or *ought* to be analysed, achieved and/or secured.

Positivism: Refers to a theory of knowledge that argues it is possible to apply scientific principles of objectivity, replication, verification/falsification and generalisation – used to study the natural world – to the study of society (and security).

Post-positivism: Refers to a series of approaches, including many critical approaches to security, that reject the idea that it is possible to analyse the natural and social world in the same way. These approaches emphasise the point that truth claims can never be grounded; there is no objective view from nowhere, outside history and politics, from which we might take a neutral position.

Security as a derivative concept: The idea, common among critical approaches to security, that the way we think about security derives from the way we think the world works more broadly.

'critical' variants are then defined. Commonly, the notion of traditional security studies refers to work associated with the broader approach to international relations known as political realism, in both its 'classical' and 'structural' (or 'neo-realist') variants. As with most categorisations of this sort, this blanket term covers over a diverse range of thinkers and ideas, but at base political realism is usually seen to emphasise the state as the main object of security, and war as the main threat to it. In the classical vein, Walter Lippmann argued in the early 1940s that 'A nation is secure to the extent to which it is not in danger of having to sacrifice core values, if it wishes to avoid war, and is able, if challenged, to maintain them by victory in such a war' (Lippmann 1943: 51, cited in Ayoob 1997: 124). Similarly, neo-realist Stephen Walt has defined security studies as 'the study of the threat, use, and control of military force', which is frequently cited as a reflection of the overall position. According to Walt's perspective, the essence of international security is competition for power among states, understood in terms of coercive capability (military strength). In this view, therefore, security is viewed narrowly in terms of the survival of the state. The state is taken to be the primary 'referent object' that is to be secured and, as the quotation from Walt illustrates, the focus is predominantly on the military sector and on other issues only to the extent that they 'bear directly on the likelihood and character of war' (Walt 1991: 212–213). Working from the basis that all states seek increased security, and will consequently seek to augment their military strength where possible, Realist security studies have focused particularly on the concept of a 'security dilemma'. Developed primarily in the context of the nuclear threat in the cold war period, the security dilemma denotes a situation whereby the move to secure one state leads to the insecurity of another – since there can always be an ambiguity over whether an increase in military capability is for protection or for conquest – and hence to a cycle of insecurity between states (Herz 1950).

Political realism, though dominant in the study of security for most of the twentieth century, is not the only 'traditional' (i.e. 'non-critical') perspective against which critical security studies has been defined, however. An assorted cohort of peace researchers, war historians, arms controllers and those working broadly within liberal traditions of international politics, might also be said to fall under the banner of traditional approaches. While these perspectives differ from realism in some respects (such as the prospects for cooperation among states), they all share a common commitment to thinking security within the context of a military security agenda. Reviewing liberal and realist approaches to security, Patrick M. Morgan concludes that, for both, 'Security has long been about the survival and physical safety of the actors and their people; by extension it concerns the *deliberate* use of force by states (and some other actors) for various purposes' (Morgan 2000: 40, emphasis in original). Liberals may make much greater allowance for potential constraint of force than Realists, but their object of concern remains fundamentally the same. In addition, these perspectives occupy similar ground theoretically. With few exceptions, this work is typically committed to a positivist problem-solving mode of inquiry that largely takes 'prevailing social and power relationships and the institutions into which they are organized' – namely states – 'as the given framework for action' (Cox 1981).

In this intellectual narrative, discussed in more detail in Chapter 2 in particular, the emergence of critical security studies as a sub-field of the discipline of security studies is bound up with various moves away from the state-centric militarism of the traditional orthodoxy. These moves can be summarised with reference to the so-called 'broadening' and 'deepening' of the security agenda. The former relates to the expansion of the analytical horizon of the study of security beyond the military sector to encompass environmental, economic, political and societal spheres (Buzan 1991). The latter is a term used to refer to extension of the referent object of security beyond simply the state to incorporate other actors such as institutions, human individuals and groups, and even the biosphere. In short, this intellectual mapping functions by defining critical security studies in terms of what it is not: namely, traditional or state-centric security studies. Traditional security studies implies a circumscribed focus on war and the state and, conversely, adoption of a critical approach entails making allowance for a more expansive agenda.

As always, the problem with such bipolar characterisations is that they tend to obscure the grey areas that often lie between and within opposed positions. Characterising 'traditional' approaches in this manner, for example, runs the constant risk of reducing and simplifying extensive and often diverse bodies of thought to function primarily as a stalking horse for the purposes of distinguishing a countervailing 'critical approach'. Some have argued, for example, that the traditions of both political realism and political liberalism in the study of international relations and security is often more complex and variegated than this (see, for example, Williams 2013). Similarly, such bipolar characterisations have the attendant risk of creating distinct oppositional categories or 'boxes' into which approaches to the study of security may not easily fit. At the hinge between traditional and critical approaches to security, for instance, we find 'constructivism', which has seen its own bifurcation into 'conventional' and 'critical' camps, as is discussed in more detail in Chapter 1. Constructivist theories of security, though often categorised with the catchall term of 'constructivism', actually diverge on several points. Whereas conventional constructivism might be said to leave key assumptions of traditional security studies fundamentally unchallenged, a more self-consciously 'critical' strand of social constructivism has also emerged and grown. At a broad level, 'critical constructivism' – which includes the work of scholars such as Jutta Weldes (1999), Karin Fierke (1998, 2007) and David Mutimer (1999) – can be said to place greater emphasis on the *constitutive* role of discourse: that is, the ways in which discourses are constitutive not only of actors' identities, but also of the power relations between them. The central concept here is 'discourse', which can be defined as 'Systems of meaningful practices that form the identities of subjects and objects' (Howarth and Stavrakakis 2000: 5). Discourse commonly refers to words, but can also include other data such as visual images, material objects and social institutions (see Chapter 5). Critical constructivists reject the proposition that discourses are merely 'neutral' or 'objective' forms of knowledge. In this sense, critical constructivism is grounded in a post-positivist approach to knowledge, as distinct from the positivism of its conventional counterpart (Weldes *et al.* 1999: 13). Critical constructivists inject a normative orientation into the study of security that is also shared by several of the approaches discussed later in this volume, and the emphasis on discourse and power blurs the boundary between this work and several of the approaches covered later (most notably feminist and gender approaches, poststructuralism, postcolonialism and securitisation theory). More important than such boundary disputes, however, is the fact that the role of social construction is not the sole purview of constructivist approaches. It is, to differing degrees, also a crucial point of analysis for all of the critical approaches discussed in this text.

From the cold war to the war against terrorism

Another common way of mapping security studies, and the emergence of critical approaches within it, is via the use of different temporal narratives. By 'temporal narratives' we mean diverse references to various timeframes, historical events and the delineation of supposedly distinct 'eras' in order to plot developments in the way that security is studied. Two particular 'ruptures' stand out in narratives used in contemporary security studies: the end of the cold war period associated with the fall of the Berlin Wall and revolutions throughout Eastern Europe in 1989, and the collapse of the Soviet Union in 1991; and the events of 11 September 2001, which saw two planes flown into the twin towers of the World Trade Center in New York and a third aircraft into the Pentagon in Washington, DC.

The cold war period (usually taken to denote the period 1945–1989) refers to the strategic environment that emerged out of the Second World War, which saw the rise of the USSR and US as the two global superpowers. With the collapse of the wartime alliance between the UK, the USSR and the US, the latter two states became embroiled in an ideological stand-off between communism and capitalism. For most of the twentieth century this ideological split led to the geographical division of Europe and a long-standing military confrontation between the superpowers and their allies. This confrontation was intensified with the development of nuclear technology. The arrival of the intercontinental ballistic missile in the 1950s meant that the USSR could be reached from US territory, and vice versa, within 20–40 minutes. While there were several moments when a clash between the superpowers seemed imminent, most notably during the 1962 'Cuban missile crisis' and in 1983 when the US deployed missiles in Europe in response to the shooting down of a South

Korean airliner in Soviet airspace, the confrontation never escalated to full nuclear warfare. Indeed, it was precisely the absence of direct military action, in the European theatre at least, that gave rise to the term 'cold' war.

With its focus on the security dilemma, states' survival and military capability, political realism was considered particularly apposite to the analysis of state behaviour under the threat of nuclear warfare during the cold war period. However, the inability of realist scholars to predict the end of this period, together with the changing reality of the strategic environment, meant that a number of scholars began to question the continuing relevance of realism and traditional security studies more generally. According to this familiar temporal narrative, the ending of the cold war era went hand-in-hand with challenges to the hegemony of the realist position in security studies, which, in turn, paved the way for the emergence of more critical approaches surveyed in this volume. It is precisely in this context that the discourses of 'broadening' and 'deepening' of the security agenda, seen as characteristic of moves away from state-centred militarism, are typically framed.

The broadening and deepening of security studies in a more self-consciously 'critical' vein can be read against the backdrop of events and changes associated with the end of the cold war. For example, the dissolution of the USSR in 1991, Yugoslavia in 1992 and Czechoslovakia in 1993, which led to heightened flows of people and the reclassification of formerly 'internal' migrants as 'international' migrants, was the specific context in which European government officials, media reporters and security analysts began to frame migration in terms of security (see Chapter 11). Similarly, the advent of the UN Development Report in 1994, with its focus on global access to healthcare, education and resources as components of 'human security' was a key milestone in the recognition of the human as a referent object of security (see Chapter 10). One way of mapping critical security studies, therefore, is in terms of the relation between the way that security is theorised and the historical context in which that theorisation takes place.

This relation is once more apparent if we consider how the events of 11 September 2001 have provided a powerful framing for the way in which security has been studied in the ensuing 'war against terrorism' and how critical approaches have developed within this context. Indeed, comparable to the fall of the Berlin Wall and the collapse of the Soviet Union, '9/11' has become another key reference point in an array of temporal narratives found in the practice and theory of security alike. Part of the significance attributed to 9/11 in security studies derives from the fact that this date has been invoked frequently by the US administration, and other Western governments, in framings of domestic and international policies. A common thread running throughout former US President George W. Bush's speeches was precisely the idea of two worlds: one *before* and one *after* the attacks on the World Trade Center and Pentagon. In his speech commemorating the fifth anniversary of the establishment of the Department of Homeland Security on 6 March 2008, for example, Bush asserted: 'The events of September the 11th, 2001 demonstrated the threats of a new era. I say "new" because we found that oceans which separate us from different continents no longer separate us from danger'.

The invocation of this date as a turning point between 'old' and 'new' eras is politically significant because it has been regularly cited by the US administration as a justification for a range of responses to the threat of international terrorism that includes military intervention in Afghanistan and Iraq, the rolling out of new homeland security measures at home and abroad, and a battery of counterterrorism policies and practices (see Chapter 9).

Arguably, one of the defining features of a range of work associated with critical security studies, however, has been a critique of the usage of 9/11 as a key turning point in global security relations. Rather than simply accepting the temporal narrative of 9/11 as ushering in a new era, this temporal narrative has come under intense scrutiny in the critically oriented literature. The very packaging of events on 11 September 2001 as '9/11' has been questioned as an oversimplified coding of a complex series of events and issues. Some scholars have also pointed to what they consider to be the media hyperbole of representations of 9/11. Repeated images and footage of the collapse of the iconic twin towers were watched globally and received unprecedented media coverage. While acknowledging the tragedy of the attacks, it has been argued that other events in global politics, such as the on-going conflict in Darfur for example, have by contrast claimed more lives yet attracted far less attention.

The tendency to take 9/11 as an unproblematised starting point in a seemingly continuous sequence of events in the 'war on terror', now known as simply '11/3', 'Bali', 'Istanbul', '7/7', 'Mumbai', has also been criticised. As well as ignoring the specificities of each of these tragedies, such a narrative implies that global history somehow *begins* with 9/11. In turn, as emphasised by those working in the postcolonial tradition, this de-historicises the various colonial legacies, Western foreign policies and global inequalities that are part of the broader context in which 9/11 and other terroristic events can be emplaced (for more see Chapter 4). Similarly, scholars associated with poststructuralism and international political sociology (IPS) approaches have sought to critically interrogate discourses of exceptionalism used by Western governments to justify the use of 'exceptional' illiberal practices in supposedly liberal democratic regimes (for more see Chapters 5 and 9). What is common to these critical commentaries, therefore, is an insistence on the importance of paying close attention to the way in which the discourse of a pre/post-9/11 world works politically in order to justify particular policies and interests.

Despite the prevalence of temporal narratives in the study of security there are good reasons to exercise caution when relying on these various historical mappings. The evolution of security studies, and critical strands within it, has not been as linear as this method of framing the field implies. The association between the end of the cold war and the rise of critical security studies obscures critically oriented work that pre-dates 1989. Richard Falk's (1975) contributions to the World Order Models Project in the 1970s and Richard K. Ashley's (1984) poststructural critiques of neo-realism in the early 1980s were, for instance, arguably seminal in the formation of critical approaches to security. Also, many aspects of critical theorising, such as the contributions of feminist and gender approaches, transcend the arbitrary divisions of pre/post-cold war and 9/11. Another key problem with the un-reflexive usage of temporal narratives is that this type of map can overlook areas of continuity between different periods said to be distinct. Thus, for example, discussions of 'homeland security' and the need for a coordinated approach to counterterrorism in the US actually pre-date 9/11 (see Chapter 9).

From Aberystwyth, to Copenhagen, to Paris

More recent attempts to map critical security studies overlay the previous intellectual and temporal mappings with distinctions between different critical approaches indicated via a set of geographical metaphors or 'schools'. Indeed, part of the initial motivation for the delineation of the 'Aberystwyth (or 'Welsh') School', 'Copenhagen School', and 'Paris School' approaches to security, as put forward by its initial proponent, emanated from a more general sense that the distinction between traditional and critical security studies failed to capture the internal variation within the latter (Wæver 2004). In a review of the field of security studies as a whole Ole Wæver, a key author of the securitisation approach discussed in Chapter 6, argued that the 'traditional/critical' distinction is generally only recognised within security studies in Europe (and to some extent Canada), and not in the US. In the US, he argued, the study of security remains concentrated on intra-realist debates and more narrowly focused on military issues, with the supposed temporal 'ruptures' discussed above leading to much less variation in intellectual approaches in American security scholarship.

In addition, Wæver also suggested that the main critical approaches to security in the European context could be distinguished by their aims and modes of analysis, thus approximating to different 'schools' of thought that might be named by their place of origin for ease of identification. At the University of Wales, Aberystwyth (now Aberystwyth University), Ken Booth and Richard Wyn Jones had self-consciously developed a brand of 'critical security studies' that challenged the definition of security purely in terms of military threats to the state, and instead linked the study of security to the expansive goal of human emancipation; Wæver, along with Barry Buzan and other colleagues linked to the Copenhagen Peace Research Institute (COPRI) put forward the concept of 'securitisation', focusing on how the invocation of the concept of security affects particular issues; and in Paris, scholars working at Science Po (or the Paris Institute of Political Studies) and connected to the journal *Cultures et Conflits*, edited by Didier Bigo, were seen to be developing a more sociological approach that concentrated on the conduct of everyday security practices ranging from policing to border control.

Although the work of each of these three schools is clearly distinct from security studies as it is generally formulated in the American academic context, Wæver also hinted at potential divergent paths emerging between the Aberystwyth, Copenhagen and Paris schools. The work of those associated with the Aberystwyth (or Welsh) School adopts an overtly normative approach to the study of security, one that questions the primacy of state security and instead seeks to ascertain the conditions for achieving individual security from the broader threats of poverty, political oppression and environmental degradation, as well as violence and conflict. By contrast, scholars associated with the Copenhagen School approach originally proposed the concept of 'securitisation' as a means towards developing a new analytical – rather than explicitly normative – approach to the study of security. Here the focus is shifted on to analysis of the consequences that follow from invoking the concept of security, particularly in relation to non-military issues (or sectors), and proponents of securitisation tend to be much more sceptical about the merits of including issues such as poverty and environmental degradation as 'security' threats. Those associated with the Paris School approach have concentrated more on the question of how security professionals and bureaucracies 'do' security: that is, how security practices are conducted across a range of different contexts, and often in ways that diminish any supposed distinction between internal (policing) and external (military) security.

On face value, this tripartite division of schools of critical security seems to achieve a neat delineation between normative (Aberystwyth), analytical (Copenhagen) and sociological (Paris) approaches. However, the idea of mapping critical approaches to security via distinct schools of thought, like the other two maps outlined above, has strengths and weaknesses in almost equal measure. At a broad level the idea of 'schools' highlights the variation between different critical approaches, resisting the temptation to lump these approaches into one category. The schools metaphor also underlines the extent to which critical approaches are products of individual and collective intellectual activity, rather than theories 'out there' that appear as if from nowhere. It draws our attention to the extent to which Western Europe has, for the most part, been the site of development for many of these approaches. In the process, it highlights the Eurocentric origins of critical approaches, and then raises valid questions over the role institutional and funding structures play in this. It is worth asking, paraphrasing

Wæver, why there is a Copenhagen School but no Calcutta School, an Aberystwyth School but not an Addis Ababa School, Paris but no La Paz?

At the same time, there are a number of potential drawbacks to mapping critical approaches according to different schools. Wæver's initial effort in this regard was largely intended as a rough sketch of the field, and he acknowledged that the schools metaphor is potentially problematic for a number of reasons – not least because each of these 'schools' usually comprises only a handful of scholars, and many more do not conveniently fit within any of these three categories. The idea of schools also risks overstating the cogency of the positions they are taken to represent. As one prominent rejoinder argued, the schools categorisation 'can be misleading if taken too seriously [. . .] Aberystwyth, Copenhagen, and Paris are dispersed locations associated with specific individuals and debates, much more than unitary schools of thought' (CASE 2006: 444). This response by a large collective of scholars under the rubric of 'Critical Approaches to Security in Europe' (CASE) argued that instead of 'schools', critical security studies in Europe is better thought of as an extensive network, with overlaps and dialogue between different schools generally outweighing their distinctions. On this reading, critical scholarship on security also extends well beyond school boundaries into anthropology, criminology, human geography and sociology rather than being restricted by school perimeters.

By taking the three schools idea as a starting point, though, the CASE collective's argument is itself indicative of the extent to which the schools metaphor has become part of the 'furniture' in debates over critical security studies. To some extent, then, reference to the schools nomenclature in later chapters is unavoidable, but we are also acutely aware of the limitations of this categorisation as a whole. In particular, the tripartite geographical distinction misses out on two important approaches that are not named as 'schools', but which nevertheless constitute significant critical approaches to security: feminist and gender approaches (discussed in Chapter 3); and approaches derived from various forms of postcolonial theory and experiences (discussed in Chapter 4). The inclusion of these two approaches in this text addresses two of the often-observed lacunae in the schools categorisation: the place of feminist and gender scholarship (see Sylvester 2007), and the potential Eurocentrism/West-centrism of critical approaches.

Travelling without maps . . . structure and features of the book

While it is clearly important to get a sense for the narratives according to which critical security studies has been mapped out in existing characterisations, we also want to restate the general point that there are various downsides to these maps and the activity of mapping more generally. An awareness of the maps to which we refer above (and return to elsewhere in the text) is in some ways obligatory, as they frequently form part of the intellectual story of individual approaches as told by their proponents. Detailed discussions of the scholars (and groups) that inform various approaches, and historical events that shape the intellectual trajectory of individual approaches are important, and this is also part of the work of the proceeding chapters. However, it is also worth noting that such maps – if rigidly adhered to – can be counterproductive in that they often impose largely artificial boundaries within and between critical perspectives. In turn, this can prevent readers from making their own connections and detecting similarities as well as differences across the entire field of ideas in critical security studies. It also leads to arbitrary and sometimes unhelpful choices about which 'school' of thought to adopt, which hinders rather than assists the task of analysing pressing issues in global politics.

What we wish to draw attention to, therefore, is a recognition of the importance of reflecting critically on the intellectual maps we often use in critical security studies. Maps are usually two-dimensional, whereas critical security studies is very much a layered body of work, with messy interconnections as well as areas of divergence. The terrain we are dealing with has a complex topography and it is precisely this messiness or variegation, as reflected in the image chosen for this book's front cover, that we seek to convey and work with rather than brush to one side. To get at this idea, we borrow both from the artist Jackson Pollock's signature style for the cover, and, from the critical security scholar Richard Wyn Jones, the idea of 'traveling without maps'. Writing about the study of security in the context of the cold war's end, Wyn Jones suggested that as well as the changes to conventional maps required by the dissolution of the Soviet Union, the landscape of security and insecurity was also rapidly changing – to the point where the intellectual maps of the cold war provided by security studies no longer had the same purchase (Wyn Jones 1996). In this sense, security scholars were deemed to be temporarily travelling without maps. Playing off this idea in a slightly different way, the structure of this book eschews the temptation to frame its overview entirely within one of the usual mappings of critical security studies covered above (including the temporal narrative alluded to by Wyn Jones). Instead, the book is divided into two main parts with the chapters in each simply arranged in alphabetical order rather than according to any unfolding intellectual, temporal or geographical narrative.

In this spirit, Part I, 'Approaches', surveys the newly extended and contested theoretical terrain of critical security studies. It covers an array of different perspectives: constructivist theories (Chapter 1); Critical Theory and its application in security studies (Chapter 2); feminist and gender approaches to security (Chapter 3); postcolonial perspectives (Chapter 4); poststructuralism and international political sociology (Chapter 5); and securitisation theory (Chapter 6). Each chapter aims to offer a clear, concise and accessible introduction to each of these positions. They are preceded by a short abstract that sets out the key themes discussed, and each chapter also contains text boxes that provide readers with explanations of key terms, background information on each approach, and relevant textual extracts. Each is then concluded with a series of points for further reflection and discussion, and a guide to further reading that gives an indication of where readers might follow up on the themes and discussions covered. In addition to providing an overview and guide to each approach and its key proponents, the chapters also highlight the intellectual heritages that these approaches in turn draw upon. Not all the approaches surveyed here operate along the same intellectual plane; several of the approaches covered in Part I reach out to and engage ideas from beyond disciplinary security studies, such as post-Marxist critical theory, feminism, theories of postcolonialism, poststructuralist ideas, sociology and speech act theory, among others. By examining these distinctive political-theoretical foundations we can gain a more sophisticated understanding of the different starting points of the various perspectives. In keeping with the argument made above, this emphasis on theoretical depth, we hope, potentially provides readers with new ways of conceiving of the various points of convergence and divergence between the different critical approaches covered here.

Part II, 'Issues', then offers an overview of how these various theoretical approaches have been put to work against the backdrop of a diverse range of issues in contemporary security practices. These encompass: environmental security (Chapter 7); the securitisation of health (Chapter 8); homeland security and the 'war against terrorism' (Chapter 9); human security and development (Chapter 10); migration and border security (Chapter 11); and technology and warfare in the information age (Chapter 12). These issues illustrate how the adoption of different critical approaches opens up the terrain of study beyond narrow militaristic threats to also include a wide range of contemporary problems. In turn, the ways in which different critical approaches focus upon and analyse these issues tells us much about how these approaches operate, what they deem to be important, and how they treat the concept of security more broadly. The dynamic interface between theory and practice in critical approaches means that such issues can be used reflexively to assess the insights (and potential limitations) of the various theoretical contentions covered in Part I of the book. To do so Part II makes use of internal references that point readers back to themes and discussion covered in Part I. As with Part I, each chapter in Part II is introduced by a short abstract and uses text boxes to augment readers' understanding. Each also provides points for further discussion and a guide to further reading.

The advantage of this mode of organising the text is that by imposing only a minimal structure, new readings of the field and the texts that comprise it may potentially emerge. Even prominent 'traditionalists' in security studies sometimes recognise that 'an active field is always a mess – fuzzy boundaries, contention, methodological quandaries', although the same commentator warns that this can 'be carried too far' (Morgan 2000: 40). We would argue that this recognition is often not carried far enough in relation to critical approaches to security, and that the merits of critical security studies as an 'active field' of precisely this sort are frequently missed. Rather than clumping approaches together, or prematurely prescribing the boundaries between and around critical approaches to security, then, we instead opt to invite readers to engage in their own critical cartography in reading this text. The chapters can be read in or out of the sequence in which they are presented on the contents page, or with chapters in Part I read in tandem with those in Part II and vice versa. The text as a whole, and its individual chapters, is designed in such a way as to allow readers to identify, engage and judge the interconnections and disjunctions between critical approaches to security for themselves. Using the text in this way will, we hope, prove a productive way of introducing and connecting readers to the subject matter of critical security studies.

Guide to further reading

Barry Buzan and Lene Hansen (2009) *The Evolution of International Security Studies* (Cambridge: Cambridge University Press). Offers a comprehensive intellectual history of security studies.

CASE Collective (2006) 'Critical Approaches to Security in Europe: A Networked Manifesto', *Security Dialogue*, 37: 443–487. A detailed overview of the state of contemporary critical approaches to security that also attempts to outline new avenues of inquiry.

Jef Huysmans (1998) 'Security! What do you mean?' *European Journal of International Relations*, 4: 226–255. Focuses on the issues associated with defining the concept of security; for contrasting discussions on a similar theme see Wolfers (1952) and Baldwin (1997), details in Bibliography.

Keith Krause and Michael C. Williams (1997) *Critical Security Studies: Concepts and Cases* (London: UCL Press). A landmark articulation of, and contribution to, the field of critical security studies.

Steve Smith (2000) 'The Increasing Insecurity of Security Studies: Conceptualizing Security in the Last Twenty Years', in Stuart Croft and Terry Terriff (eds), *Critical Reflections on Security and Change* (London: Frank Cass). Provides a comprehensive overview of critical security studies as it stood at the turn of the millennium.

Part I
Approaches

1 Constructivist theories

Abstract

This chapter provides an overview of constructivist theories, their application in the study of security, and their relation to the field of critical security studies. Rather than portraying 'constructivism' as a monolithic theoretical approach, the chapter instead makes the case that social constructivist approaches to security are best thought of as a plurality of approaches that converge around some key assumptions but diverge on others. Although they might be argued to share, at a minimum, the assumption that security and insecurity should be conceived of as socially constructed, different variants of constructivism diverge on the precise implications and significance of that claim. The chapter reviews these issues, with a particular focus on the contributions of (critical) constructivist theories to (critical) security studies.

Introduction

Social constructivist (or now simply referred to as constructivist) theories have become an established point of reference in the disciplinary study of both international relations (IR) and security over the past two decades in particular. As the use of 'theories' in the plural above already alludes to, there is a strong case to be made for distinguishing between different variants of constructivist theories. There is even an argument that a focus on social construction within the study of security is not simply limited to constructivist theories. To try and help make sense of these various issues and distinctions, this chapter begins with a general discussion of the principle of social construction, focusing initially in particular on one of the original formulations of this idea, namely in the work of Peter L. Berger and Thomas Luckmann (1991 [1966]). Although not alone in emphasising the significance of social construction, Berger and Luckmann's work remains a touchstone in this regard and introduces a theoretical lexicon that arguably still remains foundational to later variants of constructivist theories in IR and security studies. The substantive sections of the chapter then go on to outline and discuss how different those different variants of constructivist theories interpret and apply the notion of social construction. The particular emphasis here is on the distinguishing features of 'conventional constructivism' on the one hand, which arguably seeks to refine rather than fundamentally challenge key predicates of traditional security studies, and 'critical constructivism' on the other hand, which poses more avowedly and self-consciously 'critical' questions on the social construction of threats, dangers and insecurities.

On the social construction of reality

So what is social construction? Or, to put that question differently, what is it that characterises 'constructivist' or 'social constructivist' theories such that we can speak of these as relatively distinct from other theoretical approaches? At the very broadest level of categorisation, it can be argued that constructivist theories share the contention that 'human reality' is 'socially constructed reality' (Berger and Luckmann 1991 [1966]: 210–211). Those terms come from Peter L. Berger and Thomas Luckmann's aptly titled book *The Social Construction of Reality: A Treatise in the Sociology of Knowledge*. Berger and Luckmann's treatise takes as its main focus the ways in which 'the *inter*subjective common-sense world is constructed' (1991 [1966]: 34, emphasis in original). By this Berger and Luckmann mean that humans are, fundamentally, social beings: that is, humans exist (or more accurately co-exist) within societies. How we come to apprehend the world around us, Berger and Luckmann argue, is influenced by pre-existing social conventions and institutions and is filtered and mediated via pre-existing frameworks for learning and understanding, most notably language.

By claiming that human reality is socially constructed, Berger and Luckmann do not seek to deny that all members of a social group are at the same time different and distinct as individuals; nor is the claim intended to imply that human reality is completely free or independent of humans' biological being or their surrounding physical environment. Instead Berger and Luckmann argue that the formation of individuals' identities as such is crucially forged out of an individual's engagement with the social world into which they are born. And when individuals begin to adopt, consciously and unconsciously, the norms and conventions of the social world that they engage with, they undergo a process of 'socialisation'. Our notions of individual self-identity, Berger and Luckmann argue, thus emerge out of complex processes of intersubjective interaction and subtle and on-going processes of identity formation. In this context, the term 'intersubjective' means that these processes happen in the communication and interaction between different 'subjects' or individuals, each with their own constantly developing sense of self-identity (see Box 1.1).

Box 1.1   Berger and Luckmann on 'The reality of everyday life'

The reality of everyday life is organised around the 'here' of my body and the 'now' of my present. This 'here and now' is the focus of my attention to everyday life [. . .] [However] The reality of everyday life further presents itself to me as an intersubjective world, a world that I share with others. [. . .] Indeed, I cannot exist in everyday life without continually interacting and communicating with others [. . .] I also know, of course, that the others have a perspective on this world that is not identical with mine. My 'here' is their 'there'. My 'now' does not fully overlap with theirs. My projects differ from and may even conflict with theirs. All the same, I know that I live with them in a common world. Most importantly, I know there is an ongoing correspondence between *my* meanings and *their* meanings in this world, that we share a common sense about its reality.

(Abridged from Berger and Luckmann 1991 [1966]: 36–37; emphases in original)

Berger and Luckmann do not deny that humans have certain biological drives and needs and that, for example, certain physical features of the natural environment exist. However, they take issue with the idea that these drives and physical features might determine the whole of humans' reality. You, as reader, might hypothetically feel pangs of hunger reading this text having not eaten since breakfast; but the question of what you 'want' to eat for lunch is not simply based on a biological need to eat. All sorts of other factors come into play: social conventions as to when lunch is eaten as distinct from other meals; as to what is 'appropriate' to eat for lunch (ice-cream alone, for example, might be deemed by some to be inappropriate as a lunch meal, even if some might try to claim that ice-cream's nutritional value would provide enough nutritional sustenance ...). The decision of where you might go to buy lunch is not simply an issue of how far to walk and the impeding terrain (bodily and geographical factors) but of how much to you wish to pay, and when you need to get back to work in order to meet a deadline. Of the latter, financial systems that establish rates of pay, the value of particular foodstuffs, and the nature of academic deadlines can be argued to be products of social, human-made, systems as opposed to naturally occurring physical or biological features. These would all instead fall into the category of what Berger and Luckmann term as 'socio-cultural determinants', rather than biological or physical determinants, of how humans interact with each other, and act in, the world around them (cf. Berger and Luckmann 1991 [1966]: 66–67).

Security: What states make of it?

What relevance, you might be asking, does reflecting on such apparently mundane aspects of everyday life (a technique that is used recurrently by Berger and Luckmann in *The Social Construction of Reality*) have to the study of security? Taken as a whole, constructivist approaches to the study of security might be said to be underpinned by two key assumptions: first the observation that 'security' and 'insecurity' are categorisations that emerge out of and are applied to the realm of human activities; and second, following on from this, that many of the concepts, processes and dynamics identified by Berger and Luckmann – the social construction of reality, intersubjectivity, identity formation and socialisation – are as applicable to the study of security as they are to the study of any realm of social life.

More than this, those adopting or advocating a constructivist theoretical approach to the study of security would go further and argue that the study of security is not simply an area where the insights of social constructivism *can* be applied but where they *should* be applied. In particular, critics of 'mainstream' or 'traditional' approaches to the study of international security have argued that such approaches underestimate, marginalise or simply miss the crucial importance of social construction (Wendt 1995). Thus, for example, the editor of a key collection of essays that began to take seriously the 'sociocultural determinants' of national and international security cast that volume's purposes as part of a broader effort to '[make] problematic the state interests that predominant explanations of national security often take for granted [...] State interests do not exist to be "discovered" by self-interested, rational actors. Interests are constructed through a process of social interaction' (Katzenstein 1996a: 1; 2). Katzenstein's volume, *The Culture of National Security: Norms and Identity in World Politics*, advocated that 'sociological approaches' could be used to generate new insights on the roles of culture, norms and identity formation in relation to 'traditional' security issue areas such as the proliferation of conventional weapons, national military doctrines, deterrence and military alliances, using 'culture' as 'a broad label that denotes collective models of nation-state authority or identity, carried by custom or law' (Katzenstein 1996a: 6). Contributing authors made the argument that, even in relation to 'hard cases' of military security issues, mainstream (neo)realist and (neo)liberal theoretical approaches to security in particular tended to miss key pieces of 'puzzles' in world politics such as the peaceful disintegration of the Soviet Union, which both (neo)realism and (neo)liberalism are both frequently accused of failing to either foresee or adequately account for (Katzenstein 1996a: 3; 1996b: 499). Mainstream approaches instead tended to predict either the continuation of the cold war or its violent conclusion in nuclear war. Relatedly, the continuance of the North Atlantic Treaty Organization (NATO) after the Soviet Union's demise seemed to fundamentally contradict the expectation of traditional alliance theory that military alliances dissolve in the absence of a common threat (cf Ciută 2002; Gheciu 2005; Risse-Kappen 1996; Williams and Neumann 2002). In short, mainstream approaches to the study of international security appeared to be at a loss to explain issues and developments – the trajectory of the cold war and the nature of military alliances – that had somewhat ironically been their central concern for several decades.

In the wake of mainstream security studies' apparent difficulties in explaining major changes in world politics – particularly the cold war's end – multiple scholars began to advocate variants of constructivism as a superior way of understanding key issues in the study of international security. Thus, for example, Alexander Wendt argues that the 'security dilemma', which arguably remains at the core of 'mainstream' or 'traditional' approaches to the study of international security, can only be truly understood via a constructivist framework of analysis. The concept of the security dilemma, as set out originally in the work of realist IR scholars such as John Herz and Robert Jervis, argues that in the realm of international politics a state will necessarily compete to preserve its own existence as its principal objective, but that in doing so it will inadvertently increase the insecurity of other states in the international system (Herz 1950; Jervis 1978; for an extended discussion see Booth and Wheeler 2007). According to the logic of the security dilemma, particularly as read and rendered by neorealist approaches to the study of international politics, states exists in a condition of 'anarchy': that is, states are each sovereign powers within their own territorial boundaries, but exist without any overarching sovereign power above them. Traditional approaches to security, though diverse in character, thus tend to hold the baseline proposition that world politics is inter*national* politics: that is, it occurs 'between' separate nation-states rather than 'above' them, so to speak.

Such conditions, it is argued, give rise to the security dilemma as an endemic feature of world politics. Without any external government or guarantor for protection, states are forced to look to their own means first in order to assure their protection and their self-preservation. This necessarily means, according to the neorealist theorist Kenneth Waltz, that the contemporary international system is a 'self-help' system (Waltz 1979): states have to be self-reliant in their own quest for national self-preservation by investing in the military means to protect themselves. The problem this gives rise to, according to the logic of the security dilemma, is that in seeking to protect their territorial security, states may inadvertently create greater insecurity for others. Material military capabilities – land armies, tanks, navies, air-forces, nuclear weapons and so on – can be used for offensive purposes as well as self-protection. Scholars such as Herz and Jervis saw this as potentially problematic, for one state could never be entirely sure that a military build-up by another was intended purely for defensive purposes. To guard against the possibility that such a build-up may actually be geared towards invasion or military expansion, the logical option would be for all states to likewise arm themselves as far as possible as a preventive measure. This in turn would lead to the same and reciprocal insecurities for other states, leading in the worst cases to cyclical and potentially disastrous arms races. The 'dilemma' of the security dilemma, then, is argued to be the fact that states in world politics are faced with (only) two unappealing choices: either to arm for self-defence but risk creating cyclical insecurities and having to engage in cyclical arms racing; or remain unarmed, but then remain at the mercy of predatory states that might to choose to arm and invade.

Wendt, though agreeing with the existence of the security dilemma dynamic as a potential feature of international politics, argues that traditional approaches and (neo)realists in particular crucially misunderstand the nature of security dilemmas. According to Wendt, a security dilemma is a '*social structure* composed of *intersubjective* understandings in which states are so distrustful that they make worst-case assumptions about each others' intentions, and as a result *define their interests* in self-help terms' (Wendt 1995: 73, emphases added). Although Wendt agrees on the existence of security dilemmas between states, his qualifiers make important distinctions from traditional understandings. Wendt, in a manner akin to Berger and Luckmann, does not deny the existence of material (military) capabilities. But, he contends, 'material capabilities as such explain nothing; their effects presuppose structures of shared knowledge, which vary and which are not reducible to capabilities' (Wendt 1995: 73). Wendt famously illustrates this point by noting that '500 British nuclear weapons are less threatening to the United States than 5 North Korean nuclear weapons, because the British are friends of the United States and the North Koreans are not, and amity or enmity is a function of shared understandings' (Wendt 1995: 73). Although in Wendt's illustration the material capability of the British is greater than that of the North Koreans, they are interpreted by the US as being less of a threat because the British state is regarded traditionally as a friend (amity), but North Korea is not. Whereas North Korea has a history of enmity with the US that has manifested itself in outright conflict (the Korean war of 1950–1953) and in subsequent characterisation of North Korea as a 'rogue state' in US security policy discourse, Britain is routinely characterised by US policy makers as having a 'special relationship' with it, as well as having institutionalised alliance ties via bilateral relations and as a 'friend' within NATO. The US 'interest' in preventing or containing North Korean nuclearisation on the one hand and accepting Britain's nuclearisation on the other hand is thus argued to be inseparable from their identification of one as 'opponent' and the other as 'ally'.

Wendt argues that even if states exist within a condition of 'anarchy', their actual relationships within that anarchic context can vary significantly and can evolve and change over time, leading to Wendt's much cited claim that 'Anarchy is what states make of it' (Wendt 1992). While traditional accounts view the security dilemma as a 'seemingly natural social structure' (Wendt 1995: 74), Wendt argues that it is the social nature of the structure that allows scope for it to change over time. Thus, for instance, US–British relations have shifted significantly from the period of the late eighteenth and early nineteenth centuries in which, far from a 'special relationship' of amity, the US tended to regard the British state as a predatory imperialist oppressor and Britain likewise regarded the newly independent US as a rebellious upstart. Wendt thus contends that constructivist approaches remind us that even the most apparently intractable security dilemmas might be amenable to progressive improvement, and the efforts of human agents to assist such improvement. Thus, for example, the apparent 'inevitable' end of the cold war in nuclear Armageddon could instead give way to 'peaceful change'; and the history of Franco–German enmity that was at the crux of two world wars could instead evolve to become the basis, via the processes of integration that have ultimately constituted the European Union (EU), of a pan-European 'security community' (see Box 1.2).

Wendt does not argue that simply because the potential exists for 'security dilemmas' to give way to 'security communities' that this will always happen or be practically possible. As he puts it, 'to say that structures are socially constructed is no guarantee that they can be changed' (Wendt 1995: 80). But in Wendt's view constructivist theories can make a significant contribution to critical theoretical approaches to the study of IR more generally by making allowance for the potential of such progressive change in nation-states' security relations.

Box 1.2 From security dilemmas to security communities

Wendt makes the case that whereas a security dilemma is a 'social structure' distinguished and characterised by mistrust between states, a 'security community' is 'a different social structure, in which states trust one another to resolve disputes without war' (1995: 73). Wendt's use of the term presaged the work of Emmanuel Adler and Michael Barnett (1998a, 1998b) on 'security communities' and their extension of that concept as originally formulated by the IR theorist Karl Deutsch. In the 1950s and 1960s Deutsch developed a theory known as 'transactionalism' to try and understand and explain the increasing level of interaction (or 'transactions') between states globally in the post-war era. This approach is also sometimes known as 'pluralism', or the 'communications approach' because of its emphasis on communication and interaction as the basis of integration. Deutsch argued that the ultimate outcome of transactionalism was a 'security community', a situation in which the prospect of war between a group of states has been eradicated due to deeply embedded structures of communication. Deutsch's ideas were revisited by Adler and Barnett in the late 1990s. They argue that the 'logic of anarchy' can in certain instances be superseded by the 'logic of community' – the idea that 'actors can share values, norms and symbols that provide a social identity, and engage in various interactions in myriad spheres that reflect long-term interest, diffuse reciprocity, and trust' (Adler and Barnett 1998a: 3). Their approach suggests that international organisations such as the United Nations, the Organization for Security and Cooperation in Europe, the EU, NATO and the Association of South East Asian Nations all (to varying degrees) display elements of the collective values, shared identity and relations of trust and reciprocity that Deutsch expected to be characteristic of security communities. Given the emphasis on collective identity and values, Adler and Barnett (1998b: 59) argue that a constructivist approach is best suited to the purposes of assessing how and when security communities form between states, and for evaluating whether they are 'loosely' or 'tightly' integrated as such.

From 'security communities' to 'cultures of insecurity': Critical constructivism and boundary debates

The variant of constructivist theory advocated by Wendt (see also in particular Wendt 1999) is one of the most notable, influential and widely cited post-cold war contributions to the theorisation of IR. As detailed above, much of that contribution has been based on direct engagement with and interrogation of the traditional terrain and terminology of security studies: the security dilemma, military alliances and nuclear deterrence. Some scholars have, however, raised questions over exactly how much of departure from mainstream IR theory and traditional security studies Wendtian constructivism is (see Hopf 1998; Zehfuss 2001). Wendt, for his part, hopes that his version of constructivism could be agreeable to schools of 'critical' thought in IR theory – 'postmodernists', 'neo-Marxists', 'feminists', and other constructivist theorists (1995: 71). At the same time, Wendt admits in the same article to his agreement with specific key traditional realist and neorealist IR theory assumptions: 'that international politics is anarchic, and that states have offensive capabilities, [that states] cannot be 100 per cent certain about others' intentions [...] and a commitment to states as units of analysis, and to the importance of systemic or "third image" theorizing' (1995: 72). Thus, for example, Wendt does not reject the assumption that contemporary international politics is fundamentally composed of states interacting within an anarchic environment. Rather he suggests that realists and neorealist theoretical approaches (as well as other 'mainstream' liberal and neoliberal IR theoretical approaches) underestimate the importance of (variations) in state identity within that context, and the range of possible modes of state interaction that arise as result (see Wendt 1992).

This has led some scholars to argue that Wendtian constructivism is representative of a 'conventional' theoretical approach, whereby conventional constructivism is distinguished by a desire to present 'an alternative to mainstream international relations theory' by offering 'constructivist solutions' to 'mainstream puzzles' (Hopf 1998: 172, 186). Likewise, the version of constructivist theory advocated by Katzenstein, for example, welcomes 'broader' security studies in terms of an expanded range of focus but 'only if the issues and actors that it studies have some demonstrable links to states and questions of military importance' (1996b: 525). In both cases, the emphasis on states and their military relations so characteristic of traditional approaches to the study of security remain intact even as conventional constructivists suggest new ways of studying and understandings international security.

Hopf (1998: 182) suggests that we can distinguish this 'conventional' variant of constructivist theory in the study of international relations from a more avowedly 'critical' variant. Both 'conventional constructivism' and 'critical constructivism' share, he argues, 'theoretical fundamentals'. Hopf, however, distinguishes critical constructivism from its conventional counterpart on the basis that critical constructivism is argued to be 'more closely tied to critical social theory' and, by consequence, to the goal of 'unmasking' (1998: 172, 185) the hierarchies of power that inherently exist within social relations. Hopf argues that conventional constructivism of the kind espoused by Wendt and Katzenstein promises a 'research agenda' (1998: 171) that aspires to be 'analytically neutral' and can fit with both mainstream IR theory and traditional security studies, but critical constructivism is more likely to be directly and explicitly critical *of* the disciplinary foundations of both.

Weldes *et al.* (1999) explicitly make the case for a specifically critical constructivist approach to the study of security and insecurity that adopts this more critical outlook towards the study of security. Critical constructivism, they argue, is loosely identifiable by adherence to the following analytical commitments: First, that 'What is understood as reality is socially constructed'; second, that 'Constructions of reality reflect, enact, and reify relations of power. In turn, certain agents or groups of agents play a privileged role in the production and reproduction of these realities'; and third, that 'A critical constructivist approach denaturalizes dominant constructions, offers guidelines for the transformation of common sense, and facilitates the imagining of alternative life-worlds. It also problematizes the conditions of its own claims; that is, a critical constructivism is also reflexive' (Weldes *et al.* 1999: 13; and on the last point compare also Fierke 1998: 94–110). Although the first of these principles can be said to be shared with conventional constructivism and consistent with Berger and Luckmann's earlier theses, the latter two principles are more radically at odds with conventional constructivists' aspiration to create an analytically neutral research agenda that takes certain key assumptions of mainstream IR theory and traditional security studies for granted.

One way in which Weldes *et al.* (1999) seek to heighten this distinction is by emphasising a focus not on 'security' *per se* but on 'insecurity' and the social 'production of danger' as key constitutive dimensions of social relations in general and international politics in particular. As they put it:

> insecurities, rather than being natural facts, are social and cultural productions. One way to get at the constructed nature of insecurities is to examine the fundamental ways in which insecurities and the objects that suffer from insecurity are mutually constituted; that is, in contrast to the received view, which treats the objects of insecurity and insecurities themselves as pre-given or natural, and as ontologically separate things, we treat

them as mutually constituted cultural and social constructions: insecurity is itself the product of processes of identity construction in which the self and the other, or multiple others, are constituted.

(Weldes *et al.* 1999: 10)

At least two important points are notable from the view offered in this quotation. The first is that Weldes *et al.* make no direct initial reference to states in this discussion. In fact they instead suggest that we should not 'treat the objects of insecurity' as 'pre-given or natural'. In contrast to conventional constructivism, this suggests an approach that would seek to question the assumption of states as the pre-given objects of analysis in the study of international relations and security. A critical constructivist approach seeks to account for the apparent predominance of that assumption in the first place as well as the historical and contextual factors that give rise to that assumption. Weldes, for example, argues that Wendt's understanding of the state 'continues to treat states, in typical realist fashion, as unitary actors with a single identity and a single set of interests [...] The state itself is treated as a black box whose internal workings are irrelevant to the construction of state identity and interests' (Weldes 1999: 9; see Zehfuss 2001 for an extended critique of Wendt's conception of state identity along related lines). This is not to say that states are unimportant, or that we should not seek to study them as both human communities and institutionalised forms of political association. But the point is precisely that states are *human* communities – or 'imagined communities' (see Anderson 1991) – formed out of lengthy, complex, messy and uneven processes of formation and institutionalisation. Critical constructivist accounts of state identity, then, cannot simply assume the metaphorical boundaries of a state's identity or its interests, but rather seeks to question how particular forms of identity and particular conceptions of the 'national interest' come to predominate at any given moment (see Weldes 1999; Steele 2008). Further to this, scholars such as Fierke emphasise the very 'centrality of language' (1997: 225) in the construction of understandings of security and insecurity, and the employment of metaphors of family, protection and domesticity in underpinning states' national security policies and 'architectures' (see also Chapter 3).

The second notable point from the quotation in Box 1.3 is that insecurities and dangers are social constructions that are seen to have constitutive identity effects. In other words, Weldes *et al.* make the proposition that elements of 'danger' in social relationships might actually have productive effects: productive not necessarily in terms of being desirable, but in producing distinctions between self and other, between friend and foe, and between states of security and insecurity. As they argue in relation to the social construction of nuclear insecurity (see Box 1.3), Weldes *et al.* do not claim that this position amounts to a rejection of the proposition that there is material reality ('Our constructivism would not deny that nuclear weapons exist', as stated in the quote in Box 1.3). However, as Fierke (1998: 11) puts it, 'material possibility is linguistically constituted' (see also Chapter 5, Box 5.3). Humans interpret and represent the world they encounter, primarily through language. On the basis that there can be multiple ways of interpreting reality constructivists seek to question how it is that certain ways of interpreting and representing reality come into being, predominate and enable particular courses of action.

At first glance, the discussion of the social construction of nuclear insecurity in Box 1.3 would seem to simply reiterate Wendt's observation (as discussed earlier in the chapter) that, historically, for the US state North Korea's possession of nuclear weapons has consistently been regarded as much more of a danger than Britain's possession of nuclear weapons. The general example, Wendt argues, indicates that states do identify and treat each other

---

Box 1.3 On the social construction of nuclear insecurity

To refer to something as socially constructed is not at all the same as saying that it does not exist [...] Our constructivism would not deny that nuclear weapons exist, that their use could maim and kill millions of people, and that a number of states possess a nuclear capability (including the United States, Russia, Britain, France, China, Israel, India, and Pakistan, at least). On this a constructivist and the most empiricist of arms-control experts can agree. [...] In the face of the heterogeneous dangers represented by nuclear weapons, there is nonetheless an established common sense, made real in collective discourse, that foregrounds some dangers while repressing or ignoring others so that, for example, Americans are more likely to be afraid of Pakistani than of British nuclear weapons, although neither have ever been used. It is this discursive constitution of the *threat* represented by nuclear weapons that we refer to as 'construction,' and it means not that the weapons have been made up but that their meaning has been molded in discourse.

(Weldes *et al.* 1999: 12, emphasis in original)

---

differently in their assumptions and interactions. Weldes *et al.* similarly argue that 'Americans are more likely to be afraid of Pakistani than of British nuclear weapons'. But they go even further than this by arguing that 'In the face of the heterogenous dangers represented by nuclear weapons, there is nonetheless an established common sense [...] that foregrounds some dangers while repressing or ignoring others' (Box 1.3). Why is it, we might ask, that for American citizens, North Korean or Pakistani possession of nuclear weapons might be assumed to be more of a 'danger' or 'threat' than America's own possession of nuclear weapons? The US is, as Weldes *et al.* implicitly allude to, the only state to have ever used nuclear weapons in conflict to date (in the bombings of Hiroshima and Nagasaki in 1945), but is often assumed to be a 'reasonable' nuclear weapons state (Gusterson 2004: 25). The very 'existence' of nuclear weapons actually means that all states that possess such weapons run the risks of accidental use (see, for example, Schlosser 2013 for an extended discussion of 'near misses' during the cold war) that would have the same destructive effects as the use of such weapons in war, and issues over the safe maintenance of weapons materials and facilities over time and their impact upon local habitats and communities (see Masco 1999). Why, we might ask, have these 'dangers' been less prominent, both in the academic study of security and in policy terms, in historical discussions of nuclear weapons and nuclear deterrence?

A critical constructivist approach to nuclear insecurities thus illustrates Weldes *et al*'s broader contention that 'Constructions of reality reflect, enact, and reify relations of power' (Weldes *et al.* 1999: 13). Gusterson's (2004) work on 'nuclear orientalism', for example, extends the argument to make the case that Western states have historically been able, by drawing on 'orientalist' representations of the non-Western 'other', to render 'Third World' possession of nuclear weapons as inherently more dangerous than their possession by 'established' nuclear powers. Fierke in particular notes the effect of particular kinds of 'language games' (drawing on the philosopher Ludwig Wittgenstein) in the rhetoric of the NATO alliance's promise to use nuclear weapons in defence of Europe that 'replac[ed] the destructive, fearful emotions associated with nuclear war with positive emotions of safety and belonging' (1997: 247). Similarly, Weldes' examination of the Cuban missile crisis of October 1962 forensically details how practices and processes of identity construction by both US policy makers and in subsequent historical recounting not only constructed the deployment of Soviet missiles in Cuba as a global 'crisis', but also as a moment that rein-forced the 'construction of the United States as the hemispheric and global leader with both a moral obligation and formal commitments to defend freedom' (Weldes 1999: 203). As such, Weldes argues that the construction of the Cuban missile crisis generally enabled the construction of US state identity as a defender of freedom, the Soviet Union as its evil 'Other' and Cuba as the backdrop or simply a 'physical space' under 'foreign domination' (1999: 39) in which the contest between the two superpowers would take place rather than a substantive state actor in its own right. That particular construction, Weldes argues, meant that the US could portray and pursue particular courses of action as 'commonsensical', as well as reinforcing and reifying a lasting identity construction of the US as the rightful leader of the 'free world' (see also Fierke 1997: 230–231).

While critical constructivism has clear applications to the study of inter-state relations and socially constructed worlds that policy makers interact in, there is also a much more explicit sense in critical constructivist scholarship that security is not – and should not – solely be considered as 'what states', or state elites, 'make of it'. Critical constructivism is concerned, to borrow a phrase again from Berger and Luckmann, with the intersubjective construction of 'common-sense' understandings of the world. Likewise individuals' common-sense understandings of the world are informed, implicitly and explicitly, by their experiences of everyday life and by processes of socialisation. This has two potentially radical implications for how critical constructivists suggest that we should approach the study of security. The first is that even in the realm of the 'high politics' of elite-led state interaction, the cultural sources of individuals' common-sense understandings of the world are replete with concep-tualisations and beliefs that are potentially informed by a much wider range of cultural sources than just the formal policy realm. Weldes (1999: 241–242) for example argues that in order for policy makers to make their representations 'plausible and persuasive' and, ulti-mately, meaningful to broader audiences, they necessarily draw on a range of popular cultural, common-sense, discursive resources (see Box 1.4). She terms this process, drawing on the work of the post-Marxist theorist Louis Althusser (1971) and its subsequent interpre-tation by the cultural theorist Stuart Hall (1985) as 'interpellation': that is, the ways in which individuals come to recognise and associate their own identity with wider identity forma-tions that are articulated in, for example, formal policy discourses. Thus, for example, when national political leaders make a claim about what it means to be an 'American', 'French, 'South African', and so on, they will often invoke specific cultural and historical markers of that national identity, in the hope if not the expectation that a majority of an audience will recognise and agree with that articulation of national identity (a process that Althusser (1971) terms as 'hailing', likening this identity claim to the process of a shouted call to which individuals then respond to). And in the process of socially constructing and specify-ing notions of *the* national interest, and threats and dangers to the nation state and its identity, policy makers often draw on a wide range of cultural resources in attempting to specify both the nature of a threat and its referent object.

So, to continue the exemplification of this point as made in Weldes' study of the Cuban missile crisis, she argues that the representation of the 'crisis' as such was the product of a 'security imaginary', a 'structure of well-established meanings and social relations out of which representations of the world of international relations are created'. US policy makers' security imaginary of the Cuban missile crisis, she argues, drew upon pre-existing popular representations of the time of 'Red Fascism' and 'Russian oriental despotism' as ways of constructing the immediacy and seriousness of the Soviet threat in a familiar and recognis-able way (Weldes 1999: 129–136; see also Doty 1993; Campbell 1992).

Box 1.4 Popular culture and the social production of dangers

Weldes (1999: 241) makes the argument that:

> The reproduction of common sense, and specifically of the grounds upon which particular representations are constructed and make sense [...] cannot be restricted to the representational practices of state actors. [...] Representing world politics is not an unusual or extraordinary activity; rather it is a relentlessly mundane and commonplace one. A key site at which that representation takes place, then, is in popular culture, in the everyday practices of meaning making that structure the quotidian.

A representative example of the extension of this approach can be found in Rowley and Weldes (2012) where the authors use the popular US television series *Buffy the Vampire Slayer* (and its spin-off *Angel*) to engage fundamental questions of the everyday constructions of danger insecurity and, as illustrated by the key characters' development and interactions, to make the case that such constructions rarely fit neatly into clearly divided states of security versus insecurity, safety versus danger. More generally, the examination of popular cultural constructions of security and insecurity is a growing area of research. Among multiple possible examples, Grayson *et al.* (2009) make the case for substantive incorporation of the study of popular culture into IR more generally; Grayson (2012) employs a reading of the biblical story of Judith in order to critically engage with representation of political assassination in Western cultural understandings of political violence; Debrix (2008) assesses the role of visual culture and media in constituting the 'tabloid geopolitics' of the US war on terror; Lisle (2007: 334) investigates what the cultural phenomenon of 'dark tourism' – tourist visits to sites of assassinations, atrocities and wars – indicates in relation to the popular 'consumption of danger'; and Salter (2011) analyses the ways in which best-selling video games such as *Civilization* and *Grand Theft Auto IV* reproduce popular geopolitical imaginaries.

The second potentially radical implication of the approach suggested by Weldes in particular is that 'security imaginaries' pervade not only the worlds of policy makers but also the everyday lives of individuals more generally in a range of popular cultural discourses, practices and artefacts.

As discussed in Box 1.4, this opens up the spectrum of analysis of critical constructivist approaches to the study of security in a way that most proponents of traditional approaches to the study of security, and even conventional constructivist approaches, are likely to be uncomfortable with. In, for instance, using the 'Buffyverse' (Rowley and Weldes 2012) as way to interrogate and understand not only everyday constructions of insecurity and danger but also narrative constructions of the evolution of (critical) security studies, Rowley and Weldes (and others – see Box 1.4) arguably challenge the conventional boundaries of what is to be included in the study of security. While critics might argue that this risks loading the study of security with the weight of examining the wide and amorphous category of 'popular culture', this focus on popular culture and the everyday production of dangers usefully provokes reflection on the extent to which security studies, and even some variants of critical security studies, have tended to privilege analysis of 'exceptional' measures and the discourses and activities of political elites over and above the mundane, quotidian constructions of danger and insecurity or their interrelation.

Conclusion

As with all of the approaches covered in this book, a final point for consideration is the extent to which constructivist theories are distinct from or overlap with other positions considered in Part I of this text. On the question of whether constructivist theories constitute a distinct strand of approaches to the study of security, this chapter has made the case that there are least two distinctive constructivist theoretical approaches. This is not to say, however, that either conventional constructivist approaches or critical constructivist approaches are hermetically sealed off from the other approaches covered here. At a general level, it might be said, as noted already in the Introduction to this book, that adherence to the idea that reality is socially constructed is a recurrent theme across all of the approaches covered in Part I. More nuanced differences begin to emerge in ways in which each of the approaches incorporate, address and extend that assumption, and this becomes clearer in comparison with the other individual chapters: feminist and gender approaches (Chapter 3) tend to home in on the social construction of gender identities; postcolonial approaches on constructions of an oriental 'Other' (Chapter 4); poststructuralism on binary and hierarchical constructions of 'Self' and 'Other' (Chapter 5); and securitisation theory on a specific mode of constructing existential threats that is argued to be peculiar to security discourses (Chapter 6).

In relation to Chapter 2, while the exact overlap with the critical theoretical approach advocated by the Welsh School is perhaps less obvious, the notion of security as a 'derivative concept' as advocated by the latter can still be related to a broader upholding of the notion of security as socially constructed. Moreover, even if critical constructivism clearly does not necessarily sign up to the precise notion of 'emancipation' covered in Chapter 2, Weldes *et al*'s commitment to the use of critical constructivism to allow for 'facilitating the imagining of alternative life worlds' (1999:13) might at the very least be said to carry a more qualified commitment to identifying the potential for progressive social change. Fierke similarly argues that constructivist theory can be 'pushe[d] further' to include an explicitly critical and emancipatory purpose that draws on the Critical Theory of the Frankfurt School (see Chapter 2 in this book) if, rather than simply describing processes of social construction, it:

> makes us look again, in a fresh way, at that which we assume about the world because it has become overly familiar. In this way, new spaces are opened for thinking about the meaning of the past and the present, and, therefore, how we construct the future.
>
> (Fierke 1998: 11, 13)

Critical constructivism by virtue not only of its 'critical' appellation but its more general tenets and approach, thus clearly overlaps with the field of critical security studies if the latter is broadly conceived of. Indeed, critical constructivist and poststructuralist approaches are often seen to bleed into one another to such an extent that it is common to find certain authors (Jutta Weldes and David Campbell being prominent examples) identified in the literature as key proponents of both. In closing though, it is worth reiterating not just the significance of social construction to the study of security, but also the distinct contributions of different variants of constructivist theoretical scholarship as discussed in this chapter.

Key points

- Constructivist theoretical approaches to the study of security might be said to share in common a concern with the intersubjective construction of security relations.
- Beyond this, a distinction can be made between conventional constructivist and critical constructivist theoretical approaches.
- Conventional constructivist approaches tend to accept key 'puzzles' as identified in traditional security studies, such as the security dilemma and explaining the maintenance and dissolution of military alliances between states, but offer constructivist accounts in response that emphasise the roles played by intersubjectivity and identity in states' interactions.
- Critical constructivist approaches are distinguished by their attention to how questions of power are inherent within social relations and common sense understandings of the world, are by a normative concern with identifying the ways in which dominant understandings of the world preclude the articulation and production of alternative life-worlds.
- Critical constructivist approaches also allow for a more heterodox and pluralist theoretical and methodological approach that is not limited to examination of state actors, but can also include analysis of everyday representations of insecurity and danger and focus on multiple cultural sources of both state and non-state security imaginaries.

Discussion points

- What is the potential significance of the claim that security is 'socially constructed'?
- What are the political and methodological implications of adopting a social constructivist approach to the study of security?
- In relation to the study of security, what is 'critical' about 'critical constructivism'?
- How should we define and study culture in relation to security?
- To what extent do other theoretical approaches within this text share or challenge the key tenets of constructivist theories?

Guide to further reading

Alexander Wendt (1999) *Social Theory of International Politics* (Cambridge: Cambridge University Press). Provides an extended version of Wendt's argument that 'anarchy', and by implication security, is 'what states make of it'.

Jarrod Hayes (2013) *Constructing National Security: US Relations with India and China* (Cambridge: Cambridge University Press). A more recent attempt to apply and extend a modified constructivist approach to understanding processes of threat construction in relations between states.

Jutta Weldes, Mark Laffey, Hugh Gusterson and Raymond Duvall (eds) (1999) *Cultures of Insecurity: States, Communities and the Production of Danger* (Minnesota, MN: University of Minnesota Press). As well as a key introductory chapter by the editors, this edited collection offers critical constructivist perspectives in application to a wide range of issues and cases.

Karin M. Fierke (1999) *Changing Games, Changing Strategies* (Manchester: Manchester University Press). Fierke's theoretically detailed and empirically rich analysis of East–West relations in the last two decades of the cold war seeks to push constructivist approaches to the study of security further by combining a Wittgensteinian approach to 'language games' with the critical intent of the Frankfurt School tradition.

Peter J. Katzenstein (1996) (ed.) *The Culture of National Security: Norms and Identity in World Politics* (New York: Columbia University Press). Makes the case for a constructivist approach to the study of states' distinct national security cultures, with multiple contributions on specific case studies.

Peter L. Berger and Thomas Luckmann (1991) *The Social Construction of Reality A Treatise in the Sociology of Knowledge* (London: Penguin Books). First published in 1966 and in multiple editions since then, Berger and Luckmann's text remains a key starting point for further reading on the topic of social construction.

2   Critical Theory

Abstract

Among the multiple critical approaches to security, one specific variant – Critical Security Studies (CSS), or the Welsh School approach – has sought to explicitly link the study of security to Critical Theory. This chapter locates the key intellectual origins and developments in this understanding of CSS, before moving on to discuss in more detail its central ideas. Particular attention is paid to the concept of 'emancipation' as viewed from a CSS perspective and to the issue of how security theory and security practices are related to one another. The chapter also goes on to discuss some of the most prominent criticisms of Welsh School CSS before evaluating the contributions, limitations and potentialities of this particular interpretation of the relationship between Critical Theory and security.

Introduction

Although critical security studies is increasingly recognised and used as a term, the significance of appending the word 'critical' to 'security studies' has been interpreted in several different ways. One particular school of thought – known variously as 'Critical Security Studies', 'CSS' (upper case), or sometimes as the 'Welsh School' of security studies (see Box 2.1) – argues that relating the study of security to 'Critical Theory' generates a specific range of theoretical, methodological and normative implications. One proponent has summed up these implications as entailing the 'broadening', 'deepening', 'extending' and 'focusing' of security studies (Wyn Jones 1999: 166). 'Broadening' refers to a conception of security studies that includes a range of issues beyond military force under the rubric of security. 'Deepening' implies a theoretical approach to security that connects our understandings of security to deeply rooted assumptions about the nature of political life more generally. 'Extending' denotes the expansion of the security studies agenda to recognise not only a multiplicity of issues, but also a multiplicity of actors beyond the state as referent objects of insecurity including, most fundamentally, individual human beings. Finally, CSS claims to provide an approach to security that is ultimately 'focused' in the sense that it is grounded in a particular normative goal: that of human 'emancipation'.

This self-styled critical approach to security departs radically from more conventional (or 'traditional') approaches to security for reasons that are discussed in more detail later in the chapter. However, while some of the moves made by the Welsh School's Critical Security Studies/CSS project are shared by the other approaches gathered under the critical umbrella, other commitments entailed in its relation of Critical Theory and security have been more controversial and divisive. The consequent result is that this definition of CSS is far from universally accepted.

Box 2.1 'Critical security studies' – what's in a name?!

Within recent writing on security it is possible to find references to both 'Critical Security Studies/CSS' (upper case) and 'critical security studies/css' (lower case). Why is this distinction made and what significance, if any, should we attach to it?

Generally speaking, security scholars use CSS/css in a manner parallel to a broader distinction made between forms of critical social theory. 'Critical Theory' (upper case) is conventionally used to denote a Marxian tradition of theorising that includes elements of ideas first put forward by Karl Marx (1818–1883) – most notably his invocation to not only 'interpret the world' but to 'change it' – but also several efforts to reinterpret and offset some of the more deterministic aspects of Marx's thought. In particular, the thinkers associated with the so-called Frankfurt School of Critical Theory sought to extend Marx's critique of capitalism from its focus on economics to a concern with issues ranging from popular culture, psychoanalysis and technology. Proponents of CSS, such as Ken Booth and Richard Wyn Jones, tend to reserve the use of the term 'Critical Security Studies' to denote a specific approach to security that claims to draw primarily upon this Marxian tradition of Critical Theory as well as interpretations of this tradition within the study of IR more broadly (although see Box 2.6 for critiques of CSS's employment and interpretation of Marxian thought). The use of the lower-case 'critical theory' is generally used in the social sciences to identify a more diverse range of ideas and approaches that includes Marxian-inspired thought but is far from limited to it and even challenges it in some respects. Whereas the former has a particular (emancipatory) purpose, the latter is more heterogeneous in its concerns and goals. A good way for readers to get at this contrast further is to compare the interpretations of the term Critical Security Studies taken by Booth (2007) and Wyn Jones (1999) with the multiple interpretations of the term used in Krause and Williams (1997).

More recently there has been an attempt to distinguish the CSS 'school' by its geographical origin. Since the key proponents of CSS – Booth and Wyn Jones – both put forward their rendering of Critical Theory and security whilst at Aberystwyth in West Wales, some have suggested referring to it as the Welsh School of security studies (see CASE 2006) as a counterpart to various other schools of thought.

From 'traditional' to 'critical' security studies

The CSS project has its broad origins in peace studies (or peace research), which aimed to develop 'new thinking' about the cold war stand-off that threatened nuclear annihilation, and its emergence is also linked to the development of a 'critical turn' in international studies more broadly. As peace studies evolved in the 1980s it increasingly began to focus not only on the achievement of 'negative peace' (the absence of war) but also the idea of 'positive peace' – the pursuit of social and economic justice as means of addressing underlying causes of conflict. The latter goal opened peace research out to consideration of issues such as health, economic welfare and environmental stability as well as its previous focus on military issues such as nuclear weapons, and this 'broad' perspective has been a key influence in the development of CSS. The expansive agenda of peace research helped encourage a 'comprehensive' view of security within the CSS project, and simultaneously developments in 'Critical International Theory' crucially informed its attitude towards the study of security. At the beginning of the 1980s, the IR theorist Robert Cox argued that the study of world politics could be divided into two categories: 'Problem-solving theory' and 'Critical Theory'.

Problem-solving theory, Cox argued, takes the nature of world politics as a 'given'. In other words, it assumes that there are a number of actors and issues that we should always focus upon. In security studies, this was traditionally manifested in the assumption that states are key actors in world politics, and that war between states is *the* central problem to be 'solved' in world politics.

Cox argued that *Critical Theory*, by contrast, should critically interrogate the traditional assumptions made by Problem-Solving Theory. Cox argued that by assuming that world politics is simply a range of problems – such as the problem of war between states – to be resolved, we risk missing out on key dimensions of world politics that don't fit squarely into a problem-solving mindset. More than this, we also embed and hence potentially legitimate the 'problems' we set out to study. What we should be doing in many instances is critically interrogating the way that the *problem* is set up.

Fundamentally, Cox argued, Problem-Solving and Critical Theory can also be distinguished by their approaches to knowledge (Cox 1981). Whereas Problem-Solving Theory assumes that scholars can attain and produce knowledge of the world in an objective and value-neutral fashion, Critical Theory assumes that because academic analysts are necessarily embedded within the social world they seek to analyse, knowledge has an inherently social character. Hence there is no easy distinction that can be made between 'facts' and 'values'. When building a theory or presenting an argument, we necessarily concentrate on some 'facts' and not others, highlight certain issues and cover others in less detail or not at all. All of these decisions will be affected by our own social position, education, beliefs and so on. The way that we as analysts choose to piece these elements together to either frame or address a specific 'problem' in world politics is, therefore, not a neutral act: it is an act that is, consciously or not, built upon a series of choices as to what counts as important and what does not. In turn, the ways that particular theories interpret and present the world will have consequent effects for how others view it, how decisions get made, where we devote our attention, how resources get distributed and so on. This led Cox, drawing on the ideas of Antonio Gramsci (see Box 2.4), to make his now famous pronouncement that 'theory is always *for* someone and *for* some purpose' (1981: 128).

If we apply this perspective to the discipline of security studies, it has far-reaching implications. Security studies originally developed with the explicit mandate of solving the problem of war and instability in world politics. It had clear objects of analysis – states – and a clear goal – explaining why states go to war. One of the key exponents of this vision of security studies, Stephen Walt, has succinctly argued that 'security studies may be defined as *the study of the threat, use and control of military force*'. More specifically, Walt advised that security studies was best understood as the study of 'the conditions that make the use of force more likely, the ways that the use of force affects individuals, states and societies, and the specific policies that states adopt in order to prepare for, prevent or engage in war' (1991: 212, emphasis in original).

This view of security studies, which originates from neorealist IR theory, is what has become known to its critics in CSS as 'traditional security studies'. As in Problem-solving theory, the central problem to be addressed (war) is already assumed in this view, as are the key actors (states). Although Walt makes reference to individuals and societies, he leaves us in no doubt that their security is predicated upon the policies adopted by states and that states should, by consequence, be the primary area of concern for security studies.

In keeping with the Coxian approach, critics of the 'traditional' approach argue that this narrowly focused problem-solving approach has several weaknesses. They claim that traditional security studies tends to accept the world 'as it is', assuming that analysts simply produce knowledge about the world 'out there'. Traditional security studies assumes a number of 'enduring features' of world politics, most prominently it assumes war between states as *the* enduring recurrent feature of the international system. So in other words, traditional security studies accepts (1) the state, (2) the 'anarchic' nature of the international system (the idea that there is no higher authority or actor above the state level), and hence that (3) wars between states are an inherent feature of the international system. During the cold war in particular, these factors tended to be taken-for-granted starting points for the study of security.

Scholars operating within the CSS framework argue that accepting war as *the* fact of international life *is part of the problem*. Think about the logic here: if we begin from the assumption that war is a natural feature of international life, then we are perpetually limited to efforts to constrain it. Following the broader critical move within Critical IR theory espoused by Cox, what CSS argues is that we need to be sceptical about the actual benefits of an exclusive focus on war, which, though still of great importance, is but one among a multitude of contemporary security issues. Instead of the 'problem-solving approach', proponents of CSS have called for a study of security that 'goes beyond problem-solving *within* the status quo and instead seeks to help engage with the problem *of* the status quo' (Booth 2005a: 10 emphasis in original).

A primary objection to the traditional approach is that it is too narrowly focused on the military security of states (what is often referred to as 'state-centrism' or 'statism'). In doing so it paints a static picture of international life that claims to simply portray the world 'as it is', but also makes a powerful political statement in assuming that fundamental change in the nature of world politics is virtually impossible. After the end of the cold war, which radically undermined confidence in this traditional approach because of its preclusion of significant international change (see also Chapter 1), a number of criticisms emerged of this state-centric security focus and these have helped inform the emergence of CSS.

First the contention is that state-centrism is *empirically unhelpful*: in other words, that it is an incomplete description of the nature of contemporary world politics. Following the cold war, conflict between states – the central traditional focus – was arguably no longer the biggest issue in world politics. In the 1990s, the frequency of wars *within* (rather than between) states led some to coin the concept of 'new wars' (Kaldor 1999), to describe conflicts such as those that have occurred within the former Yugoslavia, Somalia, Rwanda and later in Sudan. In this context the traditional focus on wars between states seemed poorly equipped to grasp either the localised nature of new wars or the ways in which they are embedded within global complexes of militarism, aid and development (Duffield 2001).

Second is that state-centrism often acts as a *justification of the status quo*: in other words it justifies the preservation of the state system as it is. In the 'developed world' states might be argued to generally uphold the liberty of their citizens; but in many parts of the 'developing world' states can be the biggest threat to the liberty, human rights and lives of their citizens. Some peace theorists have argued that in many cases, states can be a source of *structural violence* – that states are often a major cause of poverty and repression for their citizens (Galtung 1996). Drawing on this line of thinking, scholars such as Richard Wyn Jones argue that we should approach the traditional assumption of the state as protector of its citizens with caution:

> Even if a very narrow, military understanding of security is applied, it is apparent that the arms purchased and powers accrued by governments in the name of national security are far more potent threats to the liberty and physical safety of their citizens than

any putative external threat. This is true not only of states in the disadvantaged South but also of those in the North. When a broader definition of security that includes non-military threats is applied, it is clear that many states are deeply implicated in the creation of other forms of insecurity for their own populations, for example, in such issues as food and environmental security.

(Wyn Jones 1999: 99)

Likewise, Ken Booth has noted that 'to countless millions of people in the world it is their own state, and not "The Enemy" that is the primary security threat' (1991: 318).

Third, radical political economists – such as dependency theorists and world systems theorists (see Poku and Therkelsen 2013 for an overview) – have long argued that the state system as a whole is actually a major *source of poverty, instability and violence in the developing world* because international capitalism creates a system of winners and losers in the global economy:

the relative security of the inhabitants of the North is purchased at the price of chronic insecurity for the vast majority of the world population [. . .] So, far from being a necessary condition for the good life, statism appears to be one of the main sources of insecurity – part of the problem rather than the solution.

(Wyn Jones 1999: 99)

State-centrism, on this view, tacitly justifies the existing economic status quo, which is a major source of economic deprivation and dependency in many parts of the world.

CSS: Key concepts and core ideas

With these kinds of criticisms in mind, an emerging literature in the 1990s argued that the concept of security in the post-cold war era needed to be reconceptualised, and Welsh School CSS has been at the forefront of attempts to redefine both security and security studies. CSS is based on three core ideas that links it to a broader critical move in security studies, and one additional key principle dealt with in the following section – 'emancipation' – which tends to be seen as the distinguishing feature of the CSS project and is more divisive.

Understanding security as a 'derivative concept'

The first core idea underpinning CSS is the argument that security is a derivative concept. That is, the view of security we have derives from the way in which we see the world and the way we think politics works: what we think of as the most important features of world politics will influence what we think of as threats, what needs to be protected, and hence how we define security.

The question of how we should define security is all at once deceptively simple and of fundamental importance. One would think that academics and analysts working within the field known as 'security studies' would at least be able to agree on the meaning of the term. In one sense there must be a minimal shared understanding of the term security given that we speak of the field of 'security studies'. An example of such a minimal understanding might be Ken Booth's definition in his 1991 article *Security and Emancipation* where Booth argued that '"Security" means "the absence of threats"'.

Box 2.2 Key concepts in CSS

Statism/state-centrism: An ontological assumption – challenged by CSS – that holds the state to be both the primary actor in world politics and the provider of security, which leads in turn to a political orientation that holds national (state) security to be the pre-eminent value.

Security as a 'derivative concept': The idea that understandings of security reflect 'deeper assumptions about the nature of politics and the role of conflict in political life' (Wyn Jones 1999: 166).

Emancipation: The 'freeing of people (as individuals and groups) from those physical and human constraints which stop them carrying out what they would freely choose to do' (Booth 1991: 319).

Immanent critique: 'Immanent critique', as understood by Booth, 'involves identifying those features in concrete situations (such as positive dynamics, agents, key struggles) that have emancipatory possibilities, then working through the politics (tactics and strategies) to strengthen them' (2007: 250).

Theory–practice nexus: The idea that theories of security inform security practices and vice versa, leading to the contention that 'reconceptualized understandings of security and strategy might aid the transformation of real-world practices' (Wyn Jones 1999: 167).

When we examine such a definition in more detail, however, we come up with a range of related questions that are among the most contested (and most interesting) within the subject area: what kinds of 'threats' do we want to be free from? Who or what is it that 'threatens' us? How do we define the 'we' seeking freedom from threats? Is it the individual, group, nation, state or all of the above? Even if we can answer these questions, how do we go about achieving security?

Traditional security studies, by taking the security of the state as its central concern, assumes ready-made answers to each of these questions. So, for example, the view of security that dominated the cold war – neorealism – focused on the threat of nuclear war and the security of states, because this was derived from a focus on the political conflict between the US and the Soviet Union. But, for proponents of CSS, this definition of security is itself a derivative concept: it derives its meaning from a neorealist worldview and its emphasis on the 'anarchic' nature of the international system. Different worldviews give rise to different conceptions of security. This is not something which is usually acknowledged in a realist/neorealist perspective, which assumes 'national security' to be a universal value. From a Coxian-critical perspective this worldview is itself derived from the theories of white, Western and predominantly male academics working within a particular context. 'Security', from the point of view of a refugee in Sudan, for example, is likely to mean something very different. Expanding the point, theories that challenge neorealism's emphasis on the state as *the* referent object consequently give rise to different conceptions of security.

A broadened security agenda

CSS argues that military force, although important, is not the only potential threat to security, that other threats are equally worthy of consideration, and that the end of the cold war allowed space to give consideration to these alternative threats that were previously generally marginalised. Among the first academics to put forward this argument was Barry Buzan in his book

People, States and Fear. Buzan (1991) argues that security analysts needed to think about security in five different 'sectors': military, but also environmental, economic, political and societal. The basic point that those within the CSS project borrowed from Buzan was that in the contemporary world, people *are* threatened by a multitude of issues: yes war, but also poverty, famine, political oppression and environmental degradation to name but a few.

The individual as the 'referent object' of security

Although those within CSS concur with Buzan that security studies needs to widen its focus to include non-military dimensions, they argue that he does not go far enough because Buzan's work still exclusively focused on the state as its referent object. For Richard Wyn Jones, the title *People, States and Fear* is arresting but also misleading. '"States and Fear" is a more accurate representation of Barry Buzan's ultimate focus in that work', Wyn Jones argues (1999: 112) because Buzan's broadening only accounted for the ways in which non-military issues such as environmental degradation and economic crisis might threaten the state. As we saw previously, CSS takes such state-centrism to be problematic. By contrast, what Booth and Wyn Jones want to argue is that military, environmental, economic, political and societal threats affect *people* in the first instance (see also Chapter 10). States are, at base, human communities; therefore the ultimate referents of security should be the human beings that make up the state, not the state itself in some abstract sense. In a similar vein, Bill McSweeney has asserted that 'security must make sense at the basic level of the individual human being for it to make sense at the international level' (1999: 16). In short, proponents of CSS argue that security, fundamentally, should refer ultimately to the 'corporeal, material existence and experiences of human beings' (Wyn Jones 1999: 23).

Emancipation, community, identity

These three elements – security as a derivative concept, the idea of a broadened security agenda, and challenging the assumption of the state as the referent object of security – might be said to be common points of discussion in all the 'critical' approaches to security discussed in this book. They are addressed not only by the Welsh School formed around Ken Booth and Richard Wyn Jones, but also (albeit to differing degrees) by critical constructivists, poststructuralists, proponents of securitisation theory, feminist and postcolonial approaches. However, the idea of security as a 'derivative concept' applies as much to the 'critical' approach to security as it does to its traditional counterpart. As well as originating in ideas drawn from peace studies and the 'critical turn' in IR theory, the argument for thinking of security as 'emancipation' links CSS to the broader tradition of Critical Theory and several concepts and ideas derived from Marxian thought.

As well as building on the three elements outlined in the previous section, Booth and Wyn Jones seek to add a fourth principle: the principle of 'emancipation'. They argue that Critical Security Studies should have a purpose, and that its purpose should be the transformation of society itself into a more secure and emancipated form.

Emancipation

Proponents of CSS argue that the corporeal, material existence of human beings should be the central focus of security studies: that is, security should ultimately be concerned with the 'real world' security of human beings. Consequently, for CSS, the study of security should seek to illuminate the wide range of constraints on human well-being that exist in many parts of the world, and challenge the forms of security knowledge and practices that perpetuate these constraints.

Locating this goal within a broader tradition of Critical Theory (see Box 2.3), Ken Booth outlined the contours of an 'emancipation-oriented' approach to security in a seminal 1991 article entitled *Security and Emancipation*. Here Booth argues that:

> 'Security' means the absence of threats. Emancipation is the freeing of people (as individuals and groups) from those physical and human constraints which stop them carrying out what they would freely choose to do. War and the threat of war is one of those constraints, together with poverty, poor education, political oppression and so on. Security and emancipation are two sides of the same coin. Emancipation, not power or order, produces true security. Emancipation, theoretically, is security.
>
> (Booth 1991: 319)

What Booth argues here is that if we broaden the security agenda to include issues like poverty and education, then we are necessarily getting involved in the general well-being of societies (hence the 'broadening' and 'extending' of security are inherently related). People will feel secure not just through protection from military threats, but also through protection

---

Box 2.3 CSS and Critical Theory

Although associated with several strands of political thought as well a variety of social movements (see Nederveen Pieterse 1992), the concept of *emancipation* is usually seen to hold special significance within Marxian thought. At the heart of Marx's philosophy was an attempt to rethink the relationship between 'freedom' and 'necessity'. Marx believed that under relations of capitalism, human beings subject themselves to a range of unnecessary constraints (servitude, wage labour, exploitation), which appear as 'necessities' but from which we can and should become emancipated. The concept was later taken up by a group of German social theorists in the interwar years known as the Frankfurt School – inclusive of thinkers such as Max Horkheimer (1895–1973), Theodor Adorno (1903–1969), Herbert Marcuse (1898–1979) and Jürgen Habermas (1929–) (for an overview, see Held 2004) – who sought to develop a form of 'Critical Theory' aimed at illuminating the prospects for emancipation in society.

The Critical Theory tradition, in a very broad sense, looks to identify those aspects of modern life, culture, and technology that constrain and enable human freedom, and the work of Richard Wyn Jones (1999) in particular looks to this tradition to inform the 'Critical' in Critical Security Studies. The CSS conception of emancipation is not built around a static or monolithic vision of an ideal society: 'even if a more emancipated order is brought into existence, the process of emancipation remains incomplete. There is always room for improvement; there is always unfinished business in the task of emancipation' (Wyn Jones 1999: 78). Hence the concept of *immanent critique*, also associated with the Frankfurt School, has come to be central to the CSS project both as a normative and methodological orientation. Broadly speaking, the term refers to a strategy utilising critique in order to identify potentialities that are immanent but as yet unfulfilled in any given theory or historical context by highlighting inherent contradictions. Thus, for example, the CSS project might be regarded at a general level as an immanent critique of security studies that seeks to retrieve and expand the potential of 'security' from its more conservative statist definitions by highlighting the fact that 'national security' regularly impinges upon the security of individuals.

from the threat of poverty, ill-health, environmental degradation and so on. Similarly, Richard Wyn Jones argues that the welfare of individual human beings – that is their freedom from both military and non-military threats – needs to be placed at the centre of the security studies agenda. We should study security, Booth and Wyn Jones argue, in order to learn more about how individuals can maximise their freedom from threats. The more secure people are from the threats of war, poverty and oppression, the more emancipated they will be and vice versa.

This necessarily leads to a more expansive conception of security that is more than simply 'survival'. In the traditional approach to security, state survival is assumed to equate to security for all its inhabitants. Yet for the various reasons outlined in the previous section CSS critiques opposed this assumption and the tendency to conflate the concepts of 'security' and 'survival'. Booth argues that 'Survival is being alive; security is living', or, as he puts it elsewhere, security is equivalent to *survival-plus*: security is 'an instrumental value in that it allows individuals and groups (to a relative degree) to establish the conditions of existence with some expectations of constructing a human life beyond the merely animal' (Booth 2007: 106–107). Survival merely implies the continuance of existence in conditions where life is threatened, whereas security denotes a genuine absence of threats and the consequent maximisation not only of an individual's life-chances but also of their life-*choices*. Booth and Wyn Jones therefore argue that when we think about security, we are also engaging in fundamental questions about nature of political life and, specifically, the attendant questions of roles of community and identity in the achievement of security.

Community and identity

As is discussed in Chapter 6, the focus of the Welsh School on the human being as the ultimate referent of security has left it open to charges of methodological individualism. Wyn Jones (1999) argues that this need not necessarily follow from a focus on human emancipation. He recognises that individual identity is a central aspect of what it means to be human, and that by consequence the constitutive relationship between 'identity, security and community' requires CSS to engage with the nature of political groupings that exist within concrete historical circumstances:

> Identity never occurs in the singular [. . .] The human condition is one of overlapping identities; that is, each person has a number of different identities, all (potentially) in flux, and all of which come into play at different times and in different situations. Thus a focus on individuals strongly discourages any tendency to reify human identity; it points instead to the complex, multifaceted, and even fluid nature of identity.
>
> (1999: 116)

Although the normative basis of CSS centres around the security of the individual human being, Booth and Wyn Jones recognise that individuals do not exist in vacuum; rather, 'individuals' are constituted in large part by their membership of overlapping forms of political community. The question of security is, in practice, underpinned by questions of who 'we' are and what 'we' want to be secured from. In this sense, Booth argues, 'Community is the site of security' (2007: 278).

However, the CSS approach to community is also a cautious one. Rather than celebrating 'difference' for its own sake, CSS argues that it is *emancipatory* communities – based around inclusionary and egalitarian notions of identity – that should be promoted over communities that are predicated on internal relations of domination (such as patriarchy) and chauvinistic forms of identity (such as notions of national superiority). Fundamentally, human emancipation – both that of individual humans and humanity in general – provides the guide both for relations within communities and between them. Hence 'As a political orientation [CSS] is informed by the aim of enhancing world security through emancipatory politics and networks of community at all levels, including the potential community of all communities – common humanity' (Booth 2007: 31).

Reconceptualising security, reconceptualising practice

Appeals to emancipation and common humanity are all very well, but even those operating within CSS have openly recognised that 'critical theorists must go beyond generalised exhortations concerning emancipation, empowerment, freedom, and happiness. If critical theory is to have practical relevance, it must reflect on what emancipation means in terms of actual institutions and relationships' (Wyn Jones 1999: 76). A theoretical commitment to emancipation can only be made good by a commitment to emancipatory practices, and the Marxian idea of *praxis* (see Box 2.4) indicates that theory is informed and reformed by engagement with practical issues and, conversely, that concrete situations are affected and improved by new theoretical insights (what Wyn Jones terms as a 'theory–practice nexus').

So what strategies are open to those seeking to advance emancipation? How does 'an emancipatory approach to thinking about security interact with and impinge upon emancipatory praxis?' (Wyn Jones 1999: 118). Here proponents of CSS offer general principles rather than a set framework for action. The reason for this is that CSS suggests an understanding of emancipation as 'a process rather than an end point, a direction rather than a destination' (Wyn Jones 1999: 77). The constraints and insecurities suffered by individuals vary across time and space; hence it is not possible to specify with finality abstract criteria for emancipatory action, rather these must be developed in conjunction with an analysis of specific contexts. At a more general level, Richard Wyn Jones has suggested that proponents of Critical Security Studies should seek to act as organic intellectuals (see Box 2.4) that promote progressive social change:

Box 2.4 CSS and Gramsci

As well as Frankfurt School of Critical Theory, CSS also draws in part upon the thinking of the Italian Marxist theorist Antonio Gramsci (1891–1937), in particular Gramsci's thinking on the role of intellectuals and the relationship between theory and practice (Gramsci 1971). Taking seriously Marx's admonition to not only think about the world but to change it, as Gramsci does, proponents of CSS emphasise *praxis* – the idea that theory and practice are inextricably intertwined – and the potential role of intellectuals in advancing emancipatory change. Critical scholars, Wyn Jones argues, should 'become the *organic intellectuals* of critical social movements when they exist, or encourage the creation of the political space necessary for their emergence if they do not'. As opposed to 'traditional' intellectuals, who regard the study of security as relatively autonomous from its subject matter, the concerns of organic intellectuals grow 'organically' out of the everyday struggles for security endured by 'the voiceless, the unrepresented and the powerless' (Wyn Jones 1999: 167).

through their educational activities, proponents of critical security studies should aim to provide support for those social movements that promote emancipatory social change. By providing a critique of the prevailing order and legitimating alternative views, critical theorists can perform a valuable role in supporting the struggles of social movements.

(Wyn Jones 1999: 161)

There has been a general reluctance to specify exactly what 'support' of social movements might consist of beyond this critical-educative function. However, the goal of emancipatory change itself does indicate that some alternative visions and social movements are more preferable than others. 'Let us consider the ending of apartheid in South Africa', Wyn Jones offers as an example (see also Box 2.5):

Although the citizens of that country cannot be adjudged to be free after the overthrow of the apartheid system, surely they are freer. Although the establishment of liberal democracy there offers no panacea, it is a better system than the totalitarian one it has replaced.

(Wyn Jones 1999: 43)

Booth has argued that:

We can begin or continue pursuing emancipation in what we research, in how we teach, in what we put on conference agendas, in how much we support Greenpeace, Amnesty International, Oxfam and other groups identifying with a global community, and in how we deal with each other and with students. And in pursuing emancipation, the bases of real security are being established.

(1991: 326)

In this sense for Booth, emancipation is itself '*a practice of resistance* [...] a framework for attempting to actualise both nearer-term and longer-term emancipatory goals through strategic and tactical political action based on immanent critique' (2007: 112, emphasis in original). This approach is captured in Booth's concept of 'emancipatory realism', where the Marxian origins of 'emancipation' are filtered through Kantian idealism and a focus on 'gradual reforms' as 'the only means of approaching the supreme political good' (2007: 87). In other words, scholars of security should seek to identify and foster elements of progressive social change through their work as part of a gradualist, non-violent strategy for emancipation that is ultimately more realistic than rigid blueprints for utopia that – as in the case of the French and Russian revolutions that heralded the 'Terror' and 'purges' respectively – often end up generating even more intense cycles of violence and insecurity.

CSS and its critics

As summed up by Richard Wyn Jones (1999: 5), CSS is an approach that:

- 'eschews statism'
- recognises that non-military issues have 'a place on the security agenda' as well as military issues
- and 'anchors the theory and practice of security in a broader concern with human emancipation'.

Box 2.5 CSS and the case of Southern Africa

Among the attempts to offer practical application and illustration of the CSS project, Ken Booth and Peter Vale's (1997) work on Southern Africa remains one of the most instructive accounts. As well as the end of the apartheid regime in South Africa representing the result of a concrete emancipatory struggle, Booth and Vale argue that the historical experience of South Africa and the region more generally highlights several of the key contentions of CSS:

On the perils of statism:

> The states of southern Africa [...] do not match the textbook images of Anglo-American political science. These states have not stood as reliable watch-keepers over the security of their inhabitants. In the southern African context the state is often the problem, not the solution.
>
> (333)

A broadened security agenda:

> The threat of food scarcity is, for many, more fundamental than the threat of military violence [...] In [this] and other examples (drugs, violence, falling investment, and the threat to the fulfilment of peoples' expectations in South Africa) it is evident that the major security threats in the region are intimately interconnected.
>
> (337)

On the referent object debate:

> The security of the apartheid regime [...] meant the insecurity of both the majority population of the South African state and the neighbours of their state. National security for South Africa meant security for the white minority, not the vast majority of citizens in the state.
>
> (334)

On the theory–practice nexus:

> No small part of the strategic license that enabled South Africa's minority government to destabilize the region in the 1970s and 1980s was the result of generation upon generation of South Africa's white youth learning – being taught – to look upon their neighbours as inferior.
>
> (331)

On the role of (organic) intellectuals:

> Critical security students have an important role to play, by raising the salience of different security conceptions, referents, threats, principles, institutions, and timetables [...] In the long run, security in the form of peace, order and justice must come from within the people(s) of the region. At present they do not have much of a voice in their own affairs. Consequently [C]ritical [S]ecurity [S]tudies must engage with practical politics in Southern Africa and speak up for those without security.
>
> (354)

Most fundamentally, following Cox's contention that 'all theory is for someone and for some purpose', proponents of the CSS project argue that Critical Security Studies is 'for "the voiceless, the unrepresented, and the powerless" [in world politics], and its purpose is their emancipation' (Wyn Jones 1999: 159).

However, the Welsh School emphasis on 'emancipation' is both a distinguishing and divisive feature. As Ken Booth puts it, 'emancipation is at the contested heart of Critical Security Studies' (2005b: 181). The introduction of the concept of emancipation into security studies is at the heart of the CSS project for its proponents, but they also recognise that its introduction generates a series of further commitments and complexities. CSS attaches a particular meaning (emancipation) and referent object (the individual human being) to the concept of security. It thus challenges the state-centric definition of security, but also the idea sometimes put forward that security is 'an essentially contested' concept (see Baldwin 1997: 10). The particular threats to an individual may be multifaceted and change over time, and in this sense insecurities are contingent upon time and place, but security is assumed to have a basic meaning that relates to the establishment of freedom from those threats. 'Security' thus ultimately has a positive connotation within the CSS perspective when it can be related to the improvement of individual well-being. In this sense the CSS project has been seen by its proponents to entail a commitment to progressive politics and thus, ultimately, to the spirit of the eighteenth century Enlightenment (see Wyn Jones 2005 and especially Booth 2007).

The concept of emancipation is thus one of the most far-reaching but also one of the most controversial ideas associated with CSS or Welsh School security studies, and is generally seen to distinguish the Welsh School from the other 'critical approaches' to security. The most fundamental criticism of CSS is that its commitment to 'emancipation' is misguided, and this is a primary reason why several other critical (with a lower case 'c' – see Box 2.1) approaches to security are seen to be distinct from the Critical Security Studies project. Many poststructuralist approaches to security argue that we can still be critical of traditional approaches to security without invoking a broad goal like emancipation (see Chapter 5). Emancipation, on this view, is a potentially dangerous 'meta-narrative' – a term often used in poststructuralist thought to denote overarching explanations of the world, which it regards sceptically (Lyotard 1984) – that is particular to a Western philosophical tradition rooted in European Enlightenment and liberal thought. There is no universally agreed definition of what emancipation is (and many poststructuralists argue that the pretension to universalism is part of the problem), and definitions of emancipation may be used to legitimate illiberal practices. Even sympathetic critics of the CSS project, such as Hayward Alker, note with caution the tainted historical association of 'emancipation' both with projects for Marxist revolution, Western hegemony and liberal imperialism at the global level (Alker 2005: 189). Others, such as Mohammed Ayoob have suggested the potential inappropriateness of the concept of emancipation to non-Western security contexts, where 'interpreted as the right of every ethnic group to self-determination, emancipation can turn out to be a recipe for grave disorder and anarchy' (1997: 127).

In response to such criticisms, Richard Wyn Jones has argued that the distance between the CSS project and poststructuralist approaches to security has been overdrawn (Wyn Jones 2005: 215). All critical approaches to security, and indeed the very notion of critique, he argues, are implicitly underpinned by some notion of thinking or doing security better by the very fact that they all seek to problematise and criticise traditional approaches and practices. In this sense, Wyn Jones argues, poststructuralist approaches to security are necessarily committed to some notion of emancipation – albeit emancipation with a small 'e' rather than the visions of 'Emancipation' that originate more directly from Enlightenment thought. Similarly, rather than simply rejecting the idea of emancipation as inapplicable outside of a Western context, Alker recommends instead that:

we still need to achieve the fuller inclusion of multiple Western *and* non-Western perspectives on the meanings of freedom, without giving up the distinctive and attractive appeal to human improvement and emancipatory development that is so central to the ethical/global concerns of the critical security studies project.

(2005: 200, emphasis in original)

For some critics, though, the CSS project is problematic not for its use of the concept of emancipation but for the linkage it assumes *between* security and emancipation. By simultaneously advocating a broadened security agenda and a symbiotic relationship between security and emancipation, the implication of the CSS project is that more security is required across a range of issues to achieve human improvement. In short, it assumes that security (of the individual) is a 'good thing'. A number of thinkers, whilst acknowledging the need for a broadened security agenda, worry that this encourages the practice of simply 'hyphenating' security to other issues: that is, the tendency to attach the concept of security to other issues, such as environmental degradation in the notion of 'environmental security'. For some viewing the environment in terms of security is fundamentally unhelpful (this debate is discussed in more detail in Chapter 7).

More broadly, proponents of securitisation theory argue that because 'security' carries a specific military connotation historically, its application to non-military issues such as migration and economics can be highly misguided. Rather than emancipation and security being two sides of the same coin, they argue that the logic of security may be inappropriate to certain issues and that we should instead look to 'desecuritise', as is discussed in Chapter 5. Others argue that struggles for security and struggles for emancipation – in terms of the achievement of equality at a social level – should be kept separate rather than conflated:

> When equated with security, emancipation becomes problematic as it can no longer envisage social transformations outside of the logic of security [...] The struggle for security is re-styled as a struggle for emancipation, without any qualms about the relationship between emancipation and security.
>
> (Aradau 2004: 397–398)

Once again, this is linked to the idea that security has, historically, been linked with a particular type of politics that has often inhibited rather than advanced struggles for political equality (think of the use of police and other state forces against civil rights protesters in the name of 'national security') (Peoples 2011).

As an alternative to the equivalence of security and emancipation, then, Claudia Aradau suggests that critical approaches to security might look to the understandings of emancipation found in the work of the French post-Marxists Jacques Rancière, Alain Badiou and Étienne Balibar where emancipation is considered as distinct from security and 'is linked to democratic politics, extensively defined in terms of equality and fairness, voice and slow procedures open to public scrutiny' (Aradau 2004: 401). This alternative vision of emancipation is rooted within a broader critique of contemporary capitalism in post-Marxist thought and, in a related vein, some have criticised the CSS project for failing to say enough on the functioning of contemporary capitalism as a major source of individual insecurities. The implication here is, as has been argued elsewhere (Herring 2013), that CSS is insufficiently concerned with class and economic inequalities as originally so prominent within Marxian historical materialism (see Box 2.6).

Box 2.6 Historical materialist critiques of Critical Security Studies

Karl Marx espoused what he termed as 'the materialist conception of history' in the preface of his 1859 work *A Contribution to the Critique of Political Economy*. Subsequent interpreters of Marx often use the term 'historical materialism' to denote the view that the social, political and legal 'superstructure' (as Marx would have it) of societies is fundamentally shaped by the 'base' of its economic 'conditions [or 'means'] of production', with Marx further arguing that the distinguishing feature of modern capitalist societies was the class cleavage between those who own the means of production and profit from it (the 'bourgeoisie') and those who serve it and are exploited by it (the 'proletariat') (see Marx 1971 [1859]). Herring (2013) argues that it is surprising that 'historical materialism is much less prominent [. . .] than would be expected from the fact that [it] is central to the origins of the critical theory on which much of CSS draws'. Herring's criticism is not simply limited to the Welsh School variant of CSS covered in this chapter, but its potential applicability in this respect is clear in his further claim that 'Most of CSS is so post-Marxist as to be non-Marxist: what lingers are commitments to change and emancipation (freeing people from the constraints that prevent them from living full lives) but with little understanding of how capitalism shuts down or opens up space for emancipation' (2013: 47). Although some later interpretations of Marx's historical materialism have been accused of economic determinism – that is, the argument that economic structures determine all other aspects of social life – Herring and other proponents of historical materialism as an approach (including 'neo-Gramscian' scholars such as Cox (1981, 1983)) argue that the accusation is itself based on a reductionist reading of both Marx's ideas and historical materialism. Instead they argue that historical materialist approaches to security and insecurity do allow for the significance of 'superstructural' aspects, but retain a crucial focus on how concrete material economic structures condition and create threats to individuals and communities. In the context of radical global economic inequalities that have been exacerbated by (but also precede) the impacts of the 'global financial crisis' of 2008, a strong case can be made that, for a majority of the world's population, poverty is a fundamental source of human insecurity, and that the political economic dimensions of security and insecurity must be taken seriously as a result (for related discussions see Chapter 10).

Criticising Ken Booth's recent calls for a form of capitalism that is more appropriate to individual security globally, Rens van Munster has argued that 'The world would certainly benefit from a more humane capitalism, but emancipation cannot happen through dialogue and the extension of rights alone. It also involves concrete struggles in the realm of work, production and property relations' (2008: 439). Neocleous argues that Booth's equation of 'security' and 'emancipation' is in this respect 'far closer to classical liberalism than it is to critical theory'. As such, Neocleous claims, Booth's version of CSS reinforces a 'security fetish' (2008: 5) and ultimately fails to question the ways in which security politics has, historically, served to uphold a form of social and economic order that has benefited states' governing classes. He attempts to illustrate this point by detailing the connections between the rise of the 'national security' state and the 'social security' (welfare) state in the mid-twentieth century, and by examining the 'commodification of security' under contemporary conditions of privatisation (see also Chapter 12). Invoking the spirit of Marx (see Box 2.6), Neocleous argues for a 'critique of critical criticism'. That is, he argues that CSS should itself be critically interrogated as to its own assumptions, particularly the assumption that security in its 'true', emancipatory form can be a positive condition to aspire to and attain. Viewing 'security' as an instrument of 'bourgeois politics', Neocleous exhorts us to 'return the gift' of 'security' (2008: 8, 10).

Conclusion

Critics of the CSS project have highlighted several of its potential limitations but in the process may also point to some of its own inherent potentialities, particularly in regard to the general idea of relating Critical Theory and security studies. The work of Booth and Wyn Jones is suggestive of one possible variation of that relationship, but there may be other ways of relating Critical Theory to security, for example in application to environmental degradation, human security and military technology, to enhance our understanding of key issues (see Chapters 7, 10 and 12). Indeed the question of whether and how to relate Critical Theory to the study of security continues to animate debate. Hynek and Chandler (2013: 46) argue that CSS is 'no longer productive of emancipatory alternatives' in a concrete sense as a distinctive feature of the Critical Theory tradition. Conversely, Nunes (2012: 357) argues that a 're-engagement' with the CSS focus on emancipation is crucial to the 'politicisation' of security. While acknowledging the force of several of the criticisms of CSS, Nunes makes the case that a concern with emancipation can and should still be made central to critical analysis of security politics, and to analysis of how existing structures and relations of vulnerability and disadvantage might be overcome. Otherwise, he argues, the critical study of security risks losing all sense of purpose.

To its detractors the CSS project remains fatefully wedded to an Enlightenment progressivism whose time has come and gone, a connection that recent restatements of CSS have tended to stress and defend even more forcefully. Some readers, after moving on to later chapters, may become more convinced that this is an inherent limitation of the CSS approach. Others, however, will no doubt be attracted by the appeal of an approach that focuses upon the concrete insecurities of individual human beings globally, and attempts to deal head-on with the issue of how the study of security can be focused to help address those insecurities, an approach that 'points towards a notion of critique that is committed to deconstruction but also unashamedly reconstructive' (Nunes 2012: 357). For those readers, the CSS project may well constitute an attractive basis for attempting to change global security rather than simply thinking about it.

Key points

- The 'Welsh School' of Critical Security Studies (or CSS) is built in large part around a critique of state-centric approaches to security – that is, approaches to security that tend to focus exclusively on military threats to the state.
- Proponents of CSS argue that, ultimately, human beings are the most important referent object(s) of security; as a result, CSS adopts an explicitly 'emancipatory orientation' – focused on the freeing of people (as individuals and groups) from those physical and human constraints which stop them carrying out what they would freely choose to do – as the key to achieving security.
- Rather than offering fixed blueprints for emancipation, CSS suggests that the form of emancipatory practices must be contingent upon the identification of the particular insecurities experienced by groups and individuals within a given context.
- The CSS focus on 'emancipation' is seen to distinguish it from other critical approaches to security, and CSS has attracted a significant range of criticisms over its definition of emancipation, its focus on the individual and its equation of emancipation with security.

Discussion points

- Is the CSS critique of state-centric definitions of security well-founded or misguided?
- How and why has the so-called Welsh School of Critical Security Studies sought to utilise Critical Theory in thinking about security?
- Is CSS right to focus on the individual as the referent object of security?
- What function does the concept of 'immanent critique' play within CSS?
- 'The problem with emancipation is not that it is idealistic, it is that it is dangerous.' Discuss.
- How significant are historical materialist critiques of CSS?

Guide to further reading

Bill McSweeney (1999) *Security, Identity and Interests: A Sociology of International Relations* (Cambridge: Cambridge University Press). Although not usually counted within the CSS project, McSweeney's account offers several interesting overlaps and provides useful comparative reading.

Ken Booth (1991) 'Security and Emancipation', *Review of International Studies*, 17: 313–326. The touchstone work in terms of setting out the idea of an emancipation-oriented approach to security.

Ken Booth (2005) (ed.) *Critical Security Studies and World Politics* (Boulder, CO: Lynne Rienner). An edited collection with various contributions that offer restatements of the CSS approach, sympathetic critiques and applications of the principles of CSS to empirical issues.

Ken Booth (2007) *Theory of World Security* (Cambridge: Cambridge University Press). Provides both a trenchant defence and restatement of the CSS project and attempts to use it as the basis of a more expansive 'theory of world security'.

Michael Sheehan (2005) *International Security: An Analytical Survey* (Boulder, CO: Lynne Rienner). Makes the case for theorising security with a concern for human emancipation, justice and peace in the context of an overview of the field of security studies.

Richard Wyn Jones (1999) *Security, Strategy, and Critical Theory* (Boulder, CO: Lynne Rienner). Develops the idea of an emancipation-oriented approach further, but in the process roots CSS more explicitly within the tradition and ideas of Critical Theory.

Shannon Brincat, Laura Lima and João Nunes (2011) (eds) *Critical Theory in International Relations and Security Studies: Interviews and Reflections* (Routledge: Abingdon). Brings together a series of essays on, interviews with and critical reflections by 'pioneers' of the turn to Critical Theory in IR and security studies, including Robert Cox, Ken Booth, Richard Wyn Jones and many others.

3   Feminist and gender approaches

Abstract

This chapter introduces a range of critiques of both traditional and critical security studies from diverse feminist and gender perspectives. It begins by examining the gendered politics of security studies as a field that has typically marginalised women and the significance of gender structures more generally. A variety of responses to these issues are explored, beginning with liberal and standpoint feminist perspectives that attempt to make women more visible in the context of international security. The move to increase the visibility of women is not free from controversy, however. Some gender theorists, particularly those associated with poststructuralist thought, question the very possibility of referring to the views and experiences of 'women' per se. Concerned with avoiding the essentialised categories of 'man' and 'woman', this alternative work deconstructs gender claims, problematises sex and gender as discursive construct, and politicises the (re)production of different gendered subjectivities. The chapter concludes with an assessment of the various ways in which feminist and gender approaches have stimulated new lines of enquiry in critical security studies.

Introduction

Women and gender structures have long been marginalised in the study of security. In part this is due to their relative invisibility on the terrain mapped out by dominant traditional perspectives. Yet, 'critical' work, including other perspectives in Part I of this book, has also been charged with taking gendered assumptions for granted. Over the past three decades, this gender bias has been identified, interrogated, and resisted by a collection of feminist and gender approaches within the field. This scholarship is nevertheless far from united in terms of its aims, method, or implications and reflects an array of related positions in political theory. Most notably, writers influenced by poststructuralism have questioned the liberal feminist move to simply 'bring' women into security studies. For some poststructural gender theorists, for example, the categories of 'man' and 'woman' are radically unstable and caution should be taken in essentialising and universalising notions of 'female' (and 'male') experience. Liberal standpoint feminists have countered this by emphasising the focus on what they consider to be the unique subjugation of women as a strategy for generating political programmes. As we shall see, there is increasing diversity of scholarship associated with feminist and gender perspectives. Yet, while it is important to note that there is no consensus about what a 'critical' response to gender inequalities *should* be, these debates have opened up new and important terrains of research in critical security studies relating to broader issues involving identity, violence and justice.

Box 3.1 Key concepts in feminist and gender approaches to security

Feminism: Relates historically to women's struggle for equality with men. Also refers to a diverse range of thought that draws attention to women's knowledge and experience.

Sex: Usually refers to the coding of bodies as either 'male' or 'female' on the basis of biological attributes, but often critiqued by poststructuralists as another form of essentialism.

Gender: A socially constructed identity that categorises subjects as either 'masculine' or 'feminine'.

Femininity: Attributes associated with a female identity (emotionality, dependence, caring); the social construction of women *as* 'women'.

Masculinity: Attributes associated with a male identity (strength, autonomy, aggression); the social construction of men *as* 'men'.

Standpoint feminism: A perspective that emphasises the importance of taking real women's experiences as the basis for critiquing patriarchy.

Liberal feminism: An approach that seeks legal, economic, political and social equality between men and women.

Patriarchy: Refers to the hierarchical arrangement of social, economic and political structures whereby men are privileged over women.

Performativity: The idea, developed by Judith Butler, that gendered identities are not natural, but produced through being acted out in social life.

The gendered politics of security studies

Eleanor Roosevelt, first lady of the US from 1933 to 1945, once commented that 'too often the great decisions are originated and given form in bodies made up wholly of men, or so completely dominated by them that whatever of special value women have to offer is shunted aside without expression' (quoted in Tickner 1992: 1). It is not difficult to see why she said this. The *dramatis personae* in the theatre of global security – state leaders, diplomats, soldiers and international civil servants – typically have at least one thing in common: they are almost always *men*. Moreover, the persistence of global gender inequalities means that, despite some progress since Roosevelt's era, international politics is still very much a 'man's world' (see Box 3.2).

The dominant view that the realm of the international is a 'masculine sphere of life' has meant that women have been marginalised in the study of security (Enloe 2000: 4). Much of the earlier feminist work in security studies argued that this bias resulted from the dominance of various strands of political realism in defining what studying 'security' in 'international politics' means. Indeed, with a 'top-down' focus on political elites, the state and the state system, realists have been criticised by many prominent feminists for constructing a worldview that is profoundly *un*realistic in failing to take half of the human population into consideration. This worldview has meant that, while the actions, careers and policies of men have been taken for granted as legitimate objects of study, the experiences of women, by contrast, have not been considered worthy of investigation in their own right (Enloe 2000; Tickner 1992). Rather, for the most part, the tacit assumption in realist-oriented security studies has been that men's experiences are somehow representative of human experience as a whole. Feminist and gender theorists of all hues thus converge on the basic point that research in security has been overwhelmingly the study *of* men *by* men:

Box 3.2 Global gender inequalities

In 2000 the United Nations' Department of Economic and Social Affairs published a report, entitled *The World's Women 2000: Trends and Statistics*, which illustrates the extent of gender inequality between men and women in global politics. Despite outnumbering men in most regions (with the exception of some parts of Asia), women comprise only one-third of the global workforce. While this actually represents an historic high, women's earnings remain on average only between 50 and 80 per cent of men's. Women are more likely to work in roles with little or no authority. They also experience more – and longer – periods of unemployment. For this reason it has been argued that 'poverty has a woman's face: of 1.3 billion people living in poverty, 70 per cent are women' (UNDP 1994: 4).

Resource scarcity also affects men and women differently (see also Chapter 7). For example, in the developing world women are more disadvantaged by water scarcity because they are the main water carriers. In the dry season women spend between 3.5 and 28 hours per week collecting water. Moreover, the effects of water shortage and poor sanitation result in a disproportionate burden of unpaid female labour in families across the global South. Part of the reason for their disadvantaged position in the global political economy is that women have fewer educational opportunities – two-thirds of the world's 876 million illiterate are female. More generally, there is evidence to suggest that women suffer worse human rights abuse than men. In some African states over 50 per cent of all women and girls have undergone genital mutilation. Female refugees, constituting half of the global migrant population, are also more vulnerable to sexual violence in camps and resettlement.

The possibility of tackling gender inequality is not assisted by the fact that women's representation in government still lags far behind men globally. To some extent there has been increased representation of women on the world stage since 1945: the first female prime minister was Sirimavo Bandaranaike of Ceylon and Sri Lanka in 1960; Margaret Thatcher became the first female British prime minister in 1979; and in the US three women have served in the position of secretary of state (Madeleine Albright was the first in 1996, followed by Condoleezza Rice in 2005 and Hillary Rodham Clinton in 2009). Despite this seeming 'progress', however, equal representation between men and women is still a long way off, particularly in senior positions in government (only 10 per cent of representatives are female), policy making, the armed forces and diplomacy.

In 1979 the UN adopted the Convention on the Elimination of all Forms of Discrimination Against Women (the 'Women's Convention'). This Convention aimed to shape national policies in order to guarantee equality between men and women, especially in terms of access to education, employment rights and marriage. The Women's Convention has received considerable international support with 89 per cent of all states having ratified the agreement. That said, however, 29 per cent of states expressed reservations during the ratification process and there is considerable regional variation in terms of commitment to the Women's Convention. While 100 per cent of states in Latin America and 90 per cent of states in Europe and North America ratified the Convention, these figures contrast with just 35 per cent of states in the Middle East where no government has fully adopted it. Therefore, although patriarchy is a global problem, gender inequalities are manifested in different ways locally. This illustrates an important wider point: various gender inequalities are most acute in certain parts of the world. For example, 1 in 16 women die from pregnancy-related causes in Africa compared to 1 in 65 in Asia and 1 in 1400 in Europe. In India, 75 per cent of women have been physically assaulted by an intimate partner, whereas in New Zealand this figure stands at 17 per cent.

Quite simply, and with deadly monotony, women's systematic *oppression* – and insecurity – is not taken seriously; to the extent that it is 'visible', either gender hierarchy is justified by 'nature is destiny' beliefs, mystified by apparent 'equal opportunities' options, and/or its transformation is deferred until 'after the revolution'.

(Peterson 1992: 49)

In this way, feminists have sought to emphasise that security studies are not separate from but fundamentally a part of broader gender dynamics in global politics. As such, the gendered practices of sovereignty, political identity and labour considered in Box 3.2 above have translated into a systematic bias in the way that international security has conventionally been analysed.

At base, the aim of feminist and gender approaches to security has been to identify, interrogate and resist the multifarious ways in which the views, interests and actions of men have been privileged over those of women in contemporary social life. It is precisely this systematic prioritisation of men in society that the key feminist concept of 'patriarchy' refers to (see Box 3.1). Central to the 'feminist project', if there is such a thing, is a focus on making structures of patriarchy more visible in order to better understand and ultimately challenge women's relative subordination to men. As we shall see, this involves taking seriously and acting upon the idea that the 'personal is political'. It also entails core questions such as: why are men usually in combat roles? Do states protect the security of men and women equally? What are the prospects for resisting patriarchy and improving the lives of both men and women?

While this commitment to critical engagement with patriarchy is shared among feminist and gender approaches, it is nevertheless important to emphasise that in this chapter we are dealing with a diverse and heterogeneous body of work. Indeed, there is no *singular* 'feminist' or 'gender' perspective on international security, as such. On the contrary, as we shall see in the course of the discussion, there are areas of considerable disagreement concerning the identity of 'women' and what should be done in response to gender inequalities in both theoretical and practical contexts (see, for example, Lobasz and Sjoberg 2011 and Shepherd 2013a). In other words, although feminist and gender scholarship is bound by a common criticism of patriarchy and a normative commitment to address it, the object, method and consequences of critique vary quite significantly. Such disagreement is not at all surprising (or indeed a 'negative' feature of the intellectual landscape), however, and many of the positions within feminist/gender security studies mirror the broader field of perspectives in social and political thought. As with any attempt to characterise a field of study there are inevitably areas of overlap and common political concern, with several key positions often identified in the literature: liberal feminism; standpoint feminism; and poststructural gender approaches (see Table 3.1).

As well as an increasing diversity of perspectives, the targets for critique have also been extended within feminist and gender approaches to security studies. Whereas earlier work focused primarily on the perceived failings of traditional approaches to security such as political realism, various critics have more recently pointed to what they consider to be the patriarchal and/or gendered assumptions of some of the more critically oriented viewpoints explored in Part I of this book. Lene Hansen, for example, has argued that securitisation theory (see Chapter 6) presupposes a situation in which speech is indeed possible. Yet, the very problem is that many women, like the mythical Little Mermaid in Hans Christian Andersen's fairy tale, are prevented from being subjects worthy of speaking. Thus, Hansen accuses the Copenhagen School, and other approaches reliant on the concept of securitisation, of lacking an understanding of gender-based *in*securities borne out of unequal power relations (Hansen 2000). Furthermore, poststructural feminist and gender approaches are

Table 3.1 Key positions in feminist and gender approaches to security studies

	Focus points	*Implications*	*Exponents*
Liberal feminism	• Where are the women in security?	• Make women more visible in security studies.	• Cynthia Enloe
Standpoint feminism	• Takes the views and experiences of women in global politics as basis for theorising global security relations.	• Empirical analysis of views and experiences of women.	• J. Ann Tickner
Poststructural gender approaches	• No special ontological status given to 'woman'. • 'Woman' (and 'man', 'sex') are discursive constructs.	• Analysis of instability of gender categories.	• V. Spike Peterson

suspicious of the possibility of applying abstract, universal notions of 'emancipation' associated with the Welsh School (see Chapter 2) in response to the patriarchal structures of global security.

Making women visible in international security

In 1989 US academic Cynthia Enloe published the first edition of *Bananas, Beaches, and Bases: Making Feminist Sense of International Politics*, which has since become widely acknowledged as a landmark text in feminist security studies. Writing from a broadly liberal feminist perspective, Enloe argued that 'if we employ only the conventional, ungendered compass to chart international politics, we are likely to end up mapping a landscape peopled only by men' (2000: 1). Ironically, she claimed, 'making women invisible' led to a profoundly unrealistic caricature of security relations, because it 'hides the workings of both femininity and masculinity in international politics' (2000: 11). Against the tide of 'malestream' Realist dominated approaches, therefore, Enloe dared to ask: where are the women in the study of security?

Enloe's research strategy was to focus on marginal women in order to show how the conduct of international security to some extent depends upon men's control over them. One of Enloe's case studies was the relationship between women and nationalism. She analysed the way in which, via their roles as teachers in missionary schools, women performed a vital role in helping to establish core nationalist values and institutions central to the US colonial project, for example in the Philippines during the nineteenth and early twentieth centuries (2000: 48). Through the transmission and cultivation of certain Western gendered ideals, such as notions of 'respectability', the US attempted to shape the hearts and minds of the colonised. Indeed, according to Enloe, the notion of 'lady-like' behaviour was very much seen as the 'mainstay of imperialist civilisation' (2000: 48). Moreover, in the highly gendered context of imperial rule, relationships between men and women were either tolerated or condemned according to how they were perceived to impact upon prevailing relations of power: 'Sexual liaisons between colonial men and local women were usually winked at; affairs between colonial women and local men were threats to imperial order' (2000: 48).

Another gendered site investigated by Enloe is the military base. By the mid-1980s there were around 3000 military bases across the globe controlled by one state in another state's territory. Enloe analysed the various gendered practices through which bases are produced as 'normal' places in order to make the lives of 'base women' more visible in security studies. Her study considered interactions between bases and local economies/infrastructures and she concluded that 'the normalcy that sustains a military base in a local community rests on ideas about masculinity and femininity' (2000: 67). Though usually unnoticed, the unpaid domestic work of women was fundamental to the assimilation of the base in local communities and to the support and furtherance of their husbands' military careers. The gendered division of labour at bases typifies the association of femininity with the domestic sphere and masculinity with the international domain considered above. Moreover, the presumption among many base families that sons will pursue a military career and daughters will stay at home as military wives illustrates how these values and the prevailing gender order they sustain are reproduced from generation to generation.

The marginalised position of women in international political economy, and the male dependency on this subjugation, is also explored by Enloe across various contexts. Via a gendered history of the banana, for example, Enloe demonstrates how even the most seemingly masculine of work environments, the banana plantation, fundamentally relies on women: 'behind every all-male banana plantation stand scores of women performing unpaid domestic and productive labour' (2000: 137). The labour provided by women is almost always unpaid or low paid, seasonal, and with little or no training or chance for promotion. With few other options, women end up supporting the very forms of agricultural labour patterns that perpetuate patriarchal landownership and reinforce their subjugation.

Enloe's analysis was considered path-breaking in security studies because it took the feminist insight that the 'personal is political' and applied it for the first time to the realm of international. In this way Enloe undermined the prevalent notion that the private sphere was somehow 'out of bounds' in the study of security. According to Enloe, the realisation that the personal is political is profoundly 'disturbing' because it means that 'relationships we once imagined were private or merely social are in fact infused with power, usually unequal power backed up by public authority' (2000: 195). By insisting that security impinges not only on the public but also the private sphere, Enloe was able to bring issues formally marginal to the centre stage of the study of the state and international security more generally (for example the politics of marriage, the role of unpaid domestic labour, the patriarchy of land ownership). The insight that the functioning of the international relies on 'private' divisions of labour complicates and personalises traditional approaches to foreign affairs and security. In making women more visible in global security relations Enloe drew attention to the importance of struggles between masculinity and femininity in making the world go round. Consequently, her analysis highlights the way in which gendered structures are intrinsically infused with relations of power: 'It has taken power to deprive women of land titles and leave them little choice but to sexually service soldiers and banana workers' (2000: 197–198).

While a classic text in the formation of feminist security studies, *Bananas, Beaches, and Bases* has been subject to a number of criticisms as the field has developed over the past three decades. The primary critique of Enloe and the liberal feminist position with which her work is generally associated has focused on the proximity between this perspective and some of the theoretical assumptions underpinning traditional security studies. Although Enloe defines her approach in contradistinction to 'malestream' political realism, on closer inspection there are several potential areas of common overlap. Most fundamentally, Enloe does not question the positivist foundations of realist approaches, which assume that analysts can observe and detail the nature of security and insecurity. On the contrary, she accepts that there is such a thing as the 'reality' of global security relations and claims that making women more visible offers a 'more realistic approach to international politics' (2000: 199). This has led some postpositivist critics to argue that hers is merely an 'add women and stir' perspective that takes problematic notions of 'reality', 'men', 'women' and 'gender' as givens rather than social constructs (Steans 2009). As we shall see in the light of poststructural approaches, Enloe's position is vulnerable to the charge of essentialising women's identities rather than appreciating difference according to race, class, ethnicity, and other forms of social and geopolitical stratification; although, equally, as is also noted further below, critical engagement with Enloe's initial work continues to be a productive of inspiration even for more poststucturalist-oriented feminist security scholarship.

Gendering global security relations

One alternative approach to Enloe's position is that offered by J. Ann Tickner. Whereas Enloe's book *Bananas, Beaches and Bases* largely brought women into an existing realist framework, Tickner questions that very framework as a suitable starting point for analysing international security. Instead of an 'add women and stir' approach, Tickner aims to 'think about how the discipline of international relations might look if gender were included as a category of analysis and if women's experiences were part of the subject matter out of which its theories are constructed' (1992: 5).

In general terms, Tickner's emphasis on the importance of the views and experiences of women for theorising security has been categorised as a standpoint feminist approach (see Box 3.1 and Table 3.1). In her *Gender in International Relations: Feminist Perspectives on Achieving Global Security* (1992), Tickner analyses the various ways in which women define national security and she considers how this affects the way security can be theorised. From her perspective it is not simply that women have been historically excluded from the institutions of international security. Rather, it is possible to identify how some of the most basic structures in global politics are taken for granted in realist approaches, such as the very distinction between 'international' and 'domestic', rely on acutely gendered assumptions, tropes and metaphors (see also Carol Cohn's feminist critique of the gendered nature of debates about nuclear security during the cold war, discussed in greater depth in Chapter 12).

The notion of the realm of the 'international', for example, has long been associated with specifically *masculine* traits: strength, power and autonomy (Tickner 1992: 1). According to Tickner, ideals of both manhood and the state have been mutually reinforcing throughout the history of warfare, as encapsulated in the figure of the 'citizen-soldier'. For this reason, Tickner refers to what she calls the prevalence of an 'essentialist connection between war and men's natural aggressiveness' (1992: 40). In this context, Tickner cites the observation made by Simone de Beauvoir (see Box 3.3) that the highest form of patriotism is to die for one's country – an accolade that, until very recently, women have been systematically excluded from achieving (1992: 28).

In contrast to the masculine traits of the international, domestic politics is typically portrayed in feminine terms. Indeed, it is no coincidence that the term 'domestic' – one pertaining to the home – is the sphere with which women are primarily associated. The gendered politics of international security has meant that men abroad are charged with protecting citizens (primarily women and children, who are in most need of defence) inside states' borders. Thus, while women have performed roles intrinsic to the 'functioning' of this

> **Box 3.3** Simone de Beauvoir (1908–1986)
>
> Simone de Beauvoir was a French twentieth-century philosopher, feminist and political activist. Beauvoir helped to develop a movement in philosophy called existentialism. She is perhaps best known for her path-breaking feminist work *The Second Sex* (1997) [1949]. This text examines how 'woman' comes to be a mode of existence. For Beauvoir men and women have no fixed essence, but are produced as such socially. In other words, 'woman' is a relational concept to 'man', and vice versa. Yet, however, woman has been produced historically as both less than man (other) and radically different from man (Other). On Beauvoir's view, it is therefore necessary for women to challenge the notion of their radical Otherness with men if they are to achieve equality. This is because the move to subordinate women is usually based on an appeal to their biological difference with men, which needs to be overturned. While the work of Beauvoir has been subject to many interpretations, it is has paved the way for much of the feminist theorising in security studies. In particular, it has inspired work that sought to make more women visible and draw attention to the social construction of gendered identity (Hutchings 2009).

gendered organisation of social life, their involvement in security has usually been associated with maintaining order at home. Historically female labour has involved so-called caring roles such as teaching and nursing and these have long been considered secondary to those of men. As such, women's roles are often discounted as mundane, extraneous to the serious business of state security, and unpatriotic (Tickner 1992).

There are several important implications of Tickner's analysis for the study of security. First, Tickner problematises rather than accepts the inside/outside, domestic/foreign, public/private binaries that characterise traditional approaches to security studies. Her work demonstrates that behaviour in the 'domestic' and 'international' realms are fundamentally inseparable. For example, women in militarised societies are far more vulnerable to rape and other forms of sexual violence (1992: 56; cf Shepherd 2007). Similarly, the idealised notion of the brave male citizen-soldier abroad is shown to *depend upon* the devaluation of the female subject and myths about the need for her protection at home.

Second, Tickner emphasises the importance of identity in international security. By considering women's views and experiences, she argues, it is possible to construct a less militarised account of security relations. On this view, the identity of states begins to change. Somewhat controversially, as we shall discuss later, Tickner also believes that this alternative perspective opens up the possibility of more peaceful relations: 'A feminist perspective would assume that the potential for international community also exists and that an atomistic, conflictual view of the international system is only a partial representation of reality' (1992: 63). By re-thinking states' identities from a female standpoint, it is suggested that a focus on autonomy, self-help and perpetual conflict might be replaced by one that privileges peace, togetherness and cooperation.

Third, in many ways pre-empting discourses of human security and the concept of emancipation in the Welsh School (see Chapters 2 and 10), Tickner develops an explicitly normative perspective about what *should* be done to address global gender inequalities. Part of this programme involves showing how different human insecurities often have gendered origins and histories. Above and beyond this, however, Tickner argues it is also necessary to overcome gender inequalities by establishing parity between male and female views and experiences. Since women are disadvantaged economically, she claims that critical feminist thinking demands a re-privileging of values associated with justice over those linked to order. In the final analysis, Tickner advocates a reorientation of security studies along these lines in pursuit of what she refers to as a 'non-gendered discipline': 'Only through analysis that recognises gender differences but does not take them as fixed or inevitable can we move toward the creation of a non-gendered discipline that includes us all' (1992: 144).

Tickner's commitment to a wholesale critique of realism and her insistence on analysing the production of 'gender differences' rather than simply making women more visible certainly marks her approach as different from Enloe's. Yet, while Tickner claims not to take gender differences as 'fixed or inevitable', there is a sense in which her analysis still clutches on to the notion of 'authentic' female views and experiences (Steans 2009). Other feminists, for example those working in the poststructural tradition, have fundamentally questioned the extent to which it is possible to generalise across time, space and culture in this way (Peterson 1992; Shepherd 2008). Furthermore, despite claiming to focus on gender rather than women per se, the extent to which Tickner adequately deals with the (re)production of masculinities and the subjugation/exposure to violence of particular groups of men might be called into question (Jones 2004; Parport and Zalewski 1998, 2008). Finally, we might also wish to express a certain degree of scepticism regarding the possibility – and desirability – of achieving a 'non-gendered discipline' in the study of security. Is it sufficient to wish the category of gender away or should security theorists be constantly vigilant to claims made in the name of gender difference?

Poststructuralist approaches to gender and security

When considering the contributions of poststructural feminists and gender theorists to security studies it is again necessary to bear in mind that we are not dealing with a single approach or body of thought. There are multiple strands of work associated with the label 'poststructuralism' and often these diverge (for more see Chapter 5 in this book). Nevertheless, it is possible to draw out some common themes in order to characterise the differences compared with liberal and standpoint feminist positions considered so far. Perhaps the overriding commonality among poststructuralist feminism and gender perspectives is a resistance to the 'reconstructive' projects of Enloe and Tickner (Steans 2009). In other words, whereas these authors seek to develop a feminist programme out of a critique of patriarchy, poststructuralists are hesitant to determine what should be done in such an abstract, essentialist and universalising way. This hesitation, however, should not be misunderstood as an inability or unwillingness to engage in the question of political action. Rather, it is precisely because of a broader commitment to questioning what it means to make claims about and in the name of 'men' and 'women'. At the broadest level, poststructuralists argue that it is not simply that 'gender' is constructed socially: the category of sex is produced discursively as well. This means that there is no 'essence' to being a man or woman and neither shares a particular perspective on the world per se. In this way, poststructuralists go further than standpoint feminists in claiming that we should not confer any special ontological status to 'manhood' or 'womanhood': there is no *uniquely* male or female view or experience. Instead, and often through detailed empirical work, the challenge of poststructuralism is to interrogate the politics of the construction of different gendered identities and question the stability of gender categories to show how they always breakdown or 'deconstruct' (see Chapter 5).

Politicising gender relations

The work of V. Spike Peterson in particular has been seminal in the development of post-structural feminist and gender approaches in security studies. Peterson argues that the pressing task of this work is not simply to make women more visible nor raise awareness of women's views and experiences. More fundamentally, it is about 'transforming ways of being and knowing' in the study of security (Peterson 1992: 20). Peterson takes as her starting point the idea that our understandings of the 'world' are intrinsically shaped by gendered ontologies (theories of being) and epistemologies (theories of knowing). In other words, our viewpoints are never gender-neutral, but reflective of dominant assumptions about masculinity and femininity: 'that is, we do not experience or "know" the world as abstract "humans" but as embodied, gendered beings' (1992: 20).

If we follow this logic through then it is not simply that gender, in other words masculine or feminine traits, is socially constructed. Rather, a further step is required in order to demonstrate that sex and meanings associated with it are not 'natural' either. Peterson argues that all too often a distinction is maintained between gender as a construction and sex as a biologically determined fact. Sexual identity, however, like any other, is no less socially produced. A series of interlinked factors are usually referred to in the categorisation of someone's sex as 'male', 'female' or 'intersex': phenotype (physical appearance); psychological sex (what a person feels like); gonadal sex (whether someone has ovaries, testicles or a combination of sexual organs); and chromosomal sex (how many X/Y chromosomes). In this way, the determination of sex is based upon complex interlinked factors that form a continuum of sexual characteristics. It is not necessarily the case, therefore, that sexual identity is always straightforward. Indeed, 1 in 3000 children born in the UK are categorised as being 'intersex'. The case of the South African athlete Caster Semenya, forced by the International Association of Athletics Federations (IAAF) to have a gender test to check her eligibility for entering the 2009 world athletics championship as a woman, indicates the complexity, sensitivity and politically fraught nature of this question of identity.

Peterson thus calls for a radical decentring of biological explanations of social relations. Men and women are not separate with mutually exclusive views and experiences. Instead, gendered identities are constituted and reconstituted through everyday practices. In the context of security studies this means 'asking what security can mean in the context of interlocking systems of hierarchy and domination and how gendered identities and ideologies (re)produce these structural insecurities' (Peterson 1992: 32). For example, Peterson calls for a reconsideration of the very concept of national security as it relates to marriage. Both institutions, she argues, can be interpreted as 'protection rackets' that are 'implicated in the reproduction of hierarchies and in the structural violence against which they claim to offer protection' (1992: 51). What is necessary, therefore, is much more than an analysis of women's involvement in global security relations. This perspective 'requires *politicising* structural violence as historically constituted – as contingent rather than natural – and specifying some of its implications and consequences' (1992: 50).

One method of politicising structural violence is to analyse the various gendered narratives that give rise to and maintain it. In *Feminist Security Studies: A Narrative Approach* (2011) Annick T.R. Wibben argues that while narratives are inescapable – 'they are a primary way by which we make sense of the world around us, produce meanings, articulate intentions, and legitimize actions' – they may be both violent and disruptive of violence. Narratives of *security* are of particular political significance on her view because they order social relations and have 'effects on life and death' (Wibben 2011: 39). The analysis of such narratives in both traditional and critical security studies are organised around a similar *form* even if their content varies: '1) Threats that locate danger; 2) Referents to be secured; 3) Agents charged with providing security; 4) The means by which threats are contained' (2011: 7). By contrast, Wibben argues that feminist security studies informed by poststructuralist perspectives on narratology – the study of narratives – have the potential to challenge both the form *and* content of security narratives. In turn, this not only 'broadens' and 'deepens' the field, but also 'opens' it up to already existing feminist counter-narratives and alternative, potentially non-violent, conceptualisations of security.

Performing gender security

In *Gender, Violence, and Security: Discourse as Practice* (2008) Laura J. Shepherd demonstrates how the politicisation of gender structures called for by Peterson might lead to analysis of concrete aspects of international security. Shepherd takes as her focus gendered violence as it relates to security and investigates how violence is constitutive of subjectivity and different types of bodies. In keeping with poststructuralist feminism, Shepherd's curiosity lies in the way in which gender is made meaningful in social and political interaction. She does not take for granted the existence of a pre-established female subject whose views can be accessed, experiences analysed and rights claimed. Importantly, however, this approach does not imply the abandonment of all notions of subjectivity. Rather, following the work of US poststructuralist feminist thinker Judith Butler (see Box 3.4), Shepherd argues that different performances produce subjects *as* gendered in specific contexts. Shepherd's substantive research investigates the (re)production of gendered subjectivities in relation to the case study of UN Security Council Resolution (UNSCR) 1325 (see also Pratt and Richter-Devroe 2011). This resolution was adopted in 2000 with the aim of expressing the importance of sensitivity to gendered violence and inequalities in the contexts of armed conflicts, international peace-building, and post-conflict reconstruction. Drawing on a discourse analysis

---

Box 3.4 Judith Butler (1956–)

In *Gender Trouble* (1990), Judith Butler argues that the common distinction between 'sex' on the one hand and 'gender' on the other is a misnomer. From her perspective it is not that sex is a pre-discursively constituted natural condition upon which gender is then added. Rather, following Michel Foucault (see Chapter 5 in this book), sex is the bodily effect of gendered regimes of power/knowledge in society. In other words, there is no originally sexed person who then acquires masculine or feminine traits. Indeed, those traits do not necessarily coincide with a particular type of body. The example Butler gives to illustrate her reading of sex/gender is drag. Drag queens demonstrate that gender is not static, stable or a given. Rather, it is an identity that is assumed by people and performed through their looks, behaviour and interactions. In order to grasp the production of gendered subjects in this way Butler has developed the key concept of performativity: 'Gender is always a doing, though not by a subject who might be said to pre-exist the deed. [...] Identity is performatively constituted by the very "expressions" that are said to be its results' (1990: 33).

Performativity is used to refer to the activity through which gendered subjects are (re)produced. Over time the practices that bring those subjects into being acquire a sense of permanence and normality. It is because of their repetition, rather than anything else, that they come to be seen as in some sense 'natural'.

approach influenced by Judith Butler, Jacques Derrida and Michel Foucault (see Chapter 5), Shepherd interrogates the gendered assumptions – or 'narrative' – of the text, the claims made in the name of gender, and its implications for the (re)production of female subjectivities. She argues that, in referring to and making representations of 'women' (rather than the broader category of gender), the resolution runs the risk of reconstituting the very problems relating to gendered forms of violence that presumably the UN seeks to overcome. The focus in UNSCR 1325 is on women in global politics, but women primarily understood as mothers (see also Åhäll 2012). According to Shepherd, this unproblematised association of women with motherhood and children supports rather than challenges the ideals of nationhood that are often to blame for conflict in the first place. Such an approach also fails to take account of the multifarious ways in which some women are actively engaged in the oppression of other women (and men). Moreover, in Shepherd's view, the recommendation that more women should be included in decision-making roles in the realm of international security does not deal with the key issues at stake. Rather, she argues, 'this liberal notion (re)produces the subject of "women" as a homogenous group whose interests are *essentially* peaceful and socially beneficial' (2008: 162).

Also inspired by Butler's approach to the performativity of gender is Victoria M. Basham's book *War, Identity and the Liberal State: Everyday Experiences of the Geopolitical in the Armed Forces* (2013). Basham charts the various ways in which institutionally and culturally the presence of women's bodies in the British military have posed challenges to and opportunities for the performative reinscription of gender norms. Despite various efforts to be more inclusive, as of January 2012 the total number of regular members of the British military stood at 182,080 – of whom 92.9 per cent were men, 90.3 per cent white and an unknown majority assumed to be heterosexual (Basham 2013: 7). Departing from an emphasis on narrative and discourse understood narrowly in terms of language (see also Chapter 5, Box 5.3), Basham draws on Karen Barad's (2003) reformulation of performativity to include the material dimensions of regulatory practices. Based on extensive ethnographic fieldwork into the everyday views and experiences of serving soldiers between 2003 and 2005, Basham argues that 'The practices and performances of gender that constitute women as weak, leaky, promiscuous, and so on, render their bodies logistical because they function to reinscribe the 'rightful' dominance of men in armed forces and war' (Basham 2013: 86). Basham's overall approach then is one that takes into account how various interlocking constitutive outsides – gender, race and sexuality – are embedded in discursive-material practices in such a way as to reproduce the white, male, heterosexual subject as the idealised 'norm' of the contemporary British military. In this way, and reminiscent of the earlier insights of Enloe, she argues that 'War makes [...] gender hierarchies possible and the intimate – the close, the connected, the personal – makes war viable' (Basham 2013: 86).

The work of Sarah Bulmer (2013), also on military masculinities, draws explicitly on Enloe's concept of 'patriarchal confusion' – the notion that gendered forms of power may produce 'incoherent or contradictory outcomes' – in order to study the incorporation of lesbian, gay, bisexual and transgender (LGBT) personnel in the British military. Up until 2000 such personnel were discharged if found to be serving in the armed forces, but this ban was overturned at the turn of the millennium following a ruling by the European Court of Human Rights. Since then the policy of the British military has been to view sexual orientation in terms of an exclusively 'private' matter, which has effectively made open homosexuality 'invisible' and left patriarchal heteronormativity – the assumption that only sexual relations between members of the opposite sex are 'correct' – intact. Arguing that the study of sexuality and the policing of norms around it helps us to better understand the construction of gendered identities and heteronormativity, Bulmer analyses the case of the 2008 London Pride march. She highlights the 'patriarchal confusion' that arose when, at such a 'public' display of sexual orientation, marching LGBT personnel and their commanding officers were unclear about what forms of dress and behaviour would be considered acceptable in view of the British military's stance on sexuality and privacy. Instead of framing the issue of the incorporation of non-traditional military recruits in terms of either subversion or cooption – as some feminist analyses have tended to – Bulmer (2013: 149) demonstrates that the case illustrates both – 'when LGBT personnel march at Pride they can be understood to *simultaneously* sustain and resist patriarchy'. More generally she claims that it is via the identification of such 'patriarchal confusion' that 'feminists can demonstrate where gender fails on its own terms' and show the 'radically contingent nature of patriarchy' (Bulmer 2013: 150).

Criticisms of poststructuralist approaches

The challenges of poststructural feminist and gender approaches to the study of security are considerable. The work of Peterson, Shepherd, and others draws attention to the problems of abstract universalistic generalisations about supposedly 'female' views and experiences across time, space, race, class, and culture. Not only are notions of femininity and masculinity socially constructed but so too is the concept of 'sex', which is revealed as a discursively produced categorisation. Nevertheless, despite these problematisations of some of the fundaments of liberal and standpoint feminist thinking, poststructural work has been criticised for eliminating the very grounds upon which a progressive response to patriarchy might be mounted. Tickner, for example, recognises the importance of poststructural perspectives, but counter-argues that 'to be unable to speak for women only further reinforces the voices of those who have constructed approaches to international relations out of the experiences of men' (1992: 17). From Tickner's point of view some form of strategic essentialism might be required in order to struggle for women's rights, justice, and equal opportunities. In response, the poststructural argument would be that any form of programmatic engagement with patriarchy is unable to deal the specificity with which it manifests itself at a localised level. Furthermore, while concepts of emancipation are intrinsically appealing, one needs to ask what this means in less abstract terms, who benefits, and what are the potential costs to others?

Conclusion

For some commentators the sub-field of feminist and gender approaches to security continues to be characterised by a certain 'camp politics' (Parashar 2013) that seeks to fracture feminist scholarship into distinct positions. However, others seek to inhabit multiple perspectives and complicate the kind of move made in this chapter to categorise different 'types' of scholarship ('liberal', 'standpoint', 'poststructuralist', and so on) (Basham 2013; Bulmer 2013; Zalewski 2013). When taken as a whole, work in feminist and gender approaches constitutes one of the most dynamic areas in critical security studies. While, of course, this scholarship has raised important questions about the role of women in international security, its significance stretches beyond its core thematic. Research into the gendered nature of security has opened up new insights into the behaviour and identity of the state and the sexualised politics and violence that ultimately it relies upon. It has problematised aspects of the relationship between human security and international political economy drawing our attention to inequalities otherwise relatively obscured in security studies. Such work has also cast new light on problematic distinctions between domestic/international, private/public and order/anarchy. Moreover, the insight that the personal is political has drawn attention to links between militarism and structural violence, the importance of the 'everyday' as a site in international security, and the private sphere as one no longer beyond relevance. Finally, despite fierce disagreement about the implications of these insights for critical theorising and practice, this field has brought *people* into the forefront of analysing global security relations (for potential overlaps here with the discourse of 'human security' see Chapter 10). Understanding international security 'from the point of view of subjugation' (Tickner 1992: 18) brings not only gender inequalities, but the 'interlocking' dimensions of race, class and culture into the frame (Basham 2013; Razack 2008). For this reason, feminist and gender approaches of all kinds are likely to continue to innovate, broaden, deepen and open the field of critical security studies.

Key points

- Women and gender structures more generally have been marginalised in both traditional and critical security studies.
- Feminist and gender approaches to security have attempted to address this marginalisation, but there is disagreement about the focus, method and implications of critique.
- Liberal feminists seek to make women more visible in the realm of international security, but they have been accused of an 'add women and stir' approach that does not question realist frameworks.
- By contrast, standpoint feminists draw on the views and experiences of women in political life, rather than abstract realist principles, to theorise international security.
- Poststructural feminist and gender approaches, however, criticise liberal and standpoint work for essentialising and universalising the 'female' subject, and call for a politicisation of all claims made in the name of gendered difference.

Discussion points

- In what ways have security studies marginalised women and gender structures in global politics?
- To what extent does the liberal feminist move to make women more visible in international security challenge or reaffirm the gendered assumptions of traditional security studies?
- What are the similarities and differences between a liberal feminist and a standpoint feminist perspective?
- Why do poststructuralists call the category of 'woman' fundamentally into question?
- How do feminist and gender perspectives open up the field of critical security studies?
- Is feminist security scholarship better conceived of a unitary body of thought or as a range of distinct and contending sub-positions?

Guide to further reading

Cynthia Enloe (2000) [1989] *Bananas, Beaches and Bases: Making Feminist Sense of International Politics*, 2nd edn. (Berkeley, CA, and London: University of California Press). The classic articulation of a liberal feminist approach to security studies.

Jane Parport and Marysia Zalewski (1998) (eds) *The 'Man' Question in International Relations* (Boulder, CO: Westview Press). Contains essays that analyse the production of masculinities in global politics.

Jennifer Lobasz and Laura Sjoberg (eds) (2011) 'Critical Perspectives' section of *Politics and Gender*, 7(4). An overview of current debates and controversies in 'feminist security studies'; see also a number of responses published as 'Forum: The State of Feminist Security Studies: Continuing the Conversation', *International Studies Perspectives* (2013) (14) edited by Laura J. Shepherd.

Jill Steans (2009) *Gender and International Relations: Issues, Debates, and Further Directions*, 2nd edn. (Cambridge: Polity Press). Offers an overview of theoretical positions within feminist and gender scholarship.

J. Ann Tickner (1992) *Gender in International Relations: Feminist Perspectives on Achieving Global Security* (New York: Columbia University Press). A landmark contribution to feminist security studies from a standpoint perspective.

V. Spike Peterson (1992) (ed.) *Gendered States: Feminist (Re)Visions of International Relations Theory* (Boulder, CO, and London: Lynne Rienner). An articulation of poststructuralist approaches to feminism and gender in security studies.

Weblinks

United Nations statistics and indicators on women and men: http://unstats.un.org/unsd/demographic/products/indw

UN Convention on the Elimination of all Forms of Discrimination Against Women: www.un.org/womenwatch/daw/cedaw/text/econvention.htm

Women in International Security (WIIS), Centre for Peace and Security Studies, Edmund A. Walsh School of Foreign Service, Georgetown University: http://wiis.georgetown.edu/

WomenWatch, the United Nations Inter-Agency Network on Women and Gender Equality (IANWGE): www.un.org/womenwatch/

4   Postcolonial perspectives

Abstract

This chapter evaluates critiques of traditional and critical security studies emanating from postcolonial experiences and theories. To do so the chapter outlines and discusses the multiple meanings of 'the postcolonial' in geographical, spatial and theoretical terms. It emphasises that there is no single monolithic postcolonial approach to security. Rather, there are multiple ways of interpreting the postcolonial (itself a highly contested term) and each gives rise to different, and often contrasting, approaches to security. These include 'Third World security' and the related idea of 'subaltern realism' as well as approaches to security that draw more explicitly on postcolonial theory and concepts, which are also discussed in this chapter.

Introduction

An emerging body of literature drawing on postcolonial theories and perspectives (broadly understood) has increasingly sought to critique the Western/Eurocentric bias of both traditional *and* critical security studies. Scholars such as Mohammed Ayoob have pointed to the ethnocentric tendencies of security studies in general, and Ayoob has instead proposed a brand of 'subaltern realism' that is more attuned to the security concerns of 'Third World' states than the 'fashionably expansionist definitions of the concept of security' associated with variants of critical security studies (1997: 139). From a different angle, others have argued that security studies derives its core precepts almost exclusively from European experience and is hence underpinned by taken-for-granted historical geographies of the 'Third World', the 'West', global 'North' and global 'South'. This, they contend, is again true not only of traditional security studies, but also of critical approaches to security by virtue of their commitments to varieties of (Western) Enlightenment political thought. The consequence of this has been the marginalisation of the world beyond the global 'North' and the inability of critical security studies to recognise its own particularity and ethnocentrism.

The 'Third World' in security studies

In dealing with postcolonial approaches to security, we begin first with a consideration of what the Third World means and how it has figured within security studies. This is not to say that the terms 'postcolonial' and 'Third World' are interchangeable (indeed, many proponents of postcolonial studies, particularly in cultural and literary studies, use the term 'postcolonial' much more broadly to include parts of the 'First' and 'Second' worlds as well

– see Ashcroft *et al.* 1989). However, the 'Third World' (see Box 4.1) is now often assumed to be *post*colonial even if only in a historical sense referring to the processes of decolonisation that occurred in the wake of the Second World War. Thus, Arif Dirlik argues that the word postcolonial 'claims as its special provenance the terrain that in an earlier day used to go by the name of Third World' (Dirlik 1994: 329).

As is discussed later in the chapter, many scholars now find all-encompassing 'meta-geographical' terms such as the Third World objectionable on a number of grounds. Yet for some the idea of the Third World retains its utility as a broad designation. Mohammed Ayoob, the foremost proponent of an approach to security explicitly grounded in the experience of the 'Third World', claims to use the term in a 'generic sense'. While recognising that multiple distinctions and internal cultural and political differences are skirted over by the term, Ayoob argues:

> these [Third World] countries share enough in terms of their colonial past and their unequal encounter with the European powers following the Industrial Revolution to set them apart from the European states which have traditionally formed the 'core' of the modern system of states. They also share the attributes of economic underdevelopment and social dislocation, which are at least partly attributable to their encounter with the West (and which have continued even after the formal process of decolonization has been completed).
>
> (1983/1984: 43)

Thus, for Ayoob at least, the Third World is distinguished as geographically, historically and economically postcolonial and he has retained this 'generic' use of the term in his more recent writings as well (see, for example, Ayoob 2002).

For much of the history of security studies (and related subdisciplines such as strategic studies), the study of security in the Third World played a distant second fiddle to consideration of the stand-off between the 'First' and the 'Second' worlds during the cold war. Where the Third World did feature, it too tended to be framed within the broader contours of this stand-off rather than being treated as a stand-alone concern. As Ayoob noted in the early 1980s:

> Most states in the Third World are only recently participants in the modern system of states, which is European in origin and in its defining characteristics. Until a few decades ago they were mere 'objects' rather than 'subjects' in international relations.
>
> (1983/1984: 44)

In other words, during the cold war the states of the 'Third World' were generally viewed as 'pieces' or 'objects' to be 'taken' or 'lost' in a global contest between the US and the USSR, as 'bit [part] players in the larger drama of superpower conflict' (Krause 1998: 125). Hence, as Pettiford (1996: 289) notes, the dominant political and intellectual concern with the cold war rivalry meant that, among many possible examples, the insurgency in El Salvador in the early 1980s was assumed a priori to be the product of Soviet and Cuban machinations rather than domestic social and political grievances. In short, the 'regional' conflicts of the Third World generally only became of import to the mainstream of security studies if and when they could be related to the 'central strategic balance' (Acharya 1997: 300).

The porous nature of the term 'Third World' has always led some analysts to be sceptical of its actual utility as a categorisation, and the (pejorative) connotations of underdevelopment often assumed to accompany the term (partly resultant from its use within

Box 4.1 Where is the 'Third World'?

The term 'Third World' is generally seen to have entered the political lexicon in the 1950s. Although there is some debate about the origins of the term, most pinpoint its first use to the work of the French demographer Alfred Sauvy in 1952. Sauvy, referring to the struggle for decolonisation in India and China, used the term 'Third World' as an equivalent term to the 'third estate' as used during the French Revolution to distinguish the struggle of the 'common people' against the 'first' and 'second' estates (the clergy and the aristocracy). Later the term 'Third World' came to be adopted, often self-consciously, by the leaders of decolonisation movements and it gained currency during the cold war as a descriptor for states that were neither part of the 'First World' (capitalist states) nor 'Second World' (communist states) (Weiss 1995: x; Thomas 1999: 226). As Weiss (1995) notes, the term 'Third World' has always remained open-ended with regard to membership (see Figure 4.1 for one contemporary interpretation) and subject to different users' own categorisations, although in political terms it was often associated with the states involved in the Non-Aligned Movement (primarily comprising states located in Africa, Latin America and East Asia) in much the same manner as 'First World' status was associated with membership of NATO and the OECD (Organisation for Economic Co-operation and Development) and 'Second World' status with membership of the Warsaw Treaty Organization.

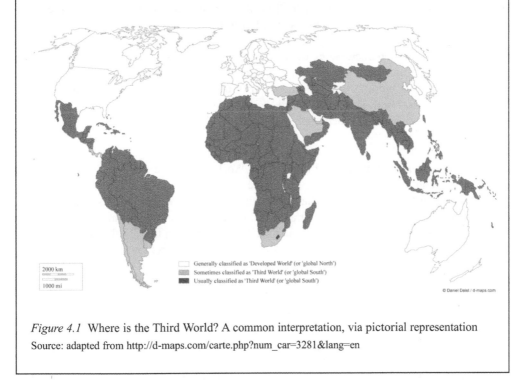

Figure 4.1 Where is the Third World? A common interpretation, via pictorial representation
Source: adapted from http://d-maps.com/carte.php?num_car=3281&lang=en

'modernisation theory') have led some states, such as China and India, to at times reject their inclusion within its scope of reference. Use of the term has, however, persisted despite the collapse of the so-called 'Second World' communist states in 1989–1991 (epitomised, for example, by the continued title of the journal *Third World Quarterly*). It now tends to be used to emphasise the disjuncture between 'First' and 'Third' worlds (and is now also broadly paralleled in distinctions made between 'developed' and 'developing' worlds, and between a global 'North' and 'South'). Indeed, far from disappearing, Caroline Thomas argues, the Third World 'is becoming global' due to processes of economic globalisation that place an ever-increasing number of people among the world's poor. In this sense, for Thomas at least, the term Third World 'still has meaning today' (1999: 225–226), although as is discussed later in the chapter many scholars within postcolonial studies critique the use of the term for a variety of reasons.

A 'subaltern realist' approach to security

Assuming, as most uses of the term 'Third World' do, that sub-Saharan Africa and Asia are included within the term, Third World security is surely deserving of more sustained attention within security studies than it received during the cold war. In terms of military conflict alone, the vast majority of wars in the post-cold war era have been fought in the Third World (Acharya 1997: 300–301), and most of these have been *intra-state* rather than inter-state in character (that is, wars that have occurred within state boundaries, rather than between states – see weblink to the Uppsala Conflict Data Program). Against this backdrop the focus on inter-state conflict is of questionable merit, and even during the cold war some scholars such as Ayoob had already begun to identify traditional security studies as insufficient to the study of security of Third World/postcolonial states. For him:

> The three major characteristics of the concept of state security as developed in the Western literature – namely, its external orientation, its strong linkage with systemic security, and its binding ties with the security of the two major alliance blocs – have been so thoroughly diluted in the Third World that the explanatory power of the concept has been vastly reduced when applied to Third World contexts.
>
> (Ayoob 1995: 6; 1983/1984: 43)

On the first point, Ayoob argues that in the Third World 'the sense of insecurity from which these states – and more particularly, their regimes – suffer, emanates to a substantial extent from within their boundaries rather than from outside' (1983/1984: 43). This does not mean that external threats to the state – the traditional concern of national security – are entirely absent. Rather, Ayoob argues, external threats to state security in the Third World are almost always bound up with *internal* threats to state structures and regimes, often to the point where it makes little sense to speak of 'external' and 'internal' threats to the state in distinct terms (Ayoob suggests that we should think in terms of a 'nexus' of internal and external threats – 1997: 128). Where inter-state wars do occur in the Third World, Ayoob argues that they are still usually closely related to domestic divisions. He cites, as just one example, the case of internal crisis in Pakistan in 1971 leading to the subsequent India–Pakistan war (1995: 49), and Amitav Acharya similarly points to the internal drivers of the Iraqi invasion of Kuwait in 1990 (1997: 309).

In this light, the traditional realist focus on external threats to national security is highly problematic. The problem, Ayoob argues, is that security studies has traditionally assumed a one-size-fits-all conception of the state in its consideration of national security. This, by its very nature, fails to recognise the fact that the type of state assumed within this conception – based around the so-called 'Westphalian' model of the state – is the product of particular historical circumstances (for example, centuries of state building, war, and then later industrialisation). The modern state was forged in Europe, and then later exported as a model (often, if not always, violently) to North America, Australia, Africa and Asia by European powers. However, as Ayoob points out, the process of state formation in the Third World is distinctive in character and, he argues, gives rise to a different type of state and, consequently, a distinct conception of security. In the Third World the process of state formation has tended to be accelerated (that is, it has occurred over a much shorter period of time than in the Western/European 'core') by virtue of its imposition by external powers; it has depended on a particular pattern of elite recruitment from along local populaces; and, in the period after 1945, it has occurred under the conditions of rapid decolonisation.

In short, for Ayoob, different experiences of state formation determine differences in the 'primary security orientations' of 'two sets of states' (1983/1984: 44): those in the West, and those of the Third World. In particular, on his account, the accelerated nature of the process of state formation in the Third World has tended to give rise to a type of state structure that has, at best, weak roots. Hence, 'The dimensions of the security problem, and of the concept of security itself, in the Third World are [...] very different from those applied to, and common in the literature of, the developed West' (1983/1984: 46).

The argument is made, therefore, that security means something very different in the Third World as compared to its meaning for other states. Third World states, Ayoob argues, tend to be 'weak' as states in comparison to their Western counterparts. This is not to say that Third World states are necessarily lacking in material resources or power (the opposite may often be the case), but that the legitimacy accruing to Western states by virtue of centuries of development is often weaker within Third World states (leading some to speak of 'quasi-states' – see Jackson 1990). In these conditions, Ayoob argues, fundamental 'internal' issues of political, social and economic organisation are equally as much of a concern to Third World regimes (i.e. those in power in Third World states) as they might lead ultimately to destabilisation of the state and regime collapse: 'security-insecurity is defined in relation to vulnerabilities – *both internal and external* – that threaten or have the potential to bring down or weaken state structures, both territorial and institutional, and governing regimes' (Ayoob 1995: 9, emphasis in original). It is for this reason, Ayoob argues, that Third World regimes have, in practical terms, always 'broadened' national security to include economic and social issues as well.

Ayoob and others focusing on Third World security consequently tend towards the view that 'If there were good reasons for the dominance of traditional security analyses in International Relations they are not, and never were, very relevant for understanding the Third World' (Pettiford 1996: 300). Ayoob, however, does not view the various critical alternatives to traditional security analyses as much of an improvement with regard to Third World contexts, and in many ways he regards them as a backward step. He rejects what he classes as the 'fashionably expansionist' definitions of security associated with some critical approaches:

> While it is essential to move beyond an exclusively ethnocentric Western definition of security to include domestic and non-military dimensions, especially issues of intra-state conflict and political legitimacy [...] one should not [...] run away with the concept to make it all things to all people.
>
> (Ayoob 1997: 139)

Many of Ayoob's concerns in this regard parallel those raised by proponents of securitisation theory in response to the 'broadening' of the concept of security (see Chapter 6). But Ayoob reserves particular ire for the 'deepening' of security proposed within Critical Security Studies (see Chapter 2). Ideas of 'emancipation' remain rooted in Western political philosophy and hence, for Ayoob, the notion of aligning 'security' and 'emancipation' is still fundamentally Western-centric in orientation (and he even goes so far as to suggest that it has a 'neocolonial bias' (1997: 140)). In regard to Ken Booth's (1991) linkage of security and emancipation Ayoob contends that:

> such semantic acrobatics tend to impose a model of contemporary Western politics – of national states that have by and large solved their legitimacy problem and possess representative and responsive governments, which preside over socially mobile populations that are relatively homogenous and usually affluent and free from want – that are far removed from Third World realities.
>
> (Ayoob 1997: 127)

As an alternative to both traditional *and* critical approaches to security, Ayoob suggests what he terms as a 'subaltern realist' approach to security. This approach argues that greater recognition of the particular positioning of Third World states within the international system is required than has generally been the case within security studies. Third World states, Ayoob argues, endure a particular 'security predicament' (1995) that encompasses three interrelated dimensions: state making (as outlined previously); regional conflict (often as a consequence of internal factors); and the position of Third World states in the international system. With regard to this last category, Ayoob argues that Third World states occupy a 'subaltern' position in the world order: they are states of 'weak and inferior rank' (1997: 121), due to the historical legacy of colonial exploitation. This legacy continues to have visible effects, such as in the weak institutional structures inherited by Third World states after decolonisation, border disputes and irredentism as a product of boundaries imposed during the colonial era and continued economic dependence. In turn, this accentuates internal social and economic instability, which leads to regional conflict – and so the predicament is perpetuated.

The 'realist' part of Ayoob's 'subaltern realism' refers to his maintenance of the state both as the referent object of security and the means of security provision. The problem for the Third World as Ayoob sees it, and here again he is at odds with the Critical Security Studies (Chapter 2) critique of 'statism', is that there is *not enough* state competence in too many cases (cf. Krasner 1981; Jackson 1990): that is, Ayoob sees many of the security issues of the Third World as emanating from 'incomplete' processes of state formation:

> The overriding importance of the state – both as a territorial unit and as an institutional complex – to the political, and therefore security, realm in the case of the large majority of countries is justified in the context of the historical juncture at which most members of the international system (that is, the large majority that is located in the Third World) currently find themselves.
>
> (Ayoob 1997: 131)

For as long as the world remains a world of states, therefore, Ayoob sees development and enhancement of state institutions (or 'adequate stateness' (1997: 140)) as the only way out of the security predicament for the countries and people of the Third World.

Criticisms of subaltern realism

Ayoob's subaltern realism offers a pointed and arguably refreshing critique of the assumptions both of traditional and critical approaches to security. However, though Ayoob makes a sustained and valid critique of Western-centrism in security studies, his own approach to security has been accused of retaining 'strong residues' of the traditional/realist paradigm that he initially sets out to critique.

One of the primary criticisms of Ayoob's subaltern realism is that it conflates security with the state and, from here, with the regime that rules the state. Although beginning from a simi-lar basis to that offered by Ayoob, Pettiford's (1996) analysis of Central America illustrates several cases where state militaries have been used to repress 'subversion' of internal order, and this often constitutes a major source of insecurity for citizens of these states. Yet, Ayoob seems to want to maintain the development of institutionally 'strong' states in the Third World as the path to ultimate security, which implies that a degree of state violence may be 'almost inevitable' in this process of development (Ayoob 1997: 133). As Keith Krause notes in this regard, 'Ayoob's understanding of security rests on a narrow conception of "the polit-ical" that privileges the state without even raising the question whether or not it should be the proper *subject* of security' (1998: 129, emphasis in original). In this sense, the 'predica-ment' of Third World security might be reread as an equation where the increasing (state) security of Third World regimes often comes at the cost of the individual liberties and lives of those that might oppose or object to such regimes. Here, Ayoob would probably counter that Western states have undergone similar processes in their trajectory of development in centuries past, and that Western observers can hardly afford to take the moral high ground on this basis. Yet, many would side with Krause in objecting that Ayoob's account focuses too heavily on security as defined by state elites in the Third World, and that it is overly permissive in terms of the methods used to achieve security defined on these terms (and here there are some parallels with criticisms of the alleged elite focus of securitisation theory – see Chapter 6). Amitav Acharya, though broadly sympathetic to Ayoob's general approach, warns that overemphasis on the security of the state often leads to a problematic conflation of national security (the security of the state) and regime security (the security of those who rule the state) (Acharya 1997: 303).

In short, Ayoob puts forward a view of security that is avowedly statist, and for critics this puts him firmly back into the ambit of the Western approaches to security that his subaltern realism is supposed to challenge. By taking the unitary Western state as a model for the development of security infrastructures, Ayoob risks prematurely ruling out the question of 'what *kinds* of states might be most appropriate to deal with the challenges diverse social and communal groups face' (Krause 1998: 134, emphasis in original).

Ayoob's use of the terms 'Third World' and 'subaltern' has also been viewed as problem-atic by several critics. Krause contends that Ayoob's generic use of the term 'Third World' 'collapses the multiple distinctions between vastly different parts of the world such as Africa, Latin America and East Asia', and to do so risks encouraging Western tendencies to 'see these regions as an undifferentiated zone of turmoil' (Krause 1998: 133). Ayoob's use of the term 'subaltern' within his subaltern realist approach is also seen as problematic. As is acknowledged by Ayoob himself, his use of the term 'subaltern' has little relation to the movement known as 'subaltern studies' within postcolonial theory (see Box 4.2), from which he borrows the term. Rather than referring to a range of subaltern 'classes' and their subjugated positions within societies (as within subaltern studies), Ayoob deliberately uses the term subaltern to refer to Third World *states* and their subordinate position relative to First World states in the international system. Once again this points to Ayoob's statist orien-tations but, to play off the title of Michael Barnett's incisive (2002) critique, it clothes his realism within a thin veil of 'radical chic' associated with the notion of the subaltern. Indeed, Ayoob himself locates the intellectual groundings of his subaltern realist approach not in postcolonial theory (see Box 4.2), but in a combination of ideas that all emanate primarily from Western traditions: (Hobbesian) classical realism, historical sociology, and – somewhat ironically – the 'English School' or international society approach (Ayoob 2002: 28–29).

A postcolonial moment in security studies?

In contrast to Ayoob's admission of a thin connection between subaltern realism and post-colonial studies, there have been more recent attempts to foster a 'postcolonial moment' (Barkawi and Laffey 2006) in security studies that is linked more explicitly to several post-colonial thinkers and ideas (see below).

In many ways, Barkawi and Laffey's conception of a postcolonial moment within secu-rity studies is animated by similar concerns to those motivating Ayoob's subaltern realism. However, their call for a 'non-Eurocentric security studies' (2006: 330) has as an additional motivation: a desire to get to grips with the rise of non-state terrorism, Al-Qaeda in particu-lar. Efforts at understanding the rise of groups such as Al-Qaeda need, according to Barkawi and Laffey, to be situated within the broader historical context of relations between the global 'North'/'First World' and global 'South'/'Third World' and a critical assessment of the functions these categorisations play (cf. Doty 1996; Lewis and Wigen 1997; Slater 2004). Traditional security studies is, they suggest, 'at best a poor basis for understanding and action in contemporary security environments' (Barkawi and Laffey 2006: 330) in this regard for at least two reasons. The first is that traditional security studies focuses upon 'great power'/inter-state conflicts and 'as a result provides few categories for making sense of the historical experiences of the weak and powerless who comprise most of the world's population' (2006: 332). Traditional security studies not only struggles with the emergence of non-state actors, it also cannot fathom the reasons for recourse to 'terrorist' acts as a potential recourse of the 'weak and powerless'. Barkawi and Laffey do not seek to justify such acts per se but rather to point out that the 'war on terror' represents but the latest vari-ation of North/South conflict in which *all* forms of resistance from the global South have been characterised as illegitimate. In keeping with the spirit of Frantz Fanon (2001 [1961]), they instead want to keep open the possibility that violent resistance may at times be the only recourse of the weak and oppressed (Barkawi and Laffey 2006: 251).

In part this relates to a second failing of traditional security studies as characterised by Barkawi and Laffey: the 'Eurocentric' nature of security studies, which 'regards the weak and the powerless as marginal or derivative elements of world politics as at best the site of liberal good intentions or at worst a potential source of threats' (2006: 332). Here the over-laps between Barkawi and Laffey's critique and ideas in postcolonial studies, most notably Edward Said's writings on 'Orientalism' (see Box 4.2), become apparent. As John Hobson notes, drawing on Edward Said (2003):

> Eurocentrism or Orientalism is a discourse that was invented in the eighteenth and nine-teenth centuries by European thinkers as they went about constructing European identity [where] Western man was elevated to the permanent 'proactive subject' of global poli-tics/economics – past, present and future – standing at the centre of all things. Conversely, Eastern 'man' was relegated to the peripheral status of global politics' 'passive object', languishing on the Other side of an imaginary civilizational frontier, stripped of history and dignity. In this Eurocentric imaginary, then, the line of civiliza-tional apartheid separates the Western heart of light from the Eastern heart of darkness.
> (Hobson 2007: 94)

Box 4.2 Theorising the postcolonial: Key thinkers and ideas in postcolonial studies

Although the term 'postcolonial' now has wide usage, there is no agreed or settled definition as to what might constitute postcolonialism (or postcolonial studies) as a distinct theoretical move-ment. As one review of the field comments 'probably no term within literary and critical studies is so hotly contested at present as is the term "post-colonial"; probably no area of study is so thoroughly riven with disciplinary self-doubt and mutual suspicion' (Slemon 2001: 100). In fact it might be argued that the only minimal common ground between postcolonial thinkers is a shared effort to come to terms with what, exactly, the nature of the 'postcolonial' condition is. In the process, the group of thinkers loosely connected under the rubric of postcolonial studies have produced 'a radical rethinking and re-formulation of forms of knowledge and social iden-tities authored and authorized by colonialism and western domination' (Prakash 1992: 8). Frequently this has entailed questioning the term 'Third World' itself as a description 'authored and authorized' by Western domination where the colonial subject is defined in contradistinction to a Western 'core'. Instead, thinkers such as Dipesh Chakrabarty (1992, 2000) point us towards an examination of colonial/postcolonial histories and experiences authored by the subjugated. Borrowing Antonio Gramsci's concept of the 'subaltern' – used to denote groups or classes within society that are subject to the authority of ruling groups – this school of 'subaltern stud-ies' attempts to make common cause with subordinated people *everywhere*, thereby linking the specific subjugation associated with colonialism to the experience of subjugated minorities globally (see Guha and Spivak 1988; Prakash 1990).

Although very different in its form and goals, this emphasis on the shared experience of subjugation (and the forms of knowledge and action it gives rise to) is also indicated in the title of Frantz Fanon's seminal (1961) work *The Wretched of the Earth* [*Les damnés de la terre*] (Fanon 2001). Fanon (1925–1961), a psychotherapist and an active member of the Front de Libération Nationale (FLN) in Algeria during the war against French colonialism, sought to illustrate the inherent and brutal violence of colonial rule and to articulate a liberating counter violence on the part of those subjected to colonialism. Where Fanon's work points to a form of postcolonial identity forged out of the violent struggle against colonialism (and has sometimes been criticised on this basis), Edward Said's (1935–2003) seminal account of Orientalism (Said 2003) takes a longer historical view of the development of the relationship between Western colonial powers and the people of the Middle East, and the forms of identity and power produced as a result. Said's work examines the ways in which particular constructions of an 'exotic' oriental 'Other' and romantic notions of the 'orient' in Western literary and cultural writings have continually underpinned imperialism, racism and, ultimately, the notion of the 'West' itself.

More recent work in postcolonial studies has exhibited a concern with whether and how a more 'authentic' version of the postcolonial experience might be rendered, and whether this is even possible. Indeed, for some, contemporary postcolonial studies, intersecting with theoreti-cal currents from poststructuralist thinkers such as Jacques Derrida (see Chapter 5), is generally distinguished by an attempt to 'abolish all distinctions between center and periphery as well as all other "binarisms" that are allegedly a legacy of colonial(ist) ways of thinking and to reveal societies globally in their complex heterogeneity and contingency' (Dirlik 1994: 329). Gayatri Chakravorty Spivak (1942–), drawing on both feminism and poststructuralism, has focused on the question of who speaks for the subaltern (Spivak 1988) in the context of unequal power rela-tions, whilst Homi Bhabha (1949–) argues that the postcolonial condition is best thought of in terms of 'hybridity' – the ways in which the cultures, languages and experiences of 'coloniser' and 'colonised' are inherently mixed and reformulated (or 'hybridised') rather than essentialist categories (Bhabha 1994).

In short, Eurocentric/Orientalist accounts assume European centrality geographically, historically, and politically, and Western development (with its roots in Europe) as the apex of 'civilisation'. Critics have suggested that such Orientalism has been a pervasive feature of traditional security studies, during the cold war in particular. Barkawi and Laffey detect strong Orientalist currents in accounts of strategic theory, the Cuban Missile Crisis, the Second World War and the Holocaust where, in each, the West has been routinely and unquestioningly configured as 'a force for good in world politics' (2006: 343). In a similar vein Bradley Klein has examined the ways in which strategic studies provided a map of the world in which the West always ended up on the 'good' side (1994: 5). In doing so it reified Western culture and values and, in the process, has helped legitimate various forms of Western intervention (military and economic) in the global South.

As with Ayoob, Barkawi and Laffey find that critical approaches are of little improvement over their traditional counterpart and often exhibit their own Eurocentric/Orientalist tendencies. They too are concerned that 'emancipation', as advocated in Critical Security Studies (see Chapter 2), is ultimately rooted in Western political theory. More substantively, and distinct from Ayoob's critique of CSS, Barkawi and Laffey argue that the problem with CSS is that it ultimately maintains a distinction between 'strong' and 'weak' where only the former are assumed to have the capacity and agency to emancipate the latter:

> The politics of critical and human security approaches revolve around the concept of emancipation, an idea derived from the European Enlightenments. In this literature, the agent of emancipation is almost invariably the West, whether in the form of Western-dominated international institutions, a Western-led global civil society, or the 'ethical foreign policies' of leading Western powers [...] Even when the concrete agents of emancipation are not themselves Westerners, they are conceived of as the bearers of Western ideas, whether concerning economy, politics or culture.
>
> (Barkawi and Laffey 2006: 350; cf. Hobson 2007)

What is problematic here, for Barkawi and Laffey, is that the non-West is often represented within both traditional and critical approaches in terms of what is 'lacking' in comparison to the West, in this case the agential capacity of those in the non-Western world. Indirectly addressing Ayoob's subaltern realism, they also critique accounts that explain conflict 'in terms of a lack of those institutions and attributes associated with European modernity, such as sovereignty, rather than as a consequence of long histories of colonial and postcolonial interaction with the West' (2006: 347) (recall Ayoob's argument that the 'Third World security predicament' emanates primarily from a *lack* of adequate state institutions). Instead of assuming such binary divisions, Barkawi and Laffey suggest a 'relational approach' that recognises the mutual constitution of the 'strong' and the 'weak' and 'begins with the assumption that the social world is composed of relations rather than separate objects, like great powers or "the West"' (2006: 348). Thus, the 'postcolonial moment' highlights 'the *interconnectedness*, rather than the separateness, of the colonial and the postcolonial and the North and the South' (Abrahamsen 2003: 196, emphasis added) as a key focus of investigation within security studies.

What this might mean, and what precisely is a 'non-Eurocentric security studies' in this vein remains to be fully fleshed out (see Box 4.3 for an indication). As is discussed in Chapter 10, several critical approaches to the issue of development and security in particular might be said to adopt a stance that seeks to emphasise the *relational* aspect – between 'metropole' and 'peripheries' – of development 'complexes' (Duffield 2001). Some scholars

---

Box 4.3 Relating the 'West' and 'the rest': Outlining a 'relational approach' to the war on terror

For many, the war on terror is a clash between the West and the Islamic world. Al-Qaeda, bin Laden and his allies are conceived as 'Islamic fundamentalists' with a passionate hatred of everything Western. The problem with this way of framing the conflict is that it ignores the long history of interconnection and mutual constitution out of which bin Laden's ideas and organisation were produced. Currents of Western, Arab and Islamic cultures and histories, modern technologies and communications, and the policies of various regimes and great powers combined to form crystallisations, amongst them bin Laden's and Al-Qaeda's particular way of being modern. Attempting to disaggregate these phenomena and squeeze them into boxes marked 'Islam' and 'the West' will not aid understanding of the dynamics of the war on terror. More importantly, policies derived from such binary understandings may create the very conditions that crystallise future bin Ladens and Al-Qaedas.

(Barkawi and Laffey 2006: 347)

---

working at the intersection of security studies and IR theory have attempted to identify and bring non-Western thought and experience into the field (Acharya and Buzan 2007; Tickner and Wæver 2009). Others argue that taking IR theory and security studies as a starting point reinforces rather than challenges the basis of the problem of ethnocentrism (Nayak and Selbin 2010; Shani 2008; and cf. Vasilaki 2012). Ultimately, what this 'postcolonial moment' might entail, at a minimum, is a refusal to treat the terms such as 'West' and 'Third World' as self-evident, even – and perhaps especially – in self-proclaimed accounts of 'Third World security'.

Postcoloniality, race and 'necropolitics'

The postcolonial critique of the Western-centric tendencies of traditional and some 'critical' approaches to security such as CSS (Chapter 2) can also be extended to poststructural perspectives within the field. Sankaran Krishna argues that, on the one hand, there are many synergies between postcolonialism and poststructuralism, such as the common focus on questions of identity and difference, notions of otherness, and the problem of universal grand narratives (see Chapter 5). On the other hand, he also claims that there are some key differences precisely around the issue of who the political subject is and where s/he is pre-supposed to be:

> Emerging from a rather comfortably self-contained view of the West, [poststructuralist perspectives] seem to contain little recognition that a totalizing critique of all forms of essentialism and identity politics might play out very differently for people situated outside putative mainstreams or that the demise of narratives such as the nation may have different political implications for those situated elsewhere.
>
> (Krishna 1999: xxix)

In a similar vein, Christine Sylvester has referred to the typically Western focus of much of the poststructural work on sovereignty, practices of exceptionalism and contemporary biopolitics. This geographical and cultural bias, Sylvester argues, is not unique to poststructuralist works specifically in security studies, but the very thinkers who have inspired this scholarship. Thus key thinkers associated with poststructuralism, such as Michel Foucault and Giorgio Agamben, typically draw on Western examples and delimit their analyses to specifically Western juridical-political order (Sylvester 2006: 66; see also Shani 2008).

Nevertheless, there have been some attempts at applying the insights of Foucault and Agamben to the postcolonial context. Sylvester refers to the work of Rajeev Patel and Philip McMichael (2004), who argue that colonial governance was in essence about controlling and managing bodies. In this sense, the colony was the epitome of a 'biopolitical' space:

> local people were routinely made to cover their bodies, subject their bodies to hygiene, fill their bodies with Western knowledge, move their bodies to different lands, use their bodies for slave and wage labour, and fight other bodies in the name of the colonizing state.
>
> (Sylvester 2006: 68)

Moreover, the point made by Patel and McMichael, as well as Sylvester, is that the prefix 'post' in the term 'postcolonial' inaccurately implies that such practices are confined to history. Rather, via contemporary expressions of the state of exception, colonial biopolitical practices are arguably very much alive in current global political life. Indeed, for Sylvester, one of the rationales for postcolonial studies is precisely to 'see and address more of the troubling biopolitics of our times' (2006: 76). The recent work of Vivienne Jabri (2011) on the production of postcolonial subjectivity and attempts by various security agendas to govern it offers one indication of how this has been addressed. Jabri argues that colonialism is no longer about direct rule, but the management and control of subjects deemed to be potential sources of danger to the neoliberal world order project of Western states: 'We might say that where the colony in modernity was subjected to conquest, the postcolony is subjected to the post-panoptic governmentalizing manifestation of power, where populations, and not simply individuals, are shaped and regulated into governable, manageable entities' (Jabri 2011: 4). One of the means by which entire 'errant populations and their movements' (2011: 5) are secured is via war waged by Western states in the name of humanitarian protection. By rendering postcolonial subjects vulnerable and in need of protection those states are able to better 'know' and therefore govern the populations they target: 'The government of populations comes to constitute a legitimate sphere of operations in a politics of protection that confers not just legitimacy but also impunity to the "protector" and negates the potential of agency in the "protected"' (Jabri 2011: 121). But while such global security projects are 'reflective of a colonial rationality of domination and dispossession', Jabri claims that they never fully succeed in capturing or securing the postcolonial subject, whose agency manifests itself in diverse forms of resistance (as illustrated, for example, in the uprisings of the 'Arab Spring' since 2010).

Thinking about various biopolitical practices through the lens of postcolonialism enables the interrogation of an otherwise neglected dimension of global security relations: race. In this context Achille Mbembe is of note in his insistence on the racial characteristics of contemporary biopolitics. Mbembe takes as his starting point Foucault's understanding of racism as a form of control based upon the distribution of the human species into different groups and the 'establishment of a biological caesura between the ones and the others' (Mbembe 2003: 17). A racist logic is one that divides, separates and distinguishes between people based upon biological characteristics so that some lives may count as worthy of living and others may not. In this way racism can be considered as a form of biopolitical economy that serves to regulate who dies and who stays alive depending on the imperatives of the state (see Box 5.1, Chapter 5). Yet, despite the overt prevalence of racism, Mbembe claims that it 'has been the ever present shadow in Western political thought and practice; especially when it comes to imagining the inhumanity of, or rule over, foreign peoples' (2003: 17).

Mbembe considers the racial biopolitics of practices in the colony. Slavery, he argues, was one of the first manifestations of biopolitical governance. On his view, the structure of the plantation, where a slave belongs to his master and is kept alive but in a permanent state of injury, is akin to the figure of the state of exception (see Box 5.4, Chapter 5). The colony does not conform to the norm of the state: the army is not a distinct entity; wars are not fought between regular armies; there is no distinction between combatants and non-combatants. 'As such', writes Mbembe, 'the colonies are the location par excellence where the controls and guarantees of judicial order can be suspended – the zone where the violence of the state of exception is deemed to operate in the service of "civilization"' (2003: 24). In other words, echoing the work of Giorgio Agamben, those who inhabit the colony find themselves living a 'bare life' banned from conventional juridical-political structures in a permanent state of exception.

For Franz Fanon colonial occupation is first and foremost about the division of space into different compartments aligned with the biological categorisation of those living within them (Fanon 2001 [1961]). Using this insight Mbembe refers to the way in which the establishment of the colony relies upon the writing of new spatial relations via new boundaries, hierarchies and classifications. If space is the 'raw material' of the sovereign, as Fanon suggests, then Mbembe argues that 'sovereignty meant occupation, and occupation meant relegating the colonised into a third zone between subjecthood and objecthood' (2003: 26).

According to Mbembe, however, the concept of biopolitics has become insufficient for an understanding of contemporary forms of subjugation of some peoples' lives to the power of death. Foucault's focus on the ability of biopower to 'make live and let die' does not take into account:

> the various ways in which, in our contemporary world, weapons are deployed in the interest of maximum destruction of persons and the creation of *death-worlds*, new and unique forms of social existence in which vast populations are subjected to conditions of life conferring upon them the status of the *living dead*.
>
> (Mbembe 2003: 40)

Under conditions of late modernity, therefore, Mbembe claims that colonialism combined what Foucault calls disciplinary power and biopower with a third form of governance: 'necropower'.

Mbembe develops the concept of necropower to characterise the way in which the dynamics of territorial fragmentation referred to by Fanon combine with a proliferation of sites of violence that result in death in the colony. The 'splintering occupation' of colonies involves the separation of communities not only in two but three dimensions. Battlegrounds are not solely located on the earth's surface: 'the underground as well as the airspace are transformed into conflict zones' (Mbembe 2003: 29). Necropolitics, on Mbembe's formulation, involves the cultivation of such spatial arrangements that put populations in daily contact with the possibility of death. Under necropolitical conditions people acquire the status of the living dead: a liminal position between life and death that means they are easier to manage (and dispose of). The concept of necropolitics thus carries deliberately macabre overtones that seek to alert us to the radical insecurities suffered in many parts of the world that are not adequately captured by accounts of security emanating from the developed 'West'. Mbembe argues that the 'most accomplished' form of necropower is the occupation of Palestine, but the idea of the 'death-world' can be applied to many parts of Africa and other areas of the global South where 'the sovereign might kill at any time or in any manner' (2003: 25). Thinking postcolonial insecurities in terms of necropolitics therefore expands the horizons of critical security studies beyond a Western frame that has typically sought to expunge both race and death.

Conclusion

As noted at the beginning of this chapter, and as evidenced in its presentation of the multiple and often-disparate 'postcolonial' perspectives relevant to security studies, the term postcolonial encompasses a variety of meanings. Whereas some scholars interpret the 'post' in postcolonial purely in terms of historical and geographical differentiation of the 'Third World' and its security predicaments, others argue the term should be more accurately deployed to critique the Western-centric biases of (critical) security studies, or to highlight the essential continuity of colonial practices in the creation of 'death-worlds' as opposed to any clean break between colonial and postcolonial epochs. The extent to which any or all of these postcolonial perspectives on security overlap or are compatible is open to question. Indeed, for some 'the term "postcolonial" seems increasingly to be straining at its seams, incorporating a proliferating set of theories with varying ontologies and epistemologies many of which are incommensurable, as even some postcolonialists recognise' (Hobson 2007: 103), and the same might well be said of the various postcolonial approaches to security outlined here.

Yet, the plurality and diversity of postcolonial perspectives might equally be cast as a particular source of interest for students of security. Taken as a whole, and in spite of their internal differences, postcolonial approaches can be said to draw our attention to the parts of the world, parts of theory and perspectives that are usually only partially considered or even absent from both traditional and critical accounts of security. In relation to critical security studies in particular, postcolonial approaches are notable not only for the extent to which they reinforce some of the moves within the critical 'turn' in security studies, but also for the ways in which they continue to challenge many of the theories and approaches covered in other chapters in this book.

Key points

- Many scholars working from a 'Third World' perspective argue that during the cold war in particular the security concerns of the Third World tended to be read through the lens of the superpower rivalry or simply neglected altogether within security studies.
- The subaltern realist approach sets out to highlight the specificity of the Third World's 'security predicament' but has in turn been criticised for its explicit statism, which many critical approaches suggest is often a source of individual insecurity.
- The idea of a 'postcolonial moment' is used to denote the opportunity for a more substantive overlap between security studies and postcolonial studies that addresses the Eurocentric/'Orientalist' biases of both traditional and critical security studies.
- Some question the term 'post'colonial, suggesting that many people continue to live under colonial conditions, and that race has been a neglected aspect of the study of global security relations in both the traditional and critical literatures.

Discussion points

*   How does security look today from a 'Third World' perspective?
*   'Interpreted as the right of every ethnic group to self-determination, emancipation can turn out to be a recipe for grave disorder and anarchy' (Ayoob 1997). Why might a 'Third-World perspective' lead to a critique of 'emancipation' as the basis of security studies?
*   What are the main strengths and weaknesses of a subaltern realist approach to security?
*   What does the 'postcolonial moment' contribute to the study of security?
*   How does thinking in terms of race affect the study of global security relations?

Guide to further reading

Amitav Acharya (1997) 'The Periphery as the Core: The Third World and Security Studies', in Keith Krause and Michael C. Williams (eds) *Critical Security Studies: Concepts and Cases* (London: UCL Press). Provides a broadly complementary account of 'Third World Security' to that espoused by Ayoob, albeit one that is more open to the 'broadening' of the security agenda.

Keith Krause (1998) 'Theorizing Security, State Formation and the "Third World" in the Post-cold war World', *Review of International Studies*, 24: 125–136; Michael Barnett (2002) 'Radical Chic? Subaltern Realism: A Rejoinder', *International Studies Review*, 4(3): 49–62. Krause's article provides a critical review of Ayoob's *Third World Security Predicament*, while Barnett makes an incisive critique of the notion of subaltern realism.

Mohammed Ayoob (1995) *The Third World Security Predicament: State Making, Regional Conflict and the International System* (Boulder, CO: Lynne Rienner). For a self-defined 'Third World' perspective on security, Mohammed Ayoob's work is still the primary point of reference within security studies.

Sankaran Krishna (1999) *Postcolonial Insecurities: India, Sri Lanka, and the Question of Nationhood* (Minnesota, MN: University of Minnesota Press). An empirically detailed and theoretically sophisticated account of the relation between nation building and ethnic conflict in Sri Lanka. A more expansive version of Krishna's arguments can be found in his (2008) *Globalisation and Postcolonialism: Hegemony and Resistance in the Twenty-First Century* (Lanham, MD: Rowman and Littlefield).

Tarak Barkawi and Mark Laffey (2006) 'The Postcolonial Moment in Security Studies', *Review of International Studies*, 32: 329–352. The most substantive attempt to relate security studies and post-colonial studies to date.

Vivienne Jabri (2011) *The Postcolonial Subject: Claiming Politics/Governing Others in Late Modernity*. Inspired by postcolonial and poststructural traditions, Jabri explores the (re)production of the postcolonial subject in global security projects and the question of agency and resistance to those projects.

As well as consulting these texts, readers are also recommended to go straight to one or more of the seminal works in postcolonial studies such as Fanon (2001) [1961], Said (2003) [1978], Chakrabarty (2000) or Bhabha (1994). Alternatively, or as an introduction to these texts, the review chapter by Slemon (2001) and the text in which it appears (Castle 2001) both provide useful overviews of key themes and work in postcolonial studies, as do Abrahamsen (2003), Loomba (1996), Moore-Gilbert (1997) and Young (2001). Critical perspectives on the use of meta-geographical terms such as 'the West', 'Third World' and 'global North/South' are to be found in Doty (1996), Lewis and Wigen (1997) and Slater (2004) (see the Bibliography for details of all these readings).

5 Poststructuralism and international political sociology

Abstract

This chapter is organised into five sections. The first offers a sketch of the term 'post-structuralism', but warns of the inherent difficulty of referring to 'it' as a coherent position or approach. The second introduces two thinkers associated with the poststructural turn in political philosophy – Jacques Derrida and Michel Foucault – to give a flavour of the range and diversity of thought under consideration. The third considers the impact of this turn on security studies via a discussion of seminal poststructural works influenced by Derrida and Foucault. The fourth offers a survey of more recent research informed by poststructural thought associated with international political sociology (IPS) and the so-called 'Paris School'. Finally, the chapter concludes with a discussion of some of the possible limitations of poststructural approaches within security studies.

Introduction

Over the past four decades, security scholars inspired by poststructuralist thought have high-lighted the politics of language, interpretation and representation in the construction of notions of danger, threat and identity in international security. More recently, especially in the context of the 'war on terror' unleashed in the aftermath of the attacks on the World Trade Center and Pentagon on 11 September 2001, this work has proliferated in new directions involving analyses of discourses of exceptionalism and risk, debates about 'liberty' and 'security', practices of security as a technique of government and the question of the mate-riality of security. It is possible to trace the emergence of a more sociologically oriented approach to security, which is producing some of the most provocative research in the field. While poststructuralism was once seen as marginal to security studies, it has become increas-ingly prominent, though has not gone without criticism, especially in the UK and European contexts.

What is 'poststructuralism'?

It is not uncommon to find the terms 'poststructuralism', 'postmodernity' and 'postmod-ernism' used interchangeably in the literature. This can be quite confusing as each refers to something potentially very different. 'Postmodernity' implies a particular historical periodi-sation: the idea that we are currently living in an era, sometimes said to have been ushered in by the Second World War, that is in some sense *after* or *beyond* the epoch known as 'modernity'. 'Postmodernism', while often related to this view of history, is more of an umbrella term for an artistic, architectural and cultural movement in the West that emerged in the 1950s/1960s. 'Poststructuralism', our primary concern in this chapter, is a fragmentary assemblage of diverse social, political and philosophical thought that engages with, but also calls into question, the 'structuralist' tradition. 'It' is commonly associated with a particular intellectual milieu, including Giorgio Agamben, Roland Barthes, Jean Baudrillard, Judith Butler, Gilles Deleuze, Jacques Derrida, Michel Foucault, Jacques Lacan and Jean-François Lyotard among other, though not exclusively, continental philosophers of the twentieth century.

A word of caution is required here, however, since many of the thinkers whose work is labelled 'poststructural' seek to distance themselves from this term. Derrida, for example, considers it inherently suspect and problematic. One of the reasons for this distancing is that the label tends to be used more by critics than supposed proponents as a way of dismissing so-called poststructuralist works without engaging with them on their own terms. Another reason, which offers a clue as to the ethos of poststructural thought, is a refusal to accept practices of labelling, categorisation and generalisation unproblematically – as paradigmatically captured by Lyotard's 'incredulity towards meta-narratives' ('progress', 'emancipation', the 'end of history' and so on).

Nevertheless, poststructuralism, if there is such a thing, pays especial attention to detail, the specificity of context and how claims about 'the world' are dependent upon certain forms of knowledge. Indeed, many of the above thinkers challenge the very idea that we can think and speak of 'the world' in any straightforward meaningful, universal sense. This is because what we might *mean* by 'the world' always already depends upon representations of 'it', which are not separate from but fundamentally a part of that world. In this context, then, the role of language is particularly significant, because any knowledge or experience of 'the world' is unthinkable outside interpretation and the politics of representation.

Language and the security of meaning

Before we delve deeper into the implications of poststructuralism for the study of security, it is instructive to briefly consider the structuralist tradition in relation to which the former is often defined. As we shall see, the 'post' part of poststructuralism does not mean a wholesale rejection of structuralism.

Structural linguistics

One route into thinking about the relation between structuralism and poststructuralism is via Ferdinand de Saussure's structural approach to language and Jacques Derrida's subsequent 'deconstruction' of it.

Saussure (1857–1913) was a Swiss linguist whose *Course in General Linguistics* (1986) [1916] was published posthumously by his students. The focus of Saussure's work was the production of meaning and he developed a theory of the structure of language. For Saussure, the structure of any language consists of a series of different sounds and ideas. The basic unit of the linguistic structure is called the 'sign' (e.g. 'chair'). Each sign comprises two component parts: the signifier (e.g. the sound of the word 'chair' when spoken); and the signified (e.g. the idea of a 'chair' as something to sit in). Crucially, Saussure argued that there is no intrinsic relationship between the signifier on the one hand and the signified on the other. In other words, there is nothing essential about the connection between the sound of the word 'chair' when spoken and the piece of furniture known as a 'chair' to which we refer when we say that word. This is because, for Saussure, there are no positive terms within the linguistic structure, only differences. Put another way, the meaning of the sign 'chair' is not present in and of itself. Rather, we only know what is meant when someone says 'chair' because it is *not* a 'table', 'footstool', 'desk' and so on. So, the meaning of the sign 'chair' is not given as such, but produced in contradistinction to other signs in the linguistic structure.

The key point of Saussure's approach to language, therefore, is that meaning depends on *difference* within the structure of language. Indeed, it is because of the very structure of language – a series of differences between signs – that there is such a thing as 'meaning' in the first place.

Deconstructing the security of meaning

Derrida's encounter with Saussure goes some way to illustrating the relationship between structuralism and poststructuralism. As we shall see, the latter engages with the former on its own terms to produce what poststructuralists consider to be a more sophisticated under-standing of language and the production of meaning. This is why many writers refer to 'poststructuralism' as one word.

Derrida (1930–2004) agreed with Saussure's fundamental insight that meaning is produced through differences within the linguistic structure. However, Derrida argued that meaning is not always as stable as Saussure's structuralist approach implies: the meaning of signs in any given sentence often remains ambiguous and can lead to confusion. How many times, for example, have you received a short text message from someone and not quite understood what has been meant? Some messages, such as those arranging a time and place, might be straightforward enough. Others, though, may leave you wondering things like: am I being asked out on a date? How much should I read into this? What does s/he really *mean* by such and such? In these instances, there is a delay between the thought of the person send-ing the message and the point of communication with the recipient of the SMS.

Derrida's overall point is that 'meaning' is often difficult to pin down: it is always already slippery, 'on the move', so to speak, endlessly differing and deferring. While Saussure paid attention to the *spatial* differentiation between signs within the linguistic structure, Derrida argued that he neglected the importance of *time* and the *deferral* of meaning. In this way, Derrida did not argue against or 'critique' Saussure. Instead, he brought the issue of tempo-ral delay to Saussure's structuralist account of the production of meaning in language.

Although Derrida wrote very little about security issues as traditionally understood, in a certain sense he can be thought of as a radical theorist of security. Having shown that mean-ing is always already differing and deferring, Derrida was interested in attempts to secure it. He argued that in Western thought the inherent instability of meaning is secured through the use of binary oppositions, for example man/woman, cause/effect, presence/absence and so on. According to Derrida, these terms are not equal, but implicated in a hierarchical relation: the first term is usually privileged over the other (man *over* woman, etc.), which gives the sense of a firm foundation for meaning. Although the first term is granted a higher status, however, it cannot function without the second term on which it relies. In other words, the superior term *depends* on its shadow: it is only through the exclusion of the secondary term that the first term comes into being.

The focus of Derrida's work, then, is not ontology or 'what *is*', but what he called *hauntology* or 'what *is not*' (and how the two are fundamentally interrelated) – in other words that which is left out or excluded in order for meaning to be secured. Despite his famous hesitation in defining it, this is what Derrida meant by a 'deconstructive' way of reading. Deconstruction is a mode of thinking that takes the instability of meaning as its starting point in order to then trace diverse attempts at securing it and the violence that is bound up with this move. Derrida's thought has inspired a number of deconstructive readings of an array of issues in the study of global security relations – including what 'security' itself might mean.

'Truth', discourse, and power

Another figure central to poststructural approaches in security studies is Michel Foucault. Foucault (1926–1984) was a historian and social theorist who, like Derrida, was drawn to marginal phenomena to analyse the (re)production of norms in Western society. He traced the way in which different understandings of insanity and sexual deviance came to define 'normal' behaviour in different historical periods. Instead of asking questions like 'What is madness?' Foucault explored how the meaning of madness is produced through different social institutions at different times. Through hospitals, universities and the scientific community more generally, a context is formed within which an understanding of madness is made possible. In such a context, the 'truth' of what counts as insanity and sanity is configured: particular 'regimes of truth' then emerge over time as certain 'facts' and become manufactured and accepted as such. According to Foucault, there is such a thing as 'truth', but what that means will inevitably vary according to social, economic and historical context. Hence Foucault focuses on the role played by prevailing 'discourses'.

In a general sense, 'discourse' is the context within which regimes of truth come to be. Importantly, Foucault's use of this term does not merely refer to 'language' (see Box 5.3). Rather, in Foucauldian terms, discourse is understood as a series of practices, representations and interpretations through which different regimes of truth, for example the boundary between sanity and insanity, are (re)produced. The realm of the discursive, then, is one in which identities are constructed, social relations established and ethical-political outcomes made possible. For Foucault, however, the study of discourse is significant not only because it permits an analysis of different regimes of truth. It also tells us about the nature of power, or more accurately what Foucault called 'relations of power', in society (see Box 5.1). What counts as 'true' is always implicated in the relationship between knowledge and power (or what is sometimes referred to as the 'power–knowledge nexus'). Discursive analyses, therefore, identify 'subjugated knowledges', which have been excluded by the regime of truth.

Box 5.1 Michel Foucault: the 'how' of power

Power

For Foucault, power cannot be approached as if 'it' were something that can be 'possessed' by someone or concentrated in an institution. Rather, we must think of power as a relation or interplay between people that is always dispersed throughout society. To study power, therefore, is to analyse the *relations of power* or the terms of that interplay. In other words, instead of thinking about the 'who' of power, it is necessary to question the 'how' of power relations in any given context. For this reason, Foucault argued that we need to cut off the king's head in political philosophy. By this, he meant shifting our attention away from the sovereign to *mechanisms of power* understood as the techniques, tactics, strategies used to influence behaviour, colonise space and enable/constrain ethical and political practice. Crucially, for Foucault, relations of power should not be conceived of as entirely repressive or about subservience. The relation between the master and the slave, whereby the latter is in total subordination to the former, is not one of *power* but of *violence*. On the contrary, specifically power relations always presuppose some form of freedom in order to operate. Hence, where there are relations of power there are always sites of *resistance* because the subject is never entirely captured. In this way, power relations are said to have a *productive* dimension.

Sovereign power

Historically, the privilege of the sovereign was the unconditional right to decide over life and death. The origin of this understanding derives from the Roman right of *patria potestas* or the right of the father of the family to dispose of children and slaves (Foucault 1998: 135). Sovereign power is therefore a term in Foucault's work that refers to putting people to death or letting them live. However, Foucault argues that there is always an imbalance in that the sovereign cannot give life in the same way as it can be taken and so this form of power is always 'tipped in favour of death' (Foucault 2002: 240). With the advent of modernity the unconditional power of the sovereign – associated with *patria potestas*, literally the authority of a father as the 'head' of the family – was gradually replaced with a conditionality. Only when someone transgressed the law or attempted to rise up against the sovereign could they then be put to death.

Disciplinary power

With increasing agricultural and industrial production in the seventeenth century and the development of new medical knowledge in the eighteenth century, Foucault argued that we see the emergence of a new type of power relation: one that brought the human body into the sphere of political calculation. This new type of power relied heavily on different forms of surveillance of individuals as represented by Jeremy Bentham's (1785) model of the *panopticon* – the perfect prison designed so that inmates in cells would feel as though they were under the constant watch of guards in the watch tower without being able to see them or each other (see Figure 5.1). Such a power, which Foucault called 'disciplinary power', focused on the training and surveillance of the individual human body or 'anatomo-politics'. It centred on the body as a machine; not only disciplining it in a controlling sense, but also optimising what it can do. This 'docility' allowed for enhanced economic production and political subjugation at the same time.

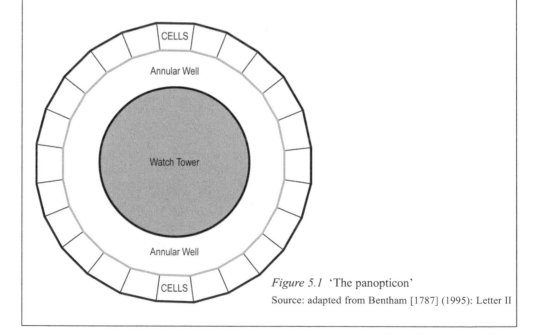

Figure 5.1 'The panopticon'
Source: adapted from Bentham [1787] (1995): Letter II

Biopower

Towards the mid-eighteenth century, Foucault identifies the rise of a third type of power relation – one that did not replace so much as dovetailed with the existing operations of disciplinary power. At this time, new statistical methods pioneered by early demographers gave rise to the idea of the *population* as a category. This enabled the development of new knowledge about birth rates, death rates, ratios of births to deaths, the rate of reproduction, fertility rates and public health (see also Chapter 8). Western societies increasingly came to think of the human as a species and the biological features of the population became the target of political strategies. In this context, new relations of power emerged, not based on man as an individual body, but a 'massifying' power addressed to man as a living being (Foucault 2002: 243). The concept of 'biopolitics' in Foucault refers precisely to the emergence of 'the population as a political problem, as a problem that is at once scientific, as a biological problem and as power's problem' (Foucault 2002: 245). Biopolitical techniques, designed not to 'take life and let live' but now to 'make live and let die', enabled new forms of governance. Instead of disciplining individual bodies, biopolitics seeks to maximise circulation, flows and movement and the health of people, in order to sift 'good' elements of the population from 'bad'.

The poststructural turn in security studies

Reflecting broader developments in social and political theory, the late 1980s/early 1990s saw the publication of several landmark texts in IR, including Richard K. Ashley's article 'Untying the Sovereign State: A Double-Reading of the Anarchy Problematique', published in *Millennium: Journal of International Studies* (1988); James Der Derian and Michael J. Shapiro's edited collection *International/Intertextual Relations: Postmodern Readings of World Politics* (1989); and R.B.J. Walker's (1993) *Inside/Outside: International Relations as Political Theory*. Taken together, these texts constitute what some surveyors of the disciplinary landscape consider to be the beginning of a 'poststructural turn' in IR and security theorising. Much of the focus of this early work was directed against the tendency of the then dominant realist/neorealist paradigm to take the social world as a given rather than understanding the role that knowledge plays in (re)producing it. More specifically, poststructural critics questioned how the image of international politics as portrayed by prominent realists like Kenneth N. Waltz came to appear natural, neutral and unchanging. Drawing on the insights of Derrida and Foucault among others, they analysed realist discourses of hierarchy/anarchy, inside/outside and self/other, in order to demonstrate how those accounts rely upon particular binary oppositions to give the impression that the structure of international politics is stable and immutable.

It is against this backdrop that the poststructural 'turn' in the disciplinary sub-field of security studies should be considered. For many writers associated with this turn, the distinction between 'IR' on the one hand and 'security' on the other is inherently problematic. Indeed, many earlier poststructuralist-inspired works in international politics, such as James Der Derian's *Antidiplomacy: Spies, Terror, Speed, War* (1992), David Campbell's *Writing Security: United States Foreign Policy and the Politics of Identity* (1992), David Campbell and Michael Dillon's *The Political Subject of Violence* (1993), and Michael Dillon's *The Politics of Security* (1996), deliberately sought to blur the terrains of IR theory, security studies, and political philosophy.

Box 5.2 R.B.J. Walker: Deconstructing international relations

In his *Inside/Outside: International Relations as Political Theory* (1993), R.B.J. Walker argues that theories of international relations are less interesting for the analyses they provide than as reflections of the ways in which we try to make sense – and attempt resolutions of – the mysteries of human existence. At the heart of these attempted resolutions in IR theory is the concept of *sovereignty*. For Walker, sovereignty is not a natural given. Rather, it is a historical construct that emerged from the seventeenth century as a principle for organising ourselves politically. Specifically, it resolves the paradox of our twin identity *both* as citizens of a universal common humanity *and* citizens of particular nation states. The principle of sovereignty, according to Walker, relies upon a spatial and temporal distinction between inside and outside. Spatially, a line is drawn between the *inside* of political community, associated with safety, security and amity on the one hand, and the *outside* of the international associated with lawlessness, insecurity and enmity on the other hand. Temporally, this demarcation provides the condition of possibility for aspirations towards justice, democracy and 'progress' within the boundaries of the state, as compared with the immutable prospect of conflict, barbarism and warfare between states. Through different discursive practices, for example in the realms of foreign policy and international law, the inside/outside dichotomy is reproduced thereby creating the effect of sovereignty and a sense of stability. According to Walker, conventional IR theories rely upon but fail to acknowledge this logic of inside/outside, which serves to reaffirm the limits of the modern political imagination.

David Campbell's *Writing Security: United States Foreign Policy and the Politics of Identity* (1992) is a seminal poststructural account of the role of identity and the production of danger in international security. Inspired by Derrida's account of language and the production of meaning, Campbell argues that *identity* is constituted by *difference*: 'The constitution of identity is achieved through the inscription of boundaries that serve to demarcate an "inside" from an "outside", a "self " from an "other", a "domestic" from a "foreign" ' (1992: 8).

He refers to this identity/difference problematic in a general sense as 'foreign policy' (small 'f' and 'p'). Applying this logic, the identities of states are never given but (re)produced in relation to other states through repetitive practices that code, constitute and discipline the boundaries on which the identity/difference problematic depends. Indeed, 'the state' does not exist as such outside the gamut of practices that bring it into being. In other words states, and their identities, are *performed* (for connections with Judith Butler's concept of 'performativity see Box 3.4). Furthermore, states are never finished political entities, but must always be considered as a work in progress.

Campbell's study explores how the identity of the US is constituted via an analysis of texts written in its name. It proceeds by offering a close, detailed, empirical examination of how those texts secure the meaning of the identity of the US as a major actor in international politics. Specifically, Campbell investigates the reliance upon notions of *danger* in order that the US can portray itself in a particular way. Danger, he argues, is not an objective condition: 'it (sic) is not a thing that exists independently of those to whom it may become a threat' (1992: 2). There is nothing that is inherently 'dangerous' and not all dangers are treated equally in international politics. Rather, danger must be understood as a 'category of understanding': 'those events or factors that we identify as dangerous come to be ascribed as such only through an interpretation of their various dimensions of dangerousness' (1992:

2). It is against the designation of state x as dangerous that the identity of state y is defined and produced. For Campbell, Foreign Policy (with a capital 'F' and 'P') – as traditionally understood in terms of the external affairs of the state – is only one of a number of discourses of danger made possible by foreign policy. He argues, however, that it has been afforded a privileged position within the discursive economy of the state, which, 'by virtue of telling us what to fear, have been able to fix who "we" are' (1992: 170).

In his reading of US Foreign Policy texts during the period of the cold war, Campbell considers how a particular view of danger and dangerousness came to be associated with communism and the Soviet Union. Following the Second World War, the US government confronted an array of domestic challenges including high unemployment, low wages and the growing demands of the trade union movement. Yet, despite seemingly having no connection with these challenges, the Soviet Union became a threat to the nation, which generated a 'red scare' whereby external threats came to be associated with internal disorder. Through the exteriorisation of the threat, and the demonisation of the Soviet Union as 'other', 'alien', 'subversive', 'dirty' and 'sick', US Foreign Policy texts attempted to secure a particular version of American identity. It is precisely this attempt at securing the meaning of the US, in contradistinction to the identity of the Soviet Union, which Campbell refers to as the practice of *writing*.

Box 5.3 Language, materiality and discourse

The early literature that brought the insights of poststructuralism to IR and security studies in the 1980s used the term 'discourse' to refer not only to language, but also to the more general context in which various phenomena are co-located and given meaning (Shapiro 1981; Der Derian and Shapiro 1989; Connolly 1974). These writers' use of 'discourse' did not discriminate between 'language' and 'materiality' because from this broad theoretical approach both are fundamentally sutured together. However, in more recent years the focus of 'discourse analysis' in IR and security studies has arguably narrowed, reinstating the language/materiality distinction and privileging the study of language over materiality (Aradau 2010; Lundborg and Vaughan-Williams 2011). This means that IR and security studies have been particularly vulnerable to the critique of the so-called 'new materialisms' turn in social and political thought of the 2010s. This body of work stresses that materiality is not a passive background or object whose content and meaning can be captured, represented or constructed by language, but rather something that is active, alive and of political significance in its own right (Bennett 2010; Braun and Whatmore 2010; Coole and Frost 2010). In the context of critical security studies this latest 'turn' has inspired diverse analyses of, for example, the agency of critical infrastructures in practices of (in)securitization (Aradau 2010), the materiality of the urban environment as both a condition of possibility for community and an object of contemporary warfare (Coward 2009, 2012), and the role of material objects and human/non-human interaction in the production of the 'migrant-health assemblage' (Voelkner 2011). The extent to which the insights of the 'new materialism's turn' are actually 'new' might be questioned in the light of 'older' forms of historical material-ism' (see Chapter 2, Box 2.6) and compared with the latter's concentration on material basis of socio-economic structures. Moreover, unlike the poststructuralism of Derrida and Foucault, in some guises New Materialist scholarship seems to merely invert the hierarchy between language and materiality (and thus maintain a distinction between the two). These caveats aside, this latest turn has reinvigorated debates about the status of discourse and material aspects of security, which are not the preserve of more traditional approaches.

International political sociology (IPS)

More recently, especially against the backdrop of the US-led 'war on terror', poststructural approaches to security have been invigorated and taken in new theoretical and empirical directions. Much of this research is associated with the so-called Paris School, which fuses a concern with discourses of security and constructions of danger with a focus on security *practices*. The focus on practices such as the role of security professionals, the conduct of policing, risk management (see Box 5.5) and the activities of private security companies, for example, aligns this work with a more sociologically oriented approach. It is in this context that the term 'international political sociology' has been used.

One of the prominent figures of the Paris School, Didier Bigo, examines the relation between liberty and security from an IPS perspective. Methodologically, Bigo takes much inspiration from the French social theorist Pierre Bourdieu, particularly his related concepts of *habitus* and the *field*. Briefly, Bourdieu developed the concept of *habitus* to refer to the framework of orientation, provided for both by formal and informal social structures, within which actors are emplaced in society. The *field* is the social universe within which actors relate to each other and those structures: a complex web of relations between different positions determined by inequalities such as power and wealth.

Applying these concepts, Bigo has analysed shifts in the *habitus* of security relations in the West. Whereas, for example, the distinction between the police on the one hand and the army on the other mapped on to and further entrenched a logic of inside/outside as diagnosed by Walker (1993) (see Box 5.2), Bigo argues that this correlation no longer holds. A new *habitus*, underpinning what he calls the 'transversal field of globalised (in)security' has emerged, whereby the traditional separation between inside/outside has become ever more blurred:

> In very simple terms, we can no longer distinguish between an internal order reigning, thanks to the police, by holding a monopoly on legitimate violence, and an archaic international order which is maintained by an equilibrium of national powers vis-à-vis the armies and diplomatic alliances.
>
> (Bigo 2008: 11)

According to Bigo, however, the border between inside and outside has not so much been eroded, but *deconstructed*, in the Derridean sense. That is to say, while the realms of internal and external are hard to discern, they have not disappeared entirely. Rather, the deconstruction of inside/outside has led to the playing-out of that binary in new and often unexpected ways (for more on this in relation to border security see Chapter 11).

In turn, this has given rise to a novel *field* of security relations, between security professionals, governmental and non-governmental institutions, the police, military and private enterprise, across an increasingly *globalised* terrain. What is specific about this *field* in the context of the war on terror is that it constitutes a 'semantic continuum' in which security actors cultivate fear, unease and (in)security. Through the development a harsher legislative climate, acts of profiling and containing foreigners, and practices of exceptionalism (see Box 5.4), *liberal* regimes create an atmosphere that both justifies and necessitates further *illiberal* practices. The extent to which these practices are 'new' or 'exceptional' is a moot point as they may be considered central to liberal forms of governance – as illustrated in the context of colonialism (see Chapter 4). Consequently, this field of (in)security opens up new possibilities as far as the governance of populations in the West is concerned. Here the concept of *(in)security* is pivotal in Bigo's diagnosis of contemporary political life.

For Bigo, security is always necessarily about *sacrifice*: the security of *x* always leads to the *in*security of *y*. In other words, the practice of securing one actor simultaneously renders other actors insecure. For this reason, and this is a crucial point, it makes little sense to think of 'security' as a positive condition and 'insecurity' as its negative correlative. Furthermore, this view holds that security and insecurity are *not* polar opposites, but fundamentally inter-related and interdependent.

On the one hand, there is a striking similarity between Bigo's formulation of (in)security and the classical 'security dilemma' in realist thought. On the other hand, however, while both point to the sacrificial logic of security, Bigo does not delimit the application of this insight to individual sovereign *states* acting independently within an anarchical system. Rather, the 'actors' in this context comprise all those who constitute the field of security rela-tions. Bigo refers to the practices through which different actors are produced as (in)secure as practices of '*(in)securitisation*'.

Despite the obvious semantic connection, overlaps with the Copenhagen School concept of 'securitisation' are minimal, however, as Bigo seeks to flesh out a 'thicker' sociological conception of securitising (speech) acts (see also Chapter 6). Along with this conception is an attempt at a more nuanced and sophisticated treatment of the affects of an (in)securitising move, which, given the multiplicity of actors in the field of global security relations, are difficult to quantify:

> The actors never know the final results of the move they are making, as the result depends on the field effect of many actors engaged in the competitions for defining whose secu-rity is important, and by the acceptance of different audiences of their definition.
>
> (Bigo 2008: 124)

The ultimate task of a more sociologically oriented critical security studies, then, is to address the question: 'Who is doing an (in)securitization move, under what conditions, towards whom, and with what consequences?' (Bigo 2008: 124). However, from an IPS perspective this must be addressed on the basis of the critique of communication and of the subject informed by earlier poststructural thought. This challenges more simplistic notions of a linear or causal transmission between the 'source' of an (in)securitising move and its 'audience' (see also Balzacq 2011).

Security and discourses of exceptionalism

Discourses of exceptionalism have become a major concern of recent poststructural-inspired work in security studies. The concept of the 'exception' has a rich political, philosophical (and theological) heritage within the tradition of Western thought. Different thinkers have used the concept of the exception/exceptionalism in various ways (see Box 5.4).

Today it is not uncommon to find the phrase 'exceptional times call for exceptional meas-ures' used by politicians who seek to justify an array of illiberal practices such as those identified above. Indeed, throughout the war on terror, this phrase has been especially popu-lar. Former US President George W. Bush, for example, used it to justify the indefinite detention of 'unlawful enemy combatants' at the US naval base in Guantánamo Bay, Cuba. Clearly, however, the usage of this phrase is not something new or unique in the context of Western politics post-9/11. Rather, there is a long history of declarations of emergency conditions said to necessitate exceptional measures in the West. During the 1920s, for example, successive governments of the Weimar Republic in Germany repeatedly invoked emergency powers under Article 48 of the constitution. What this kind of move enables is a suspension of the normal rule of law and its replacement with a 'state of exception'.

While formal declarations of states of emergency are few and far between in the West, many contemporary security analysts argue that a *logic of exceptionalism* nevertheless pervades contemporary counterterrorist policies. Such a logic enables techniques of governance, often of a biopolitical nature (such as torture, rendition or indefinite detention) that would otherwise be stymied by normal liberal democratic checks and balances on coercive and authoritarian regimes. Indeed, by invoking discourses of exceptionalism, such as the notion that in any given context it is precisely the security of the nation that is at stake, it is arguably more likely that populations in liberal democracies will not only sanction but in fact *demand* further illiberal practices.

In recent years the work of Italian philosopher Giorgio Agamben (1942–) has become popular among security analysts seeking to analyse discourses and practices of exceptionalism in the context of the War on Terror, though his work has not gone without criticism. Agamben (1998, 2005) takes his inspiration from the debate between Schmitt and Benjamin in the 1920s and sides with the latter, arguing that the state of exception has become the dominant paradigm of government in contemporary politics. That is to say, the exception is no longer exceptional because it is indistinguishable from – indeed part of – the norm. In support of this view, Agamben refers to contemporary sovereign practices that blur the otherwise taken-for-granted threshold between democracy and absolutism. One example is former US President George W. Bush's 'military order' authorising the indefinite detention and trial by military commissions of non-citizens suspected of terrorist activities. This order works to secure sovereign power by blurring the legal and political status of a suspected individual thereby producing a legally unnameable and unclassifiable being. In Guantánamo, for example, the use of the term 'unlawful enemy combatant' is not recognised by the UN or any other international institution. In contravention of Article 5 of the Third Geneva Convention, none of the detainees have been classified as prisoners of war and, as such, there is a deliberate ambiguity surrounding their status. Such ambiguity deprives those detained from access to a competent tribunal in order to establish who they are and what their rights might be. Agamben argues that detainees in Guantánamo reflect a form of life that is mute and undifferentiated: what he calls a 'bare life'.

Bare life does not exist before or outside power relations: it is not something we are all born with and can be stripped down to. Any attempt to qualify life as 'bare' or otherwise is necessarily a move away from what the Greeks referred to as *zoē* (the simple biological fact of life common to all living things). Rather, bare life is a form of life that is deliberately *banned* from law and politics – an operation that Agamben links with the inner workings of sovereignty. The fact that bare life has such an unclear juridical and political status means that it is more amenable to the sway of sovereign power, which Agamben claims is more prominent today than Foucault's account allows for and has always worked in a biopolitical mode. Caught in a vacuum, bare life is exposed and vulnerable to exceptional practices – such as torture – that may eventually become considered as 'normal' given the imperatives of national security. Under biopolitical conditions in which the paradigm of security has become the normal technique of government, Agamben argues that the distinction between the citizen and bare life is increasingly blurred: 'Living in the state of exception that has now become the rule has [...] meant this: our private body has now become indistinguishable from our body politic' (2000: 39).

What this means is that, on Agamben's view at least, it is ever more difficult to maintain a rigorous distinction between the 'norm' of citizenship and the 'exceptional' existence of

---

Box 5.4 Thinkers of the exception

Carl Schmitt (1888–1985)

Schmitt was a German legal theorist and sympathiser of the Third Reich who wrote a number of influential works of political philosophy, including *Political Theology: Four Chapters on the Concept of Sovereignty* (1922). In this text Schmitt argued that the essence of sovereignty was the ability to decide on the exception: 'For a legal order to make sense, a normal situation must exist, and he is sovereign who definitely decides whether this normal situation actually exists' (Schmitt 2005 [1922]: 13). Such a decision involves two steps: first the decision that an emergency has emerged beyond the scope and provisions of the existing legal order; and second the decision about what can be done to remedy the situation. The sovereign, he who makes a double decision on the exception, has an unusual relationship to the juridical-political order. At once the sovereign both *belongs to* and *stands above or outside* that order in his capacity to decide when the constitution no longer applies. According to this formula, therefore, the law is paradoxically outside itself, since the sovereign who is outside the law declares that there is nothing outside the law. Schmitt refers to the strange situation arising from the suspension of existing legal norms and practices in this way as the 'state of exception'.

Walter Benjamin (1892–1927)

Benjamin was another early twentieth-century German thinker who engaged critically with Schmitt's theory of sovereignty in an attempt to move the concept of the exception away from emergency provisions towards a more original function within Western political structures. In his 'Eighth Thesis on the Concept of History', Benjamin (2003) responded to Schmitt's theory of exception by arguing:

> The tradition of the oppressed teaches us that the 'state of exception' in which we live is the rule. We must attain to a concept of history that accords with this fact. Then we will clearly see that it is our task to bring about the real [...] state of exception, and this will improve our position in the struggle against fascism.

Benjamin points to the way in which, for example, the Third Reich thrived precisely on confusing the difference between norm and exception, law and fact, and order and anomie. On this basis, as the quotation above highlights, Benjamin suggested that the task of the oppressed is to bring about a state of exception proper since it is only then that fascist rule might be overcome.

---

bare life. In other words, the generalisation of the state of exception potentially puts entire populations under the perpetual threat of insecurity. We are all, potentially, bare life, Agamben argues. This claim, and Agamben's argument more generally, has been used by analysts to examine the shooting of electrician Jean Charles de Menezes in Stockwell Station (Vaughan-Williams 2007), the treatment of victims of terrorist attacks in New York and London by authorities (Edkins 2007) and the biopolitics of life and death in the war on terror more generally (Dauphinee and Masters 2007).

Conclusion

The poststructural turn in IR and security studies is not without its critics. Indeed, some of the fiercest intra-disciplinary debates have centred not only on the implications but even the validity of poststructuralist scholarship. For some outspoken critics, such as Robert Keohane (1988), poststructuralism does not constitute a bona fide approach to international security

---

Box 5.5 Risk, preemption and catastrophe

The concept of 'risk' is now ubiquitous in contemporary global politics and there are various registers in which it is used (Petersen 2011): economists model risk in terms of maximising profit; sociologists have focused on risk as central to modern industrial and capitalist societies; and anthropologists have sought to analyse cultural factors in the shared meaning of risk. In recent years the work that risk does in structuring contemporary relations and imaginations of (in)security has been a particular concern of scholars associated with poststructural and IPS approaches.

Whereas the concept of 'threat' was understood in the cold war context largely in terms of the physical safety and survival of the state, 'risk' connotes a broadening of the landscape of issues to include climate change, health and other so-called new security challenges (Aradau *et al.* 2008). Thinking in terms of risk also deepens the referent object beyond the state and human to encompass vulnerable populations (Elbe 2005), financial architectures (de Goede 2007; Lobo-Guerrero 2012) material infrastructures (Aradau 2010) and ways of life (Duffield 2010).

Intelligence-led risk-management has attempted to make a range of risks measurable and therefore more manageable (Amoore and de Goede 2005). In this context, various forms of 'dataveillance' have emerged in order to map complex and evolving data and identify 'risky' individuals, groups and behavioural types within and across suspect populations (Amoore and de Goede 2005; Aradau and van Munster 2007) (see also Chapter 12). Moreover, the risk management cycle is no longer the preserve of national governments as private security companies now provide risk profiling and analysis services (Amoore 2006; Leander 2005).

Conceptually, risk-based approaches to security focus not on eliminating threats, per se. Rather, the role of strategy is to devise ways of living with (often now termed as 'resilience') rather than trying to overcome a spectrum of complex and interconnected risks. Thinking in terms of risk shifts attention towards the identification and management of uncertainty – particularly unforeseen, unspecific and unpredictable 'low-probability-high impact' events. As such, there is a strong temporal dimension to risk management, which is geared towards precautionary and increasingly preemptive principles of governance (Aradau and van Munster 2007; de Goede 2007).

Aradau and van Munster (2011) have traced the emergence of catastrophe as a specific problematisation of securing the future. On their view the concept of catastrophe – associated with a disruptive incident that emerges suddenly and without warning – is increasingly used in order to make unknown futures actionable. Whereas more traditional biopolitical modes of governance rely on 'collective, serial and probabilistic' phenomena, the biopolitics of catastrophe is informed by exceptional events and the spectacle (Aradau and van Munster 2011: 10). Thus, the framing of security increasingly in terms of catastrophic futures has given rise to new forms of governance where imagination and sensory experience play an enhanced role in attempting to simulate the next event: 'the politics of catastrophe emerges in the disputes between what can be known and what cannot and how the unexpected lays bare structures and dispositions and challenges them' (Aradau and van Munster 2011: 120).

---

because 'it' fails to have a cogent scientifically rigorous research agenda. Others have criticised what they consider to be a relativistic and nihilistic 'anti-foundational' attitude (Brown 1994).

These criticisms, however, are problematic because they rely upon caricatured (mis)readings of some of the main characteristics of poststructural thought. For example, many of the authors associated with this genre have set out to call into question the very framework within which Keohane's notion of 'bona fide' research can make any sense.

Similarly, Brown's charge is problematic because it mistakes a questioning of foundations for their rejection (Fagan 2013). Derrida, for example, does not seek to *destroy* but rather *politicise* the foundations of Western knowledge. Nevertheless, while poststructuralism has attracted a number of hackneyed criticisms, there are several limitations (and counter-arguments) worth taking seriously.

First, while poststructural inspired scholarship offers a number of diagnoses of contemporary global security relations, the extent to which it privileges critique over praxis might be called into question. On the one hand, a defence would be that it is inherently troublesome to imply that critique and praxis are somehow separate or separable to begin with. On the other hand, an aversion to making abstract, generalised prescriptions arguably entails few prospects for generating security policy advice in the traditional 'problem-solving' sense. That said, scholarship influenced by poststructuralism and critical thought might engage productively with policy-making communities by questioning the way certain problems are framed as such and how these framings may entrench particular 'solutions', and by holding a mirror up to the ethical-political implications of a given position or practice. Inevitably, these issues call into question the role of the security analyst more generally: why do we study security? Is it sufficient to comment critically on global security issues? Do scholars have a responsibility to think about the practical 'real-world' implications and societal impact of their research?

Second, others have pointed to the way in which, by focusing on the dominant assumptions of specifically Western thought, poststructural scholarship is in danger of being Western and/or Eurocentric in its outlook. For example, Giorgio Shani (2008: 723) has argued that the 'secular Eurocentric historicism deployed by most critical theorists places limits on the degree to which transnational non-Western actors can fully participate in "critical" international politics'. On the one hand, it might be counter-argued that the motivation for an internal or 'immanent' critique of the Western/European foundations of knowledge is a deliberate move and indeed one that is motivated by a desire to identify, interrogate and ultimately even resist this cultural dominance. On the other hand, a number of postcolonial scholars highlight the possibility that starting with a focus on Western/European foundations, values and practices ultimately end up reproducing their centrality in global politics (see Chapter 4).

Third, a number of scholars, including many of those associated with poststructural work in critical security studies, have raised criticisms specifically of Agamben and approaches to the politics of exceptionalism inspired by his thought. One high-profile critique is that of Judith Butler (2004), who has argued that Agamben fails to offer an account of how power functions differentially among populations. Focusing on issues of race and ethnicity, Butler accuses Agamben of ignoring the ways in which different people are more likely to be produced as 'bare life' than others. Cristina Masters (2009) has claimed that the figure of *homo sacer* is inadequate to the task of identifying women's experiences in the war on terror and she critiques the 'lack of explicit engagement with gender' in the biopolitical literature more generally. Andrew Neal (2009) has pointed to what he considers to be the ahistorical treatment of sovereignty in Agamben's account of the production of bare life and Matthew Coleman and Kevin Grove (2009) question his treatment of political space. Others have doubted the extent to which law is 'suspended' entirely in Guantánamo Bay, as Agamben claims, or whether it is more accurately a site of hyper-intensive legal efforts and authorities (Johns 2005). For an example of how some scholars have developed Agamben's approach to take account of the gendered, racialised and class logics of sovereign power in the context of the war on terror, see Sherene Razack (2008).

Key points

- 'Poststructuralism' is a diverse and heterogeneous body of intellectual thought that engages with, but does not reject, the 'structuralist' tradition.
- Saussure developed a structuralist theory of language that says meaning depends upon differences between units in the linguistic structure. Derrida pushed Saussure further, however, by emphasising that meaning not only differs between static units, but is also deferred across time.
- Foucault analysed the way in which 'truth' is always a product of the relation between knowledge and power. A Foucauldian approach to power does not see 'it' as something that can be possessed. Rather, power is always *relational* and where there is power there is always *resistance*.
- David Campbell's *Writing Security* was a pioneering application of poststructural thought to the study of security in which he argues that states' identities are not given but (re)produced through discursive practices.
- In recent years poststructural approaches to security have embraced a more sociological focus on practices – particularly those associated with the politics of exceptionalism, risk management and preemption.

Discussion points

- What different aspects of the study of security are opened up by a poststructuralist/IPS perspective?
- How significant is the (re)production of identity in global security relations?
- What is more threatening to civil liberties: international terrorism or responses to it?
- What is meant by the concept of 'exceptionalism' and how does this contribute to an understanding of contemporary practices in the global 'war on terror'?
- Does the Paris School offer security practitioners any policy guidelines?

Guide to further reading

Andrew Neal (2009) *Exceptionalism and the Politics of Counter-Terrorism: Liberty, Security, and the War on Terror* (Oxford and New York: Routledge). An instructive starting point on the concept of the exception and contemporary usages of it in relation to terrorism and counterterrorism.

Claudia Aradau and Rens van Munster (2011) *Politics of Catastrophe: Genealogies of the Unknown* (London and New York: Routledge). An exploration of the role of catastrophe and preemption in the attempt to govern future events.

David Campbell (1992) *Writing Security: United States Foreign Policy and the Politics of Identity* (Manchester: Manchester University Press). A seminal contribution to poststructural approaches that emphasises the politics of identity in international security.

Didier Bigo and Anastassia Tsoukala (2008) (eds) *Terror, Insecurity and Liberty: Illiberal Practices of Liberal Regimes after 9/11* (London and New York: Routledge). An analysis of the liberty/security relation from an IPS/Paris School perspective.

Michael Dillon (1996) *The Politics of Security* (London: Routledge). A significant application of a range of poststructuralist thought to the study of security.

Weblinks

The 'InfoTechWarPeace' project at the Watson Institute, Brown University: www.watsoninstitute. org/infopeace/index2.cfm

The website of the CHALLENGE project on the relation between liberty and security in Europe: www.libertysecurity.org

The 'Histories of Violence' website: http://historiesofviolence.com/

6   Securitisation theory

Abstract

This chapter outlines the main features of 'securitisation theory', its theoretical underpinnings and its applications. It begins by introducing the concept of securitisation and establishing its intellectual origins. After outlining the meaning of the concept of securitisation in more detail, the chapter then goes on to address the issue of how securitisation occurs at a general level, before examining the dynamics of securitisation in specific 'sectors' (military, environmental, economic, societal and political). Following this it discusses the related concept of 'desecuritisation' and several other key debates in securitisation theory. Finally, the chapter assesses the place of securitisation theory within the broader category of critical security studies.

Introduction

The notion of 'securitisation' is one of the most significant conceptual innovations to emerge out of debates over the nature of security in recent decades. It is primarily associated in security studies with a group of scholars commonly referred to as the 'Copenhagen School', which is usually taken to consist of Barry Buzan, Ole Wæver and the collective authors of works such as Wæver *et al.* (1993) and Buzan *et al.* (1998). The term Copenhagen School, actually first employed in a critique of works by these authors (see McSweeney 1996), derives from the association of this school of thought with the Centre for Peace and Conflict Research (latterly known as the Copenhagen Peace Research Institute or COPRI) in the Danish capital. Like so many of the ideas discussed in this text, however, the concept of securitisation has been employed, and generates debates, far beyond the geographical or intellectual confines suggested by the idea of a 'school'. By consequence, the term 'securitisation theory' is generally preferred in this chapter as it is increasingly possible to argue that although work produced by those associated with the Copenhagen School remains *the* key point of reference in discussions of securitisation (particularly the Buzan *et al.* (1998) text *Security: A New Framework for Analysis*), the core idea of securitisation has also been adopted, adapted and developed by other scholars beyond the immediate original circle of the Copenhagen School, sometimes even in ways – as is discussed later – that challenge and test the limits of the framework originally outlined by Buzan *et al.* and Wæver *et al.* (see, for example, Balzacq 2011). Paralleling this line of development, this chapter begins by examining the core understanding of securitisation as originally put forward by the Copenhagen School and then moves to a consideration of challenges to this particular vision of securitisation, as well as critiques of the very notion of securitisation itself.

What is 'securitisation'?

The work of the Copenhagen School and their initial development of the concept of the concept of securitisation as the basis of 'a new framework for analysis' (Buzan *et al.* 1998) can, at a very simplistic level, be said to represent the fusion of two major theoretical and conceptual innovations in security studies: Barry Buzan's notion of different sectors of security (first put forward by Barry Buzan in the book *People, States and Fear* in 1983 and then later in an updated version in Buzan 1991) and Ole Wæver's concept of 'securitisation' (see Wæver 1995 for an early iteration). Buzan *et al.* endorse the widening of the security agenda as identified and advanced by Buzan's earlier work, but their development of a theory of securitisation emanates from a concern that there are 'intellectual and political dangers in simply tacking the word *security* onto an ever wider range of issues' (Buzan *et al.* 1998: 1, emphasis in original). For Buzan *et al*, then, the main question is how to define *what is and what is not* a security issue in the context of attempts to 'broaden' the definition and usage of security as a concept. Given that context, they argue, we need some sort of analytical grounding or principle to judge what is and what is not a security issue; otherwise there is a danger that the concept of 'security' will become so broad that it covers everything and hence becomes effectively meaningless.

So how do we judge *what is and what is not* a security issue? Buzan *et al.* argue that security, as a concept, is fundamentally about survival: it is when an issue is represented as posing an *existential threat* to the survival of a referent object. Here the term 'referent object' can be defined simply as 'that to which one can point and say, "It has to survive, therefore it is necessary to..."' (Buzan *et al.* 1998: 36). This is the same basic principle that underpins the conventional focus of national security and defence: war threatens *the very existence* of a referent object, the state (hence the term 'existential threat'). Within the concept of national security it is assumed that the state 'has to survive', therefore it is assumed that it is necessary for the state to maintain standing armies, weapons production and procurement, intelligence agencies and so on.

One of the ways we can distinguish an existential threat, then, is the level of response it generates. When an issue is successfully presented as an existential threat, it legitimises the use of exceptional political measures. A classic (military) example in IR is a state's right to self-defence: if a state is under attack, it can legitimately use extraordinary measures that go beyond routine day-to-day politics. A state under attack can declare a state of emergency during which it suspends or changes its functions. It may declare martial law, for example, ration the provision of certain services, close roads and schools, and so on. Commonly, Wæver argues, existential threats set in chain a number of effects that characterise the specific quality of security problems: urgency – the issue takes priority; and extraordinary measures – authorities claim powers that they would not otherwise have, or curtail rights and liberties that might otherwise apply (1995: 51). So, ultimately, we have a seemingly simple formula: *Existential Threat to a Referent Object = A Security Issue*. Identifying the presence (or absence) of this formula allows us to get an analytical handle of what is and what is not a security issue.

How does securitisation occur?

This leads to the question of how the process of securitisation happens, and the conditions required for successful securitisation to take place. According to securitisation theory, when an issue comes to be treated as a *security* issue, it is justifiable to use exceptional political

---

Box 6.1 Key concepts in securitisation theory

Securitisation: Shifting an issue out of the realm of 'normal' political debate into the realm of emergency politics by presenting it as an existential threat.
Securitising speech act: The act of 'saying security' in relation to an issue.
Securitising move: An attempt to securitise an issue by labelling it as a *security* issue.
Desecuritisation: Shifting an issue out of the realm of securitisation and emergency politics back into the realm of 'normal' political or technical debate.
Asecurity: A condition in which issues tend to remain unsecuritised, and are dealt with primarily as political issues or considered as non-political.

---

measures to deal with it. In other words it is *securitised*: we treat it with the same degree of urgency as we would a military threat. Buzan *et al.* argue that we can think of this process of securitisation in terms of a spectrum that runs from nonpoliticised (meaning that an issue is not a political issue), through politicised (meaning it is part of a public policy debate) to securitised (meaning that the issue is thought of as an existential threat and therefore justifies responses that go beyond normal political practices).

Nonpoliticised ------------------------→ Politicised ------------------------→ **Securitised**

Figure 6.1 The securitisation 'spectrum'
Source: adapted from Buzan *et al.* 1998: 23

How does this occur? Simply put, securitisation begins by 'saying security': 'Traditionally, by saying "security", a state representative declares an emergency condition, thus claiming a right to use whatever means are necessary to block a threatening development' (Buzan *et al.* 1998: 21). Building on this template, Wæver argues that this process of securitisation has to be initiated through what is known as a 'speech act': a securitising 'move' occurs when an issue not previously thought of as a security threat comes to be *spoken of* as a security issue by important political actors (see Box 6.2).

On this basis, Buzan *et al.* argue, the meaning of security is in many ways secondary to 'the essential quality of security in general' (1998: 26) that resides in the *act* of saying 'security' rather than in any essential meaning of the word:

> That quality is the staging of existential issues in politics to lift them above politics. In security discourse, an issue is dramatized and presented as an issue of supreme priority; thus, by labelling it as *security*, an agent claims a need for and a right to treat it by extraordinary means. For the analyst to grasp this act, the task is not to address some objective threats that 'really' endanger some object to be defended or secured; rather, it is to understand the process of constructing a shared understanding of what is to be considered and collectively responded to as a threat.
>
> (1998: 26, emphasis in original)

Box 6.2 Speech act theory and securitisation

As formulated by Wæver, the idea of securitisation draws heavily on the theory of language, in particular the branch known as 'speech act theory':

> What then *is* security? With the help of language theory, we can regard 'security' as a *speech act*. In this usage, security is not of interest as a sign that refers to something more real; the utterance *itself* is the act. By saying it [security] something is done (as in betting, giving a promise, naming a ship). By uttering 'security,' a state-representative moves a particular development into a specific area, and thereby claims a special right to use whatever means are necessary to block it.
>
> (Wæver 1995: 35)

Here Wæver draws upon speech act theory as formulated in the work of the philosopher John L. Austin (1911–1960). In his 1962 book *How to do Things with Words*, Austin proposes that many utterances are equivalent to actions; when we *say* certain words or phrases we also *perform* a particular action. Classic examples of 'doing things with words' are cited by Wæver in the example above. For instance, when we give a promise ('I promise to . . .') we are not simply promising to do something in the future, the promise is itself a type of action.

Certain speech acts are known as 'performatives' whereby saying the word or phrase effectively serves to accomplish a social act (what Judith Butler (1996) terms as a kind of 'social magic'), as in the act of naming a ship. Of course, not just anyone can name a ship! For this type of performative speech act to work, certain conditions have to be met: the words have to be said by someone in authority, in the right context and according to certain pre-established rituals or conventions. These are what are known as 'felicity conditions' in speech act theory – conditions required for the successful accomplishment of a speech act.

In this sense there is an explicitly constructivist (see Chapter 1) component to securitisation theory: issues can become *security* issues by virtue of their presentation and acceptance as such, rather than because of any innate threatening qualities per se (although Buzan *et al.* do retain a sense that some threats are easier to present as existential threats than others, as is discussed below). Hence, 'the exact *definition* and *criteria* of securitization is constituted by the intersubjective establishment of an existential threat with a saliency sufficient to have substantial political effects' (Buzan *et al.* 1998: 25, emphases in original). Successful securitisation, Buzan *et al.* argue, requires some degree of acceptance between the perpetrator of the securitising speech act and the relevant audience that is appealed to otherwise, a securitising move remains incomplete.

Securitisation thus has a certain 'modality' (a general pattern or mode of operation) that is constant and identifiable, even if the context in which securitising speech acts occur may vary. Yet not every 'securitising move' is successful, even if they are presented in a way that adheres to the general pattern of operation required for securitisation. As Buzan *et al.* stipulate:

> Threats and vulnerabilities can arise in many different areas, military and non-military, but to count as security issues they have to meet strictly defined criteria that distinguish them from the normal run of the merely political. They have to be staged as existential threats to a referent object by a securitizing actor who thereby generates endorsement of emergency measures beyond rules that would otherwise bind.
>
> (1998: 5)

As this formulation indicates by noting the condition of endorsement, in any securitising speech act there is always a speaker and an audience (hence, securitisation is an 'intersubjective' process between human political subjects). In order for securitisation to work, an audience has to accept a threat as credible. Hence successful securitisation, Wæver argues, not only requires a securitising speech act, but also the presence of what he terms (drawing again on speech act theory) as 'felicity conditions' (2000: 252; see Box 6.2) – conditions that increase the likelihood of successful securitisation.

The first of these conditions, as already outlined, is that the internal logic of a securitising speech act follows the conventional 'plot' of securitisation: an existential threat is presented as legitimating the use of extraordinary measures to combat that threat.

The second condition entails the requirement that the securitising actor – the actor attempting to securitise a given issue – is in a position of authority and has enough social and political capital to convince an audience of the existence of an existential threat. Typically, for example, those designated as 'security experts' are assumed to have the capacity to speak authoritatively on what constitutes a security issue due to their background and qualifications, whereas non-experts are not usually assumed to have the same capacity to 'speak security'.

Third, it will be easier to present an issue as an existential threat if objects associated with the issue carry historical connotations of threat, danger and harm, or where a history of hostile sentiments exists. So, for example, tanks are generally held to be threatening owing to their status as weapons and historical experience of their use in war; so the massing of tanks along the border of a state is relatively conducive to securitisation by elites and security experts. Similarly, where there is a history of conflict between two states, a rapid increase in the production of, for example, nuclear weapons by one will be relatively easy for the other to present as a potential existential threat.

In short, certain actors and institutions are better at securitising than others, because they are perceived as being more credible by the relevant audience, and certain issues and objects are easier to securitise than others depending on the associated connotations. However, no one of these conditions on their own is sufficient to achieve securitisation, nor are they ever entirely assured. Perceptions of actors' credibility can fluctuate significantly over time for instance (credibility can be won or lost), and this can radically impact upon the chances for success in any securitising move (think of the extent to which the credibility of the US and British governments on security issues was affected by the failure to find weapons of mass destruction following the invasion of Iraq in 2003). Likewise, representations and perceptions of historical threats or enmities can change over time. Securitisation theory thus emphasises the importance of the speech act component, and the ultimately political and intersubjective nature of securitisation:

> No condition (any number of tanks at the border) or underlying cause (motivation of leaders), not even a solid position of authority of the speaker of security, can make for a securitization – they can only *influence* a political interaction which ultimately takes place among actors in a realm of politics with the historical openness this entails.
>
> (Wæver 2000: 252, emphasis in original)

The dynamics of securitisation

Securitisation theory seems to make sense when thought of in the familiar terms of military security. But can we apply this formula outside the military realm? Buzan *et al.* argue that we can, but that we need to be aware that the types of interaction, referent objects, and threats to referent objects associated with non-military sectors (which they identify as environmental, economic, societal and political following Buzan's earlier (1991) categorisation) can be very different from those associated with the traditional military focus. Understanding securitisation as a 'mode of thinking' allows the security analyst to investigate how 'the *same* logic' might apply to non-military issues (Wæver 1995: 51). But what constitutes an 'existential threat' in one sector may not necessarily be identical to threats in other sectors, even if Buzan *et al.* caution that these sectors should be treated as distinct and separate only to make the analysis of securitisation more manageable. In reality, as they acknowledge, sectors frequently overlap; but they also argue that the disaggregation of security into different sectors allows us to discern distinctive patterns or dynamics of security that are found in each, as well as allowing us to identify the likely securitising actors and prospects for securitisation.

Security: A New Framework for Analysis (Buzan *et al.* 1998) provides an initial attempt to identify how these dynamics operate in relation to the military, environmental, economic, societal and political sectors, and this is summarised initially in Table 6.1.

With regard to the *military* sector, unsurprisingly the traditional/military conception of security prevails. Security is 'about survival' (Buzan *et al.* 1998: 21), and in this sector the security agenda is geared towards the goal of *national* security. With the rise of the nation state, the priority became the preservation of the state such that the concepts of security and 'national security' became virtually interchangeable for much of the twentieth century. Defence of the nation was seen to legitimate extraordinary measures. Hence, for example, the US targeting of the Soviet Union with nuclear weapons that could wipe out millions of people (and vice versa) was legitimated in terms of maintaining national security.

Securitisation theory makes two important assumptions in relation to the *military* sector of security. First is that, as noted previously, military security is not the only sector worthy of consideration in security studies or analysis of securitisation. Even state militaries increasingly carry out a range of activities and functions, such as humanitarian intervention and peacekeeping, associated with a 'broadened' security agenda. Indeed, owing to processes of institutionalisation, state militaries tend to be maintained even in the absence of an obvious existential threat. However a second and equally important point to note is that the traditional

Table 6.1 Dynamics of securitisation according to sector of security

Sector	Type of interaction (Buzan et al: 7)	Dynamic of securitisation
Military	Relationships of forceful coercion	Existential threat to state/populace/territory/military capacity
Environmental	Relationships between human activity and the planetary biosphere	Existential threat to biosphere/species/natural environment
Economic	Relationships of trade, production, and finance	Existential threat to markets/finance/resources
Societal	Relationships of collective identity	Existential threat to collective identity/language/culture
Political	Relationships of authority, governing status and recognition	Existential threat to sovereignty/organisational stability/ideology of a social order

Source: adapted from Buzan *et al.* (1998)

conception of security operative in the military sector is in many ways paradigmatic for other non-military sectors. Non-military threats do not necessarily have to be as dangerous as war, but they do have to follow a logic (existential threats to a referent object) and have effects (the use of emergency powers) that parallel the traditional military–political understanding of security. As Wæver (1995: 47) argues, the concept of security – like any other concept – carries with it historical connotations. In the case of the concept of security, these connotations relate to practices of war, threat and defence. Hence invoking the term security potentially initiates what Wæver has termed elsewhere as the 'Clausewitz effect', that is, dynamics of threat and defence that parallel those conventionally associated with warfare (Bagge Laustsen and Wæver 2000: 724; Wæver 1995: 53).

Certain *environmental* issues, such as global warming, pollution and overuse of limited energy resources may be construed by securitising actors as threatening the very existence of animal species or even human life itself. For example, it could be argued that the very existence of Bangladesh is threatened by rising sea levels globally, and an environmental issue such as this can also have knock-on effects in other sectors: refugees from Bangladesh might be seen to threaten the societal, economic and political integrity of neighbouring states. Some within the scientific community have sought to securitise the issue of climate change on this basis, and these can be characterised as securitising actors within this sector. But as Buzan *et al.* note, 'Crucial for environmental security is whether states, major economic actors, and local communities embrace the scientific agenda' – in other words, successful securitisation of environmental issues requires acceptance by the relevant audience (1998: 91).

National or global markets might be threatened by financial collapse, and hence equate to an issue of *economic* security on a large scale with direct consequences for communities and individuals. It is worth remembering, however, that even though we speak quite commonly of our personal 'economic security', this needs to be an *existential* threat to meet the criteria of securitisation. In extreme cases, a financial crisis can compromise or remove access to basic necessities such as food, water, clothing and shelter and hence could be presented as an existential threat to individuals. At a broader level, threats to the existence of large firms and companies might also be presented as issues of security. Buzan *et al.* tend to focus on 'security spillovers' from the economic sector (1998: 117). Thus, for example, state actors may present financial crisis or collapse as a potential threat to the funding of national defence.

Within the *societal* sector, which is discussed in more detail below, securitisation occurs when issues are accepted as threatening the existence of a group's identity. For instance, an influx of migrants who hold rival and potentially competing values could be presented by securitising actors (such as state or community leaders) as threatening the very existence of a 'way of life', a language or a community.

In the *political* sector, the referent object is usually the constitutive principle of a political unit, the thing that makes a political unit 'hang together' – such as sovereignty in the case of states. Anything that threatens the existence of this principle can be presented as a security issue. One example Buzan *et al.* give is that the European Union could be existentially threatened by events that might reverse the process of European integration, which can be said to function as its constitutive principle. Or, at the state level, threats to state sovereignty that are non-military in nature could fall into this category.

As we can see, Buzan, Wæver and de Wilde, in their *Security: A New Framework for Analysis*, do seek to make the case that non-military issues can be considered as security issues under certain circumstances. What they try to do is to distinguish what types of referent object and what types of threats should fall under the heading of security. But they reject the idea that the study of security should focus purely on the welfare of individual human beings; even though this may seem like an attractive ideal, this would stretch the study of security too far. Wæver cautions that 'the individual has various needs and can be hurt by threats to those needs, and this makes everything a potential security problem'; hence, in his view, 'the concept of security becomes all-inclusive and is thereby emptied of content' (1995: 49). Focusing on the individual level simply perpetuates the over-expansion of the meaning of security, Wæver argues, which is what the analytical tool of securitisation seeks to avoid.

Wæver illustrates this with what he terms as the 'hourglass' model of security (Figure 6.2), arguing that whilst it can be accepted that ' "security" is influenced in important ways by *dynamics* at the level of individuals and the global system' (1995: 49), terms such as individual security and global security remain fundamentally opaque and impractical for the purposes of analysis.

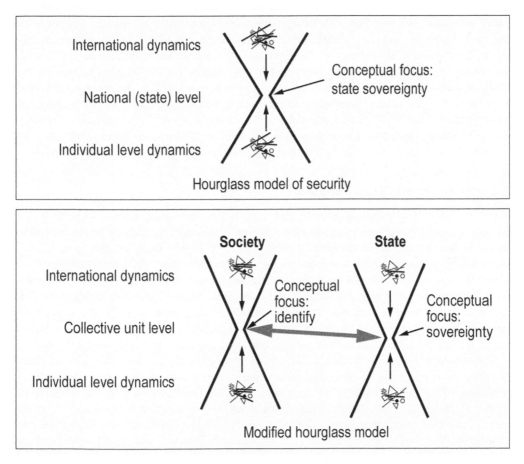

Figure 6.2 Wæver's 'hourglass' models of security

Source: adapted from Wæver 1995: 49

Buzan *et al.* hence maintain a commitment to methodological collectivism – a focus on the dynamics of collective units – and have conversely charged other critical approaches to security (such as those concerned with 'emancipation' – see Chapter 2) with an ill-judged resort to methodological individualism. For Buzan *et al*, the state remains an important (and possibly the most important) 'level of analysis' in security studies. Further to this, they also concentrate attention on the role securitisation of external threats plays in the formation of regional 'security complexes': subsystems of states within the international system whose major security concerns are inextricably linked and where the securitisation of an external threat lends internal coherence and unity to an otherwise diverse group of states (see Buzan *et al.* 1998: 15–19; Buzan and Wæver 2003, 2009).

However, Buzan *et al.* do acknowledge that referent objects other than the state can be subject to securitisation. In particular they have sought to explore the concept of 'societal security' as a 'new referent object' (Wæver *et al.* 1993: 17), arguing that societal identities have the degree of consistency and tangibility to function as a referent object in processes of securitisation (see the 'modified hourglass model' of security illustrated in Figure 6.2, which implies that society can be treated as a collective unit in a way that parallels the state, albeit with a different conceptual focus). Societal security denotes the security of 'large-scale "we" identities' (Wæver *et al.* 1993: 21) such as national ('we Germans'; 'we Irish') and religious ('we Christians'; 'we Muslims') identity groups. Since the boundaries of states and societies are rarely identical, and since state boundaries may contain multiple identity groups, focusing on the state alone fails to capture the dynamics of securitisation within the societal sector. As is explored in more detail in Chapter 11, securitisation theory has been applied to the study of migration in particular in order to assess how, when and by whom migration has been securitised as an existential threat to group identities (see Wæver *et al.* 1993 and more recently Huysmans 2006). Here it is usually some notion of 'society', as opposed to the state, that is claimed to be under threat: migrants may not be presented as direct threats to state institutions or political stability, but instead as threats to conceptions of national identity.

Securitisation and desecuritisation

In contrast to the traditional assumption that security is an intrinsic good and something that we would instinctively want more of, one of the most striking implications of securitisation theory is that security is not always a 'good thing'. On this view more security is not necessarily better as securitisation of an issue brings with it a particular type of emergency politics where the space (and time) allowed for deliberation, participation and bargaining is necessarily constricted and brings into play a particular, militarised mode of thinking. Thus, for instance, many have argued that the securitisation of migration actually has a negative impact in limiting the political space required to think through this complex issue and instead introduces an unhelpful degree of enmity and urgency (Aradau 2004; Huysmans 2006).

Consequently, Wæver in particular has argued that we should in most cases 'aim for *desecuritisation*: the shifting of issues out of emergency mode and into the normal bargaining processes of the political sphere' (Buzan *et al.* 1998: 4, emphasis added). The question of what desecuritisation means and what it might involve in practice is the focus of much current attention in debates on securitisation theory. It is generally acknowledged that the concept of desecuritisation figures more prominently in Wæver's individual work (such as Wæver 1995, 2000) than in the collective efforts of the Copenhagen School, which spend less time on exploring desecuritisation. In his early work on securitisation and desecuritisation, Wæver gives a clearer sense that the rationale for developing securitisation theory as an approach is not simply analytical but is also motivated by a concern that 'radical' or 'critical' approaches to security have fostered a tendency to simply append the term security to an ever-increasing variety of issues (environmental, economic, societal and political) without altering the substantive meaning of security from its traditional military origins. In so doing, Wæver argues, such approaches unwittingly risk facilitating and exacerbating the introduction of threat–defence dynamics and emergency politics into non-military realms of activity, and this is of questionable merit.

Nonpoliticised ------------------→ Politicised ------------------→ **Securitised**
                                                    <<------**Desecuritisation?**------<<

Figure 6.3 Desecuritisation?

   As an illustration of this point, some have argued that the securitisation of environmental degradation (via the presentation of processes such as climate change as an existential threat to the planetary biosphere and species survival) could have a positive effect in motivating emergency measures to alter human and state activities that may well lead to such degradation. As Buzan noted in the context of increasing use of the term 'environmental security' by environmental campaigners in the early 1990s, 'The security label is a useful way both of signalling danger and setting priority, and for this reason alone it is likely to persist in environmental debates' (cited in Wæver 1995: 63).

   Wæver has, however, questioned the appropriateness of introducing the 'grammar of security' into environmental debates for several reasons. First is that intentionality is more difficult to ascribe in environmental issues than in traditional military issues. Whereas conflict takes place between warring parties, it is difficult to make the case that processes of environmental degradation, even if produced by human activities, are deliberately aimed at creating a threat to others. Second, because the label security is traditionally associated with the state, the term 'environmental security' implies that a state response is most appropriate. This implication, however, overlooks the fact that environmental problems frequently transcend and traverse state boundaries both in their likely causes and their impact. Third, securitisation of environmental issues brings with it an increased likelihood of militarised thinking, that is, of thinking in terms of threat and defence. Doing so might well encourage a reactive approach to environmental problems, whereas what might well actually be required is a more fundamental consideration of the extent to which environmental problems are the product of patterns of human activity that require substantial rethinking and deliberation (Wæver 1995: 65; see also Deudney 1990). The issue of the 'securitisation' of the environment is explored in more detail in Chapter 7. Others have similarly argued that the securitisation of issues such as health, aid and development is actually unhelpful in attempting to deal with these issues (Grayson 2003; Abrahamsen 2005).

   Wæver thus expresses his preference for *not* securitising issues where possible, and for desecuritisation, that is, shifting issues from the realm of emergency politics back into the realm of 'normal' political deliberation and haggling. In some of his work, Wæver suggests the condition of 'asecurity', rather than security, is in fact optimal. Asecurity denotes a condition where actors 'who do not feel insecure, do not self-consciously feel (or work on ing) secure; they are more likely to be engaged in other matters' (Wæver 1998: 71). security thus describes a condition where the occurrence of securitisation (and hence any consequent requirement for desecuritisation) is minimal or absent, and issues are not conceptualised in terms of security.

Yet this still leaves the question of how issues that have already been securitised might be downgraded or moved back to the status of 'normal' political issues. Several authors have noted this as a potentially under-theorised aspect of securitisation theory. As Claudia Aradau notes, the concept of desecuritisation has received 'comparatively scant attention' within securitisation theory as compared with the more prominent concept of securitisation (2004: 389). Examining the securitisation of migration in the EU, in which migrants are presented as a threat to existing forms of identity, Huysmans (1995: 66–67) suggests three possible strategies of desecuritisation: an 'objectivist strategy' (we might try to prove that migrants are not really a threat to 'our' identity); a 'constructivist strategy' (developing a broader understanding and awareness of how migrants are constructed as threats in processes of securitisation as a possible means of undercutting the potency of securitising moves); and a 'deconstructivist strategy' (where we might try and listen to the voices and experiences of migrants themselves as means of breaking down exclusionary notions of 'us' and 'them'). However, Roe (2004) has argued that in some cases (such as the securitisation of minority rights), securitisation is so entrenched (in, for example, constituting and perpetuating the identity of minorities) that it becomes virtually impossible to conceive of viable strategies for desecuritisation. In sum, while the concept of securitisation has been developed in a way that allows for clearly identifiable speech acts, securitising actors and conditions for success, the equivalent concept of desecuritisation, and what that might entail, remains much less well specified in securitisation theory and is a source of continuing intellectual ferment.

Debates, dilemmas and developments in securitisation theory

As well as debates over the nature of desecuritisation, there are several other debates, dilemmas and developments in securitisation theory that distinguish it as one of the most vibrant areas of research in contemporary security studies.

One of the initial points of contention over the development of securitisation theory concerns the concept of 'societal security'. In particular, the Copenhagen School has been accused of essentialising identity in its rendering of securitisation theory. Criticising the notion of societal security, McSweeney (1996) argues that identities (even national identities) are fluid and change over time. He consequently suggests that the concept of societal security 'will make claims for the protection of national identity all the easier to substantiate, without investigation of the interests underlying them or of the moral choices involved in any decision to authenticate them' (1996: 91). In short, McSweeney worries that the concept of societal security risks legitimating and hardening notions of 'us' and 'them' that in turn tend to fuel identity conflicts. Buzan and Wæver have countered this by arguing that they do not treat identities as objective or given, but that 'once mobilized, identities have to be reckoned with as something people perceive that they belong to, and act upon as objective, given' (1997: 246). Although we might find the practice objectionable or regrettable, securitising actors frequently speak *as if* group identities exist as hard facts for purposes of mobilisation, and hence it is argued this is something that the analysis of securitisation should take account of.

Others have, however, questioned whether even the distinction between securitising actor and the analyst of securitisation is so easily made (see Eriksson 1999). Securitisation entails the analysis of when actors 'speak security' in relation to a particular issue. But logically, the analyst of securitisation ends up reproducing this 'security talk' in the process of analysis, as well as privileging the role of elite actors. As Wæver has acknowledged, this creates something of an ethical dilemma for the prospective analyst of securitisation as 'Even when talking security in order to achieve desecuritisation, it is possible that one contributes to securitisation by the very fact of producing more security talk' (2000: 252).

The issue of 'speaking security' and the emphasis on speech acts within Wæver's conception of securitisation is a further key point of debate within securitisation theory. For one thing, as Lene Hansen has argued, 'reliance on speech act theory presupposes the existence of a situation in which speech is indeed possible' (2000: 285). Examining the case of honour killings in Pakistan, Hansen argues that the version of securitisation theory put forward by Buzan *et al.* in their *New Framework for Analysis* is blind to the ways in which gender can have a major impact upon our social position and hence our ability to speak security. She also points to the ways in which the discursive aspect of securitisation is often accompanied by practices targeted against the body (stoning to death, flogging and bride burning in the case of honour killings) that 'exceed' speech acts given that they are physical and corporeal, rather than discursive, in nature.

From a different direction, Williams (2003b) argues that an exclusive focus on speech acts is ill advised when so much of contemporary political communication takes place through primarily visual media such as television and the internet. In this context, Williams suggests that an analysis of the securitising potential of images to accompany the analysis of speech acts is a necessary development in securitisation theory, and Hansen (2011) proposes the extension of securitisation theory to include analysis of visual depictions of threats and dangers. Watson (2012), in a related vein, makes the case that securitisation theory can and should be thought of as subfield of 'framing': that is, the study of the ways in which political actors frame and communicate their interests. Others have recommended that greater attention to the non-discursive aspects that facilitate securitising speech acts is also needed (see Chapter 5, Box 5.3). Bigo (2002) advocates a focus on the key role played by security 'experts' and institutions in securitisation (see Chapter 5), while Balzacq (2005: 173) suggests that the focus on speech acts needs to be supplemented by awareness that audience, political agency and context are 'crucial' to successful securitisation (see also McDonald 2008).

More recently, debate in securitisation theory has centred on the relationship between politicisation and securitisation, and the vision of politics that underpins the concept of securitisation. Buzan *et al.* declare that ' "Security" is the move that takes politics beyond the established rules of the game and frames the issue either as a special kind of politics or as above politics' (1998: 23). However, the question has been raised as to whether politicisation (the treatment of an issue within the 'normal' sphere of political haggling) and securitisation (where issues are given priority and responded to with emergency measures) can be treated as distinct and separate (Acharya 2006: 250), and this raises a further analytical question about the possibility of a distinctive 'political' sector of security.

Some have suggested that rather than plotting politicisation and securitisation on a spectrum, as illustrated in Figure 6.1, the distinction between politicisation and securitisation is better represented in terms of a 'sliding scale' where issues move only very gradually from 'normalcy' to 'emergency', and are usually conceived of as 'security risks' rather than existential threats in between these two stages (Abrahamsen 2005: 59; see also Nunes 2012). More fundamentally, the question arises as to how we conceive of 'normal' politics in distinction to the politics of emergency associated with security: what is 'normal' politics? For some this question can only be answered by assuming conditions in which 'exceptions' actually define the normal day-to-day workings of politics (see Williams 2003b; Huysmans 2004), and that this in turn brings securitisation theory into the ambit of 'exceptionalism' as discussed within recent poststructural approaches to security (see Chapter 5). And as several authors have pointed out, discriminating between what constitutes 'normal' political life and the instances in which 'exceptional' measures can be invoked in the name of security is itself a highly fraught activity that involves major political and ethical claims (see, amongst others: Aradau 2004; Browning and McDonald 2013; Burke 2007; Nunes 2012). Some have made the case for a 'normative extension of securitisation theory' on the grounds that can be instances where it is 'morally legitimate' (Floyd 2011: 434) to engage in practices of securitisation. Floyd argues that this can apply in cases where only securitisation can provide the degree of political mobilisation required to, for example, address human practices of environmental degradation. On a consequentialist basis, she contends, some instances of securitisation can be regarded as 'positive' if it can be shown that they lead to progressive outcomes (and thus Floyd seeks to 'bridge' the Welsh School – see Chapter 2 – and securitisation theory approaches – see Floyd 2007). Other scholars, though, remain sceptical in this regard (Browning and McDonald 2013: 236) and question the extent to which securitisation theory itself provides or contains a sufficient ethical framework on which to make judgements on whether practices of securitisation should be welcomed or feared.

Conclusion

Securitisation theory has had such a significant impact on the way security is studied partly because it seems to offer a clearly identifiable research agenda: when, where and why do securitising speech acts occur? Why are some successful and others not? How do dynamics of securitisation differ across different sectors? For various reasons, though, this agenda in itself raises questions as to whether or not securitisation theory should be counted within the category of 'critical security studies' (and, once again, what the latter entails). Although securitisation theory shares in common with many critical approaches a concern with a 'broadened' security agenda in examining issue areas other than traditional military security, its development is also motivated out of desire to circumscribe the range of issues considered under the rubric of security lest the study of security becomes 'the study of everything, and hence the study of nothing'. Similarly, most proponents of securitisation theory (particularly those associated with the Copenhagen School) have largely resisted calls made by some critical approaches to 'deepen' the study of security to the individual level. Allowance has been made for the study of societal security as an alternative to focusing solely on the state, but many have argued that securitisation theory still encourages an analytical commitment to the state level and to those who already occupy positions of power (Eriksson 1999; Wyn Jones 1999: 111–112).

Against potential charges of conservatism and elitism, or 'not being critical enough', Wæver counters that securitisation theory:

> may be a more serious challenge to the established discourse [of security studies] than a critical one, for it recognizes that a conservative approach to security is an intrinsic element in the logic of both our national and international political principles [...] the dynamics of securitisation and desecuritisation can never be captured so long as we proceed along the normal critical track that assumes security to be a positive value to be maximized.

(1995: 57)

In addition, more recent applications and developments of securitisation theory (see 'Guide to further reading') have sought to explore the ethical dimensions and implications of securitisation. If – as Buzan, Wæver and other proponents of securitisation theory have suggested – successful securitisation entails the suspension of processes of deliberation and democratic procedures then, as Aradau argues, 'the dynamics of securitisation/desecuritisation raise questions about the type of politics that we want' (2004: 388): the 'emergency politics' associated with securitisation, the identification of existential threats and the likely corollary of closed decision-making processes that are the purview of security experts; or a form of politics that emphasises the virtues of desecuritisation as means of creating transparency and enhancing democratic participation in political processes. In this sense securitisation theory offers not only an analytical framework but also a site of critical opportunity for thinking through larger questions about the nature of contemporary security politics.

Key points

- Proponents of securitisation theory (such as Buzan and Wæver), acknowledge the broadening of security beyond traditional military issues to include environmental, economic, societal and political 'sectors', but they have tried to develop an analytical framework for judging what is and what is not a security issue in each of these sectors.
- To do this they employ the concept of 'securitisation', which denotes the process by which an issue, military or non-military, comes to be presented as existential threat to a referent object.
- Securitisation takes place through a 'speech act'; this is known as a 'securitising move', which requires that certain 'felicity conditions' are present in order to succeed.
- Some variants of securitisation theory also consider the prospects for 'desecuritisation', the process of moving an issue out of the realm of security and back into the realm of normal political deliberation, although whether and how desecuritisation can occur is still a keenly contested issue.

Discussion points

- What is meant by 'securitisation'?
- What are the arguments for and against the securitisation of issues?
- Does the concept of 'societal security' add to our understanding of security?
- What are the potential limitations of securitisation theory?
- Does the analysis of securitisation necessarily entail an ethical dimension?

Guide to further reading

Barry Buzan, Ole Wæver and Jaap de Wilde (1998) *Security: A New Framework for Analysis* (London: Lynne Rienner). The key starting point for those wishing to explore securitisation theory further. As well as detailing the theoretical underpinnings of an approach that focuses explicitly on securitisation, the book also examines the dynamics of securitisation within different sectors of security with relevant illustrations.

Claudia Aradau (2004) 'Security and the Democratic Scene: Desecuritisation and Emancipation', *Journal of International Relations and Development*, 7: 388–413, and Rita Taureck (2006) 'Securitisation Theory and Securitisation Studies', *Journal of International Relations and Development*, 9: 53–61, offer contending perspectives on whether securitisation theory is inherently political, or simply a tool for practical analysis.

Holger Stritzel (2007) 'Towards a Theory of Securitisation: Copenhagen and Beyond', *European Journal of International Relations*, 13: 357–383, offers a broadly sympathetic critique of securitisation theory as formulated by Buzan *et al.* and suggests possible revisions and extensions of their theoretical framework, as do Williams (2003b), Balzacq (2005) and McDonald (2008) (see Bibliography for full details).

Jef Huysmans (2006) *The Politics of Insecurity: Fear, Migration and Asylum in the EU* (London: Routledge). Advances a more sociologically grounded version of securitisation theory with reference to how migration and asylum are dealt with in the European Union.

Mely Caballero-Anthony, Ralf Emmers and Amitav Acharya (2006) (eds) *Non-Traditional Security in Asia: Dilemmas in Securitisation* (London: Ashgate). Discusses the merits and limitations of securitisation theory with reference to several empirical studies drawn from South and East Asia.

Ole Wæver, Barry Buzan, Morton Kelstrup and Pierre Lemaitre (1993) *Identity, Migration and the New Security Agenda in Europe* (London: Pinter). Provides an extensive exploration of the concept of 'societal security'.

Ole Wæver (1995) 'Securitisation and Desecuritisation', in Ronnie D. Lipschutz (ed.) *On Security* (New York: Columbia University Press). Offers an explicit discussion of desecuritisation, as well as reflections on the ethics of securitisation/desecuritisation.

Thierry Balzacq (2011) (ed.) *Securitisation Theory: How security problems emerge and dissolve* (Abingdon: Routledge). Offers a collection of essays that seek to review, critically engage with and extend securitisation theory at both a theoretical level and in application to different empirical contexts.

Part II
Issues

7 Environmental security

Abstract

This chapter offers an introduction to the main contours of recent debates about environmental security. It begins with an overview of some of the most pressing ecological issues facing humanity in contemporary political life. From here the analysis then turns to examine the way in which environmental degradation and resource scarcity have been produced as security threats in recent years. The next section interrogates the nature of the link between the environment and violent conflict drawing on research that seeks to question whether a connection can ever be made between the two straightforwardly. After a summary of arguments in favour of the desecuritisation of the environment, the discussion moves on to consider what critical alternative resources exist in green theory for thinking outside the ambit of national security imperatives.

Introduction

Since the 1980s environmental degradation and resource scarcity have become increasingly incorporated under the rubric of security by national governments, the media and academics. This has prompted many heated debates about the merits and disadvantages of linking two domains formerly perceived to be separate from each other in global politics. In particular, the framing of environmental issues and resource scarcity in terms of security offers an apposite case for an assessment of the Copenhagen School or 'securitisation' framework (for more see Chapter 6). On the one hand, some environmentalists argue that a move to 'securitise' the environment is rhetorically powerful because it draws states' attention to problems that would otherwise be left unaddressed. On the other hand, scholars such as Daniel Deudney have questioned the appropriateness of thinking about the environment through the lens of security, effectively calling for a 'desecuritisation' of the issue.

Environmental degradation, resource scarcity and population growth

Environmental degradation encompasses a vast range of issues from carbon emissions to deforestation. While a minority of scientists still disagree about the long-term implications of environmental damage, the 2007 Intergovernmental Panel on Climate Change (IPCC) concluded that it was 90 per cent likely that the increase in the global average temperature was due to human activity, and has continued to reiterate that basis for that finding (see IPCC weblink). Statistics illustrating the scale of environmental problems abound, as is well documented by international organisations such as the UN and noted in particular by scholars that focus on the issues of environmental degradation and resource depletion within security studies (e.g. Homer-Dixon 1999; Klare 2002). These illustrations provide an important backdrop against which debates in the field of environmental security have taken place, with, for example, Tuchman Matthews (1989) amongst the first to argue the case that the profound scale and scope of global environmental change required a corresponding effort to 'redefine security'. In order to establish the gravity of the situation, attention is typically drawn to three areas of concern: rates at which the earth is said to be in decay; levels of consumption of natural energy resources; and the extent to which an increase in the global population is likely to further exacerbate these trends.

If current rates of emissions from fossil fuels are maintained then IPCC scientists predict that, by 2100, the temperature on the earth's surface will increase between 1 and 6.4 degrees Celsius (°C). While this rise may seem negligible it is useful to consider that the earth has only warmed by 5 °C since the coldest period of the last ice age 18,000 years ago. According to the IPCC, the atmospheric concentration of carbon dioxide increased from a preindustrial average of 280 parts per million cubed (ppm^3) to 379 ppm^3 in 2005. Emissions are not distributed equally over the globe, however, with the highest cumulative output coming from the industrialised states of the global North (US estimated 27 per cent, EU estimated 18 per cent). Conversely, much lower rates of carbon output are to be found in states of the global South such as in Africa, South America and South East Asia.

Related to the increase in carbon emissions are the historically unprecedented levels of resource consumption. Between 1970 and 1995 alone, for example, one-third of all the earth's natural resources were depleted as a result of human activity (Klare 2002). Again, however, it is important to note that rates of consumption are up to 40 times higher in the world's most industrialised states (including the US, Western Europe, Russia and a rapidly industrialising China). While populations of the wealthiest states rely heavily on oil and gas, 3 billion of the world's poor live in rural areas dependent on local resources such as wood, charcoal, straw and cow dung as their main source of fuel.

At the current rate of consumption, oil reserves are estimated to run out in 2040 and an increase of just 2 per cent could bring this date forward to 2025–2030 (Klare 2002). Similarly, fresh water supplies are under strain. In 1997 there were 430 million people living in areas with chronic water shortage; the Food and Agriculture Organization (FAO) of the UN and UN-Water predict that by 2025, on current trends, 1.8 billion people will be living in parts of the world with absolute water scarcity. Already, there are 250 million cases of waterborne diseases reported each year leading to 10 million deaths annually. Another area of concern is the decline in total fish stocks – between 1950 and 1990 total fish production increased fivefold from 20.7 million to 101.27 million metric tons (Homer-Dixon 1999: 69). The UN FAO currently categorises only 3 per cent of the world's marine fish stocks as 'underexploited'; of the remainder 52 per cent are 'fully exploited', 7 per cent 'depleted' and 1 per cent 'recovering from depletion'.

Deforestation contributes to a rise in so-called greenhouse gases and affects biodiversity and vital food chains. During the 1990s tropical deforestation took place at the rate of 17 million hectares annually across the globe. Areas of forest roughly equivalent to the size of England and Wales are lost each year (Klare 2002). This is twinned with a decline in the total surface area of high-quality croplands and virgin forests reducing farmers' ability to grow food. Between 1985 and 2000, for example, there was a global loss of 100 million hectares of arable land equivalent to the combined areas of Texas and California (Homer-Dixon 1999: 56).

As we shall go on to see, some analysts argue that these trends are only set to worsen as the total global population continues to rise. According to the UN, the current global population stands at 6 billion; this figure is predicted to grow to 8 billion by 2050 and to 9.4 billion by 2050. In broad historic terms there has actually been a recent dip in the annual percentage population increase. However, the UN calculates that the total population of the world is still expanding at a rate of over 80 million people per year. Moreover, 90 per cent of this growth is taking place in developing countries of the global South.

The securitisation of the environment

Today, issues relating to environmental degradation and resource scarcity are commonly incorporated into states' national security strategies (see Box 7.1). In this way, along with other issues considered in this book such as migration, it is possible to identify the way in which the environment has become increasingly seen through the lens of security. Earlier in the twentieth century many of the problems now associated with environmental degradation were not considered to be even of popular concern. From the 1970s onwards, however, there has been an increasing politicisation of environmental issues, as illustrated by the high-profile campaigns of Greenpeace and other green pressure groups. To borrow the language of the Copenhagen School (see Chapter 6), the environment was then 'securitised' in public policy, popular media and academic contexts from the late 1980s/early 1990s. At this time, we see the gradual incorporation of environmental issues within a range of security thinking.

During the cold war there were relatively few explicit articulations of the environment–security nexus. One of the first academics to call for the theorisation of environmental problems within the ambit of security was Norman Myers (1986). He argued that food shortages, fisheries depletion, water scarcity, climate change and deforestation were likely to induce violent conflict. Such a view was also articulated in the influential report of the UN World Commission on Environment and Development, published as *Our Common Future* in 1987 (United Nations 1987) (also known as the 'Brundtland Report' after Gro Harlem Brundtland who chaired the Commission).

After 1989, variations on this argument became common as the study of security broadened. In this context, Robert Kaplan's 'The Coming Anarchy', published in the *Atlantic Monthly* in February 1994, remains a paradigmatic portrayal of the environment as a security threat. Kaplan's 1994 piece, said to have been read in the White House, is a doomsday prophecy about the turmoil resulting from environmental degradation and resource scarcity in the global South (see Box 7.2). Kaplan argued that global population growth would exacerbate the effects of disease, conflict and civil instability arising from environmental disruption. These effects, he claimed, are already visible in parts of West Africa, which have led to unprecedented levels of refugee migration, the erosion of nation states and the empowerment of private armies, security firms and international drug cartels. According to Kaplan, such developments are not likely to be contained in the South and 'will soon confront our civilization'. On this basis, he asserted that the global North was highly vulnerable to these dynamics and proclaimed the environment to be 'the national-security issue of the early twenty-first century' (Kaplan 1994).

A similarly pessimistic account of the future of global politics can be found in Michael T. Klare's book *Resource Wars* (2002). Like Myers and Kaplan, Klare begins with the premise that rising population levels and increased resource scarcity will lead to ethnic, religious and tribal violence. Indeed, writing in the aftermath of the attacks on the twin towers of the World Trade Center on 11 September 2001, he argues that struggles over resources along inter-ethnic lines have already begun on a global scale. Klare points to the way in which states' security ultimately depends on their energy supplies: oilfield protection, the defence of

---

Box 7.1 The incorporation of environmental issues into national security strategies

Extracts from *The National Security Strategy of the United Kingdom: Security for the Next Generation*, June 2009: 8–9:

Climate change:

> Climate change will increasingly be a wide-ranging driver of global insecurity. It acts as a threat-multiplier, exacerbating weakness and tensions around the world. It can be expected to worsen poverty, have a significant impact on global migration patterns, and risk tipping fragile states into instability, conflict and state failure. From a security perspective, it is important to act now to reduce the scale of climate change by mitigation, such as emissions reduction, and by being able to adapt to climate change that is now already unavoidable. The Government is determined to play a leading role and, over the past year, the Climate Change Act has come into force, setting a legally binding target to reduce the UK's emissions by at least 80 per cent by 2050, from 1990 levels, and introducing the world's first carbon budgets.

Competition for energy:

> Global energy demand, on the basis of governments' existing policies, is forecast to increase by around 45 per cent between 2006 and 2030. Internationally, competition for energy and other resources can act as a driver of insecurity in a number of ways: through fostering increased state-led competition for resources; through increasing the economic and political leverage of producer states; and through tension arising from the exploitation of resources as a source of internal instability. The Government recognises the importance of tackling these issues.

Extract from the *National Security Strategy of the United States of America*, March 2006: 47:

> Globalization has exposed us to new challenges and changed the way old challenges touch our interests and values, while also greatly enhancing our capacity to respond. Examples include:

> • Environmental destruction, whether caused by human behavior or cataclysmic mega-disasters such as floods, hurricanes, earthquakes or tsunamis. Problems of this scope may overwhelm the capacity of local authorities to respond, and may even overtax national militaries, requiring a larger international response.

These challenges are not traditional national security concerns, such as the conflict of arms or ideologies. But if left unaddressed they can threaten national security.

---

maritime trade routes and the ability to export energy products are all vital to the economic competitiveness and ultimate survival of a given state (cf. Ciută 2010).

Adopting a realist logic, Klare argues that the fight for states' survival in an anarchic system will increasingly come to depend upon their ability to secure resources under conditions of heightened global scarcity. In this context, he predicts a higher incidence of resource wars defined as 'interstate conflicts that revolve, to a significant degree, over the pursuit or possession of critical materials' (Klare 2002: 25). Klare recognises that inter-state conflict over resources is not a new phenomenon, but argues that such violence is likely to resurface

Box 7.2 Extract from Robert D. Kaplan, 'The Coming Anarchy', *Atlantic Monthly*, February 1994

For a while the media will continue to ascribe riots and other violent upheavals abroad mainly to ethnic and religious conflict. But as these conflicts multiply, it will become apparent that something else is afoot, making more and more places like Nigeria, India, and Brazil ungovernable.

Mention the environment or 'diminishing natural resources' in foreign-policy circles and you meet a brick wall of skepticism or boredom. To conservatives especially, the very terms seem flaky. Public-policy foundations have contributed to the lack of interest, by funding narrowly focused environmental studies replete with technical jargon which foreign-affairs experts just let pile up on their desks.

It is time to understand the environment for what it is: the national-security issue of the early twenty-first century. The political and strategic impact of surging populations, spreading disease, deforestation and soil erosion, water depletion, air pollution, and, possibly, rising sea levels in critical, overcrowded regions like the Nile Delta and Bangladesh – developments that will prompt mass migrations and, in turn, incite group conflicts – will be the core foreign-policy challenge from which most others will ultimately emanate, arousing the public and uniting assorted interests left over from the Cold War. In the twenty-first century water will be in dangerously short supply in such diverse locales as Saudi Arabia, Central Asia, and the southwestern United States. A war could erupt between Egypt and Ethiopia over Nile River water. Even in Europe tensions have arisen between Hungary and Slovakia over the damming of the Danube, a classic case of how environmental disputes fuse with ethnic and historical ones. The political scientist and erstwhile Clinton adviser Michael Mandelbaum has said, 'We have a foreign policy today in the shape of a doughnut – lots of peripheral interests but nothing at the center.' The environment, I will argue, is part of a terrifying array of problems that will define a new threat to our security, filling the hole in Mandelbaum's doughnut and allowing a post-Cold War foreign policy to emerge inexorably by need rather than by design.

with heightened intensity in the years ahead. Indeed, he envisages that instability resulting from resource scarcity will become the most distinctive characteristic of the international system and that a new landscape of global conflict will emerge.

Problematising the environment-conflict thesis

While some writers such as Kaplan and Klare take the link between environmental degradation and conflict for granted, a number of other authors have adopted a more sceptical stance. Indeed, the debate between the two sides has become a defining faultline in the literature on environmental security over the past three decades. In this section we turn to consider a range of arguments that we call the 'environment-conflict' thesis – and in some cases the securitisation of environmental issues more generally – into question.

Critiquing the 'environment-conflict' thesis

Thomas Homer-Dixon has sought to investigate whether environmental scarcity (as an independent variable) can be said to affect the incidence of violent conflict (as a dependent variable) in global politics. On the one hand, Homer-Dixon agrees with Kaplan and Klare that environmental disruptions are likely to be increasingly linked with violence: 'In coming decades the world will probably see a steady increase in the incidence of violent conflict that is caused, at least in part, by environmental scarcity' (Homer-Dixon 1999: 4). On the other hand, though, Homer-Dixon seeks a more nuanced and methodologically sophisticated approach to interrogating the complexity of the environment-conflict thesis: 'Sensationalist claims about "water wars", "food wars", and "environmental refugees" in the popular literature are – almost without exception – simplistic and flawed' (1999: 73).

First, Homer-Dixon argues that the causal link between environmental degradation and violent conflict is not as straightforward as writers such as Kaplan and Klare assume it to be. Environmental problems *may* be associated with violent conflict but, on his view, they are 'neither a necessary nor a sufficient cause' for it to occur (1999: 7). Rather, Homer-Dixon has identified five negative social effects of environmental scarcity and degradation that can be linked with outbreaks of violent conflict in specific developing countries: (1) constrained agricultural productivity; (2) constrained economic productivity; (3) migration of those people affected by (1) and (2); (4) greater segmentation of societies; and (5) disruption of civil society and state infrastructure. However, Homer-Dixon stresses that it is always the interaction of these with other non-environmental factors that may lead to violence.

Second, while inter-state resource wars may appear to be intuitive in the context of the realist paradigm, Homer-Dixon argues contra Klare that 'there is, in fact, virtually no evidence that environmental scarcity is a principle cause of major war among states' (1999: 138). Moreover, taking an opposing view to that of Kaplan, Homer-Dixon claims that North–South violence induced by environmental degradation is also unlikely (cf. Acharya 1997: 312). Rather, he suggests that environmental factors are most likely to be indirect causes of ethnic clashes and civil strife within states, as illustrated by recent conflict in South Africa, Mexico, Pakistan, India and China. For example, in South Africa chronic shortages of land, water and wood have led to the internal migration of poorer members of the black community into squatter settlements around major cities such as Johannesburg. This, in turn, has created conditions for inter-ethnic rivalry and violent feuds over competition for basic resources. Similarly, the migration of the rural poor to Karachi and Hyderabad has led to civil unrest and social instability in Pakistan.

Homer-Dixon notes that the relationship between natural resource scarcity, population growth and prosperity is not a new concern. Rather, in many ways the arguments of Klare and Kaplan were prefigured in the work of the eighteenth-century British clergyman and political economist Reverend Thomas Malthus (1766–1834) (see Box 7.3). Malthus argued that without constraint, human population growth was exponential whereas food production only grows linearly (Winch 1992). On this view, famine is seen as a natural check on population growth. Today, neo-Malthusians make a similar point that finite natural resources put limits on the growth of human population and that if such limits are broken then poverty and social degradation are likely. According to Homer-Dixon, this is a position that prevails in mass-media representations of global scarcity. However, he argues that empirical studies do not support these outmoded and sensationalist arguments. The link between population growth and poverty is not clear and the effects of population growth are arguably mitigated by technological change, which enables increased labour productivity. Moreover, there is evidence to suggest that larger populations can lower levels of environmental degradation depending on farming techniques and consumption patterns.

An alternative position adopted in the literature is that of the so-called 'economic optimists', who argue that the opportunities for profit act as stimuli for technological innovation. In other words, the central idea here is that ultimately there is no cause for concern as the

---

Box 7.3 Extract from Thomas Malthus, *An Essay on the Principle of Population*

I think I may fairly make two postulata.

First, that food is necessary to the existence of man.

Secondly, that the passion between the sexes is necessary and will remain nearly in its present state.

These two laws, ever since we have had any knowledge of mankind, appear to have been fixed laws of our nature, and, as we have not hitherto seen any alteration in them, we have no right to conclude that they will ever cease to be what they now are, without an immediate act of power in that Being who first arranged the system of the universe, and for the advantage of his creatures, still executes, according to fixed laws, all its various operations.

[…] Assuming then my postulata as granted, I say, that the power of population is indefinitely greater than the power in the earth to produce subsistence for man.

Population, when unchecked, increases in a geometrical ratio. Subsistence increases only in an arithmetical ratio. A slight acquaintance with numbers will show the immensity of the first power in comparison of the second.

By that law of our nature which makes food necessary to the life of man, the effects of these two unequal powers must be kept equal.

This implies a strong and constantly operating check on population from the difficulty of subsistence. This difficulty must fall somewhere and must necessarily be severely felt by a large portion of mankind.

This natural inequality of the two powers of population and of production in the earth, and that great law of our nature which must constantly keep their effects equal, form the great difficulty that to me appears insurmountable in the way to the perfectibility of society. All other arguments are of slight and subordinate consideration in comparison of this. I see no way by which man can escape from the weight of this law which pervades all animated nature. No fancied equality, no agrarian regulations in their utmost extent, could remove the pressure of it even for a single century. And it appears, therefore, to be decisive against the possible existence of a society, all the members of which should live in ease, happiness, and comparative leisure; and feel no anxiety about providing the means of subsistence for themselves and families.

---

market will always respond in new ways to ensure the supply of enough resources. This position is one adopted by the World Bank, which illustrates how such economic paradigms are not abstract phenomena but frameworks for practical action in the 'real world'. Yet, as Homer-Dixon explains, this perspective is also not without its problems. For example, it assumes that natural resources are homogeneous and that the human species is an exceptional form of life. Furthermore, like the neo-Malthusian approach, it arguably sidelines the politics of distribution.

Distributionists, often those approaching international political economy from a Marxist or neo-Marxist perspective (see Chapter 2), claim that the problem is not with 'scarcity' so much as the unequal distribution of resources and wealth in the first place. From this viewpoint, poverty is a cause – rather than a consequence – of high population growth and practices that lead to environmental scarcity. What this perspective emphasises, contrary to both neo-Malthusianism and liberal economic optimism, is that famines are the outcome of political decisions about who gets what, when, where and why (see Homer-Dixon 1999: 35–36). In many instances 'scarcity' of food, for example, exists in the countries and regions where the use of arable land is prioritised for the growth of 'cash-crops' intended for export, such as coffee and cacao, rather than domestic food production. Hence, on this view, more attention should be given to structural inequalities built into the international system that privilege those whose interests are best served by maintaining the status quo.

Homer-Dixon claims to add to the debate between the three positions outlined above by offering a synthesis of their claims. He argues that scarcity is an important factor but focuses on the way in which it affects human ingenuity, and thus the technologically innovative responses presupposed as possible by the optimists: 'Rather than speaking in terms of limits, it is better to say that some societies are locked into a race between a rising requirement for ingenuity and their capacity to supply it' (1999: 44). In other words, for Homer-Dixon the main bifurcation is not between the 'haves' and the 'have nots', but rather a division separating societies able to respond well to scarcity versus those who cannot. While the focus on ingenuity certainly marks out Homer-Dixon's distinctive contribution to the debate, however, other writers have criticised what they consider to be the politically anodyne implications of his analysis (Barnett 2001).

The case against the securitisation of the environment

By contrast, the work of Daniel Deudney has consciously sought to provocatively question the efficacy of thinking about environmental degradation and resource scarcity through the lens of national security, even in the more 'sophisticated' forms suggested by scholars such as Homer-Dixon. In an influential essay entitled 'Environmental Security: A Critique', Deudney (1999) sets out three key reasons for a more sceptical approach to the securitisation of the environment in academic and policy-making arenas.

At base, Deudney argues that to treat environmental issues as a security threat is conceptually confused and misleading (see also Deudney 1990). This is because 'the traditional focus of national security – interstate violence – has little in common with either environmental problems or solutions' (1999: 189). Significantly, environmental issues and traditional military threats differ in four key respects:

1   Environmental issues may affect human well-being but this is an *insufficient basis for the definition of a threat to national security* as such;
2   There is *nothing particularly national* about the ecological problems because most 'affect the global commons beyond state jurisdiction';
3   Inter-state violence reflects intentional behaviour whereas *environmental degradation is largely the result of unintentional activity* since 'people rarely act with the [...] goal of harming the environment';
4   While military threats necessitate the response of 'secretive, extremely hierarchical, and centralized' organisations, *environmental concerns need to be met with altogether different approaches and institutions* based upon global citizenly 'husbandmanship'.

(Deudney 1999: 193–194)

Deudney notes that, irrespective of conceptual or empirical accuracy, some environmentalists *do* seek to portray ecological degradation in terms of a national security threat as 'part of a rhetorical and psychological strategy to redirect social energies now devoted to war and interstate violence toward environmental amelioration' (1999: 195; cf. Booth 2007: 327–336). In other words, he recognises the fact that some environmentalists will seek to securitise environmental issues in the hope of mobilising the levels of attention and resources that are usually reserved by states solely for military security issues (cf. Floyd 2007). Yet, he argues, the move to present environmental destruction in security terms may backfire as it runs counter to the sort of globalism required to develop workable solutions for a sustainable future: 'in short, if environmental concerns are wrapped in national flags, the "whole earth" sensibility at the core of environmental awareness will be smothered' (Deudney 1999: 200). Rather, Deudney calls for the abandonment of the security framing (or a 'desecuritisation' in Copenhagen School terms – see Chapter 6) in favour of fostering a globalist green sensibility as 'the master metaphor for an emerging post-industrial civilisation' (1999: 201).

Significantly, unlike Kaplan and Klare, Deudney dismisses the core assumption that ecological decay is likely to cause inter-state wars. This assumption, he argues, unfairly characterises international political life as a context of unending conflict and violence. Methodologically most accounts of the environment-conflict thesis are highly problematic because they fail to cross-reference all cases of resource scarcity with incidence of conflict. Moreover, the extent to which environmental degradation can stimulate international cooperation between states has often been glossed over in the literature. Three further issues cast doubts on Klare's hypothesis about new landscapes of violence: the global market means that states no longer experience resource dependency as they once did; territorial conquest is too costly to pursue in search of new resources; and industrial technology is developing at a rate that mitigates the effects of the depletion of non-renewable energy sources (Deudney 1999: 206). On this basis, Deudney concludes:

> Environmental degradation is not a threat to national security. Rather, environmentalism is a threat to the conceptual hegemony of state-centred national security discourses and institutions. For environmentalists to dress their programs in the blood-soaked garments of the war system betrays their core values and creates confusion about the real tasks at hand.
>
> (1999: 214)

Despite Deudney's systematic critique of the appropriateness of thinking about the environment in the register of security, however, this line of argument does little to engage with the politics of securitizing moves. Furthermore, while Deudney points to the desirability of fostering a 'green sensibility', it ultimately remains unclear in his analysis what this might entail for practical politics or indeed how a desecuritisation of environmental degradation might occur.

Environmental security and the modern geopolitical imagination

The problem of environmental degradation and resource scarcity does not only raise thorny political and ethical questions about the appropriateness of solutions within a security framework. Rather, it is also an issue that confronts and problematises some of the dominant assumptions about space, identity and territory underpinning the modern geopolitical imagination. While this issue has primarily concerned political geographers, critical inter-disciplinary writers such as John Agnew, Simon Dalby and Jon Barnett have pointed to the way in which this imagination conditions the way we think about the world within security studies.

John Agnew has famously argued that the modern geopolitical imagination constitutes a 'territorial trap' (1994). It is predicated upon three highly contentious starting points: first, that states have exclusive power within their territories as represented by the concept of sovereignty; second, that domestic and international spheres are distinct; and third, that the borders of the state define the borders of society so that the latter is constrained by the former. Agnew claims that, despite structuring prominent conceptualisations of global politics, there is a tendency for these premises to go largely unexamined in IR, security studies and related disciplines. Moreover, these starting points are 'contentious' precisely because they are not facts but rather represent certain ideals about the way things *should* be. Yet, in some regions of the world (such as Africa, for example), this specifically Western conception about the organisation of political community bears little resemblance to historical or contemporary experience (see Chapter 4). On a more abstract level, while these principles enable a host of epistemological and ontological claims about the way the world is, Agnew suggests that they tell us more about our own imagination of geopolitics than anything else. For this reason, he argues that it is important to interrogate this imagination as a historically and culturally determined phenomenon in its own right.

Applying Agnew's insights, Dalby (2002) and Barnett (2001) have examined how certain geopolitical assumptions shape debates about the environment–security nexus. Dalby, for example, reminds us that Malthus' arguments cannot be divorced from the geopolitical context of the industrial revolution, the American and French revolutions, and contemporary fears about the dissolution of political order. In the face of such fears the reactionary move was naturally to attempt to restore civil stability at all costs. By focusing on a lack of resources Dalby suggests that Malthus was able to distract attention from the more structural causes of inequality: 'A general assumption of scarcity [...] works as an ideological move to preclude the necessity of probing distributional questions' (2002: 24). Barnett also emphasises that the Malthusian position assumes it is simply numbers of people that are cause for ecological concern rather than the way they choose to live. He highlights that, rhetorically, the presentation of population growth as an issue that requires management creates a role for some people to control others. It also, he argues, reduces people to impersonal demographic statistics so they might be monitored and analysed more easily (2001: 60).

According to Dalby, many of the geopolitical assumptions of Malthus are carried over into the work of Kaplan, whose essay assumes a similarly bifurcated world between aspiration and fear. Like Malthus, Kaplan ignores structural inequalities and the colonial histories that produced them in the first place, which, in Dalby's view, constitutes a very narrow geopolitical horizon – 'one that focuses solely on local phenomena in a determinist fashion that ignores the larger trans-boundary flows and the related social and economic causes of resource depletion' (2002: 34). From Barnett's perspective, neo-Malthusian arguments such as Kaplan's and Klare's fail to grasp the obvious point that rather than causing violent conflict population growth leads to famine, which, in turn, reduces the ability of a society to go to war. Like Homer-Dixon, Barnett takes issue with the environment-conflict thesis: 'There is little if any evidence to suggest that environmental problems do cause violent conflict, instead what is presented are theories that have intuitive appeal but empirically fail to convince' (2001: 50). In a further step, however, Barnett also questions the very concept of scarcity and the work it does in geopolitical discourses on environmental security, pointing out that it is ultimately relative to expectations of abundance. Furthermore, critiquing the concept of 'resource wars', Barnett complains that much of the literature on environmental security mistakenly conflates 'scarcity' with 'degradation', a move that 'offers strategic rationality a beachhead on the environmental agenda because resources and conflict are central to the strategic stock-in-trade' (2001: 51; see also Litfin 1999). This, together with the ethnocentric and primordialist assumption that people in the global South will automatically take to arms in periods of dearth, illustrates the extent to which the neo-Malthusian position is not neutral nor natural but ethically and politically loaded in favour of the maintenance of particular interests.

More broadly, Dalby has also sought to investigate how environmental problems have come to challenge some of the basic predicates of the modern geopolitical imagination as outlined by Agnew. Dalby is critical of the way in which the geopolitical vocabulary of traditional security studies is in his view stuck in the 'territorial trap'. He argues that this continued reliance upon territorially defined modes of thinking renders traditional approaches to the study of security particularly unable to grasp the complexities of environmental degradation. Analysis and rectification of phenomena such as population displacement, transnational pollution, and ecological decay do not fit within the statist vision of the modern geopolitical imagination:

> If there are no insides and outsides in a planetary predicament driven by the flows of resources, exploitation of remote ecosystems, and global traffic of wastes, then [...] ecological security cannot be understood in the conventional geopolitical parameters of territorial states.
>
> (Dalby 2002: 141)

Instead, Dalby calls for a change of geopolitical horizons within which environmental security is thought about (see also Dalby 2007). To do so he draws on the work of Barry Commoner (1971) who has sketched out four basic 'laws of ecology': first, everything is interconnected with everything else and therefore isolation of phenomenon is an impossibility; second, everything must go somewhere and, on this basis, there is no such thing as 'waste'; third, nature knows best, in other words, human attempts at improving conditions artificially are more likely to result in further deleterious results; finally, there is no such thing as a free lunch, that is to say there is a price to be paid ecologically for every aspect of human behaviour. Thus, Dalby argues that, as well as taking into account the historical domination of humanity over nature and the particular European imperialist iteration out of this phenomenon, thinking in terms of ecological systems is necessary unless security studies is to run the risk of reproducing some of the very problems it presumably wishes to solve.

The greening of critical security studies?

The final section of this chapter considers what resources exist in green theory in order to pave the way for such an alternative to the various environment-conflict theses, as called for by Dalby and others. Most notably, Jon Barnett has sketched out his vision for a 'critical' perspective on environmental security informed by 'green theory'. This vision is animated by four mutually supporting principles. First, it is motivated by a 'suspicion that modern anthropocentric and utilitarian cosmology is responsible for environmental degradation' (2001: 2). In other words, many of the problems that have become labelled as 'environmental issues' stem from an attitude towards the world that puts the human and his/her needs first. Therefore, an alternative perspective is required; one that questions the privileging of the human in order to search for different ways of prioritising more sustainable ways of living.

Second, and related to the above, Barnett refers to the need for a fundamental shift in the philosophy of space and scale. Typically, in traditional approaches to IR and security studies, the state is taken as the primary actor in the international system. Each state is presumed to be sovereign and treated as a separate entity from other states. Similarly, under domestic and international law, people are treated as distinct individuals each responsible for them-selves. A further division is that between society on the one hand and the natural world on the other. On this basis, we can see how different entities are commonly boxed off so that the relations between them can then be analysed in the study of global politics. What a green theory perspective challenges us to do, by contrast, is to see everything as being always already inextricably interlinked to begin with. From this perspective, all entities are part of complex interdependent systems. So, for example, the distinction between humans and animals makes little sense when the earth is rethought of in terms of one ecosystem. Instead of separate beings humans/animals are recast as part of a continuum of life whose common future is invested in the sustainability of that ecosystem as a whole.

Third, Barnett emphasises that an approach to environmental security inspired by green theory is one that takes on board the problems of the uncertainty of knowledge. Echoing many of the insights of Michel Foucault (see Chapter 5), green theorists are acutely aware of the problematic status of all 'truth' claims. This is not to say that there is no such thing as truth, but rather that notions of what is 'true' are always bound up in relations of power that require close interrogation. Such an approach recognises that environmental problems are not a given but defined by scientific communities. Moreover, the way in which a given prob-lem is identified affects the range of possible solutions available. Since those solutions are in effect only ever particular responses to particular understandings of the problem, attention needs to be given to the way that problem is diagnosed in the first place.

Finally, in the manner of critical theorising as outlined by Robert Cox (see Chapter 2), Barnett emphasises that green theory encourages not a pretence to objectivity but an outwardly normative dimension to the study of environmental security. In this vein, Barnett argues that his own work reflects 'a mode of theorising and critiquing which explicitly acknowledges and purposefully deploys the beliefs and values of the theorist' (2001: 3). More specifically, and reflecting many aspirations of writers associated with the Welsh School (see Chapter 2), Barnett urges a move from thinking in terms of national/state to the human/individual level, based on a conception that recognises that the human species exists in and not against, nature (see also McDonald 2003: 70). In his view, environmental security refers to 'the process of minimising environmental insecurity', and a focus on the individual enables welfare, justice and peace to be the ultimate goal (Barnett 2001: 129). Similarly, Ken Booth has suggested a 'holistic' approach to the environment as an aspect of Critical Security Studies that, grounded in 'deep ecology', would view human beings as part of nature rather than distinct from it, and the security of individuals and the ecosystem as intricately inter-twined rather than separate (Booth 2007: 327–336; see also Dalby 2007). In this way, it might be possible to see how an explicitly normative commitment to emancipation offers one route for thinking environmental degradation out of the framework of securitisation.

Conclusion

The linking of environmental degradation and resource scarcity with discourses and appara-tuses of security is a highly controversial terrain in both the theory and practice of global politics. Even if a consensus has emerged that the rate of ecological decay is one of the most pressing features of the current era there is little agreement about how this connects – or should connect – with security. The issue of the relationship between the environment and security provokes further questions investigated elsewhere in this book about what we mean by security, what is at stake when a given issue is 'securitised', and whether 'desecuritisa-tion' is possible and/or desirable.

Those who adopt a more traditional view of security, epitomised by Stephen Walt's definition of it as 'the threat, use, and control of military force', may question whether it makes any sense to think of the environment as a security issue at all (Walt 1991). Moreover, some writers on environmental security such as Homer-Dixon continue to doubt the existence of a straightforward causal connection between ecological damage and violent conflict. Yet, as we have seen, since the 1980s environmental degradation has been framed in terms of the language of security by states, international institutions such as the UN and non-governmental organisations (NGOs). On the one hand, some environmentalists have argued that this strategy works to raise the profile of ecological destruction and inspire action. On the other hand, writers such as Deudney question whether this logic runs contrary to their aims.

One way out of this impasse is to move the debate forward by analysing the politics of framing environmental degradation in security terms. What actors 'securitise' the environment, why and with what effect? What 'work' does the concept of security do in environmental discourses (and vice versa)? Whose interests might a securitising/desecuritising move of the environment serve? It is precisely through investigating such questions that a more critical stance has made a significant contribution to the literature. Analysts such as Dalby and Barnett seek to interrogate the positivistic, neo-Malthusian, ethnocentric and often realist assumptions upon which accounts of the environment–security nexus typically rest. Moreover, adopting Agnew's critique of the modern geopolitical imagination, these authors demonstrate how such accounts serve to reproduce a particular vision of global politics that serves to maintain the status quo. By taking their lead from the array of issues associated with environmental degradation green theorists are also able to question the appropriateness of orthodox thinking in IR and security studies. From a green perspective, for example, the referent object debate is opened once more and extended to include not only the state, or the individual, but also the planet as an ecosystem. In this way the anthropocentrism of security studies is not only brought into full relief but might fundamentally be challenged as a sustainable horizon.

Key points

- The rate of consumption of the earth's natural resources has been at an historic high during the twentieth century and developed states consume up to 40 times more than developing states.
- From the 1980s onwards, environmental degradation and resource scarcity was increasingly presented by national governments, the popular media and some academics through the lens of security.
- Deudney (1999) makes the case against the securitisation of environmental degradation on the grounds that: (1) environmental issues are not a national security threat; (2) presenting those issues in terms of security may backfire on environmentalists; (3) arguments about resource wars fail to grasp international cooperation in environmental affairs.
- Scholars working in critical geopolitics demonstrate how a neo-Malthusian approach glosses over significant ethical and political issues such as the colonial histories that produced structural inequalities in the distribution of resources globally.
- A critical green theory approach is one that calls for four key moves: a questioning of the anthropocentrism of security studies; a shift in space and scale to encompass a more holistic perspective on the earth as an interconnected biosphere; an appreciation of the uncertainty of knowledge and the relationship between knowledge and power; and an overtly normative position that seeks to find more sustainable ways of living.

Discussion points

- To what extent do environmental problems lead to violent conflict?
- Should environmental campaigners seek to encourage or avoid the 'securitisation' of environmental degradation?
- How does the environment–security nexus challenge traditional assumptions about the study of security?
- What is the referent object of environmental security?
- What are the implications of green theory for the study of global security relations?

Guide to further reading

Daniel Deudney (1999) 'Environmental Security: A Critique', in Daniel Deudney and Richard Matthews (eds) *Contested Grounds: Security and Conflict in the New Environmental Politics* (Albany, NY: SUNY Press). An influential critique of the securitisation of the environment.

Kate O'Neill (2009) *The Environment and International Relations* (Cambridge: Cambridge University Press). Offers a general introduction to some of the key theoretical positions on the environment in IR theory.

Michael T. Klare (2002) *Resource Wars: The New Landscape of Global Conflict* (New York: Henry Holt and Company). A realist-oriented analysis of the relation between resource scarcity and international conflict.

Lorraine Elliott (2004) *The Global Politics of the Environment* (Basingstoke and New York: Palgrave Macmillan). A significant contribution to green theory in the context of IR.

Richard A. Matthew, Jon Barnett, Bryan McDonald and Karen L. O'Brien (2010) (eds) *Global Environmental Change and Human Security* (Cambridge MA: MIT Press). Brings together a series of perspectives on the potential overlaps between environmental and human security.

Simon Dalby (2002) *Environmental Security* (Minneapolis, MN, and London: University of Minnesota Press). An account of the relationship between environmental degradation and security from a critical geopolitical perspective.

Thomas Homer-Dixon (1999) *Environment, Scarcity, and Violence* (Princeton, NJ, and Oxford: Princeton University Press). A seminal critique of the environment-conflict thesis.

Weblinks

Institute for Environmental Security, The Hague: www.envirosecurity.org/ Intergovernmental Panel on Climate Change: www.ipcc.ch/

World Resources Institute for statistics on global environmental degradation: http://earthtrends.wri.org/miscell/citing.php?theme=0

8   Health

Abstract

This chapter examines the ways in which health is increasingly linked to conceptions of security and insecurity in modern political discourses. Though related to broader discussions of human security and development, 'health security' has more recently emerged as a distinctive and burgeoning area of policy-making and research in its own right. The identification of health 'risks' such as global pandemics, infectious diseases, and the potential for the utilisation of biological agents as weapons in the form of 'bioterrorism' have proliferated among the security policies and agendas of states, supranational institutions and non-governmental organisations alike. The following discussion outlines and assesses the multiple ways in which health is now constructed as a substantive security issue – ranging from the argument that infectious diseases such as HIV/AIDS threaten militaries' ability to maintain territorial security in sub-Saharan Africa, to more expansive conceptions of the relationship between health, security and populations at a broader level. Against this backdrop, it also critically evaluates a range of concepts and approaches found in Part I as a means for engaging with recent efforts to articulate and 'contain' health risks and reflecting more generally on the implications of the 'medicalisation of (in)security' for critical security studies.

Introduction

According to the World Health Organization (WHO) (2007), the most prevalent diseases in contemporary global health are malaria, tuberculosis (TB) and HIV/AIDS (see Figure 8.1). In 2013 it was estimated that half of the world's population is at risk of becoming infected with malaria; in 2010 alone 660,000 people died from this disease (WHO 2013: 15). While the incidence of TB is declining globally, in 2011 there were approximately 8.7 million known cases (WHO 2013: 15). In the same year, 34 million people are thought to have contracted HIV and 1.7 million people died from AIDS-related illnesses – 70 per cent of whom lived in sub-Saharan Africa (WHO 2013: 16). Attracting less attention is a group of so-called 'neglected tropical diseases' – these include dengue, leprosy, rabies, schistosomiasis and 13 other conditions, and affect more than 1 billion people worldwide (WHO 2013: 16). Less prominent still, in excess of 1.1 billion people lack access to safe water and 2.6 billion people do not have proper sanitation – more than 4500 children under the age of 5 years die every day from diarrhoea as a direct result (WHO 2007: 28).

Against this backdrop, a number of authors have argued that health has become increasingly 'securitised' in global politics. That is to say, the concept of security has been 'broadened' to include health issues and global public health is increasingly viewed through

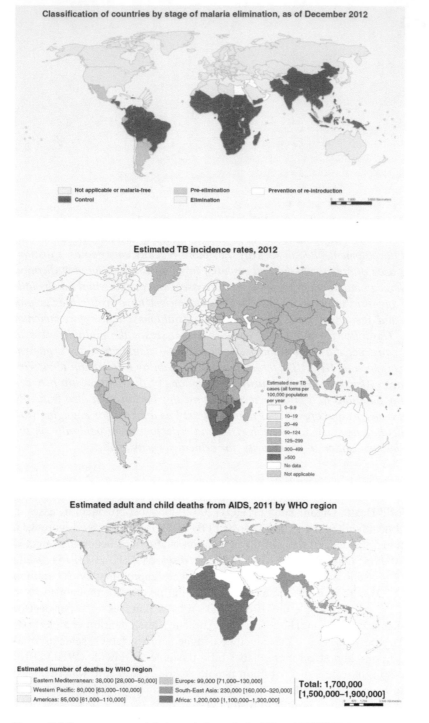

Figure 8.1 Contemporary global trends in malaria, TB and HIV/AIDS

Source: World Health Organization, Global Health Observatory, available online at:
http://gamapserver.who.int/mapLibrary/

the lens of security. Debates in both public policy and academic contexts highlight that the securitisation of health is nevertheless a contested issue. For some commentators the linking of health with security is a positive move towards generating attention to otherwise neglected problems and increasing funding necessary for their alleviation. Others view the 'health–security' nexus as a retrograde step in dealing with problems of inequality and poverty underlying many health issues. Either way, health-related issues not only broaden thinking about what security might mean in the context of the state – in certain accounts they posit 'the human' and 'vulnerable populations' as referent objects of security. The high incidence of many diseases in Africa and the global South also potentially challenges the dominant geopolitical frame within which security is commonly understood. In addition, scholars informed by poststructural and IPS approaches argue that the 'medicalisation of security' and rise of 'therapeutic interventions' have transformed the very notion of (in)security. Finally, work inspired by the concept of emancipation claims that the issue of health deepens how we view the relationship between security and the concept of the political, and raises the fundamental question of what purchase – if at all – *critical* security studies has (or *should* have) in addressing structural inequalities.

The securitisation of health

In this opening section we consider two interrelated dimensions of the securitisation of global health. On the one hand, concepts of national and international security have broadened not only to include environmental degradation (Chapter 7), development (Chapter 10) and migration (Chapter 11), but also major health issues such as HIV/AIDS. On the other hand, global public health discourses – particularly those shaped by the work of the WHO – increasingly draw on the language of security, risk and fear. We consider these dimensions in turn before exploring what is at stake in securitising health – whether such a move is desirable or not, whose interests it may serve, and the extent to which it may ultimately be necessary to think about the relationship between health and security beyond the dominant securitisation frame.

Health and national security

Traditionally, health has been viewed as a domestic political issue and largely unrelated to matters of national and international security. Links between health issues and security were typically confined to the context of armed conflict (McInnes and Lee 2012). For example, the potential impact of infectious diseases on serving military personnel and its capacity to affect the relative power of states has been a long-standing concern (Curley and Herington 2011). However, it is only relatively recently that a range of health issues have been incorporated into national security strategies and international public policy debates about peace and security.

Many scholars cite the year 2000 as a pivotal moment in the securitisation of health because the UN Security Council declared HIV/AIDS to be a threat to international peace and security in Africa (Brown and Harman 2011; Elbe 2006, 2008; McInnes and Lee 2012). In July the Security Council unanimously adopted the US-sponsored Resolution (1308) entitled 'The Responsibility of the Security Council in the Maintenance of International Peace and Security: HIV/AIDS and International Peace-Keeping Operations' (see Box 8.1). This was the first time in its history that the Security Council made a resolution on a matter of public health and the move immediately elevated the issue of HIV/AIDS in national and

---

Box 8.1 UN Security Council Resolution 1308 (2000) on the Responsibility of the Security Council in the Maintenance of International Peace and Security: HIV/AIDS and International Peace-keeping Operations

17 July 2000

Resolution 1308 (2000) Adopted by the Security Council at its 4172nd meeting, on 17 July 2000

The Security Council,

Deeply concerned by the extent of the HIV/AIDS pandemic worldwide, and by the severity of the crisis in Africa in particular,

Recognizing that the spread of HIV/AIDS can have a uniquely devastating impact on all sectors and levels of society,

Reaffirming the importance of a coordinated international response to the HIV/AIDS pandemic, given its possible growing impact on social instability and emergency situations,

Further recognizing that the HIV/AIDS pandemic is also exacerbated by conditions of violence and instability, which increase the risk of exposure to the disease through large movements of people, widespread uncertainty over conditions, and reduced access to medical care,

Stressing that the HIV/AIDS pandemic, if unchecked, may pose a risk to stability and security,

Bearing in mind the Council's primary responsibility for the maintenance of international peace and security,

1. Expresses concern at the potential damaging impact of HIV/AIDS on the health of international peacekeeping personnel, including support personnel;

2. Recognizes the efforts of those Member States which have acknowledged the problem of HIV/AIDS and, where applicable, have developed national programmes, and encourages all interested Member States which have not already done so to consider developing, in cooperation with the international community and UNAIDS, where appropriate, effective long-term strategies for HIV/AIDS education, prevention, voluntary and confidential testing and counselling, and treatment of their personnel, as an important part of their preparation for their participation in peacekeeping operations;

3. Requests the Secretary-General to take further steps towards the provision of training for peacekeeping personnel on issues related to preventing the spread of HIV/AIDS and to continue the further development of pre-deployment orientation and ongoing training for all peacekeeping personnel on these issues;

4. Encourages interested Member States to increase international cooperation among their relevant national bodies to assist with the creation and execution of policies for HIV/AIDS prevention, voluntary and confidential testing and counselling, and treatment for personnel to be deployed in international peacekeeping operations;

5. Encourages, in this context, UNAIDS to continue to strengthen its cooperation with interested Member States to further develop its country profiles in order to reflect best practices and countries' policies on HIV/AIDS prevention education, testing, counselling and treatment;

6. Expresses keen interest in additional discussion among relevant United Nations bodies, Member States, industry and other relevant organizations to make progress, inter alia, on the question of access to treatment and care, and on prevention.

international security agendas. The 2002 US National Security Strategy, for instance, pledged to 'secure public health' in order to support economic growth in developing countries. Similar references to the importance of health issues appeared in the foreign policies of Australia (from 2003), Canada (from 2002) and the UK (from 2003) (McInnes and Lee 2006). With these developments, as Stefan Elbe puts it, 'the securitization of HIV/AIDS had begun in earnest' (Elbe 2006: 121).

In 2001 the infamous 'anthrax letters' – sent one week after the 9/11 attacks to news media offices and politicians in the US – killed 5 people, injured 17 others and drew fresh attention to the imminent threat of 'bioterrorism' from terrorist organisations and 'rogue states' (WHO 2007). This threat was not entirely new – the use of biological weapons by Iraq against its Kurdish population in 1988 and the sarin attack on the Tokyo subway by the Aum Shinrikyo cult in 1995 provide two earlier examples of bioterrorism (McInnes and Lee 2006: 13). However, the anthrax scares of 2001 attracted considerable media attention, exacerbated the fears of an already anxious population in the US, and gave added impetus to the securitisation of health nationally and internationally. In this context, as Colin McInnes and Kelley Lee (2006) have shown, public health infrastructure came to occupy a privileged site in foreign policy terms as both a target and first line of defence.

In addition to HIV/AIDS and bioterrorism, fears of globally transmitted diseases threatening the health of national populations and economies were intensified following the outbreak of severe acute respiratory syndrome (SARS) in 2002–2003 and the H5N1 strain of avian influenza in 2008 (WHO 2007). The paradigmatic case of SARS, which originated in China in November 2002 and spread to Taiwan, Singapore, Vietnam and Canada by March 2003, typifies the kind of international threat feared most by foreign policy communities (McInnes and Lee 2006; WHO 2007). While death rates were relatively low compared with diseases such as TB – there were 908 fatalities by August 2003 – the disease was not constrained by national borders, spread quickly from person to person, displayed symptoms that were hard to detect and disrupted the global economy to an estimated value of US$100 billion (McInnes and Lee 2006; WHO 2007).

What are the factors that lead states to securitise health issues in this way? And why are some health issues securitised but not others? McInnes and Lee (2012) refer to three explanations that are typically used to explain why a health issue may become taken out of the realm of ordinary political debate and framed in the language of security: (1) its potential to threaten international stability (via economic disruption, migration contributing to the spread of disease and risks posed to military and peacekeeping personnel); (2) its potential to affect the internal stability of a given state (the disruption of the national economy may exacerbate class inequalities and lead to societal tensions); and (3) its potential to kill large numbers of people (aside from human security concerns, the effective functioning of the state may be compromised).

McInnes and Lee (2006, 2012) are ultimately sceptical about the extent to which these kinds of causal connections can be made, but they are evident in Robert Ostergard's (2002) seminal discussion of HIV/AIDS in Africa, which illustrates how health and national security agendas may converge. According to Ostergard, by 1999 24 million people in Africa were infected with the HIV-2 strain of the virus with some states such as Botswana experiencing higher rates of infection than others. On his view, the HIV/AIDS epidemic constitutes 'the greatest security threat from disease since the bubonic plague ravaged Europe between 1346 and 1351' (Ostergard 2002: 346). But while Ostergard notes the emergence of the discourse of human security in the 1994 UN Development Programme, his focus remains primarily on traditional state-centred military issues. For Ostergard, the most 'obvious security problem' with HIV/AIDS is the potential it has 'on the military's capacity to carry out its duties' (2002: 342). Moreover, soldiers' weakened immune systems are presented in his account not only as threat to military performance, but also to 'security and stability in the continent' because their role in spreading the disease may lead to economic instability, loss of productivity, worker illness, heightened government spending, higher insurance costs and the loss of trained workers (2002: 344).

If viewed through the lens of national security then the securitisation of health may reflect a broadening of the security agenda without necessarily challenging the state as its primary referent object. On this view, one reflected in Ostergard's analysis, the emergence of the health-security nexus in global politics is one that is entirely compatible with more 'traditional' ways of thinking about security. However, another way of approaching the health–security nexus emphasises the role that non-state actors such as the WHO have played in securitising the global public health agenda and the growing significance of the idea of human security (see also Chapter 10).

Global public health security

When the constitution of the WHO came into force in 1948 it concentrated on just three infectious diseases: cholera, plague and yellow fever. These priorities had not changed since the first International Sanitary Convention was held almost a century beforehand in 1851 in Paris to organise international cooperation between states on cross-border health issues (Kamradt-Scott and Rushton 2012). David Fidler (2005) refers to the period from the second half of the nineteenth century to the first half of the twentieth as the 'classical regime' in public health, which sought largely to protect Europe and North America from 'quarantiable' diseases. With the advent of the WHO states became obliged to notify each other of known infectious diseases within their borders and to attempt to contain them through the restriction of trade and travel. An international surveillance system was established and there were attempts to harmonise norms and procedures. Smallpox and typhus – common in Europe in the early twentieth century – were added to the watch list, although the geopolitical bias of containing diseases in Asia and the Middle East for the large part remained.

In 1951 the International Sanitary Regulations – renamed the International Health Regulations (IHR) in 1969 – were established to codify collective efforts to achieve the highest standard of health as a fundamental human right (Kamradt-Scott and Rushton 2012; WHO 2007). However, according to Fidler (2005), the mid-twentieth century was characterised by stagnation and a loss of interest in international health initiatives among nation-states. Consequently, the IHR suffered from a lack of compliance and many disease outbreaks went unreported during this period (Kamradt-Scott and Rushton 2012). By the early 1980s the epidemiological agendas reflected in the IHR and classical regime were increasingly seen as out of date. The onset of globalisation, urbanisation, mass migration, the earlier eradication of smallpox and the arrival of new health issues outside the narrow scope of the IHR and global surveillance system – most notably HIV/AIDS, malaria, TB, meningitis, dengue fever and later bioterrorism – demanded a new approach (Fidler 2005; Davies 2008).

The collapse of the classical regime and the rise of 'global public health security' at the turn of the century therefore go hand in hand (Fidler 2005). Between 1995 and 2005 the IHR underwent a process of transformation in view of the above challenges. Whereas the old IHR related only to communicable diseases, the revised guidelines – which became legally binding for 193 signatories in 2007 (McInnes and Lee 2012: 137) – expanded to include non-communicable, accidental and intentional diseases: 'illness or medical conditions, irrespective of origin or source that could present significant harm to humans' (WHO 2007: 41). As well as expanding the scope of health issues covered by the IHR, the new regime introduced context-specific measures at the source of outbreaks and for the first time made non-state sources of information permissible as part of a strengthened global surveillance system. In contrast with the greater part of the twentieth century, evidence suggests that most states have been largely compliant with the post-2005 IHR regime (Kamradt-Scott and Rushton 2012).

More recently, the WHO has identified a constellation of factors that are said to pose an historically unique set of risks to public health globally today: population growth; the use of previously uninhabited areas; urbanisation; intensive farming practices; environmental degradation; the misuse of antimicrobials (substances used to curtail the growth of, or kill, microorganisms); new diseases; and increased global air travel (WHO 2007). In this context, the primary health issues facing the twenty-first century are categorised by the WHO as: (1) epidemic-prone diseases (e.g. HIV/AIDS, SARS and avian influenza in humans); (2) food-borne diseases (e.g. Creutzfeldt-Jakob disease); and (3) accidental and deliberate outbreaks (e.g. radio-nuclear accidents and environmental disasters) (WHO 2007: ix).

In this evolving context, national and international security agendas have not only broadened to encompass health issues: global public health has also been increasingly viewed through the lens of security in global politics. Since the publication of the WHO's 2007 World Health Report, *A Safer Future: Global Public Health Security in the 21st Century*, the discourse of 'global public health security' has gathered considerable momentum. Global public health security is defined by the WHO as: 'the activities required, both proactive and reactive, to minimize vulnerability to acute public health events that endanger the collective health of populations living across geographical regions and international boundaries' (WHO 2007: ix). These 'activities' include the revision of the IHR in view of the newly identified global health 'risks' above, the deployment of a Global Outbreak and Response Network (GOARN), and the move from 'containment' strategies to 'proactive risk management' before a health issue comes to threaten a population (WHO 2007).

Many scholars agree that the WHO has been the primary agent in the securitisation of infectious diseases globally and that it has largely been successful in bringing security and public health discourses together (Curley and Herington 2011; Davies 2008; Fidler 2005; McInnes and Lee 2012; Rushton 2011). Simon Rushton (2011) has highlighted the way in which the international public health community led by the WHO has sought to deploy the language of security strategically. Similarly, Garrett Wallace Brown and Sophie Harman (2011: 773) have noted the 'utilisation and framing of fear and susceptibility to risk' as a deliberate strategy in the shaping of public health discourse. Elbe (2008) has detailed how the language of risk has been central to the securitisation of HIV/AIDS in at least three ways: the disease is presented as a longer-term potential risk for the future; it has become associated with certain 'risk groups' such as the armed forces; and certain 'risk factors' such as 'being sexually active, being mobile, being away from homes and partners for a long period of time, valorising risk-taking behaviour, and being a population with many occupational opportunities for casual sexual encounters' (Elbe 2008: 180).

However, there is less consensus about the reasons for the 'success' of the securitisation of global public health and the nature of the relationship between the WHO and nation-states. For Fidler (2005) the ascendancy of the WHO and its ability to securitise health globally is reflective of the broader decline of the nation-state and rise of a so-called 'post-Westphalian' order. Allied to this position it might be argued that the successful securitisation of health – with its perceived advantages for public health initiatives above – represents the accomplishment of a more globalist approach to human security. By contrast, Davies (2008) argues that while there has been some transfer of authority to the WHO in the area of global disease management this has been made possible only with the cooperation of states acting chiefly out of self-interest. In her view, the WHO's securitisation of health has been successful because states have felt increasingly threatened by the proliferation of infectious diseases, partly arising from globalisation (Davies 2008: 308). Thus, one of main drivers of the securitisation of health in the US context was the link made between epidemics, state failure and regional instability on the one hand, and US national security interests on the other.

Melissa Curley and Jonathan Herington (2011) argue that the state continues to be the main referent object in global health protection, despite the rise of global governance and human security discourses. For Rushton (2011), the revised 2007 IHR merely ushered in a system of 'states+' – human security 'has in fact had only a marginal policy impact' (2011: 792) and the management of health in international politics remains 'stubbornly state-centric' (2011: 789). This view is also shared by McInnes and Lee (2006: 5) for whom 'the emphasis to date has been on public health as a foreign policy and security risk, rather than on how foreign and security policy can facilitate or hinder public health'. More generally, as the next section outlines, a number of authors have questioned the securitisation of health and whether this frame is adequate or normatively desirable.

Problematising the securitisation of health

On the one hand, it might be argued that moves to securitise health by states and the global public health community are a positive development in normative terms. Such steps are often said to have given greater attention to health issues on global political agendas, attracted more financial investment, generated new policy initiatives and benefited from the involvement of a wider range of stakeholders (Brown and Harman 2011; Curley and Herington 2011; Elbe 2006). Thus, for example, Elbe (2006) highlights several arguments that might be made in favour of the successful securitisation of AIDS/HIV. First, in some African states there has been an historic 'absence of a meaningful state response' to the disease and the securitisation of it internationally has provoked action domestically – as can be seen in the cases of Nigeria, Cote d'Ivoire and South Africa (Elbe 2006: 132). Second, by invoking national security interests certain NGOs and other civil society actors have been strengthened in their ability to call for the relaxation of patents on AIDS-related drugs in order for them to be made available more cheaply in poorer countries (Elbe 2006: 133). Third, Elbe notes that 'the appeal to the naked self-interest of states' may ultimately be 'the only strategy left' if efforts driven by humanitarian arguments fail to gain traction despite the urgency of the pandemic (Elbe 2006: 134).

On the other hand, a number of writers have expressed a series of major concerns with the whole securitising agenda. Rushton (2011) argues that any study of the politics of global health security should ask 'security for whom?' and 'security from what?' – a set of normative questions not usually addressed by conventional securitisation theories. A common argument against the securitisation of health is that it serves the interests specifically of Western states (or the 'global North'). Davies (2008) claims that the 'success' of the WHO in linking health and security together has only been made possible because the global surveillance and emergency response system is aligned with their priorities. In her view, both Western states and the WHO have sought to safeguard the health and well-being of Western citizens by developing and maintaining a system 'that aims to prevent epidemics from reaching their borders' (Davies 2008: 309). In a similar vein, Rushton suggests that when viewed from the perspective of the 'global South', the current emphasis given to rapidly spreading infectious diseases, HIV/AIDS and bioterrorism appears somewhat narrow. He claims that this is because, despite purporting to be 'global' in outlook and scope, the conception of 'risk' with which public health initiatives have developed is in fact based on Western ideals and interests. This is said to reflect the groupthink of leading policy entrepreneurs who – with the exception of Mexico – largely comprise a Western security community of representatives from Canada, France, Germany, Italy, Japan, UK, US and the European Commission (Rushton 2011: 790).

An additional problem with the dominant discourse of 'global public health security' is that it captures only some of the most pressing health issues and fails to encompass issues that have not been securitised. Brown and Harman (2011: 774) argue that the securitisation of specific health risks has 'led to a distorted focus on key diseases' rather than an approach that might tackle underlying relationships between 'causal risk factors and core health systems that support effective responses'. Rushton (2011: 184) expresses a similar concern that the treatment of global health issues under the rubric of security has led to a common response and general agreement on what should be done – surveillance and emergency response – rather than a debate about possible policy alternatives. This means that the current regime is one centred on containment – and therefore orientated to the benefit of Western interests as above – rather than on dealing with prevention at source and other more radical solutions. In sum, Davies (2008: 296) points out that the 'social construction of infectious disease' by the WHO and leading (Western) states 'crowds out alternative, potentially more effective, response mechanisms'.

Elbe's (2006) discussion of the normative case against the securitisation of HIV/AIDS provides an instructive illustration in this regard. Despite the apparent benefits of an instrumental approach, he highlights some of the political and ethical dilemmas that otherwise tend to go unnoticed. First, as with the securitisation of any issue, the framing of HIV/AIDS as a security threat 'pushes responses to the disease away from civil society' and brings them into the orbit of 'the much less transparent workings of military and intelligence organizations' (Elbe 2006: 128). Second, the elevation of HIV/AIDS to the realm of security means that people infected with the disease face greater likelihood of social exclusion – for example, in the early phase of HIV/AIDS Haitians were treated as outcasts in US society and denied access to certain social benefits (Elbe 2006: 128). Third, the logic of 'threat-defence' implicit in securitisation means that humanitarian concerns are less likely to feature as highly as the specific interests of individual nation-states and certain groups (e.g. members of the armed forces) are more likely to gain access to medical resources (Elbe 2006: 129–130). State sponsorship of moves to combat specific diseases may fuel 'further suspicion and rivalry between states' instead of addressing their causes and effects (Elbe 2006: 122).

Ultimately Elbe argues that there is not a clear-cut answer to the normative question of whether HIV/AIDS should be securitised or not: 'at this stage [...]', he writes, 'it could justifiably be both "yes" and "no"' (Elbe 2006: 138). What we are left with then is an ethical dilemma with potentially major consequences for both framing HIV/AIDS as a security issue and not doing so. In order to move beyond this impasse another strand in the literature – particularly that drawing upon poststructural and Critical Theory perspectives – has sought to step outside the framework of securitisation when analysing the relationship between health and the global politics of (in)security. It is to this literature that the discussion now turns.

Beyond the securitisation of health

A number of studies have recently put forward alternative frames for understanding the health–security nexus. Here we consider the works of Elbe (2010) on the 'medicalisation of security', Alison Howell (2011) on the rise of 'therapeutic interventions' in global politics, and João Nunes (2013) on emancipatory approaches to security and the politics of health. We first explore each of these perspectives in turn – and the theoretical approaches underpinning them – before evaluating the overall significance of health as an emerging issue in the field of critical security studies.

The medicalisation of security

So far we have considered the ways in which security agendas have broadened to integrate a number of health issues and how health has come to be framed in terms of security. What both of these dimensions of the securitisation of health arguably underplay, however, are the transformative effects of these dynamics on the contemporary politics of (in)security. The focus of Elbe's book *Security and Global Health: Toward the Medicalization of Insecurity* (2010) is: 'How do health security debates also begin subtly to shape our understandings of security and insecurity in international relations?' (Elbe 2010: 14). Elbe argues that existing approaches to securitisation – particularly, though not exclusively, those associated with the Copenhagen School (see Chapter 6) – are largely inadequate to the task of addressing this question. This is because, on his view, such approaches assume a 'fairly static understanding of security' – one that 'offers us no account of how the practice of security may itself also become transformed as a result of a growing association with non-military issues' (Elbe 2010: 15).

In search of an alternative framework for the analysis of the health–security nexus, Elbe turns to theoretical resources found in sociology – particularly accounts of the process of medicalisation. According to leading sociologist Peter Conrad, the concept of medicalisation refers to 'a process by which non-medical problems become defined and treated as medical problems, usually in terms of illnesses or disorders' (quoted in Elbe 2010: 16). The definition of a social issue as a medical problem is accompanied by both an expansion in the scope of doctors' duties and the rise of medicine as a means for understanding and controlling bodies. Doctors and health professionals gain enhanced roles in society – often involving increased moral decision-making – and this dynamic pushes out lay or non-medical knowledge thereby entrenching specialists' privileged positions (Elbe 2010: 18).

In an expanded understanding of the medicalisation process, Michel Foucault has shown that the notion of 'social medicine' overflows the hospital environment and work of medical professionals to society as a whole (Elbe 2010: 19). Modern medicine gives rise to particular knowledge and practices, which target both individuals in the form of disciplinary power and populations in the form of biopower (for more on these concepts see Chapter 5 and Box 5.1). For example, one interpretation of the securitisation of HIV/AIDS is that it seeks to maximise the health of certain populations (e.g. citizens of Western states) by intervening in and disciplining the lives of others (e.g. those infected in sub-Saharan Africa) (Elbe 2005). Inspired by these insights, particularly the work of Foucault, Elbe applies medicalisation theory in order to diagnose what is at stake when practices of security start to transform via their increased interconnection with health issues – a process he calls 'the medicalization of security' (Elbe 2010: 23).

Elbe's core thesis is that our understanding of (in)security in contemporary global politics is becoming increasingly redefined as a medical problem. He argues that the medicalisation of security is not complete, but that the signs are readily identifiable across a range of practices. In order to illustrate this argument he explores four key sites where it is possible to discern the intensification of medical intervention and surveillance: pandemic threats; biosecurity; human security and development; and so-called 'lifestyle' diseases chiefly associated with the West. For Elbe, the rise of certain health issues such as HIV/AIDS, SARS and H5N1 avian influenza is not so much a symptom of the broadening of security agendas as a fundamental redefinition of what counts today as the basis for global *in*security.

Whereas for decades insecurity was associated with 'military capabilities and hostile intentions of other states' he argues that this condition has been medicalised: 'it is now also seen to stem from the proliferation of medical conditions brought about by the rapid spread of potentially lethal infectious diseases brought within the population' (Elbe 2010: 30). One of the most pronounced illustrations of the medicalisation of (in)security is the effort to which states will go in order to protect their citizens against the likelihood of a bioterrorist attack. In the context of the war on terror Elbe argues that there has been an increase in the role that doctors and health professionals play in the formulation and execution of states' foreign and security policies. There has been an opening of a 'medical front' in which terrorists are 'potentially weaponising a range of infectious diseases' and biomedical researchers are attempting to 'develop rapidly new medical counter-measures to protect their populations against such possible attacks' (Elbe 2010: 83).

With the emergence of human security discourses the medicalisation of security is further entrenched because 'virtually any lethal disease […] can become considered as a source of insecurity' and when allied with development this process expands beyond the West (Elbe 2010: 99). Finally, though non-communicable 'lifestyle' diseases – such as alcoholism, smoking and obesity – are not traditionally framed in the language of security, Elbe argues that they are increasingly viewed in public health discourses as one of the greatest threats facing Western populations. This dramatically extends the scope of medicalisation, treats lifestyles as diseases and sees a 'secure society' as one that 'requires citizens to engage in healthy behaviours' (Elbe 2010: 133).

Elbe's account is therefore one that emphasises the ways in which the concept and practice of security may be said to have changed as a result of these processes of medicalisation. From his perspective, the intensification of medical intervention and rise in surveillance and screening of human populations for disease – not only of those who are currently ill, but those who are at higher risk of developing illness in the future – means that 'the body becomes the battlefield of the twenty-first century' (Elbe 2010: 166).

Therapeutic interventions

The medicalisation of security is also the backdrop against which Howell explores the use of psychosocial approaches in contemporary global governance. In *Madness in International Relations: Psychology, Security and the Global Governance of Mental Health* (2011) she argues that knowledge and practices drawn from the 'psy disciplines' are increasingly deployed in a range of security projects. Her analysis explores three examples of this phenomenon: the pathologisation of detainees at the US naval base in Guantánamo Bay; the use of mental health programmes in post-conflict settings; and the treatment of Canadian soldiers diagnosed with post-traumatic stress disorder (PTSD). Taken together, these reflect diverse contexts where subjects – produced as 'security threats', 'victims of security' and 'providers of security', respectively – are diagnosed with mental health problems and in need of psychosocial responses.

Sharing similar conceptual ground with Elbe, Howell takes inspiration from Foucault – both in terms of Foucault's method of problematisation and his study of the history of madness. Instead of seeking to define security, Howell's primary aim is to analyse 'the emergence of security problematisations, and their political effects in order to move beyond an anti-politics of the desire for security' (Howell 2011: 25). Here the Foucauldian concept of 'problematisation' refers to the 'work of thought' that transforms a group of difficulties or obstacles into problems to which diverse solutions attempt to respond – for example the process of medicalisation described above (Foucault 1991: 389). Like securitisation theorists, Howell is interested in how certain issues become framed in terms of the logic of security, but she takes a step further in order to consider the ethical-political implications of that move and ways in which it might be reproblematised (or 'desecuritised'). Echoing Foucault's historicisation of the way that madness has been separated from reason in Western thought (see Chapter 5), Howell traces the problematisation of individuals and entire populations as sufferers of mental health disorders requiring medicalised responses in the name of security (Howell 2011: 48).

One of the most prominent sites where it is possible to see the problematisation of a security threat in psychological terms is in the case of the treatment of detainees at Guantánamo Bay. Howell details the ways in which detainees have been frequently portrayed as 'mentally ill madmen' in US security narratives. This characterisation of detainees is used by the US both to explain suicide attempts by detainees and also to justify their indefinite exclusion from the rest of 'normal' society. In drawing on the language of mental health, the US simultaneously renders detainees as a threat to national security and authorities as rational, benevolent carers – 'the absence of psychiatric care marks the backwardness or underdevelopment of the countries of origin of the detainee, and implicitly of Islam more generally (Howell 2011: 74). Ironically, humanitarian discourses ostensibly critical of the US detention facilities also end up reproducing the same pathologising logic – their tendency to explain suicides in terms of the actions of 'psychologically impaired victims' draws on the language of mental health and likewise denies detainees any political agency (Howell 2011: 65).

In addition to the disciplining of individual detainees, Howell also discusses the use of psy interventions in the context of the biopolitical management of post-conflict populations. Since the 1990s national populations have been diagnosed with PTSD – including most recently those in Afghanistan and Iraq. In this context, Howell argues that '*the psychologization of development has run parallel to its securitization*' (Howell 2011: 93, emphasis in the original). For example, the WHO MIND (Mental Health Improvements for Nations Development) project seeks to alleviate what it considers to be the cycle of mental health issues and poverty in South Africa, Ghana, Zambia and Uganda (Howell 2011: 93). However, while both development and medical experts claim this link between mental health and poverty, Howell argues that an alternative problematisation would be to say that poor people are more likely to be diagnosed as being mentally ill. The diagnosis of entire populations as in need of therapy is a deliberate strategy – one that permits surveillance of and intervention in people's lives on a scale that would otherwise be difficult to justify (Howell 2011: 108).

Lastly, Howell refers to the case of the high incidence of PTSD among soldiers in the Canadian military as an example of how psy interventions may also target non-civilian populations. Here we see not only the experiences of war being rendered technically resolvable, but also the emergence of security as being inherently linked to fitness – a point echoed in Elbe's discussion of lifestyles. Howell argues that the medicalisation of trauma among military personnel diverts attention away from the missions of overseas action to the health and well-being of soldiers and their families (Howell 2011: 128). Such a problematisation 'individualizes the experience of soldiering' and helps to shield 'the use of force in global governance from critique' (Howell 2011: 133). This point reflects the broader argument stemming from Howell's research. As part of the medicalisation of security, the use of the psy disciplines to manage diverse sites of trauma ultimately depoliticises global governance – '[i]mportant questions about war and violence are closed down when trauma or pain are treated merely as technical problems: disorders to be cured through therapeutic interventions' (Howell 2011: 148). By drawing attention to the ways in which security practices operate according to a logic of psychologisation Howell shows how it might be possible to reproblematise – and therefore repoliticise – the knowledge and practices through which this depoliticisation has taken place.

Security and the politics of health

Nunes' book *Security, Emancipation and the Politics of Health: A New Theoretical Perspective* (2013) explores the conceptual, historical and normative relationship between health, security and politics. While extant research on the health–security nexus has shown how the securitisation of health has come about and how it has also transformed our understanding of security, Nunes (2013: 5) argues that what is missing in the debate so far is 'an engagement with the ways in which ideas and practices of health and can be challenged and transformed'. While Nunes agrees with Elbe that the framework of securitisation offers little account of the transformation of security, the former wants to go further than the latter in examining the potential of health to promote broader political change: 'it is not enough to identify the dangerous consequences of predominant security arrangements; the purpose of repoliticization should be to contribute to transforming these arrangements if they are deemed undesirable' (Nunes 2013: 8).

Underpinning this argument, which to some extent is aligned with Howell's call for a repoliticisation of the health–security nexus, is a deeper theoretical/philosophical commitment to rethinking security as emancipation (see Chapter 2). However, wary of several long-standing criticisms of the so-called Welsh School of CSS, Nunes also draws on the insights of poststructuralism – particularly the work of Foucault – to offer a modified account of the reality of security, the question of the subject of security and the concept of power. For example, while he notes that for CSS the concept of security 'is ultimately tied to the experience of being insecure', Nunes argues that there is always a politics of reality surrounding that experience (Nunes 2013: 28). It is therefore necessary from his perspective to move 'beyond the moral condemnation of "insecurities"' and to analyse and explore how 'political processes [...] can be questioned, judged and eventually transformed' (Nunes 2013: 28).

Nunes claims that the idea of security is in many ways lodged historically in the way that public health is imagined – the threat of disease is not only lined to the violation and protection of the subject, but also the 'political fate of a society' (Nunes 2013: 81). The concern with integrity and the dread of disease is illustrated by recurring medicalised discourses surrounding the perceived threat of immigration and possible infection of the body politic. But in addition to the point that health issues shape and structure social relations and subjectivities, Nunes emphasises that health is also a fundamentally political issue 'inasmuch as it deploys power and advances the interests of certain groups' (Nunes 2013: 102). To illustrate the argument he gives the example of colonialism (see Chapter 4).

The rise of medical knowledge and practices was intimately related to growing concerns about the impact of disease on European colonisers since the fifteenth century. In this health imaginary the colonised were framed – or problematised – as a security threat and ideas about health became 'enveloped by a racialized form of anxiety' (Nunes 2013: 103). Nunes uses the example to demonstrate how medicine acted as a bordering device that sought to manage the relationship between Europe and the rest, and Europeans in the tropics: 'The colonized body – its strength, ability to work, propensity to fall ill, its movements, functions, and excretions – became the centre of a medical system of knowledge-production and inter- vention' (Nunes 2013: 105). Such a device was of course highly political because it involved intensive surveillance, the management of behaviour and the promotion of behavioural change – features, we might add, that are also characteristic of today's global public health security regime.

If viewed through the lens of security then the politics of health can result in exclusion, violence and the kind of border-making practices illustrated in the example of colonial medi- cine. However, even in that example the relations of power were not only repressive, but also productive in the Foucauldian sense – the colonial encounter laid the basis for modern medical knowledge. For these reasons, Nunes stresses that health has an 'open and mutable character' (2013: 109) and so if the ends of security are recalibrated toward emancipation then, he argues, it might be possible to view it as a 'bridge for peace' (2013: 117). Indeed, Nunes views health issues as occupying something of a privileged position because they force political questions about structural inequalities – and indeed exclusion, violence and harm of the kind referred to by Howell (2013) – onto a range of agendas:

> By raising some of the most contentious questions relating to the body and to the power of state authorities to manage and control it, and by placing individual and group inter- ests in a sometimes uneasy dialogue, health issues bring to the fore the most complex questions in political theory and practice.
>
> (Nunes 2013: 123)

Ultimately, Nunes' challenge to critical security studies is that in order to be 'critical' it is necessary not only to assist in the task of raising those questions, but also to make sugges- tions for how they might be addressed.

Conclusion

A shocking statistic cited by Elbe (2005) – that every day three times as many people die globally from HIV/AIDS than the number of those killed as a result of the 9/11 attacks – brings into focus the scale of the impact of poor standards of health in contemporary global politics. That health has been 'securitised' in recent years – both in terms of the incorpora- tion of certain health issues onto national and international security agendas and the framing of global public health via the language of security – is beyond doubt. However, as with other new security challenges explored in this book, there is far less consensus about whether this securitisation has been a positive development – whether it has ultimately benefited those people who are more likely to die from preventable diseases due to persistent struc- tural inequalities. As many of the authors considered in this chapter have sought to point out, the frames we use to attempt to analyse and understand the complexities of the health–security nexus are not innocent, but can contribute either to the entrenchment of certain positions or the possibility of articulating alternatives – each with potentially signif- icant ethical and political implications. Of course, this may be true of the framing of any issue, but health – with its focus on the body, its vulnerability and the inevitability of its demise – arguably has greater immediacy and salience than any other, which in turn raises the stakes even higher. Perhaps for this reason, some of the most interesting and promising research seeking to move beyond the securitisation frame – via concepts such as 'reproblematisation', 'desecuritisation' and 'politicisation' – can be found in contemporary debates about the relation between security and health. These debates not only offer alternative ways of rethinking that relationship, but also pose questions back to critical security studies scholarship via its encounter with health issues – not least the question concerning what it might mean to be 'critical' in this context.

Key points

- Whereas traditionally health was linked to security in the context of the potential impact of disease on serving members of the armed forces, the national security strategies and foreign policies of many states have recently broadened to include health issues such as HIV/AIDS.
- The discourse of global public health has increasingly been framed using the language of security and the World Health Organization is often regarded as a key securitising actor in this context.
- There is no consensus on whether the securitisation of health is a normatively desirable move: some argue that it brings greater attention and funding to issues that are otherwise neglected; others claim that it privileges Western interests, limits the range of policy solutions and fails to address underlying structural inequalities.
- A number of studies have sought to move beyond the securitisation framework when addressing global health, for example, via the lenses of medicalisation, therapeutic intervention and politicisation.
- Health issues raise the question of the relationship between theory and practice, and challenge scholars of critical security studies to reflect on what it means to be 'critical'.

Discussion points

- In what ways can health be considered a security threat?
- Should HIV/AIDS be securitised for the benefit of those infected by the disease?
- What are the strengths and weaknesses of securitisation as an approach to understanding the health–security nexus?
- How has the concept of security been transformed via its connection with international health issues?
- In what ways do 'therapeutic interventions' depoliticise war and violence?
- What does it mean to approach the issue of health from a 'critical' perspective?

Guide to further reading

Stefan Elbe (2010) *Security and Global Health: Toward the Medicalization of Insecurity* (Cambridge: Polity Press). Applies insights from the sociology of medicalisation and the work of Michel Foucault to study the changing nature of security and insecurity in contemporary political life.

Alison Howell (2011) *Madness in International Relations: Psychology, Security, and the Global Governance of Mental Health* (London and New York: Routledge). Examines the role of psychosocial approaches in global security relations and the politics of medicalised interventions.

Colin McInnes and Lee Kelley (2012) *Global Health and International Relations* (Cambridge: Polity Press). Offers a constructivist account of the relationship between health and IR and explores security as one of a number of framings of that relationship.

João Nunes (2013) *Security, Emancipation and the Politics of Health: A New Theoretical Perspective* (London and New York: Routledge). Highlights the politics of health and advances an agenda for rethinking security via a reformulated approach to emancipation.

World Health Organization (2007) *A Safer Future: Global Public Health Security in the 21st Century*, Geneva: WHO. Sets out the WHO's understanding of major health challenges and vision for the future of global public health security.

Weblinks

World Health Organization: http://www.who.int/en/

Centre for Health and International Relations (CHAIR), Department of International Politics, Aberystwyth University: http://www.aber.ac.uk/en/interpol/research/research-centres-and-institutes/chair/

Centre for Global Health Policy, University of Sussex: http://www.sussex.ac.uk/globalhealthpolicy/

9 Homeland security and the 'war against terrorism'

Abstract

This chapter introduces the concept of homeland security, and practices carried out in its name, against the backdrop of the global war against terrorism. It begins with a brief overview of the concept of terrorism in comparative and historical context. The discussion then turns to consider two cases of the response to the perceived threat of terrorism by Western governments: the rise of the Department of Homeland Security (DHS) in the US; and parallel counterterrorism initiatives in the UK. Connecting the study of homeland security and the war against terrorism with some of the theoretical perspectives outlined in Part I, the chapter then introduces two prominent 'applications' of critical thinking in security studies: 'critical terrorism studies' and the CHALLENGE project. Finally, especially in the light of the changing imperatives of the Obama presidency, the chapter ends by questioning the future direction of the war against terrorism.

Introduction

On 11 September 2001 ('9/11') two passenger jets were flown into the twin towers of the World Trade Center (WTC) in New York and a third plane crashed into the Pentagon in Washington, DC. In total the two attacks led to the deaths of approximately 3500 people. Within hours of the first attack on the WTC, US President George W. Bush declared a global 'war against terrorism'. Al-Qaeda, a radical Islamist network led by Osama bin Laden, was held responsible for the atrocities, but the US responded militarily by targeting specific *states* thought to harbour terrorists and weapons of mass destruction (WMD). On 7 October 2001 operation 'Enduring Freedom' was launched against the Taliban government in Afghanistan; and on 20 March 2003 operation 'Iraqi Freedom' began with the aim of toppling Saddam Hussein's Ba'athist regime.

Since 9/11, 'terrorism' has taken centre stage in debates about new security challenges facing the West. On the one hand, we might want to question whether this focus is warranted. After all, every day three times as many people die of HIV/AIDS in the global South as those who were killed on 9/11 (see Chapter 8). By concentrating too much on the perceived terrorist threat, it might be argued that other, more pressing security issues (such as those discussed in other chapters in Part II of this book) are wrongly marginalised. On the other hand, however, irrespective of whether we agree with the prominence given to terrorism in global security relations, the human costs of the war against terrorism should be underlined. Data on the number of Afghan civilian fatalities resulting from operation Enduring Freedom were not collected rigorously before 2007 and precise numbers remain unknown. As of March

2011 the total is estimated to be 8832, according to the Independent Human Rights Commission and the United Nations Assistance Mission in Afghanistan. In addition, more than 4000 Taliban soldiers have died and as of January 2014, coalition military fatalities stood at 3416 (www.icasualties.org). Operation Iraqi Freedom claimed between 97461 and 106348 civilian deaths up to July 2010 and more than 15,000 Iraqi military lives (BBC); as of January 2014 a total of 4804 coalition service personnel had been killed in Iraq (www.icasualties.org). The financial costs of the war against terrorism are also worthy of note, though equally difficult to calculate: the Congressional Research Service estimates that the US spent nearly $802 billion on the Iraq war by the end of the fiscal year 2011.

In addition to human and financial costs, the threat of terrorism has also led to a series of responses by governments that affect citizens' everyday lives: enhanced airport security measures; heightened levels of surveillance; new forms of identity capture and management; the cultivation of a climate of fear and suspicion; more vigorous policing and use of 'stop and search' measures; harsher legislative conditions; the rise of the 'resilient society'; and moves to prioritise national security imperatives ahead of personal liberty. These practices, which enable particular forms of governance of populations as a means of dealing with the perceived terrorist threat, have increasingly come to be defined in terms of homeland security and resilience. As Ole Wæver (2008) has argued, the idea of homeland security is not simply yet another name for territorial defence within the confines of the state, but rather a new set of logics increasingly focused on individuals and networks across the globe.

Terrorism in context

When thinking about the prominence given to terrorism in debates about security since 9/11 it is important to bear in mind that the concept of 'terrorism' is not something new. 'La Terreur' was used to describe the period of violence after the French Revolution, between 5 September 1793 and 27 July 1794, which saw the killing of enemies of the new Republic. More recent examples of terrorism in the twentieth century include the campaigns of the Tamil Tigers in Sri Lanka, the Basque separatist group Euskadi Ta Askatasuna (ETA) in Spain and the Provisional Irish Republican Army (PIRA) in Northern Ireland. Al-Qaeda's operations also pre-date 2001, as the group claimed responsibility for the bombings of US embassies in Nairobi and Dar es Salaam in August 1998, which killed over 200 and injured over 5000 people. More generally, variants of Islamic terrorism were perceived to be a threat prior to 9/11 in Russia, Israel, Thailand, the Philippines and Indonesia.

What is an act of 'terrorism'? Some scholars argue that it is possible to distinguish terrorism as a particular form of political violence. Paul Wilkinson (2000), for example, has identified what he considers to be the defining characteristics of a terrorist attack: a premeditated intent to create fear; a target audience beyond those who are victims; a deliberately random choice of (particularly civilian) victims; a motive to affect political behaviour especially that of governments; and a perception by the society within which it has taken place that something 'extra-normal' has occurred. While these characteristics seem intuitive, however, the more we probe the concept of terrorism the more complex it becomes. Who decides what and/or who is a terrorist? Are there different forms of terrorism? Must terrorists always be non-state actors?

As well as a lengthy history, the use of the concept of terrorism is also deeply political. It is not the case that a particular individual, group or organisation is ever self-evidently 'terroristic'. Rather, the label 'terrorist' is something that is *applied* and as such it can be highly controversial. Much depends on particular circumstances and sometimes the designation of someone as a 'terrorist' can change dramatically over time. At the height of 'the Troubles' in Northern Ireland, for example, Martin McGuinness was considered by the British government to be an outlaw due to his involvement with the activity of the PIRA. Yet, 30 years or so later, McGuinness became deputy leader of the Northern Ireland Assembly at the heart of new power-sharing arrangements under devolution. Similarly, as the leader of the African National Congress, Nelson Mandela was found guilty of sabotage during the apartheid

---

Box 9.1 'Official' definitions of terrorism

1   UN Security Council Resolution 1566 (passed in October 2004) defines terrorism as:

Criminal acts, including [those] against civilians, committed with the intent to cause death or serious bodily injury, or taking of hostages, with the purpose to provoke a state of terror in the general public or in a group of persons or particular persons, intimidate a population or compel a government or an international organisation to do or to abstain from doing any act, which constitute offences within the scope of and as defined in the international conventions and protocols relating to terrorism, are under no circumstances justifiable by considerations of a political, philosophical, ideological, racial, ethnic, religious or other similar nature.

2   The official American definition of terrorism can be found in US Code Title 22, Section 2656f(d) (1983):

The term 'terrorism' means premeditated politically motivated violence perpetrated against non-combatant targets by sub-national groups or clandestine agents, usually intended to influence an audience.

The term 'international terrorism' means terrorism involving the citizens or the territory of more than one country.

The term 'terrorist group' means any group practicing, or that has significant subgroups that practice, international terrorism.

3   The UK Terrorism Act (2000) defines terrorism as follows:

(1)   In this Act 'terrorism' means the use or threat of action where–
  (a)   the action falls within subsection (2),
  (b)   the use of threat is designed to influence the government or to intimidate the public or a section of the public, and
  (c)   the use or threat is made for the purpose of advancing a political, religious, or ideological cause.

(2)   Action falls within this subsection if it–
  (a)   involves serious violence against a person,
  (b)   involves serious damage to property,
  (c)   endangers a person's life, other than that of the person committing the action,
  (d)   creates a serious risk to the health or safety of the public or a section of the public, or
  (e)   is designed seriously to interfere with or seriously disrupt an electronic system.

(3)   The use or threat of action falling within subsection (2) which involves the use of firearms or explosives is terrorism whether or not subsection (1)(b) is satisfied.

regime in South Africa and was imprisoned for 27 years. Four years after his release from prison in 1990, however, Mandela became the country's first president to be elected democratically. Indeed, Mandela is one of four former 'terrorists' who have gone on to win the Nobel Peace Prize (the others being Menachim Begin, Sean McBride and Yassir Arafat). Shifts in political contexts, therefore, can radically alter who and what gets labelled as a 'terrorist'.

Another complicating factor in thinking about the phenomenon of terrorism is that it tends to act as an umbrella term for many diverse political causes. One form of terrorism, as in the cases of the Tamil Tigers, ETA and the PIRA, is *ethno-national* terrorism. What is common to these groups is a series of claims on (usually a portion of) the territory of an existing sovereign state based upon familiar narratives of 'blood and soil'. Another type is *ideological* terrorism, which, for example, is illustrated by the activities of the so-called 'Red Brigades' during the 1970s and 1980s in Italy, who attempted to establish a neo-communist state. There are also examples of *issue-based* terrorism such as the wave of (often violent) animal rights protests across the UK during the 1980s. Al-Qaeda, with its expressed intentions of evicting 'foreign' forces from the Middle East, replacing 'corrupt' pro-Western governments such as those in Saudi Arabia, Egypt and Pakistan, and establishing a pan-Islamic caliphate, are usually thought of (in the West, at least) as a kind of *religio-political* terrorist organisation.

The *referent object* of terrorism also demands consideration. Traditionally, it has been assumed that terrorists are either individuals or groups labelled as such. More recently, however, some analysts of terrorism have sought to emphasise that states can be terrorists too (see, for example, Blakeley 2007). Indeed, given the apparatuses available to it, the state has historically cultivated fear and relied upon repressive measures. In this context, for example, we might point to the colonial period in Africa, the era of the purges in Stalin's Russia, state terror in Latin America, or, perhaps most obviously, the Third Reich in Germany. In the context of the war against terrorism, President Bush famously denounced Iraq, Iran and North Korea as terroristic states forming an 'axis of evil'. More subtly, though, state terrorism can also take the form of strategic bombing, certain forms of governance and even counterterrorism. On this expanded view, given the range of often illiberal and anti-democratic measures used to combat the threat of terror, Western democratic states have been accused of acquiring the 'terroristic' characteristics of the enemies they seek to overcome. Thus, according to Noam Chomsky (2000), the US has become the greatest of all rogue states. Again, these examples highlight the enormous political capital of the concept of terrorism.

While the phenomenon of terrorism is clearly not something new or straightforward, some writers argue that the specific threat faced from Al-Qaeda is nevertheless qualitatively different from its historical forebears. Wilkinson (2007b), for instance, points to key differences between Al-Qaeda and other terrorist organisations in terms of scope (it is not territorially delimited to one state but a global network), method (it opts for mass killing as demonstrated by attacks in New York, Washington, Kenya, Bali, Casablanca, Saudi Arabia and Iraq) and aims (it seeks nothing less than a change in the nature of the international system). Crucially, whether or not we see Al-Qaeda as a unique threat, a distinctive range of counterterrorist measures has emerged in response under the banner of homeland security.

US homeland security

The use of the term homeland security in the US context pre-dates the events of 9/11. Discussions about the provision for a new national homeland security agency took place following the publication of the Hart–Rudman Commission Report in February 2001. The attacks later that year expedited the process of establishing the agency. In his 'Fear and freedom are at war' speech to Congress on 20 September, President Bush announced the creation of a new Office of Homeland Security (OHS). Tom Ridge, the then governor of Pennsylvania, was appointed as its first director. The stated aim of the OHS was to oversee and coordinate a comprehensive national strategy to safeguard the country against terrorism and respond to any future attacks. In June 2002, however, President Bush proposed the upgrading of the OHS to a Cabinet-level DHS. With the passing of the 2002 Homeland Security Act, the DHS became fully operational on 24 January 2003, with an annual budget of $100 billion.

Prior to the establishment of the DHS, homeland security activities were spread across 40 different federal agencies. Indeed, the '9/11 Commission Report' cited the lack of a coordinated approach as a factor in the failure to prevent the attacks (National Commission on Terrorist Attacks upon the United States 2004: 384–385). As such, the DHS constituted a major reorganisation of US federal government. In terms of its remit, the Department was tasked with four main 'mission' areas from the outset:

1   *Border and Transportation Security* – to control the borders and prevent terrorists and explosives from entering the country.
2   *Emergency Preparedness and Response* – to work with state and local authorities to respond quickly and effectively to emergencies.
3   *Chemical, Biological, Radiological and Nuclear Countermeasures* – to bring together the country's best scientists to develop technologies that detect biological, chemical and nuclear weapons to best protect citizens.
4   *Information Analysis and Infrastructure Protection* – to review intelligence and law enforcement information from all agencies of government, and produce a single daily picture of threats against the homeland.

Taken together these missions indicate the extent to which, above and beyond the institutional shifts inaugurated by the DHS, the concept of homeland security represents a fundamental shift in the organisation of American society. Many of the legal foundations for this shift were provided for in the US Patriot Act, which President Bush signed into law on 26 October 2001. This act allowed for a range of new measures such as an increase in powers of state surveillance, national search warrants, the detention of foreigners without trial for up to seven days without charge and the deportation of suspected terrorists. The extent and depth of homeland security, as further outlined in the 'National Strategy' published in July 2002 (see Box 9.2), places the US nation on a quasi-war footing. Indeed, the controversial colour-coded Homeland Security Advisory System, introduced in 2002 by the DHS and abandoned in 2011, indicated the perceived level of risk from terrorist attack and served as a daily reminder to US citizens of their nation's involvement in the war against terrorism.

Since its inception, the Advisory System was not lowered beyond the yellow or 'elevated' level. Effectively, the 'normal' state of affairs in the US became one where the 'significant risk of terrorist attacks' was permanent. The extent to which the Advisory System offered a sense of security among the US population is a vexed question, however. A permanently 'elevated' state implied heightened vigilance to combat potential risk, which may have offered some citizens peace of mind. However, the traffic light system itself may have also created fear, panic and a sense of insecurity among people. Of course, we cannot be completely sure what affect the Advisory System had (it was interpreted by different people

---

Box 9.2 The National Strategy for Homeland Security

The White House released the first National Strategy for Homeland Security in July 2002. Below is an extract from President Bush's preface to the document.

> My fellow Americans:
> [...] We must rally our entire society to overcome a new and complex challenge. Homeland security is a shared responsibility. In addition to a national strategy, we need compatible, mutually supporting state, local, and private-sector strategies. Individual volunteers must channel their energy and commitment in support of the national and local strategies. [...]
>   The *National Strategy for Homeland Security* is a beginning. It calls for bold and necessary steps. It creates a comprehensive plan for using America's talents and resources to enhance our protection and reduce our vulnerability to terrorist attacks. [...]
>   Our enemy is smart and resolute. We are smarter and more resolute. We will prevail against all who believe they can stand in the way of America's commitment to freedom, liberty, and our way of life.
>
>   George W. Bush

The National Strategy defined what is meant by the term 'homeland security' through the identification of three objectives:

> Homeland security is an exceedingly complex mission. It involves efforts both at home and abroad. It demands a range of government and private sector capabilities. And it calls for coordinated and focused effort from many actors who are not otherwise required to work together and for whom security is not always a primary mission. This strategy establishes three objectives based on the definition of homeland security:
>
> 1   Prevent terrorist attacks within the United States
> 2   Reduce America's vulnerability to terrorism
> 3   Minimize the damage and recover from attacks that do occur.

---

in multiple ways), but it was striking as a particular political method of governing the population via a politics of fear (Massumi 2005).

As well as mobilising domestic society in the US, efforts to secure the homeland have implications for the globe as a whole. The National Strategy for Homeland Security makes it clear that defending the US against the threat of terrorism is necessary 'both at home and abroad':

> In a world where the terrorist threat pays no respect to traditional boundaries, our strategy for homeland security cannot stop at our borders. America must pursue a sustained, steadfast, and systematic international agenda to counter the global terrorist threat and improve our homeland security.
>
>   (2002: xii)

Thus, in a speech celebrating the fifth anniversary of the DHS, President Bush declared it was better to face enemies '*over there* than here in the US'. In this way, operations Enduring Freedom and Iraqi Freedom can be read precisely as acts of homeland security, albeit overseas. This raises an interesting geopolitical question about what and where the limits of the

US homeland actually are. These limits are not necessarily coterminous with the physical territorial borders of the US. Rather, in the light of the so-called 'Bush Doctrine' of pre-emption, military strikes in defence of the US homeland can occur virtually anywhere in the world. According to this doctrine, the US claims the right to take military action against any state it believes to be harbouring or supporting terrorists. For this reason, some writers have argued that it is now impossible to maintain any rigorous distinction between the 'internal' and 'external' dimensions of US security policy (Bigo *et al.* 2007). Instead, an image of the US homeland is arguably being projected on to the globe in its entirety, as satirised by the film *Team America: World Police* (2004).

UK counterterrorism

While homeland security has become the headline term for an array of policies and practices in the US context, it has not been embraced to the same extent in the UK context. The UK does not have a direct equivalent to the US DHS nor a single-response framework for dealing with emergencies such as the bombings in London on 7 July 2005. Rather, the UK's response to the threat of terrorism consists of civil contingencies legislation, specific counterterrorism measures and a civil protection capabilities enhancement programme. According to some writers, this difference is symptomatic of other divergences between the US and the UK concerning views of radical Islam, levels of commitment to military action and 'strategic culture' in response to the threat of terrorism more generally (Rees and Aldrich 2005). Of course, one of the potentially significant differences between the US and UK is the broader historical perspective in which this threat is perceived. Whereas terrorism is a relatively recent phenomenon in the US, the UK has a longer history of terrorism and counterterrorism on its own territory.

Between 1967 and 1998 over 3500 people, both civilians and military personnel, were killed during 'the Troubles' in Northern Ireland. The activities of the PIRA, which sought a united Irish Republic on the island of Ireland, included car bombings, mortar attacks, assassinations, letter bombings and kidnappings. On 21 November 1974, for example, the group claimed responsibility for an attack on a pub in central Birmingham that killed 20 civilians and injured over 180. In a spiral of violence, loyalist groups, those in favour of the Union of Northern Ireland and Great Britain such as the UDA (Ulster Defence Army), UFF (Ulster Freedom Fighters) and UVF (Ulster Volunteer Force), were equally engaged in campaigns of terror throughout the same period. Among the atrocities carried out by the UDA was the so-called 'Greysteel massacre' on Halloween in 1993, which killed 8 people and injured a further 19. Beyond paramilitary violence, some writers also draw attention to what they consider to be British state terror during the 'long war'. Wilkinson (2007a), for instance, highlights the way in which, primarily in response to the Republican threat, a range of repressive measures were introduced. In this context, the zenith of state terrorism in the Northern Irish context was the shooting of 14 unarmed Catholic civilians by British soldiers in Londonderry on 30 January 1972, known as 'Bloody Sunday'.

The basis of post-9/11 counterterrorism legislation in the UK has its roots in the 'the Troubles' (Bigo and Guittet 2011). In 1973 the Northern Ireland Emergency Provisions Act provided for special police powers and criminal justice procedures including scheduled offences (trial by judge without jury) and internment (detention without trial). One year later, in the aftermath of the Birmingham pub bombing, the Prevention of Terrorism Act extended these measures by allowing for: the exclusion of suspected terrorists either through refusal of entry to Britain or deportation; the enhancement of 'stop and search' powers granted to port police; the extension of detention without charge to seven days; and the permission to arrest without a warrant anyone 'reasonably suspected' of being a terrorist or associated with terrorism. In 1998 the signing of the Good Friday Peace Agreement brought devolved government to Northern Ireland. Despite the Agreement, however, it is still not clear that 'the Troubles' are fully over, as evidenced by on-going intra-community violence and the murder of two army personnel and an officer of the Police Service of Northern Ireland (PSNI) in separate incidents during March 2009. Nevertheless, more recent legislation takes as its starting point the assumption that the more pressing threat comes from international terrorism, specifically: (1) Al-Qaeda and its associates, located mainly on the Pakistan/Afghanistan border; (2) groups affiliated to Al-Qaeda in North Africa, the Arabian Peninsula, Iraq and Yemen; (3) self-starting cells or individuals with no relation to Al-Qaeda; and (4) groups similar to Al-Qaeda but with their own identity and/or regional agenda (Home Office 2009, 2011).

The shifting focus on international terrorism in the UK was evident before 9/11 with the 2000 Terrorism Act, which exported anti-terror measures designed initially for Northern Ireland across the UK as a whole. This was followed by the 2001 Anti-Terrorism, Crime and Security Act, providing for additional powers to freeze and seize terrorists' financial assets and detention pending the deportation of foreign nationals suspected of terrorist activity. In 2003 the Civil Contingencies Act was accompanied by greater capital investment in emergency response, operational facilities and business contingency arrangements. Since 2003, UK counterterrorism policy has been coordinated through the so-called 'CONTEST' strategy. CONTEST incorporates four primary 'workstreams' – PURSUE, PREVENT, PROTECT and PREPARE – and its stated aim is 'to reduce the risk to the UK and its interests overseas from international terrorism, so that people can go about their lives freely and with confidence' (Home Office 2009: 8). The 'PURSUE and PREVENT' workstreams relate to the reduction of the threat of terrorism while 'PROTECT and PREPARE' aim to enhance the UK's resilience (see Box 9.3) against attack.

Following the London bombings on 7 July 2005, in which 52 people were killed along with four suicide bombers, there has been a broadening of the scope and an intensification of the activities of CONTEST. A particular focus under the PREVENT strand has been on countering the so-called 'process of radicalisation' whereby formerly moderate British Muslim citizens come to support violent extremism and/or join terrorist groups (Heath-Kelly 2013). This controversial approach to the perceived threat of 'homegrown terrorists' has led scholars to argue that there has in effect been a 'securitisation of Islam' in Britain (Croft 2012). The 2006 Terrorism Act made the preparation of terrorist attacks, the giving and receiving of training for terrorist purposes, and the attendance at a place used for terrorist training new offences under UK law. More recently, the 2008 Counter-Terrorism Act gave the police stronger asset-freezing powers, enhanced powers of entry into private property, the right to remove documents and take DNA and fingerprints from those on control orders, permission to question terrorist suspects after they had been charged, tougher sentences for convicted terrorists, and new controls on those who have been released after serving their sentence.

Despite the differences that some writers perceive between the US and UK, however, there are similarities across the Atlantic in the emerging field of homeland security. Emulating the DHS threat advisory system, the UK Home Office has made its assessments publicly available since August 2006. As in the US, there are five levels of threat in the UK: critical (an attack is expected imminently); severe (an attack is highly likely); substantial (an attack is a strong possibility); moderate (an attack is possible but not likely); and low (an attack is unlikely). Innovation in the field of border security, whereby borders are

---

Box 9.3 Security, citizenship and resilience

The increasing propensity for Western governments to frame security in terms of risk and preemption (see Box 5.5) has also given rise to the closely related notion of resilience (Brassett *et al.* 2013). Derived from the Latin *resilio* – meaning to 'jump back' – resilience is increasingly viewed by policy-makers as the horizon for living with a range of risks including terrorism, cyber crime, financial crisis, flooding and critical infrastructure collapse. In the UK, for example, the first stated objective of the 2010 National Security Strategy is to 'ensure a secure and *resilient* UK by protecting our people, economy, infrastructure, territory, and ways of life from all major risks that can affect us directly'.

Whereas emergency planning in the context of the cold war era involved the prediction of events and the protection of society against known threats, the idea of resilience pays greater emphasis to societal adaptation in the face of potentially unknowable risks (Walker and Cooper 2011). For this reason, resilience is associated with broader socioeconomic changes linked with neoliberalism: citizens, communities and businesses are enjoined by governments to be entrepreneurial in taking steps to manage their own risks. A resilient society is therefore not only able to 'jump back' from disorder wrought by high-impact, low-probability events, but one that is able to exploit the opportunities of risk in order to emerge stronger.

In security studies the concept of resilience has been studied as an integral part of the risk management cycle in multiple contexts, including: civil contingency planning (Adey and Anderson 2011, 2012); critical national infrastructure protection (Lundborg and Vaughan-Williams 2011; Zebrowski 2009); cities and public spaces (Coaffee 2010; Coaffee *et al.* 2008); international state-building, aid and development (Chandler 2013; Duffield 2012; Reid 2012). Against this backdrop, there is also an increasing interest in the role of the citizen in counterterrorism measures and the extent to which government attempts at cultivating societal resilience have gained traction at the level of the everyday (Jarvis and Lister 2013b; Malcolm 2013).

---

increasingly based upon off-shore identity capture and management, is another example of convergence between the two countries (for more see Chapter 11). The launch of the UK's first ever 'National Security Strategy' in 2008 also reflects shared thinking with the US about how it might be possible to involve society at large in the common task of fighting the war against terrorism.

Critical perspectives on the war against terrorism

The rise of homeland security and the global war against terrorism more generally has stimulated new thinking and research agendas in critical security studies. Here we consider two prominent developments in the field: 'critical terrorism studies'; and international political sociology inspired scholarship on the relationship between liberty and security.

Critical terrorism studies

Richard Jackson refers to 'critical terrorism studies' (CTS) not as a 'precise theoretical label', but rather in terms of 'a sceptical attitude towards state-centric understandings of terrorism […] which does not take existing terrorism knowledge for granted but is willing to challenge widely held assumptions and beliefs' (Jackson 2007: 246).

According to Jackson, the CTS project is partly animated by four areas of critique of traditional approaches to the study of terrorism. First, it is claimed that much of the conventional terrorism literature suffers from an 'embarrassing list of methodological and analytical weaknesses' such as: a paucity of reflection on research methods; an over-reliance upon secondary rather than primary sources of information; an absence of any rigorous analytical definition of terrorism; a privileging of description over analysis; a lack of inter-disciplinarity; the dominance of orthodox approaches to IR; the tendency to see terrorism as something 'new' since 9/11; a lack of attention given to forms of state terror; and an overly policy-prescriptive agenda. Second, the reliance of traditional terrorism studies on orthodox security studies and counterinsurgency literature is highlighted as a problem: as well as a privileging of the state as the referent object of study this work also reproduces a very narrow set of narratives and assumptions about the causes of and responses to terrorism. Third, the 'embedded' and self-referential nature of terrorism expertise is identified as a limited horizon within which 'terrorism scholars are directly linked to state institutions and sources of power that make it difficult to distinguish between the state and academic spheres' (Jackson 2007: 245). Finally, CTS is critical of what is considered to be the 'problem-solving' logic of traditional terrorism studies, which takes the world as it finds it rather than questioning the status quo and relations of power/knowledge that (re)produce it.

Beyond critique, the CTS project seeks to contribute to terrorism studies via three epistemological, ontological and ethical-normative commitments. Epistemologically, CTS acknowledges that knowledge is a social process that is produced inter-subjectively in different contexts. As such, knowledge claims are always implicated in what Michel Foucault referred to as 'regimes of truth': what counts as 'true' will depend on hegemonic understandings of 'facts' that by definition exclude alternative thinking and practice (for more on Foucault see Chapter 5). On this basis, Jackson argues that 'CTS starts by asking: who is terrorism knowledge for and what functions does it serve in supporting their interests?' (2007: 246). The view that knowledge is fundamentally bound up with power means that CTS deems the pursuit of objective research in terrorism studies to be impossible. Instead, what is called for is an approach that focuses on *how* knowledge claims work in different contexts in order to establish particular regimes of truth. This locates CTS within a post-positivist framework, which is methodologically pluralist drawing on perspectives such as deconstruction, genealogy, ethnography, historical narratives, Gramscianism and constructivism. In a similar manner, although less explicitly positioned within CTS, Stuart Croft (2006) has examined the ways in which the meaning of the war against terror was constructed in the aftermath of 9/11 via various cultural artefacts – television, billboards, bumper stickers and even jokes. Croft does this by using methods drawn from cultural studies and discourse analysis that are well beyond the methodological toolbox of conventional terrorism studies, examining how, for example, the television show *24* became a cultural resource and referent point for justifications for the use of torture in the war against terrorism.

Ontologically, CTS is committed to adopting a sceptical stance in relation to the concept of terrorism. That is to say, 'terrorism' is not anything in and of itself, but a 'tool employed at specific times, for specific periods of time, by specific actors and for specific political goals' (Jackson 2007: 248). While the effects of terrorism constitute 'brutal facts' often involving the loss of life, what counts as terrorist behaviour is a 'social fact' established through inter-subjective practice. Therefore, CTS does not work with a particular definition of terrorism against which it can 'test' certain scenarios. Rather, CTS takes its lead from the political economy within which the label 'terrorism' circulates and is applied: 'CTS is committed to questioning the nature and politics of representation – why, when, how, and for what purposes do groups and individuals come to be named as "terrorist" and what consequences does this have' (Jackson 2007: 248).

Finally, the recognition that the definition of an individual, group, institution or event as 'terroristic' is also a judgement about who may be legitimately killed or tortured, leads CTS scholars to reflect on the ethical-normative dimensions of terrorism studies. Again, rather than pursuing 'objectivity', their aim is to foreground their expressed commitments to 'the values and priorities of universal human and societal security, rather than traditional, narrowly defined conceptions of national security in which the state takes precedence over any other actor' (Jackson 2007: 249). Jackson argues that the CTS project aims to 'go beyond critique and deconstruction' in order to offer a perspective that positively constructs an agenda for social change (2007: 249). It is here that the 'critical' dimension of CTS most obviously overlaps with the tradition of Critical Theory in social and political thought and the so-called Welsh School of security studies (see Chapter 1). In this vein, Matt McDonald identifies the key ethical-normative question posed by CTS as: 'What are the imminent possibilities for emancipatory change in the context of contemporary practices of terrorism and counter-terrorism?' (McDonald 2007: 256).

What is clear is that the theoretical foundations of CTS are deliberately broad, drawing on an array of different understandings of what it means to be 'critical' (see also Jackson *et al.* 2011). On the one hand, this is perhaps to be celebrated, as it mobilises the insights of many of the perspectives introduced in Part I of this book. On the other hand, such is the breadth of influence that some authors have expressed a concern that the movement runs the risk of lacking coherence (Gunning 2007).

Liberty and security in Europe

Reflecting an IPS approach to security studies (as outlined in Chapter 5), the CHALLENGE project offers an examination of the relation between liberty and security against the backdrop of the war against terrorism in Europe. In the 'Mid-Term Report on the Results of the CHALLENGE Project', Didier Bigo, Sergio Carrera, Elspeth Guild and R.B.J. Walker articulate the overall aim of the research programme as follows: 'CHALLENGE seeks to provide a critical assessment of the liberties of citizens and others living within the EU and how they are affected by the proliferation of discourses about insecurities and the exchange of new techniques of surveillance and control' (Bigo *et al.* 2007: 2).

The project takes as its starting point the observation that in the post-9/11 context liberal democratic governments have resorted to illiberal practices in response to the perceived threat of international terrorism.

By 'illiberal practices' the authors refer to: the rise of a more severe legislative climate; heightened levels of unease; declarations of emergency conditions; the disestablishment of the importance of human rights; the justification of the development of more sophisticated technologies for mass surveillance and exchange of individual data; and the merging of the vision and role of the police, military and intelligence agencies.

Bigo *et al.* argue that there are various defining characteristics of the model of governance underpinning these practices, which can be summarised as: a privileging of the logic of security over liberty; the emergence of a new paradigm of generalised suspicion; and the justification of illiberal practices through references to 'exceptional' national security imperatives. It is worth paying closer attention to these three dimensions in turn as they have come to influence recent scholarship on the war against terrorism associated with the so-called Paris School approach to security (see Chapter 5).

First, the Treaty of Amsterdam, which came into force in European law in 1999, provided for the establishment of an 'Area of Freedom, Security and Justice' (AFSJ) within the territorial borders of the member states of the EU. In order to implement the provisions of the Treaty the accompanying Tampere Programme adopted the rule of law as the core of the development of the AFSJ. Five years later, however, following the attacks of 9/11 and the bombings in Bali and Madrid, The Hague Programme adopted a new policy agenda that revised this basic principle. Instead of putting the rule of law first it was claimed that an alternative approach was required in the light of the heightened threat posed by international terrorism: one that seeks to *balance* liberty on the one hand, with *security* on the other. According to Bigo *et al.* (2007), this approach constitutes a 'major weakness' in the EU's on-going efforts to promote itself as an AFSJ. The 'balancing' metaphor implies, contrary to the Tampere formulation, that 'liberty' and 'security' are antithetical values to begin with. In turn, such a framing permits discussion about what sort of 'equilibrium' *should* be reached between the two, depending upon the circumstances of the day. Consequently, it *relativises* what was formerly an *absolute* commitment to the rule of law and this move opens the way for a privileging of security *over* liberty. Indeed, according to the authors of the CHALLENGE Report, this is precisely what has happened in the EU since 2004: 'The over-all priority which guides the [Hague] programme remains clear: strengthening security understood as coercion' (Bigo *et al.* 2007: 16).

Second, the CHALLENGE Report identifies what it refers to as a paradigm of generalised suspicion in the West, which accompanies governments' counterterrorist initiatives. Central to the emergence of this paradigm is the decoupling of practices of policing from judicial control. Such a move has enabled the intensification of surveillance techniques, which involve not only the watchful gaze of the state *over* the citizen but also vigilance *among* citizens. The central question facing the security sector in the EU and US has thus become how to deploy suspicion broadly enough to catch unknown people while not suspecting every-body. On the one hand, Bigo *et al.* argue that the US has lurched towards a generalised form of suspicion whereby every US citizen may be a potential terrorist. On the other hand, it is claimed that the response in the EU has been more measured by comparison, even after the attacks in Madrid and in London. Despite this qualitative difference in response, however, a common reliance upon the cultivation of fear and unease has nevertheless become a routinised practice of the intelligence services and police forces in both regions. By foster-ing a climate of suspicion groups of people can be risk profiled, assessed as 'friends' or 'enemies', and then dealt with accordingly (see also Bigo and Guittet 2011). As the CHALLENGE Report highlights, such an approach potentially marks a significant departure from traditional evidence-based modes of policing. Rather, it is argued, what has emerged in the West under the banner of the paradigm of suspicion is a more *anticipatory* logic based upon worst-case scenarios. In this way, *security* has become increasingly synonymous with *surveillance* and control rather than maintaining human rights and the rule of law.

Third, the CHALLENGE Report highlights the way in which illiberal practices of liberal regimes come to be justified with reference to discourses of *exceptionalism*. The concept of the exception has a rich political, philosophical (and theological) heritage within the tradi-tion of Western thought. Different thinkers have used the concept of the exception/exceptionalism in various ways (see Chapter 5 and Box 5.4). Today it is not uncommon to find the phrase 'exceptional times call for exceptional measures' used by politicians who seek to justify an array of illiberal practices such as those identified above. Indeed, throughout the war against terrorism, this phrase has been especially popular: former US President George W. Bush, for example, used it to justify the indefinite detention of 'unlawful enemy combatants' at the US naval base in Guantánamo Bay, Cuba. Clearly, however, the usage of this phrase is not something new or unique to the context of Western politics post-9/11 (Neocleous 2008). Rather, there is a long history of declarations of emergency conditions said to necessitate exceptional measures in the West. During the 1920s, for example, successive governments of the Weimar Republic in Germany repeatedly invoked emergency powers under Article 48 of the constitution. The use of discourses of exceptionalism in order to train populations to be suspicious of each other is also something far from new: Walter Benjamin, writing in 1938, argued that 'in times of terror, when everyone is something of a conspirator, everybody will be in the position of having to play detective' (Benjamin 2003: 21).

While formal declarations of states of emergency are few and far between in the West, the authors of the CHALLENGE Report argue that an intensified *logic of exceptionalism* nevertheless pervades contemporary counterterrorist policies. Such a logic enables techniques of governance, often of a *biopolitical* nature (such as torture, rendition or indefinite detention) that would otherwise be stymied by normal liberal democratic checks and balances on coercive and authoritarian regimes. Indeed, by invoking discourses of exceptionalism, such as the notion that in any given context it is precisely the security of the nation that is at stake, it is arguably more likely that populations in liberal democracies will not only sanction but in fact *demand* further illiberal practices.

An IPS-inspired approach to security thus shifts our analysis of the global war on terrorism on to a more *everyday* or 'vernacular' setting (see also Bubandt 2005; Jarvis and Lister 2013a). While the war on terror has involved large-scale military operations such as those in Afghanistan and Iraq, the CHALLENGE project enjoins us to also think about the ordinary or even banal ways in which it impacts on society. Through the training of populations to be suspicious, for example, the logics of the war against terrorism are (re)produced: 'good' citizens are trained to be on the lookout for 'risky' terrorist subjects. Such practices are not neutral but politically and ethically laden since, as Judith Butler has pointed out, the cultivation of an objectless suspicion all too easily translates into 'a virtual mandate to heighten racialised ways of looking and judging' (Butler 2004: 77). Furthermore, racialised forms of suspicion often lead to acts of violence in public places such as railway stations, as illustrated by the shooting of Jean Charles de Menezes in Stockwell Station, London, on 22 July 2005 (Pugliese 2006; Vaughan-Williams 2007).

Conclusion

For some scholars, the war against terrorism is more than simply a phase in post-cold war international politics. According to Richard Jackson, writing in the first half of the 2000s, 'the war has taken on a life of its own and any administration would find it extremely difficult to unmake or alter to any significant degree, even if they wanted to' (2005: 3). Nevertheless, with the end of the Bush administration and the election of Barak Obama as the 44th president of the US, it is possible to identify shifts away from the rhetoric of the war against terrorism. Indeed, during his period in office Obama has rarely used the sort of language favoured by Bush, preferring a more subtle framing. Similarly, in the UK context, there was a move to abandon the 'war against terrorism' phrase during the premiership of Gordon Brown. A Home Office 'phrase book' produced in 2008, for example, called upon civil servants instead to speak in terms of 'assisting vulnerable communities in building resilience against violent extremism and criminal murder' (quoted in Amoore 2008: 130; see Box 9.3). To this extent, we might question whether 'war against terrorism' is an increasingly outdated horizon within which to analyse global security relations.

However, despite what appears to be a rhetorical shift, the extent to which security practices have changed remains somewhat less clear. There are no signs of an intention to downgrade the elaborate homeland security infrastructure constructed largely in the aftermath of 9/11. Indeed, the DHS continues to be a funding priority of the Obama administration and, as we have seen, ever-more sophisticated methods of securing the homeland are being rolled out. Louise Amoore has written about the responsibility of critical scholars in being too quick to go along with the 'official' rejection of the language of the 'war on terrorism' in both the US and UK contexts. Amoore cites Foucault, who argued that 'the role of political power is perpetually to use a sort of silent war to reinscribe the relationship of force, and to reinscribe it in institutions, economic inequalities, language, and even the bodies of individuals' (quoted in Amoore 2008: 131). On this basis, she argues that the worry about simply rejecting or forgetting about the war against terrorism is that it serves to mask the less spectacular and yet often no less violent ways in which it continues to be played out. Given the extent to which such violence affects the everyday lives of vast numbers of the globe's population, it is precisely the 'normalisation' of the war against terrorism that critical security analysts should arguably be wary of.

Key points

- Terrorism is a political label: definitions of who and/or what are 'terroristic' can change dramatically according to context.
- The limits of the US 'homeland' stretch beyond the geographical territory of America and increasingly over the globe.
- The term 'homeland security' has not been embraced in the UK as much as in the US, but there are parallels between these states' responses to terrorism as reflected in their respective national security strategies.
- CTS is a movement that questions the methodology, state-centrism and conservatism of traditional approaches to terrorism.
- The CHALLENGE project explores the relation between liberty and security via a sociological interrogation of practices at the level of the everyday.

Discussion points

- To what extent is the current threat of international terrorism qualitatively different from historical precedents?
- What is the greatest threat facing Western populations: international terrorism or governments' responses to it?
- Where are the geographical limits of the US 'homeland'?
- How applicable are notions of 'emancipation' to the analysis of terrorism?
- What does a shift in focus to an analysis of the 'everyday' mean for the study of security?
- Is the war against terrorism a short-term reaction to 9/11 or a more substantive phase in global security relations?

Guide to further reading

Angharad Closs Stephens and Nick Vaughan-Williams (2008) (eds) *Terrorism and the Politics of Response* (Abingdon and New York: Routledge). A set of essays on the London bombings from poststructuralist perspectives.

Didier Bigo, Sergio Carrera, Elspeth Guild and R.B.J. Walker (2007) 'The Changing Landscape of European Liberty and Security: Mid-Term Report on the Results of the CHALLENGE Project', Research Paper No. 4, online, available at: www.libertysecurity.org/article1357.html (accessed 10 April 2009). An articulation of the aims of the CHALLENGE project.

European Political Science, 6 (2007). A symposium on CTS featuring key articles by Ruth Blakeley, Marie Breen Smyth, Jeroen Gunning and Richard Jackson.

Richard Jackson (2005) *Writing the War on Terrorism: Language, Politics, and Counter-Terrorism* (Manchester: Manchester University Press). A good starting point for an introduction to a CTS perspective on the war against terrorism.

Stuart Croft (2012) *Securitizing Islam: Identity and the Search for Security* (Cambridge: Cambridge University Press). Develops a post-Copenhagen School approach to trace how acts of securitisation shape the identity of securitiser and securitised against the backdrop of the war on terror in Britain.

Weblinks

The EU-funded CHALLENGE project: www.libertysecurity.org
US Department for Homeland Security: www.dhs.gov
UK Home Office: www.homeoffice.gov.uk

10 Human security and development

Abstract

The concept of 'human security' has achieved near-ubiquitous status within contemporary security discourse. For this reason alone it deserves critical scrutiny, but beyond its sheer prevalence the concept is especially deserving of attention as it seems, on the surface at least, to touch upon several key ideas and debates within critical security studies. These include: debates over the 'broadening' of security to encompass non-military issues; the relationship of security to freedom; and, most fundamentally, the idea of prioritising individual humans over the state in understandings of security. This chapter begins by detailing the rise to prominence of the idea of human security and the inroads it has made into both security policy and development practices globally. From there it assesses how the concept of human security fits within the broader notion of a 'security–development nexus' wherein human development and the management of security threats are seen to be inextricably linked. The latter sections of the chapter then engage critical debates on the meaning of human security, the scope of its application in development practices, and the question of whether human security ultimately challenges or reinforces traditional understandings of security.

Introduction

Of all the ideas covered within the pages of this book, few have generated as much attention – and contention – as the notion of 'human security'. In connecting security to the issue of human development, human security has aroused a range of responses. For some the concept holds the promise of 'security with a human face': that is, an understanding of security that is focused explicitly on the well-being and welfare of individuals rather than on the protection of states exclusively. For others, human security is at best an unhelpful chimera, and at worst an understanding so broad it both voids the concept of security of any substantive meaning and simultaneously subjects a whole new range of human activities to 'security' practices unnecessarily. Similarly, for those scholars grouped under the broad umbrella of critical security studies, the idea of human security provokes mixed feelings. Aspects of human security discourse seem to resonate with the 'emancipatory' impulse of some approaches, yet the practices associated with human security and development have still aroused much critical debate over whether the concept is simply a way of managing perceived risks to global security – most prominently the 'global South' – through new modes of intervention and administration. Is the idea of 'human security' a source of promise or peril? What are its potential pitfalls? This chapter engages these questions first by outlining the emergence of the concept of human security and its incorporation into development practices, and then by turning to a discussion of key critical perspectives on human security.

Human security: Assessing the concept

Whereas many elements of critical debates about security have tended to remain solely at a level of academic debate the notion of human security has become, in some contexts at least, part of a broader political discourse. Proponents of human security argue that human security is a 'people-centred' approach to security, and in this regard the concept seems to resonate with academic attempts to reassess – and redefine – the 'referent object' of security (see the Introduction to this text for an overview of this debate). However, advocates of human security, although engaging to some extent with broader academic arguments about security, have generally been less focused on theoretical debates about the nature of security and have instead concentrated more on trying to influence policy to take greater account of the security of individuals in a more practical sense (see Newman 2010). In fact, the concept of human security is frequently seen to have its basis not in academic debate but in the realm of policy, specifically the 1994 United Nations Development Programme (UNDP) Report, which is often pinpointed as a key original statement of the concept. Reference to the concept emanated initially not in the academic study of international security but in development studies and amongst bodies such as the UN.

As is noted elsewhere (see Chapter 2 and Chapter 4), one of the main criticisms of traditional, state-centric approaches to security that emerged in the 1990s was that traditional security studies was empirically unhelpful, in so far as its concentration on *inter*-state conflict has become less appropriate to the post-cold war world. For UNDP practitioners in the developing world during the 1990s and up to today, this limitation of traditional security studies was particularly evident. Since the mid-1990s, the vast majority of conflicts have taken place *within* rather than between states. Moreover, the majority of these *intra*-state conflicts have taken place in sub-Saharan Africa, with more people killed in conflicts in this region than any other part of the world in the post-cold war era (even though the total number of deaths from conflict globally have dropped off since the end of the cold war). In this context, programmes such as the UNDP have sought to shift the emphasis away from inter-state conflict exclusively towards issues of development, and the consequences that underdevelopment can have for the liberty and security of individuals. Echoing the general tenor of several critiques of 'traditional' definitions of security, the 1994 UNDP report asserted that:

> The concept of security has for too long been interpreted narrowly: as security of territory from external aggression, or as protection of national interests in foreign policy or as global security from the threat of nuclear holocaust. It has been related to nation-states more than people [...] Forgotten were the legitimate concerns of ordinary people who sought security in their daily lives. For many of them, security symbolized protection from the threat of disease, hunger, unemployment, crime, social conflict, political repression and environmental hazards. With the dark shadows of the Cold War receding, one can see that many conflicts are within nations rather than between nations.
>
> (UNDP 1994: 22)

The UNDP proposed the concept of 'human security' as an alternative to the traditional focus on state security. This interpretation of human security was famously formulated in the 1994 UNDP report as 'freedom from fear and freedom from want': freedom from fear denoting the aspiration that people should be secure from the threat of violence; and freedom from want denoting the aspiration that people should be free from poverty and destitution and entitled to basic means of survival. This is clearly distinct from the traditional focus of

---

Box 10.1 Human security: Policy impact and inroads

Several states have sought to make the case that enhancing the basic level of human security through development can encourage stability and act as a form of conflict prevention. Of particular note here is what is known as the 'Human Security Network', a coalition of states and non-governmental organisations that endorse the concept of human security. The human security network has been championed by Canada and Norway in particular, two states that have historically been particularly active in advocating the concept of human security (among the other 13 states involved in the network are Japan, the Netherlands, Ireland, Greece, Chile, Jordan and Mali). The Human Security Network has set itself the goal of 'strengthening human security with a view to creating a more humane world where people can live in security and dignity, free from want and fear, and with equal opportunities to develop their human potential to the full'. Issues that have been addressed (with varying degrees of success) by the network include: 'protection for civilians'; a ban on landmines; a permanent International Criminal Court; children's issues (including the optional protocol on the Rights of the Child on minimum ages of recruitment and deployment of soldiers); control of small arms and light weapons; and curtailment of drug trafficking, people trafficking and organised crime networks.

Canada in particular has been a driving force in developing the human security agenda at the international level, and the concept of human security has been a prominent one in Canadian foreign policy rhetoric. In 2000, Canada became one of the first states to devote dedicated funding to the issue of human security, and the landmines treaty – a Canadian-backed initiative signed as part of the Ottawa Convention of 1997 – is still regarded as one of the primary accomplishments of the human security agenda.

Norway has similarly identified an agenda of preventive action, control of small arms, and peace operations as the core components of its approach to human security. Japan has adopted an expansive conception of human security as a key aspect of its foreign policy to ensure 'human freedom and potential'.

The UNDP has been at the forefront of the promotion of the human security agenda, and other international organisations such as NEPAD (the New Partnership for African Development), the AU (African Union), and the EU have also begun to incorporate and use the concept.

---

security. As the UNDP report puts it, 'Human security is not a concern with weapons – it is a concern with human life and dignity' (1994: 22).

Beyond this the 1994 UNDP report identified four key characteristics of human security:

1   that human security is a *universal concern*, i.e. that applies equally to all people;
2   that the components of human security are interdependent, i.e. military and non-military sources of insecurity overlap;
3   that there is an emphasis on prevention rather than intervention;
4   that human security is 'people-centred'.

This in turn seems to parallel the 'broadening' of the security agenda within the academic study of security. In the developing world violent conflict still constitutes a major source of insecurity for people living in, for example, sub-Saharan Africa. But organisations such as the UN have also recognised that many of the threats facing people in the developing world are non-military in nature: political instability leading to state oppression and breakdown in basic provisions such as education and healthcare is also a major threat to individuals;

environmental degradation (such as processes of desertification) also threatens residents of sub-Saharan Africa in particular; and in the same region epidemics and pandemics such as HIV/AIDS have a devastating effect (on the latter, see Chapter 8).

For the original proponents of the human security concept, all of these factors – internal conflict, state breakdown, environmental degradation and disease – threaten the welfare and lives of individuals as much if not more than the threat of inter-state conflict. By consequence the UNDP 1994 report identified seven specific elements that comprise human security: (1) economic security (freedom from poverty); (2) food security (access to food); (3) health security (access to healthcare) (4) environmental security (protection from factors such as degradation and pollution); (5) personal security (physical safety from systematic use of violence); (6) community security (protection of traditional cultures and physical security of ethnic groups); and (7) political security (protection of civil liberties and freedom of political expression). At the fundamental core of this expansive conception of human security is a notion that all individuals, as human beings, have a right to exist free of such threats. As Thomas and Tow put it, the 'most fundamental application' of the concept of human security 'is to concentrate upon enhancing the physical security and economic welfare of *all* the world's inhabitants, notwithstanding their sovereign status or individual identity' (2002: 181, emphasis in original).

Development and security

As noted above, the concept of human security in principle applies equally to the security of *all* human beings irrespective of geographical location. In practice, though, the primary focus of human security as an academic and policy concern has been on the 'developing world'. In this sense the concept of human security emerges as much from the field of development studies as it does from security studies; as one prominent commentator notes, 'war and its effects are now an important part of development discourse' while, conversely, 'development concerns have become increasingly important in relation to how security is understood' (Duffield 2001: 1). Consequently, the issues of security and development have come to be merged in a number of important respects (see Box 10.2 and Box 10.4).

The concept of human security and its emergence is intimately related to the emergence of the idea of 'human development'. The early 1990s saw a shift away from conceptualising improvement in global standards of living in terms of economic growth towards a focus on the more holistic concept of 'human development', an idea first put forward in the UN's *Human Development Report* of 1990 (UNDP 1990). The concept of human development refers to the broad approach to expanding people's choices or capabilities not only in terms of income, but also in areas such as health, education, the environment and employment. This understanding of human development was influenced by the thinking of Amartya Sen, Harvard professor and a former honorary president of the charity Oxfam, who has created the so-called theory of capabilities or 'capability approach' based around the extent to which human beings have access to the basic facilities to maximise their potential. The UNDP also later developed the Human Development Index as a composite measure of income per capita, life expectancy at birth and educational attainment (see King and Murray 2001). Although we might debate the accuracy and basis of such measures (how would we define an acceptable level of educational attainment for example?), it is again notable that virtually all the countries described as having low human development indicators are located in sub-Saharan Africa.

Box 10.2 Enlightened self-interest? Development as security

Development and security are intimately related – one cannot be achieved without the other. DFID's [the UK Department for International Development] approach must be guided by this [...] While the link between conflict and development is a relatively new field, the Government must prioritise it in order to improve development outcomes among the poorest. Preventing and ending conflicts will do more to create a climate for poverty reduction than any amount of costly aid programmes.

(UK House of Commons International Development Committee, *Conflict and Development: Peacebuilding and Post-Conflict Reconstruction* 2006: 3–4)

Poverty in all its forms is the greatest single threat to peace, security, democracy, human rights and the environment.

(Michael Moore, head of the World Trade Organization (WTO), speech to WTO delegates in 2002)

Development co-operation [has] an important role to play in helping to deprive terrorists of popular support and addressing the conditions that terrorist leaders feed on and exploit. Many conditions that allow terrorists to be politically successful, build and expand constituencies, find recruits, establish and finance terrorist organisations, and secure safe havens fall within the realm and primary concerns of development co-operation.

(OECD Development Assistance Committee (DAC), *A Development Co-operation Lens on Terrorism Prevention* 2003: 11)

Addressing causes of conflicts (poverty, disease, lack of governance and rule of law) is an essential first step for the EU to help promote peace and development'.

(website of the European Commission on development policies, 2009)

This links back into the issue of human security – which argues that military and non-military threats to security are interdependent – as conflict is seen to be one of the most frequent inhibitors of human development. It not only poses a direct threat to the lives of those living in conflict zones, but also indirectly inhibits their access to food, health and educational facilities. This is what is sometimes termed as the 'development–security nexus' or 'development–conflict nexus': the idea that underdevelopment leads to conflict and vice versa.

Again sub-Saharan Africa is seen to be particularly prone to the worst effects of this development–security nexus. The Human Security Centre's *Human Security Report* of 2005 argues that violent conflicts in Africa (such as those that have occurred in the Democratic Republic of Congo and in Sudan) risk giving rise to a 'conflict trap' in which conflict tends to exacerbate the condition of poverty, thus leading to greater political instability and, consequently, a higher risk of violence. In sub-Saharan Africa this prospect is exacerbated by pervasive poverty, commitment to servicing external loans and the legacies of colonial rule. The last of these is often seen to have perpetuated weak administrations, poor-infrastructure, external interventions, readily available and cheap small arms as a legacy of cold war supply by the superpowers, and the frequent lack of fit between the old-colonial boundaries and the multi-ethnic make up of many African states. The occurrence of conflict thus only serves to compound existing problems and potential state instability far beyond the direct impact of war. In the case of the Democratic Republic of Congo, it is estimated that of the 2.5 million war deaths between 1998 and 2001, only 6 per cent of these (145,000) were as a direct result of the conflict itself. The majority of deaths actually resulted from the broader societal impact of the war in terms of war-related disease and malnutrition. Similarly, the effects of conflicts frequently outlast the immediate period of violence. The 1994 Rwandan conflict, for example, generated 1.4 million 'internally displaced persons' and sent 1.5 million refugees into neighbouring Zaire (now the Democratic Republic of Congo), Tanzania and Burundi, with consequences that have long outlasted the cessation of violence.

Critical debates in human security

On the face of it, the rise of human security as a concept that traverses both policy practice and academia is remarkable. Few of the theories or concepts discussed in this textbook can boast such a degree of crossover between academic and policy realms. There are, however, several heated debates that have emerged over the issue of human security, how it should be defined and understood, and how it shapes security practices.

As a qualifier to the seeming rise in prominence of the concept it should be noted that although the term human security is increasingly a feature of policy discourses, this has not equated to universal acceptance. Cynics note that the concept of human security has largely been adopted by 'middle powers' such as Canada and Japan (as opposed to 'great powers' such as the US and China) as a means of increasing their influence on debates in international security. Even states and organisations that employ the concept diverge over its exact meaning leading to a fundamental question: what does human security actually mean? Although states operating within the human security network (see Box 10.1) all agree that they are in favour of something called 'human security', consensus on exactly what human security is has been difficult to find. In general, states are seen to favour either a 'broad' or 'narrow' interpretation of human security (see Box 10.3).

These broad and narrow conceptions can in turn be understood in terms of the original UNDP definition of human security as 'freedom from fear' and 'freedom from want'. The first commitment – freedom from fear – is generally seen as the more narrow definition of human security as this is usually interpreted to mean protection from violence and political oppression. Canada, for example, is seen to endorse this narrower conception of human security, as are the majority of other states in the human security network. The general implications of this are that Canadian security policy places an emphasis on strengthening legal norms and building the capacity to enforce them, as exemplified in the 1997 Ottawa Convention (the landmine ban) and the 1998 Rome Treaty (which established the International Criminal Court). This also leads to an emphasis on protection of civilians, peace support operations, and conflict prevention as goals, and much the same is true of Norway's security policy which has also tended to emphasise the freedom from fear aspect of human security. By contrast Japan, like the UNDP, views human security as made up of freedom from fear *and* freedom from want. This latter commitment – freedom from want – has much more expansive implications. The vision of human security employed in Japanese foreign policy, by its own previous definition, 'covers all the menaces that threaten human survival, daily life and dignity', thus potentially including factors such as environmental degradation and the spread of infectious diseases. These two interpretations of human security thus have radically different ramifications for policy practice.

Similarly, the academic community is divided over the exact definition of human security. Andrew Mack advocates a narrow interpretation that emphasises the effects of conflict, directly and indirectly, on human beings. Others, such as Ramesh Thakur, Amartya Sen,

---

Box 10.3 'Narrow' versus 'broad' definitions of human security

'Narrow' definition	*'Broad' definition*
Emphasis on 'freedom from fear' (conflict prevention and resolution).	Emphasis on 'freedom from fear' *and* 'freedom from want' (conflict prevention and resolution + broader social issues such as health and education).
In policy discourse: Canada, Norway.	*In policy discourse*: The UNDP, Japan.
'Human security is a people-centred approach to foreign policy which recognizes that lasting stability cannot be achieved until people are protected from violent threats to their rights, safety or lives' (from the Canadian government's Human Security website, www.humansecurity.gc.ca, 2009).	'Human security comprehensively covers all the menaces that threaten human survival, daily life and dignity [...] and strengthens efforts to confront these threats' (Japanese Ministry of Foreign Affairs, 1999, restated on its website, www.mofa.go.jp, 2007).
Intellectual proponents: Mack (2002); Thomas and Tow (2002).	*Intellectual proponents*: Nussbaum (2000), Sen (2000), Caroline Thomas (2002).
'[Human security] could be especially useful for explaining and justifying humanitarian interventions by underscoring the causes that generate the conflicts that invite such action' (Thomas and Tow 2002: 189).	'Human security describes a condition of existence in which basic material needs are met and in which human dignity, including meaningful participation in the life of the community, can be met' (Thomas 2002: 3).

Caroline Thomas and Martha Nussbaum advocate more expansive definitions. Nussbaum, for example, argues that human security in its fullest sense should include bodily health, senses and emotion (2000). Critics contend that even the narrow understanding of human security is much too elastic to be a workable concept. They argue that the concept of human security is:

> too broad and vague a concept of to be meaningful for policymakers, as it has come to entail such a wide range of different threats on the one hand, whilst prescribing a diverse and sometimes incompatible set of policy solutions on the other.
>
> (Owens and Arneil, cited in Paris 2001: 92)

Roland Paris has been particularly vocal in his criticism of the concept, arguing that 'everyone is for it, but few people have a clear idea of what it means' (2001: 88). Moreover, Paris argues that the broad definition of human security is effectively meaningless, since the broad understanding of human security could encompass virtually anything that causes us discomfort. For those operating within the framework of securitisation theory (see Chapter 6), this aspect of human security is especially problematic as it opens up issues such as poverty, ill-health, and poor education to dynamics of securitisation where 'in the vast majority of cases, securitization will not lead to any significant improvement [in the lives of individuals]' (Khong 2001: 233).

A further key debate in human security concerns the relationship between human security and state (or national) security. Although the concept of human security is ostensibly 'people-centred' rather than 'state-centric', the role played by states in the provision of human security varies according to different definitions of the concept. Some proponents of human security generally tend to acknowledge a role for state forces and a need for state capacity to maintain – and on certain occasions restore – peace by upholding or re-establishing state authority where it has broken down. For those of a more radical persuasion, this allowance for coexistence between state and human security undermines the ability of human security to question the global status quo, the North–South divide and the insecurities that follow from it. This disjuncture is neatly captured in a 2002 debate (see further reading) between Thomas and Tow (2002) and Bellamy and McDonald (2002). Although both sets of authors endorse the idea of human security, the former argue that a more narrowly defined concept of human security 'would accrue greater analytical and policy value' (2002: 178), whereas Bellamy and McDonald argue that a 'narrow' definition of human security is itself 'largely inconsistent with the normative concerns inherent in the human security agenda' (2002: 373). In common with the variant of critical security studies covered in Chapter 2, Bellamy and McDonald argue that 'viewed from a human security perspective, states are more often part of the problem than the source of the solution' (2002: 373).

Finally, one of the continuing debates over human security is the extent to which the human security discourse may be moving away from a focus on prevention to *intervention*. This debate has arisen particularly in the aftermath of the publication of the *Responsibility to Protect* report in 2001 (a.k.a. R2P) by the International Commission on Intervention and State Sovereignty (ICISS). The R2P report is seen by many as representative of a 'new humanitarianism' identifiable in some elements of the human security discourse. The report addressed 'the question of when, if ever, it is appropriate for states to take coercive [military] action against another state for the purpose of protecting people at risk in that other state'. It therefore deals with the issues of when and where states fail to fulfil their obligation to their citizens, and even actively contravene their human rights. This takes it into the natural territory of the human security agenda, which the R2P report refers to explicitly: 'Whether universally popular or not, there is growing recognition worldwide that the protection of human security, including human rights and human dignity, must be one of the fundamental objectives of modern international institutions' (ICISS 2001: 1.28). On this basis the report argues that commitment to the idea of human security will (or should), on occasion, necessitate military intervention in support of that ideal.

The R2P was welcomed and endorsed by UN Secretary-General Kofi Annan and his successor Ban Ki-moon. However, the R2P principle continues to be highly controversial. For much of the post-Second World War era non-intervention has been the perceived norm in international affairs (although we should note that both the US and the USSR intervened militarily on a frequent basis, often by covert means, in the global South during the cold war) and some worry that the R2P will simply encourage greater intervention by Western powers in the developing world. With regard to the human security agenda there is also a fear that the R2P over-emphasises military means and intervention, rather than issues of poverty and ill health as also covered by broader understandings of the term, and prioritises a 'top-down' interventionist approach to security that returns the state to the fore (Chandler 2012).

Critical perspectives on the 'security–development nexus'

On one level it might appear that 'human security' and 'development' are desirable almost to the point of being unobjectionable: who wouldn't want human security, one might be tempted to ask? Why not intervene where human security is at risk? Yet for many scholars operating within the ambit of critical security studies, the emerging practices associated with human security and development are a source of both critical opportunity and concern (see Christie 2010). For some operating from a self-consciously critical perspective, such as Bellamy and McDonald (2002), the problem is that in many cases the policies and practices enacted in the name of human security frequently fail to fulfil the normative, progressive potential inherent in the idea. Peterson (2013) likewise makes the case that it is the ways that human security has been operationalised in policy practices that fundamentally inhibits its 'emancipatory potential'. Others, however, argue that what is problematic is the fact that ideas of human security and human development give rise to a range of practices that are less explicitly concerned with achieving 'human security' per se than they are with enacting and perpetuating particular modes of governance, particularly in those regions of the world designated as the 'developing world' or 'global South'. Here the argument is made that rather than being motivated purely by benevolence or altruism, contemporary development practices – and associated ideas such as human security – are also designed to prevent threats to global stability from 'dangerous' parts of the underdeveloped world: 'The threat of an excluded South fomenting international instability through conflict, criminal activity and terrorism is now part of a new security framework. Within this framework, under-development has become dangerous' (Duffield 2001: 2).

In keeping with many of the assumptions of recent postcolonial approaches covered in Chapter 4 of this book, the argument has been made that the end of formal colonialism has not severed fundamental continuities with the colonial past. Ironically, Duffield argues, the 'radicalisation of development' – the argument that underdevelopment is a security concern and hence has to be addressed by radical measures (see Box 10.4) – means that Northern organisations (state and non-state) now operate in the global South to an extent that surpasses even the colonial period. 'The idea of underdevelopment as dangerous and destabilising provides a justification for continued surveillance and engagement' (Duffield 2001: 7): extensive new modes of governing the global 'peripheries' have come into being beyond the formal trappings of colonialism, and here the notion of a 'development–security nexus' has been crucial. The idea that underdevelopment potentially leads to threats, which gained increasing currency from the early 1990s onwards and became further embedded after the events of 9/11, has been key in the formation of what has been termed as 'liberal development complexes' (Duffield 2001). These 'strategic complexes' encompass UN agencies, international NGOs, governments, military establishments, private military companies and business interests. They are 'liberal' in the sense that, though the elements of these strategic complexes appear disparate on the surface, they are ultimately united in a few basic assumptions: that the spread of liberal governance encourages peace; the spread of economic liberalism (in the form of free markets) encourages development; and that these two elements combined ultimately create the conditions for security. Hence the basic logic is that where individuals have access to avenues of political participation and monetary income, they are much less likely to resort to activities such as terrorism and violent crime that may ultimately spread beyond the global South. Through development, so the logic goes, the underdeveloped world becomes less 'dangerous' in security terms.

Box 10.4 Mark Duffield on the merging of development and security

The commitment to conflict resolution and the reconstruction of societies in such a way as to avoid future wars represents a marked radicalisation of the politics of development. [It is now assumed that] Societies must be changed so that past problems do not arise, as happened with development in the past; moreover this process of transformation cannot be left to chance but requires direct and concerted action [...] The radicalisation of development in this way is closely associated with the reproblematisation of security. Conventional views on the causes of the new wars usually hinge upon their arising from a developmental malaise of poverty, resource competition and weak or predatory institutions. The links between these wars and international crime and terrorism are also increasingly drawn. Not only have the politics of development been radicalised to address this situation but, importantly, it reflects a new security framework within which the modalities of underdevelopment have become dangerous. This framework is different from that of the Cold War when the threat of massive interstate conflict prevailed. The question of security has almost gone full circle: from being concerned with the biggest economies and war machines in the world to an interest in some of its smallest.

(Duffield 2001: 15–16)

Importantly, where some have claimed that development practices simply represent a new mode of imperialism (e.g. Chomsky 1999) Duffield maintains that these 'liberal complexes' are not uni-directional: they are shaped and modified by their engagement with the developing world. Again, as emphasised by many recent postcolonial approaches to security as discussed in Chapter 4, such critical approaches to the development–security nexus avoid depicting development practices as something that is simply imposed on the global South, instead looking to the ways in which liberal complexes of governance also encompass and integrate local actors, subjects and existing patterns of authority in order to secure 'fragile' states (see Duffield 2005).

Ultimately, some are left to wonder as to whether the acceptance of the idea of a development–security nexus in the discourse of states, NGOs and development agencies is self-defeating with respect to the ostensible goals of development practices. Abrahamson, (2003) drawing on securitisation theory as discussed in Chapter 6, argues that the securitisation of underdevelopment in relation to Africa is both undesirable (it risks simply embedding and embellishing the divide between 'developed' and 'underdeveloped' worlds) and inadequate (it risks the militarisation of social and economic problems where the efficacy of such militarisation is highly questionable). Duffield surmises that the emphasis on 'sustainable development' and 'self-reliance' in development discourse is seriously undermined by a range of development practices that are predicated on the expectation of recurrent crises – or 'complex emergencies', as in the current lexicon – as justification for intervention and constant surveillance. Echoing Achille Mbembe's (2003) pronouncements on 'necropolitics' (discussed in Chapter 4), he argues:

a small part of the world's population consumes and lives beyond its means within the fragile equilibrium of mass society while the larger part is allowed to die chasing the mirage of self-reliance. Rather than addressing these divergent life chances, the securitization of development is further entrenching them.

(Duffield 2005: 142)

On this reading development is 'better understood as a liberal technology of security for containing and managing the effects of underdevelopment', rather than as an effort to transform the underdeveloped world into the equivalent of its developed counterpart (Duffield 2005: 142).

(En)gendering human security?

As noted in the section above, although the idea of human security ostensibly points to a concern with individual security and development, others suggest that the concept is inherently bound up with a broader liberal mode of global governance that aims at the management of whole *populations* (Duffield 2007; De Larrinaga and Doucet 2008). In this vein, a key aim of many critical approaches to the concept is to shift the terrain of debate away from the question of what 'human security' *is* to a question of what it *does*. That is, rather than focusing on the definitional merits of 'narrow' versus 'wide' interpretations of the concept, the alternative suggestion is to focus attention on the range of practices enacted and legitimated in the name of human security. More often than not, it is argued, the practices associated with the promotion of human security are targeted at a societal level – the level of populations – rather than individual human beings in spite of pretensions to the contrary in much human security discourse. For many this places human security firmly within the ambit of what Michel Foucault calls 'biopolitics', where humans are thought of as a species in biological terms rather than as individuals (see Chapter 5 for an extended discussion). In this light, human security is viewed primarily as a technology in the sense that security is reduced to a series of technical considerations: indices of health and containment of disease; measurement of standards of education; tracking population and refugee movements.

Although conscious of the biopolitical logic that is potentially inherent within practices of human security and development, some perspectives emanating from gender theory nevertheless maintain the hope that human security also contains more positive immanent potentialities. Gender theory, applied to security studies, emphasises the need for a 'bottom-up' perspective of security rather than a 'top-down' approach: in other words, it stresses the need to take into account the 'everyday' insecurities that are experienced by people, but which have conventionally been marginalised by the statist focus of traditional security studies (see Chapter 3). In this light the idea of beginning security analysis at the level of the individual human might be worth retaining, notwithstanding the way this general idea has been rendered and applied in human security and development practice.

Bringing gender to bear on human security means much more than simply including gender issues within the remit of human security. Gunhild Hoogensen and Kirsti Stuvøy (2006) note that both academic and policy discourses on human security do occasionally make reference to 'gender issues', usually flagging up instances where gender differences become a source of individual insecurity (such as in cases of the contravention of women's rights and instances of gender inequality – see McKay 2004 for an overview). Domestic and sexual violence and violence against marginalised groups have also been traditionally beyond the gaze of security studies, and such concerns are usually given greater salience within discourses of human security. In this sense, the concept of human security has already been gendered, but the manner in which this has tended to occur is often used simply to differentiate human security concerns from the 'real' stuff of security studies: human security is often seen to encompass 'soft' security issues such as health and welfare, with connotations of 'feminine' qualities, which are to be distinguished from the traditionally male-dominated realms of military security. On a practical level, we might simply note that even for states at the forefront of the human security agenda, such as Canada, 'the traditional notion of security has not disappeared – it has simply found a new home elsewhere' (Neufeld 2004: 115): in other words, even states propounding the idea of 'human security' continue to maintain and differentiate it from a more traditional notion of national, military security policy and practices. Hence:

> This 'feminization' of human security or a widened security concept is not meant to be complementary. It means that human security does not measure up, and traditional security sets the standard. As such, security must be rooted within the eradication of largescale violent conflict, and anything else – 'everyday security' or the securities and insecurities of individuals themselves, such as health, food, economic or environmental issues – is *not* security, at least not by the standards of those who matter [including] most policymakers who work with the concept.
>
> (Hoogensen and Stuvøy 2006: 210)

What Hoogensen and Stuvøy argue, by contrast, is that gender theory potentially provides a more fundamental rethinking of human security. Focusing on the individual/human means more than simply substituting the individual for the state within existing frameworks of analysis, it also brings those very frameworks into question. *Human* security, from a gender theory perspective, cannot simply be limited to the inclusion of new 'issues' such as poverty and educational attainment. A more substantive understanding of the concept, drawing on gender theory and feminist perspectives, potentially constitutes a new 'epistemological perspective for security studies' (2006: 209): that is, it makes allowance for forms of knowledge derived from individual and personal human experience of security and insecurity at an everyday level, and seeks to simultaneously unpack the reasons why such forms of knowledge have been treated as illegitimate by mainstream security analysis (see Chapter 3; and also Grayson 2004). It also alerts us to the extent to which practices associated with the provision of human security – such as the 'peace support operations' enacted by the UN – uphold and enact particular notions of both masculinity and femininity in their very enactment (see Higate and Henry 2004).

By focusing on the personal, everyday dimensions of human security, gender approaches therefore seek to counteract the extent to which existing human security practices are targeted at the collective level of population. At the same time gender approaches to human security thus also aim at a greater degree of individual empowerment than is often allowed for within discussions of human security. Where a tendency exists within mainstream discourses of human security to treat – and objectify – individuals as 'victims' to be saved, a gendered concept of human security seeks to reinstate the agency of individuals by linking personal accounts of insecurity to broader social contexts and structural factors. It also refocuses our attention on the corporeal nature of human security: the extent to which the physical body is very often the site of security/insecurity behind the statistics that detail the extent of conflict and poverty, and the ways in which bodies often function as nodal or connection points in networks of security that are global in their scale. Although not explicitly focused on human security, Carolyn Nordstrom's work on 'shadow industries' serves as a good exemplar here. It carefully weaves together the personal accounts of three girls variously affected by wartime violence in Mozambique in the 1990s with a wider account of the transnational linkages surrounding illegal labour and sex-trafficking (Nordstrom 1999). Networks of migrant labour and sex-trafficking ferry victims of conflict into 'peacezones' where their bodies are further exploited and abused; but these 'shadow industries' can only be sustained via a complex network of transport housing, and maintenance that ultimately allow such profiteering and exploitation to take place. The individual human insecurities of war victims and refugees, rather than being somehow limited to the 'developing world', are thus often embedded within and sustained by global networks to a degree that is not accessible simply by reviewing statistics on human rights abuses within zones of conflict. Taking this viewpoint reiterates the connection between 'every day' practices – including, for example, the work of illegal migrants that sustains the day-to-day running of many developed economies – and human insecurities (see also Steans 1998). Similarly, Lemanski makes the case that policy discourse of human security tend to begin from a top-down global level that treats individuals as an aggregate category, where, by contrast, starting from the local level of 'everyday human (in)security' produces a more fine-grained picture. Employing empirical examples of cities in the global South and drawing on individuals' own experiences, she shows how citizens are affected in their daily lives by specific issues of crime, physical security and financial insecurity that are not well captured by the catch-all categorisation of poverty as a human security issue (Lemanski 2012).

Conclusion

In many ways, as we have seen, the concept of human security is one of the most challenging contemporary ideas that critical approaches to security are trying to come to terms with. This is the case precisely because the idea itself seems to incorporate at least some of the aspects of critical debates in security and feeds them into policy discourse, yet the range of practices enacted in the name of human security and development only seems to raise numerous further concerns for many critically minded scholars. So where does this leave critical perspectives on human security and development? The ubiquity of human security in contemporary global security discourse is likely to mean that it will be a focus of much critical scholarship for years to come and, it might be speculated, the key debate will continue to be over whether the concept of human security has by now effectively been co-opted as a new model of statist security practices, or might be reinvigorated as a site of critical potential. In this sense at least the concept of human security provides a continuing source of debate. The guide to further reading below gives readers some indication of where they might follow up on this question, and, as indicated above, each of the approaches covered in the first section of the text also offer different resources for reflecting on the merits and limitations of human security in the twenty-first century.

Key points

- The concept of 'human security' has gained increasing prominence and recognition within global security discourse since the idea first emerged in the early 1990s.
- Although the idea has potentially universal application, in practice it has been used primarily in relation to issues of development and in reference to the global South.
- Critics of the notion of human security argue that it deprives the concept of security of any substantive meaning, and even proponents of the term are split over the merits of 'narrow' versus 'broad' understandings of security.
- Critically minded scholars have paid particular attention to how the concept of human security informs and is shaped by contemporary development practices.
- Some argue that the term has largely been co-opted by states as a new 'technology' of security aimed at managing populations in the global South; others hold out hope that

the basic idea of human security nevertheless opens the way to an understanding of security concerned with the 'everyday' insecurities experienced by individuals in many parts of the world.

Discussion points

- What does human security mean in theory and practice?
- Does the human security literature reproduce the assumptions of traditional security studies?
- What is at stake in claiming that poverty is a security issue?
- What is assumed in the idea of a 'development–security' nexus? Does it simply perpetuate Western intervention in the developing world?
- Does the 'human security agenda' simply perpetuate Western intervention in the developing world?

Guide to further reading

Caroline Thomas (2000) *Global Governance, Development and Human Security* (London: Pluto Press). Addresses the issue of whether and how development might be 'done' differently to achieve human security.

David Chandler and Nik Hynek (2012) (eds) *Critical Perspectives on Human Security: Rethinking Emancipation and Power in International Relations* (Abingdon: Routledge). Brings together a wide range of critical assessments of human security.

Mark Duffield (2001) *Global Governance and the New Wars* (London: Zed). Provides an expansive assessment of the development and deployment of 'liberal complexes' of global governance in the name of development. See also his (2007) *Development, Security and Unending War: Governing the World of Peoples* (London: Polity), which focuses more explicitly on the role and impact of 'human security' on development practices.

Martha C. Nussbaum (2000) *Women and Human Development: The Capabilities Approach* (Cambridge: Cambridge University Press). An empirically rich and theoretically sophisticated account of the human insecurities created by relations of patriarchy.

Ryerson Christie (2010) 'Critical Voices and Human Security: To Endure, To Engage or To Critique?', *Security Dialogue*, 41:169–190 offers a comprehensive overview of the literature on human security and responses to its rise within the critical security studies literature. Christie's ultimate assessment is that human security in itself should not be regarded as a 'critical concept' or critical approach in its own right, even if it is a discussion point on which both policy-makers and academics can 'converge'. Newman (2010) and Peterson (2013) – see Bibliography for full details – suggest greater critical potential in the concept and study of human security and offer interesting comparative reading in this respect.

Security Dialogue (2004) 35(3). Special issue of the journal that offers a series of academic perspectives on human security.

Weblinks

United Nations Development Programme: www.undp.org/
Human Security Centre/Human Security Report: www.humansecurityreport.info/
Commission on Human Security: http://www.unocha.org/humansecurity/chs/

11 Migration and border security

Abstract

This chapter introduces the crossover between the securitisation of migration and innovations in border control as a significant nodal point in the field of global security relations. It begins with an overview of some of the dominant trends in global migration and a commentary on how states go about classifying different types of migrants. From here the discussion moves on to consider how migration has been rendered a security problem in relation to the politics of insecurity in Europe, human trafficking and the gendered dimension of migration, and the relationship between critical security studies and 'critical migration studies'. Moves towards new forms of border security practices in response to the threat of migration are then traced and illustrated against the backdrop of US and EU contexts. The changing nature and location of borders in global politics poses a number of conceptual challenges for theorists of security and the chapter ends by discussing what these are and how current research in 'critical border studies' seeks to address them.

Introduction

More and more people are moving around the globe. According to United Nations data, in 1960 there were 75 million international migrants (UN 2013). By 2005 this figure had more than doubled to 191 million. As of 2013, 232 million people – 3.2 per cent of the globe's total population – are international migrants living abroad. There are many different reasons why people move between states. Some do so because they are in search of better economic prospects. Others seek to join families who have moved abroad. A significant number, 13.5 million or 7 per cent of all migrants, are in search of refuge from war, oppression and persecution.

While the phenomenon of international migration is not something new, rising numbers of migrants have led to changes in the way they are treated by states and viewed by non-migrant populations. Following the Second World War, for example, migrant workers from India, Pakistan and the Caribbean were welcomed as part of the economic reconstruction of Europe. Yet, in subsequent years the same migrants came to be associated with threats to European public order, cultural identity, and domestic labour markets. Especially since 9/11, migration has been linked by Western governments to global terrorism and transnational crime. In this way the movement of people, once encouraged as a 'good' thing, has been 'securitised' (see Chapter 6).

Throughout the global North in particular the main response to the 'problem' of migration as constructed above has been tougher border controls, which nevertheless affect people all over the globe. Traditional forms of securing the borders of sovereign states, such as the issuing of visas, the checking of passports and other forms of monitoring movement in and out of states, have been enhanced and this is transforming the relationship between mobility and (in)security. Border control is no longer solely to be found at ports, airports, and other conventional crossings, but also offshored to the point of departure. New biometric technologies, such as iris scanning, fingerprinting and automated entry/exit systems have been rolled out to capture and manage people's identities digitally (see Chapters 9 and 12). Via this kind of 'dataveillance' individuals and populations are now risk assessed and managed according to various categories of 'dangerousness', which are often calculated in advance of their travel. Thus, the identification of migration as a security issue has stimulated new border security practices that challenge conventional ideas of what and where 'the border' is.

Migration in global politics

Why are there so many international migrants? While the globe's migrant population is at an historic high, there are particular trends in the movement of people that deserve closer attention. Part of the reason for the huge growth in international migration towards the end of the twentieth century was the effect of the dissolution of the USSR in 1991, Yugoslavia in 1992 and Czechoslovakia in 1993. The breaking up of these states transformed formerly internal migrants (people who move around within a particular state) into international migrants (people who move across different states). Indeed, this reclassification accounts for more than one-fifth of the increase in numbers of international migrants between 1960 and 2005 (UN 2006). Other factors contributing to the increase since 1960 include population growth, technological development, easier and cheaper transportation and better communication networks under globalising conditions.

Who are international migrants, where are they from, and where to they go? According to the UN Department of Economic and Social Affairs the globe's migrant populations are generally concentrated in more developed states – the North is home to 136 million international migrants compared with 96 million in the South (UN 2013). However, South–South migration is just as common as North–North migration. Of 232 million international migrants, 74 per cent are of working age (between 20 and 64 years) and 48 per cent are women. As of 2013, Europe hosted the largest number of international migrants (72 million), followed by Asia (71 million) and North America (44 million). Overall, the US is the state that receives the largest number of migrants (38 million) followed by the Russian Federation (11 million), Germany (9.8 million), Saudi Arabia (9.1 million), United Arab Emirates (7.8 million), UK (7.8 million), France (7.4 million), Canada (7.3 million), Australia (6.5 million) and Spain (6.5 million). Although there is a greater density of international migrants in the global North, there is evidence to suggest that the pattern of settlement is changing. By 2005 37 per cent of all migrants lived in less developed states and the migrant population in Africa was 17 million. Having said this, different types of migrants are typically found in different parts of the globe. In Africa, for example, there is a far higher proportion of refugees (18 per cent of total migrants) than elsewhere (average 7 per cent). Moreover, as Squire (2011) has cautioned, knowledge of certain kinds of migration is always incomplete and often highly politicised and so this should always be borne in mind when confronting statistics on population movements.

How are migrants classified? We have already started above with a distinction between 'international' and 'non-international' (domestic) migrants. A number of further categories are used by states in order to manage global flows of people. This categorisation is not an innocent activity but a very significant political move because individuals – and sometimes entire populations – are treated differently according to which group they are labelled as and put into. 'Regular migrants' are those who are considered to have entered the state legally at official border crossings and are recognised as 'legitimate' individuals within that territory. 'Irregular migrants' are those who are deemed not to have met the criteria for admission into a given state: these individuals can be further classified in terms of 'clandestine immigrants' (because they are found to have crossed the border illegally) or 'irregular immigrants' (if they have outstayed a formerly legal visa).

Another important distinction to which we have already implicitly referred is that between 'voluntary' and 'involuntary' migrants. The category of voluntary migrants refers to people who are said to have chosen to move from one state to another, such as economic migrants. Within this category, further sub-divisions are often made between 'legal permanent settler' migrants (for example the Afro-Caribbean migrants who came to work in the UK during the 1950s/1960s), 'legal temporary settler' migrants (including business travellers, tourists, students, workers) and 'illegal permanent' or 'temporary settler' migrants (such as the thousands of Mexican migrants who attempt to cross the US border each year).

The label 'involuntary migrant' is applied to those whose movement from one state to another is recognised as being forced in some way. Under the terms of Article 14 of the 1948 UN Declaration on Human Rights, all people have the right to *seek* asylum from persecution in other states. This provision is reaffirmed by the 1951 Refugee Convention, which asserts the right of all to freedom from natural disaster, civil war, ethnic, religious and political oppression. Importantly, however, these international human rights conventions do not guarantee everyone the right of refugee status, only the right to be able to seek it.

The term 'asylum seeker' is used to refer to those who claim to be fleeing from persecution under those conventions. In practice, the principle of state sovereignty means that states decide whom they will admit and recognise as a legitimate asylum seeker. Those who are recognised as such are granted the status of a 'refugee', which entitles them to the same rights of hospitality and protection as citizens of the host state. However, if an individual is deemed to be a 'bogus asylum seeker' then he or she is likely to be deported back to the country from which s/he travelled in the first place.

The securitisation of migration

Is migration a 'good' thing? The answer to this question very much depends on who you are, where you are and what your interests might be. There can be obvious advantages to the migrant if s/he is successful in fleeing from persecution and/or achieving a better standard of living. The host state might also benefit economically in terms of attracting cheaper labour, enhancing productivity and adding skills to the workforce. Original states often stand to gain as well if money is sent home and/or pressure is eased on social benefits such as housing and employment.

Taking the opposite view, however, it is sometimes argued that migration can lead to the spread of conflict and forms of civil unrest between original and host states. Competition between migrants and citizens of a host state for jobs, housing and other welfare resources can lead to enmity and inter-communal rivalry and violence. Social instability, often stoked by right-wing media and political groups, can arise from the perception that migrants pose a 'threat' not only to economic well-being, but cultural identity, national heritage and the social cohesion of the host state. Whether accurate or not, migration is often associated by various state and civil actors with disorder, crime and increasingly, as we shall see below, with terrorist activity. As such, migration is a deeply contested issue.

Today, migration can be located within a security continuum that connects it with issues such as terrorism, international crime and border control. Host populations are often fearful of immigrant communities and racial tensions sometimes lead to violent confrontations (such as the 'race riots' in Oldham near Manchester in the UK in 2001 and violence against undocumented migrants from Zimbabwe and Mozambique and elsewhere in South Africa). Yet, this has not always been the case – in Europe's recent past, for example, migration was not only tolerated but actively encouraged. What has changed and how has migration been produced as a security threat?

Immigration and the politics of fear

Jef Huysmans (2006) has examined the securitisation of migration against the backdrop of European Union integration. According to Huysmans, during the 1950s and early 1960s immigrants were treated as a valuable workforce in most European states. The post-war economic climate required a cheap and flexible workforce that could not be found among domestic populations. Permissive and even promotional migration was common in France, Germany and the Netherlands, for example. Furthermore, the arrival of migrants was met with ambivalence by host populations for whom their settlement was not a salient political issue.

Towards the end of the 1960s and into the 1970s, however, Huysmans argues that migration was increasingly a public concern in Europe. The inward movement of people became associated with the destabilisation of civic order and challenges to the welfare state model. Prominence was given to immigrant communities as they started to enlarge with the arrival of workers' families. A formerly permissive stance gave way to a new tougher attitude that sought to control who came to settle. During this period, to use the language of securitisation theory (see Chapter 6), the issue of migration became 'politicised' as a pressing concern. Indeed, this is well illustrated by British MP Enoch Powell's infamous 'Rivers of Blood' speech delivered amid heightened public tensions over immigration to the UK in April 1968 (see Box 11.1).

For Huysmans, the further transition from the politicisation to the securitisation of migration in Europe occurred from the late 1980s/early 1990s onwards. At this time we see the gradual incorporation of migration and asylum policy into the constitutional structure of the European Economic Community (EEC)/European Community (EC). In 1990 the Convention designed to implement the lifting of internal borders in Europe connected immigration and asylum issues with terrorism, transnational crime and border control for the first time. While this was not a 'speech act' as conventionally understood, Huysmans argues that it constituted a significant securitising move because it placed migration within the institutional framework of the internal security of European member states. In this way, Huysmans draws our attention to the way in which an issue does not have to be literally 'spoken about' or 'written of' in the language of security for it to be securitised. Rather, the placing of an issue like migration into the technocratic institutional realm of security also has the effect, albeit one that is perhaps more subtle, of securitisation. What is at stake here, according to Huysmans, is the production of a 'domain of insecurity' in which something formerly considered resolvable in the sphere of politics has shifted to that of security (Huysmans 2006: 4).

Moves towards the securitisation of migration were thus already well underway prior to the events of 9/11. Since then, however, Huysmans points to the way in which these dynamics have been intensified and further entrenched (see also Bigo *et al.* 2007; Bigo and Guittet

Box 11.1 Extract from Enoch Powell's 'Rivers of Blood' speech, delivered to a Conservative Association meeting in Birmingham, 20 April 1968

A week or two ago I fell into conversation with a constituent, a middle-aged, quite ordinary working man employed in one of our nationalised industries.

After a sentence or two about the weather, he suddenly said: 'If I had the money to go, I wouldn't stay in this country.' I made some deprecatory reply to the effect that even this government wouldn't last for ever; but he took no notice, and continued: 'I have three children, all of them been through grammar school and two of them married now, with family. I shan't be satisfied till I have seen them all settled overseas. In this country in 15 or 20 years' time the black man will have the whip hand over the white man.'

I can already hear the chorus of execration. How dare I say such a horrible thing?

How dare I stir up trouble and inflame feelings by repeating such a conversation?

The answer is that I do not have the right not to do so. Here is a decent, ordinary fellow Englishman, who in broad daylight in my own town says to me, his Member of Parliament, that his country will not be worth living in for his children.

I simply do not have the right to shrug my shoulders and think about something else. What he is saying, thousands and hundreds of thousands are saying and thinking – not throughout Great Britain, perhaps, but in the areas that are already undergoing the total transformation to which there is no parallel in a thousand years of English history.

In 15 or 20 years, on present trends, there will be in this country three and a half million Commonwealth immigrants and their descendants. That is not my figure. That is the official figure given to parliament by the spokesman of the Registrar General's Office.

There is no comparable official figure for the year 2000, but it must be in the region of five to seven million, approximately one-tenth of the whole population, and approaching that of Greater London. Of course, it will not be evenly distributed from Margate to Aberystwyth and from Penzance to Aberdeen. Whole areas, towns and parts of towns across England will be occupied by sections of the immigrant and immigrant-descended population.

As time goes on, the proportion of this total who are immigrant descendants, those born in England, who arrived here by exactly the same route as the rest of us, will rapidly increase. Already by 1985 the native-born would constitute the majority. It is this fact which creates the extreme urgency of action now, of just that kind of action which is hardest for politicians to take, action where the difficulties lie in the present but the evils to be prevented or minimised lie several parliaments ahead.

The natural and rational first question with a nation confronted by such a prospect is to ask: 'How can its dimensions be reduced?' Granted it be not wholly preventable, can it be limited, bearing in mind that numbers are of the essence: the significance and consequences of an alien element introduced into a country or population are profoundly different according to whether that element is 1 per cent or 10 per cent.

The answers to the simple and rational question are equally simple and rational: by stopping, or virtually stopping, further inflow, and by promoting the maximum outflow. Both answers are part of the official policy of the Conservative Party.

2011). Moreover, we might add, security practices in response to fears of the effects of migration have taken on increasingly racialised characteristics. The linking of immigration and asylum with security threats in the 1980s and 1990s had already singled out Third World nationals as many asylum seekers in Europe have historically come from the global South. A more recent trend, especially in the aftermath of 9/11 and the bombings in Madrid and

London, has been the particular focus on Muslim communities (Basham and Vaughan-Williams 2013). In this context, the granting of asylum to Muslim clerics has been cited as one of the conditions of possibility for the so-called 'radicalisation' of Muslim youths in Western Europe.

Huysmans' work not only considers the production, but also the political implications of the securitisation of migration. By invoking the very notion of a community that is endangered by migration a securitising actor reinstates that community as a sovereign political entity. In other words, fear of migration and asylum can be mobilised politically in order to reaffirm the existence of a particular community: 'The securitization of migration reproduces a myth that a homogenous national community or Western civilisation existed in the past and can be re-established today through the exclusion of those migrants who are identified as cultural aliens' (Huysmans 2006: x). On this basis, Huysmans powerfully highlights what is at stake politically in the rendering of migrants as an existential security threat.

Gender, categorisation and human trafficking

In his treatment of the securitisation of migration, Huysmans adopts a Foucauldian approach that reads knowledge as constitutive of global politics (for more on the thought of Michel Foucault see Chapter 5). That is to say, security is 'not simply an analytical lens' through which we study global politics in a passive sense (Huysmans 2006: xii). Rather, on this view, security is understood more dynamically as a 'political technique of framing' that structures social relations (2006: xii). The framing of migrants in different ways, through the use of various categorisations considered earlier, has significant implications. If an individual is framed in humanitarian terms then s/he may be dealt with compassionately as a holder of particular rights. However, if a migrant is seen in terms of security (threats) then they may be subject to exclusionary practices.

Like Huysmans, Claudia Aradau pays attention to the ethical and political implications of the categorisation of different types of migrants. Aradau takes human trafficking as a case study for further analysing the way in which the naming of people constitutes their relationship with apparatuses of security. According to Aradau, there are 2.5 million people recorded as being caught up in practices of human trafficking globally (Aradau 2008). Of course, given the underground nature of these practices, there are many more undocumented cases. Irrespective of the 'true' figures, however, the majority of those trafficked from one state to another are women in the sex industry, which highlights an important gender dimension to migration.

Aradau examines how, depending on the categorisation of trafficked women, different possibilities for action are opened up and closed down. The labelling of women as illegal migrants, prostitutes, victims or the abused bearers of human rights each leads to different outcomes. Women classified as 'victims' are either admitted to rehabilitation centres or deported voluntarily, whereas 'illegal' female immigrants are typically held in detention centres and then forcibly returned to their country of origin. Yet, as Aradau shows, the line between the two is often unclear and in practice suspicion of illegality hovers over all trafficked women who are 'caught' and duly 'processed' (2008: 4).

Significantly, Aradau does *not* argue that the labelling of women is systematically 'inaccurate' in recording their 'true' status. Indeed, she emphasises that such a status does not exist straightforwardly: many women are *both* victimised *and* caught up in illegal cartels; they are not *all* dangerous, but some are; trafficking is neither entirely forced nor voluntary. Drawing on a Foucauldian perspective, Aradau is more interested in how it is through the very act of classification that the logic of security works. In other words, it is precisely the activity of making divisions, drawing lines and distinguishing between people, in this case trafficked women, that enables security to function as a method of governing populations.

From here, Aradau raises the normative question of how it might be possible to think about the trafficking of women in such a way that avoids the security trap. She rejects notions of desecuritisation (see Chapter 6), emancipation (see Chapter 2) and other forms of ethics, because she argues that these all lead to a 'humanitarian impasse'. By this Aradau refers to the way in which any approach built around the construction of victimhood leads back into the sort of line drawing that security relies upon. Instead, Aradau draws on the work of Alain Badiou to argue that a common struggle needs to be identified in order to establish the grounds for 'equality' between all those caught up in trafficking. On this view, it is through the identification of such a commonality that the situation of trafficked women might be politicised and the grounds for further differentiated classification refused. One such commonality according to Aradau is that, irrespective of how they get categorised, all trafficked women are essentially workers. Thus, by making the claim that prostitution is a form of work, Aradau argues that such women are remade as political subjects who are then better positioned to challenge 'the security practices governing the situation of trafficking' (2008: 143).

Critical migration studies

As we have seen, both Huysmans and Aradau share a commitment to the analysis of the production of different types of migrants by the state as a security practice. For Elspeth Guild this commitment underpins what she refers to as 'critical migration studies' (CMS). CMS is Guild's term for a growing body of literature that seeks to challenge the assumption that 'we know what migration is and which actors are entitled to determine the political in respect of migration' (Guild 2009: 2). Influenced in part by an IPS perspective (see Chapter 5), CMS seeks to move away from a realist-inspired state-centric approach to migration. Rather than treating migration as the mass flow of differentiated groups of people from one state to another, and therefore as an object of dispassionate statistical analysis, CMS focuses on how individual movement becomes framed in particular ways: 'How does the individual fit into a set of state structural frameworks and become categorised as a threat to security and to state control of migration?' (Guild 2009: 3; see also Squire 2011).

As the quotation above indicates, one of the key moves Guild makes is to argue for the increased prominence of the *individual* in the study of migration. All too often, she claims, analysts buy into the statist language of 'flows', 'stocks' and 'tidal waves' of particular types of migrants. An alternative focus on people and their experiences allows for a more nuanced and politically engaged mode of analysis: 'By refusing to accept the disappearance of the individual into an undifferentiated flow of people which is then directed [...] by state actors or processes, I seek to reveal the construction and deconstruction of assumptions about migration, identity, and security' (2009: 5).

According to Guild, the problem with a conventional state-centred study of migration is that it treats migrants as confronting the state as if it were a pre-existing monolithic political community. This obscures the way in which, as Huysmans' work demonstrates, it is at least partly through the securitisation of migration that the state is reaffirmed and reproduced as a distinct political community in the first place. Moreover, such an outlook distracts attention from the 'political agency' of migrants, who not only play a role in constituting regimes of border control but may also resist and/or disrupt the system in which they find themselves (see also Squire 2011; Stierl 2012).

Taking the individual as the starting point for analysing migration does not 'do away' with the state. Rather, it enables a different form of enquiry that considers how the individual and state interact. Neither is taken as a priori given, but understood to be co-constitutive of each other. This view problematises the state, which is no longer assumed to be a fully formed 'complete' sovereign entity. Rather, a more dynamic approach is implied that draws attention to how, paradoxically, the state relies on migration in order to continually perform its sovereign authority.

Although not necessarily framed explicitly in terms of Guild's use of the term, CMS might also be linked to a number of interdisciplinary currents. A particular hallmark of this research is its focus on the experiences of individual migrants: Shahram Khosravi (Khosravi 2010) analyses 'illegal immigration' from the perspective of asylum seekers travelling from Iraq and Afghanistan; Alison Mountz (2010) has explored the encounter between the state and migrants in the Australian and US contexts; Nicholas de Genova and Nathalie Peutz (2010) investigate the global deportation regime from a 'bottom-up' perspective; and Jennifer Hyndman's (2012) collection considers the role of border-crossers in shaping the relationship between mobility and (in)security.

Border security practices

There is an important connection between migration and states' borders. Indeed, it is the very act of crossing the border that produces the international migrant in the first place, as someone who is in transit from one sovereign territory to another. At the border key decisions are made about who is 'legitimate' and who is 'illegitimate'; who is 'trusted' and who is 'risky'; who can be allowed to cross freely and who is excluded. Traditionally, the image of 'the border' is of a thin line located at the geographical outer edge of the state. Today, however, the line is increasingly 'thick': it is the site of many rituals such as the checking of the passport, body searches and questioning. Through these border security practices the state performs and thus (re)asserts its authority.

Realist approaches within security studies, and IR more generally, have long been interested in the defence and transgression of states' borders. While important, however, this work has tended to take borders for granted merely as part of the 'fixtures and fittings' of the international system (Williams 2003a: 27). By contrast, more recent work, typically of a critical vein, has sought to investigate borders as sites of intellectual enquiry in their own right. In this section we consider recent research on the evolution of border security practices in the US and EU contexts, as well as more theoretical insights produced by the growing interdisciplinary field of critical border studies.

The US–Mexico border

Migration to the US has grown considerably in recent decades. In 1986 permanent legal residency was granted to 601,708 migrants (Doty 2009). By 2006 this figure had risen to 1,266,264. Of course, these numbers only illustrate the extent of successful, legitimate, recorded migration. There is also a much darker set of statistics, which show that between 1996 and 2006 approximately 4000 people died trying to get into the US illegally. Most of these deaths were of Mexican migrants heading north and their shrines are a striking feature of the border landscape.

The US–Mexico border, which spans over 2000 miles, is the longest and busiest contiguous border between the 'first' and 'third' worlds. Soon after 9/11 an explicit connection was emphasised by the US administration between immigration in the south and the threat of international terrorism. Indeed, the 9/11 Commission Report identified the border as a weak link in US security and called for tougher controls. In response, the DHS has pursued an aggressive approach to Mexican immigration as part of its overall counterterrorism strategy (see Chapter 9). Yet, as the research of Peter Andreas (2000) demonstrates, the securitisation of migration in the US–Mexico borderlands has a much longer history (see also Nevins 2010).

Andreas (2000) points out that for centuries there has been a clandestine border economy between Mexico and the US. Smugglers have long crossed the border with an array of goods from money, precious metals and stones, and antiquities to drugs, pornography and waste. The first US Border Patrol was established in 1924, with 450 officers and a budget of $1 million (Andreas 2000: 31). The number of apprehensions at the border increased from 182,000 in 1947 to 1,600,000 by 1986, which stimulated heightened control from the late 1980s/early 1990s. In 1995 Operation Hard Line was launched to curb drug trafficking and at the same time new initiatives were developed to limit illegal immigration. Tougher border security was thus already well underway during the 1990s with the enforcement budget rising from $354 million in 1993 to $877 million by 1998 (2000: 89).

At this time, the border was 'thickened' using new fencing equipment and surveillance devices, such as infrared night-vision scopes, low-light TV cameras, ground sensors, helicopters and all-terrain vehicles (2000: 90).

Writing at the turn of the millennium, Andreas' work ran counter to globalisation theorists' claims about the existence of a 'borderless world'. Rather, drawing on the US–Mexico border as a case study, he pointed to the continued significance of stubborn territorial divisions between states. Moreover, Andreas argued that, while partly aiming to deter drug traffickers and illegal immigrants, the escalation of border security in the US during the 1990s was also a political move. By constructing an impression that the border was 'under siege', local and national politicians could then present themselves as guardians of the nation. Thus, for example, Pete Wilson's campaign for re-election as governor of California in 1994 arguably focused on the border for political gain. More generally Andreas emphasises that the creation of a lawless borderland in need of control presents the state with an opportunity to reproduce its authority. Historically the US–Mexico border has never been 'sealed' and never will be. This is not the point, however. Rather, the border must be seen as a political stage: 'Border policing […] is not only the coercive hand of the state but a ceremonial practice, not only a means to an end but an end in itself' (2000:11). On this view, even though complete control of the border is impossible, the 'border games' states play are themselves politically significant security practices.

While Andreas focuses on the role of the state as a securitising actor, Roxanne Lynn Doty (2007) has shown how some US citizens are also involved in border work. In October 2004 retired businessmen Jim Gilchrist and Chris Simcox founded an anti-immigration group called the Minute Men Project (MMP). This unofficial and unauthorised, though not illegal, group was set up in order to promote citizen-led border security initiatives. It is named after the so-called 'minutemen' of the American Revolution, who were highly mobile rapid response teams mobilised to help fellow soldiers under threat. The MMP claims that, despite the gradual intensification of border control, the US state is still not doing enough to control the US–Mexico border. On this basis, it organises vigilante border protection and MMP squads go in search of illegal Mexican immigrants in order to deter and/or report them to official border guards. Doty uses this example not only to highlight the phenomenon of border vigilantism, but also to problematise what she refers to as the Schmittian decisionism of securitisation theory (see Chapters 5 and 6). She argues that the MMP, though a good example of what the Copenhagen School refers to as 'societal security', illustrates how sovereign decisions on what and/or whom is allowed to cross the border are made by diverse actors at multiple sites:

> Everyone is potentially 'the police', faceless creators and upholders of the social order. Border vigilantes 'found' a society and identity that never existed, but which they claim to want to preserve. Their practices supplement a sovereign that remains indeterminate, reminding us that any promise of an ordinary sovereign foundation can only ever be a promise.
>
> (Doty 2007: 132)

In other words, Doty uses the case of MMP border vigilantism to show how the ability to securitise an issue is not the sole preserve of the state and that in practice sovereign decisions are made by those who simply claim the authority to do so.

As we have seen, in their study of the border both Andreas and Doty focus on the geographical line that separates the US from Mexico. Louise Amoore's work adds to this analysis by considering how US border security practices do not only occur at the geographical outer edge of the state (Amoore 2006, 2007). Amoore has shown how the raft of new bordering practices rolled out by the DHS challenges straightforward distinctions between domestic/foreign, national/international, inside/outside. The Smart Border Alliance initiative, unveiled in 2004 by the DHS in response to the threat of international terrorism, prompted a shift in the conceptualisation of border security in terms of risk management. Amoore traces how the US has developed new forms of pre-emptive borders that assess risky travellers *before* they leave their country of origin to travel in the first place. In this way Amoore argues that: 'The management of the border cannot be understood simply as a matter of the geopolitical policing and disciplining of the movement of bodies across mapped space' (2006: 337). Rather, Amoore draws on the thought of Michel Foucault (see Chapter 5) to suggest that the US border is 'more appropriately understood as a matter of biopolitics, as a mobile regulatory site through which people's everyday lives can be made amenable to intervention and management' (2006: 337). It is 'biopolitical' precisely because of the focus on the body of populations through the encoding of travellers to allow for their classification according to perceived levels of risk. Moreover, rather than fixed at a specific territorial site, Amoore refers to the mobility of the US border, 'carried by mobile bodies at the very same time it is deployed to divide bodies at international boundaries, airports, railway stations, or subways, or city streets, in the office or the neighbourhood' (2006: 338). In this way, Amoore uses the US case to illustrate how borders are not what or where we might expect them to be in contemporary political life.

The EU and its borders

On the one hand, as we have already noted, the EU hosts the largest number of international migrants globally. On the other hand, the ever more sophisticated and intensive policing of member states' borders has been a significant theme in research on migration and security in the EU context. Yet, while earlier work referred to the sharp edges of 'fortress Europe' (Geddes 2000), more recent scholarship has pointed to the increasing complexity and diffusion of Europe's borders.

In 1985 the Schengen Agreement was signed between France, Germany, Belgium, the Netherlands and Luxembourg. The Agreement pledged to apply the principle of the free movement of people, services and goods, as originally provided for under the 1957 Treaty of Rome, by abolishing border controls between those states. In 1990 a Convention implementing the Schengen Agreement was signed and within six years the original states were joined by Italy, Spain, Portugal, Greece, Austria, Denmark, Finland and Sweden. The body of law accompanying the implementation of the Agreement, known as the Schengen *acquis*, was formally incorporated into the Amsterdam Treaty in 1999. This incorporation was central to the expressed aim of the EU to establish a borderless 'area of freedom, security, and justice' (Article 2, Treaty of the European Union).

Although Schengen sought to enhance the freedom of movement for European citizens into and between the territories of the EU's member states this was accompanied by harsher controls on non-European nationals. A series of 'compensatory measures' were put in place including a tougher asylum and immigration regime to prevent illegal entry from the outside. As William Walters (2002) has pointed out, however, these measures formed a continuum with checks inside the EU to monitor movement within Europe via identity cards, hotel registers, employment registers, customs and excise legislation, health certificates, social security data, and the establishment of EU-wide information databases such as the Schengen Information System (SIS). On this basis, Walters argues that the EU's borders must be read not merely as a sharp line at the outer edge of member states' territories but as 'a more diffuse, networked, control apparatus' (Walters 2002: 573).

Similarly, Didier Bigo (2000) has emphasised the increasing intertwinement of internal and external security in the context of the EU. Surveillance of the sort to which Walters refers means that the domestic and foreign policies of member states are now inseparable. Accompanying these shifts is a blurring of high-intensity policing and low-intensity military activity so that the formerly distinct realms of police inside and army outside no longer hold purchase. Rather, new forms of transnational government have led to a blurring of the categories of the inside and the outside and a destabilisation of the concepts of sovereignty, territory and security. Whereas, Bigo claims, traditional notions of security were conceptualised in terms of a 'given territory delimited by state borders', what we see in the EU is a more complex field of (in)securitisation (for more on this concept see Chapter 5):

> Security checks are no longer necessarily done at the border on a systematic and egalitarian basis, but can be carried out further downstream, within the territory, within the border zone or even upstream with police collaboration in the home country of immigrants, through visa-gathering systems and through readmission agreements.
>
> (Bigo 2000: 185)

Bigo thus abandons a simple understanding of the border as a line between sovereign territories. Instead, he develops the idea of a 'field of (in)security' to refer to the fundamentally interconnected network of security relations in the EU (cf. Burgess 2011). Such a field involves the security of some at the expense of the insecurity of others: it is a method of 'unease management' that combines practices of exceptionalism, acts of profiling, containment and detention of foreigners, together with enhanced mobility for trusted liberal subjects (see Chapter 9).

Other recent work, in many ways further illustrating the insights of Walters and Bigo, has investigated the 'off-shoring' and 'out-sourcing' of Europe's borders (Bialasiewicz 2011, 2012.) In an additional stage in the Europeanisation of member states' borders, the Frontex agency was established in 2004 to promote a pan-European model of integrated border security. Added impetus was given to the coordination of Europe's borders in the wake of the attacks on 11 September and subsequent bombings in Madrid and London. Indeed, the

Revised EU Terrorism Action Plan of 9 March 2007 refers to the role of Frontex as central to counterterrorism initiatives by conducting effective risk analyses of threats to Europe's borders, maximising the capacity of existing border systems to detect suspected terrorist activity and to impede terrorists' movement into and within the EU. Sergio Carrera (2007) has examined how, in addition to traditional forms of borderwork at conventional sites such as ports, airports and peripheral territories, Frontex operations have also taken place hundreds of miles away from member states' territories.

In 2006, for example, the Spanish government approached Frontex to help with what it characterised as unprecedented levels of illegal immigration from Western Africa to the Canary Islands. Operation HERA II brought together technical border surveillance equipment from numerous member states with the objective of preventing migrants from leaving their shores on the long sea journey in the first place. To achieve this, Frontex mobilised patrol boats supplied by Italy and Portugal off the West African coast near Mauritania, Cape Verde and Senegal. Surveillance planes borrowed from Finland and Italy were also flown along the coastline and deeper into African territory in an attempt to deter would-be immigrants from travelling. Moreover, evidence from NGOs alleges that the naval interception of migrants at sea and their subsequent return to third countries – often with requests for humanitarian assistance denied – has become another strategy pursued by Frontex. On 21 June 2009, for example, it is claimed that Operation Nautilus IV picked up 74 migrants and handed them over to a Libyan patrol vessel marking the 'first forced return operation coordinated by Frontex on the high seas (PICUM 2010: 58).

Population movements arising from the Arab Spring have set the scene for an intensification of EU border security practices. According to the BBC, between January and March 2011 an estimated 25,000 'illegal immigrants' arrived on the Italian island of Lampedusa from North Africa. In response Frontex launched Operation Hermes, which pushed migration routes further eastwards and an unknown number have sought entry into the EU via Greece's border with Turkey. Despite the launch in 2011 of the EU's humanitarian-focused Global Approach to Migration and Mobility (GAMM), NGOs working in the region claim that the increasingly pre-emptive, off-shored, out-sourced and militarised nature of EU border security has not only exposed many more migrants to death at sea, but also to inhuman, degrading and often life-threatening conditions in detention centres throughout member states, north Africa, west Africa and the Greece–Turkey borderlands (PICUM 2010).

In these ways, the activities of Frontex constitute a European border performance that complicates the traditional geopolitical imaginary of the EU. The territorial limits of the EU on the one hand are increasingly decoupled from the stretch of the EU's attempts to control movement on the other hand.

Critical border studies

The idea that 'the border' is not what or where it is supposed to be according to traditional conceptions of global politics is a theme that Étienne Balibar (1998), among others, has written about. According to Balibar, the concept of the border is itself undergoing considerable transformation:

> We are living in a conjecture of the vacillation of borders [...] borders are no longer at the border, an institutionalised site that could be materialised on the ground and inscribed on the map, where one sovereignty ends and another begins.
>
> (1998: 217–218)

Crucially, reflecting on the insights of recent empirical work on the US–Mexico and European borders, Balibar is not arguing that the vacillation of borders means their disappearance. On the contrary, in his view borders are not melting away under conditions of globalisation, but are increasingly 'multiplied and reduced in their localisation [...] no longer the shores of politics but [...] the space of the political itself' (1998: 220).

The observation that borders are complex assemblages that are ever more dislocated, offshored and as mobile as the people, services and goods they seek to control, has prompted new directions in the inter-disciplinary field of border studies. Limology, the formal study of borders, first emerged as a branch of geography in the late nineteenth century and the focus was almost exclusively on empirical case studies of particular land borders (Kolossov 2005). Traditional geopolitical scholarship in this vein took as a given the existence of borders between states as territorial markers of jurisdiction and sovereignty. From the 1990s onwards, however, the influence of the postpositivist turn in social sciences led to a more nuanced treatment of borders in global politics. The field of critical geopolitics sought to problematise the modern geopolitical imagination of which the traditional image of the border has been central in carving divisions between inside/outside (Agnew 1994; Ó Tuathail 1996; Walker 1993). Instead of taking borders between states as a static given, this work has analysed the symbolic value of borders, the work that they do in various social, political and economic discourses, and how borders get (re)produced through 'signs, identifications, representations, performances, and stories' (van Houtum 2005: 672).

A more recent development in the study of borders, especially against the backdrop of the war on terror, has been a shift from a geopolitical to a biopolitical horizon of analysis. Thus, as we have already seen, Amoore draws on Foucault to diagnose what she calls the 'biometric border': a 'mobile regulatory site through which people's everyday lives can be made amenable to intervention and management' (Amoore 2006: 337; see also Muller 2010). Developing the thought of Giorgio Agamben (see Chapter 5), Nick Vaughan-Williams has identified a logic that he refers to as the 'generalised biopolitical border' (Vaughan-Williams 2009). Instead of viewing borders as fixed and at the outer edge of the state, Agamben offers critical resources for reconceptualising 'the border' as a mobile, pre-emptive and biopolitical decision about the worthiness of different lives. Such a 'decision', which is not necessarily taken by a singular sovereign source (or even a human, necessarily), attempts to performatively produce and secure the borders of political community. It does so by defining the politically qualified life of the citizen in contradistinction with those whose lives are deemed to be 'bare'. On this view, it is precisely this sovereign dividing practice – one that is not always 'successful', but rather always only an *attempt* – that constitutes the primary activity of border security across a global biopolitical terrain. Bigo (2007) also draws on the insights of Agamben to develop the concept of the 'ban-opticon', which can be understood as another alternative biopolitical border imaginary. This concept, a play on Bentham's figure of the panopticon as featured in the work of Foucault (see Chapter 5), refers to logics of surveillance that help to create a transnational field of unease and (in) security management that transcends divisions between inside and outside. The use of 'ban' is a reference to Jean-Luc Nancy's concept of the 'abandoned being' (Nancy 1993), which Agamben uses to characterise bare life. Lives that are produced as 'bare' by sovereign power are effectively banned from juridical-political structures: they are subject to them but do not benefit from any of the rights of the citizen. In this context we might think of various 'exceptional' figures caught up in the biopolitical border politics of the war on terror such as the detainees in Guantánamo Bay, Jean Charles de Menezes who was shot dead by UK counterterrorist officers in Stockwell Station on 22 July 2005, and in some contexts entire communities deemed to pose a security risk purely because of their ethnic background (see also Chapter 9).

But while there has been a spirited uptake of Agamben in some quarters of critical migration and border studies (Diken 2004; De Genova and Peutz 2010; Khosravi 2010; Rajaram and Grundy-Warr 2004), other scholars have expressed caution when focusing on sovereign power, the politics of exceptionalism and the 'bare life' thesis more generally. Vicki Squire argues that 'while Agambenian analyses of border practices generally focus on the exceptional moments of a politics of control, an analytics of irregularity examines a range of processes of (ir)regularization that are manifest across various sites through various rhythms and in various forms – the standard and the everyday, as well as the extraordinary and the spectacular' (Squire 2011: 14). Agamben may offer tools for theorising border security as a technique of government, but his work is arguably less instructive – even ignorant of – the daily experiences of migrants and how they in turn shape regimes of border control. For Squire 'borderzones may be marked by struggles around abjectification, but do not necessarily produce abject subjects' and for this reason she argues that it is important to recover sites of contestation and migrant agency (Squire 2011: 14; see also Johnson 2013; McNevin 2013; Shewly 2013).

A growing literature associated with the broad label of CBS has sought to problematise the conception of 'the border' as a 'thin' line demarcating the sovereign territory of member states (Johnson *et al.* 2011; Parker and Vaughan-Williams 2009, 2013; Squire 2011). According to Parker and Vaughan-Williams (2009: 2), one of the tasks of critical border studies is to 'extrapolate new border concepts, logics, and imaginaries that capture the changing perspective on what borders are supposed to be and where they may be supposed to lie'. For example, by adopting a biopolitical perspective that reads borders as mobile controls on and through the bodies of individuals, new ways of thinking 'the border' are opened up. Surveillance technologies and other methods of monitoring movement can be incorporated in a broader conception of what bordering practices consist of (see Dijstelbloem and Ameijer 2011). In turn, this also allows for analysis of how the agents of many contemporary border security practices are not exclusively those employed by the state, but citizens who adopt the role of temporary sovereigns in performing borderwork (Rumford 2008, 2012). Moreover, the research foci on the changing nature of borders as they relate to broader spatial, governmental and legal shifts, the ethical and political implications of border controls, and the multiple violences and injustices implied by increasingly preemptive border security practices, means that there are significant areas of overlap between critical security, border and migration studies.

Conclusion

The movement of people across the globe has increased with growing populations, easier and cheaper forms of transportation, and new technologies that enhance communication. Yet, while migration to some of the most popular destinations such as Europe and North America was once welcomed by host governments, the issue has arguably become securitised. The securitisation of migration in the West began in the 1980s, although this process was given added impetus by the attacks of 11 September 2001. Migration has become ever more closely associated with the threat of international terrorism, transnational crime and the dissolution of traditional forms of political community. Critical approaches to the study of migration have sought to trace the production of mobility as a security threat, emphasise the ethical and political implications of the categorisation of different forms of migrants, and argue for a shift in the referent object of analysis away from statist perspectives on 'tides' and 'swarms' of migrants to the individual and his/her experiences and political agency.

As part of the securitisation of migration we have witnessed the rise of new forms of border security practices. These practices are not, however, designed merely to *stop* the circulation of people, services, and goods. Rather, borders are increasingly designed to maximise flows of legitimate traffic while at the same time filtering out illegitimate movement. The traditional geopolitical imagination views the border as a territorial marker of the limits of sovereign power at the outer geographical edge of the state. Innovations in border security practices, such as the Smart Border Alliance in the US or the activities of Frontex in the EU, in many ways challenge this imagination and call for alternative ways of conceptualising what and where borders are.

Key points

- Migrants are classified by states in different ways to manage flows of people and each classification has important implications for individuals.
- A range of writers in critical security studies has shown how migration has become produced as a security threat, or 'securitised', in the West.
- Critical approaches to border and migration studies have argued that borders are ever-more complex phenomena, not only to be found at the territorial outer edge of the state but increasingly dispersed across a global terrain.

Discussion points

- What and/or whom does migration threaten?
- Should migration be securitised? How could it be desecuritised?
- What is the relation between the securitisation of migration and the politics of fear?
- In what ways are borders central to the securitisation of migration?
- What and/or where are borders in contemporary political life?
- Does the distinction between inside and outside still apply in the study of global security relations?

Guide to further reading

Claudia Aradau (2008) *Rethinking Trafficking in Women: Politics Out of Security* (London and New York: Palgrave Macmillan). Offers a detailed empirical engagement with the gendered dimension of human trafficking and a theoretical critique of 'desecuritisation' and 'emancipation'.

Elspeth Guild (2009) *Security and Migration in the 21st Century* (Cambridge: Polity). An excellent introduction to the historical, conceptual and empirical phenomenon of migration and its relation to critical security studies.

Jef Huysmans (2006) *The Politics of Insecurity: Fear, Migration and Asylum in the EU* (London: Routledge). An important account of the securitisation of migration in the European context.

Nick Vaughan-Williams (2009) *Border Politics: The Limits of Sovereign Power* (Edinburgh: Edinburgh University Press). A poststructuralist critique of the concept of the border in the modern geopolitical imagination.

Vicki Squire (2011) (ed.) *The Contested Politics of Mobility: Borderzones and Irregularity* (London: Routledge). An agenda-setting collection of essays analysing contemporary border struggles via the lens of 'irregularity'.

Weblinks

United Nations, Department of Economic and Social Affairs, Population Division, International Migration: http://www.un.org/esa/population/migration/index.html
Minute Men Project: www.veteransforsecureborders.us
No Borders Network: http://noborders.org.uk/
United for Intercultural Action: www.unitedagainstracism.org/
Nijmegen Centre for Border Research, Radboud University, Nijmegen: http://ncbr.ruhosting.nl/
International Boundaries Research Unit, Durham University: www.dur.ac.uk/ibru/

12 Technology and warfare in the information age

Abstract

This chapter engages arguments and evidence that suggests that developments in both technology and warfare in the 'information age' have significant implications for practices of war and the way we think about them. Here it looks particularly at the idea of a 'Western way of war', the related discourse and developments associated with the 'revolution in military affairs', and the increasing mediation of warfare as a key feature of contemporary conflict. Having established this context, the chapter then goes on to examine ways in which scholars working from various theoretical positions have addressed specific features of contemporary practices and discourses of warfare: virtual war, technostrategic discourse and dataveillance. In closing, the chapter evaluates the current state of critical scholarship on technology and warfare, and questions where this scholarship might go from here.

Introduction

The issue of whether and how technological change impacts upon warfare – and vice versa – forms a perennial debate in security studies. 'War', Carl von Clausewitz declared in his oft-cited maxim from *On War* (Clausewitz 1976 [1832]), 'is the continuation of politics by other means'. This has been interpreted by some modern advocates of Clausewitz as indicating that war has a fundamental, eternal nature that remains essentially constant in the face of technological change. The view is summed up in the title of an article by one self-proclaimed 'Clausewitzian': 'Clausewitz rules, OK? The future is past – with GPS' (Gray 1999). Not all analysts of contemporary warfare, however, are as convinced as Colin S. Gray that the nature of conflict remains fundamentally as it was when Clausewitz wrote during the Napoleonic era, or that technologies such as GPS (global positioning systems) are mere 'add-ons' to traditional means and methods of organised violence. Within security and war studies there have recently been several attempts to characterise the nature of contemporary warfare as a distinctive form. Some have argued that the study of conflict needs to take into account the emergence of 'new wars' (Kaldor 1999) where 'old' forms of state-based conflict have given way to the prevalence of intra-state wars and where private use of force – in the form of militias, criminal organisations and private military companies (PMCs) – undercuts the state's supposed monopoly of violence. Others have seen similar dynamics as heralding the advent of 'postmodern war', additionally marked by reliance on technology and increasingly sophisticated means of destruction but, paradoxically, most prominent within the 'post-military' societies of the US and Western Europe that tend to be predominantly war averse (Gray 1997; Shaw 2005: 37). Box 12.1 offers a brief introduction to some of the key concepts associated with these debates. The rest of the chapter then proceeds to an overview

---

Box 12.1 Key concepts: Technology and warfare in the information age

Western way of war: The idea that Western states and militaries have developed a way of battle that emphasises technological superiority as a means to assure both military victory and minimisation of casualties.

Revolution in military affairs (RMA): Refers, broadly speaking, to the use and incorporation of information technologies to enhance US warfighting capacities.

Spectator-sport war: Used to denote the extent to which Western publics in particular primarily 'spectate' (through visual media) rather than participate in war.

Virtual war: Indicates a form of warfare where for the users of certain military technologies war is experienced primarily as a series of visual images and representations.

Technostrategic discourse: Used to describe the way in which the language of military planners tends to mimic and legitimate military technology itself.

Dataveillance: The monitoring and 'mining' of multiple forms of data – including financial transactions, patterns of international travel and behavioural data – by security professionals with the aim of identifying potentially 'risky' groups and individuals.

---

of these debates and to outline key critical positions on technology and warfare in the information age.

The 'Western way of war' and the revolution in military affairs

In tandem with the notions of 'new' and 'postmodern' wars, the concept of a new *Western way of war* has also become increasingly common in current debates over the nature of contemporary conflict. The idea of a Western way of warfare is used to capture the way in which Western militaries – the US in particular and many Western Europe states – have shifted their emphasis away from a reliance on armies based on mass conscription, to militaries based around smaller numbers of professionalised troops, but with an increased level of technological capability and greater employment of 'private' military forces (see Box 12.2). In part this trend might be seen to be driven by technological development; but it is also a reflection of the extent to which the populations of the US and Western Europe are increasingly 'risk averse'. Martin Shaw argues that since the Vietnam war, Western publics have become increasingly intolerant of military fatalities (owing in large part to the effects of the so-called 'body-bag' syndrome), and statistics show that the number of people signing up for military service in Western states has tended to decline in recent decades.

Hence, Western militaries have increasingly used technology to achieve 'risk transfer' – the minimisation of fatalities by transferring the risk of death to enemy combatants as far as possible. The employment of 'precision' weapons is one of the main ways that Western militaries have attempted to achieve this, although as Shaw notes the frequent corollary is that the risk is transferred to innocent civilians as well as enemy combatants (Shaw 2005).

This move towards an emphasis on hi-tech military methods is identified in particular with the US and its post-cold war emphasis on establishing a 'revolution in military affairs' (RMA): that is, using civilian and military technological innovations – particularly information technologies – to provide the US military with an enhanced strike capability that allows it in turn to rely on smaller troop numbers. Undoubtedly the US is the world's most advanced

---

Box 12.2 The privatisation of warfare

Described by some as 'the new business face of war' (Singer 2001: 187), the rise of 'private military companies' (PMCs), or 'private military firms' (PMFs), is one of the more notable features of contemporary warfare. The employment of PMCs has been an issue for consideration in the study of security for some time, but became particularly prominent as a result of the high reliance of the US on private contractors to provide 'military support' functions in its post-2003 occupation of Iraq. In such instances PMCs – for a fee – increasingly 'conduct tasks in the fields of logistics, maintenance and force application that were once thought to be the sole preserve of a state's security sector' (Spearin 2003: 27). 'Private' forms of organised violence are, of course, not entirely novel: the use of paid mercenaries has been common historically, and warlords routinely employ private forces to sustain their power against formal state authorities. Whereas those examples of privatised military force are often seen as illegitimate under international law, though, PMCs are a grey area. PMCs generally tend to be hierarchically organised corporations that operate as (military) service providers on the international market. And far from necessarily competing with states' security provision, in many instances states have actually encouraged the growth and operations of PMCs. Some argue that PMCs are a symptom not just of growing privatisation of state functions at a general level, but also a consequence of efforts by states in North America and Europe in particular to 'downsize' their militaries and 'outsource' military security functions in the post-cold war era. Abrahamsen and Williams (2009), for example, argue that the privatisation of warfare and of states' security sectors should be viewed as part of a broader reconfiguration of global–local and public–private relations predicated in turn on the 'commodification' of military and physical security provision. They illustrate that case by detailing the development of a 'global security assemblage' (2009: 3) of oil companies, private security firms and state authorities in the Niger Delta to 'secure' the extraction of the region's oil resources for international consumption. The rise of PMCs thus raises the troubling prospect that, in some instances at least, 'security' is thought of as a commodity to be bought and sold.

---

military force today in terms of its technological superiority. It has consistently led the way in the development of new military technologies: predator drones – pilotless planes, which have been used not only for surveillance but also for destroying targets (see Box 12.3); 'precision-guided munitions' (PGMs) – missiles that can be used to destroy targets with increased accuracy and can be remotely targeted (often referred to as 'smart weapons'); stealth technologies such as stealth bombers, largely undetectable to radar; what are known as non-lethal technologies such as EMP (electro-magnetic pulse) weapons that can be used to disable an opponent's electricity supply without actually using physical force; battlefield missile defence systems such as the Patriot system; the use of GPS for reconnaissance and munitions guidance... and so the list goes on.

There is an extensive academic debate over whether US technological innovation does actually constitute a fundamental change in the way war is fought, whether it should be considered as an 'evolution' rather than a 'revolution', or whether the nature of warfare has remained essentially the same in spite of the RMA (see Gray 2004). What is less debatable, though, is the extent to which the idea of the RMA and its associated terminology has become a staple of American military and security policy discourse. At the core of this RMA idea is the belief that advances in information technology lead to far-reaching changes in the organisation, equipment and training of military forces resulting in an entirely new way of warfare. In the 1990s, US military planners began to look at ways in which the 'information

---

Box 12.3 A new way of war? The rise of the drones

One of the most prominent and controversial products of the US RAM is the Predator drone unmanned aircraft – a remotely piloted aircraft whose primary mission is 'interdiction and conducting armed reconnaissance against critical, perishable targets' (GlobalSecurity.Org 2009: 1). Equipped with Hellfire missiles (see weblink) and state-of-the-art targeting systems, the pilotless drone plane is flown by an operator in a ground control station. Cameras in the nose of the plane relay video images via satellite to the pilot on the ground and, with no human component in the plane itself, Predators can be kept airborne for much longer periods than manned aircraft. Drones operating over Afghanistan and Pakistan have been piloted from Nevada in the western US, and the same basic principle underlies the operation of other drones (or unmanned aerial vehicles – UAVs) available to the US, such as the Reaper and the Global Hawk.

Drones have now been in operation for several years. In 2008, these 'robo-craft' flew almost 400,000 combat hours in US operations in Afghanistan and Iraq and generated an exponential increase in the amount of surveillance coverage available to US forces (Shactman 2009: 1). Drone planes have also controversially been used for purposes of 'targeted killing' by the US in its counterterrorism operations in Afghanistan and its border regions with Pakistan, raising controversy over accusations of contravention of Pakistani sovereignty as well as allegations of the killing of civilians in several drone attacks.

UAVs essentially provide the US military with unprecedented potential for 'war at a distance' with enormous 'strike capabilities', but with no risk to a drone's human operator. As such they are a far remove (literally) from any traditional notion of face-to-face combat, and raise complex questions about the nature of contemporary warfare: is recourse to war more likely when the risk of human fatalities for the attacker is virtually non-existent? How similar or different are drones to other forms of 'remote' warfare from a distance, such as the use of cruise missiles or high-altitude strategic bombing?

---

revolution' – innovation in civilian computer technology and communication systems epitomised by the growth of the internet – could be used to enhance military effectiveness. For proponents of the RMA, information is key. With more information available, it is assumed, military decision-makers will be less prone to what Clausewitz called 'the fog of war': the lack of 'situational awareness' on the battlefield that arises from unforeseen events. The more we know about the battlefield, so the argument goes, the easier it is to control it by minimising the possibility that such unforeseen events will arise.

Technological innovation in areas such as satellite surveillance, communications and the 'information super-highway' are thus seen to promise avenues of greater control for American military planners. This technological optimism has arguably been dealt a significant blow by the actual nature of the US-led military campaigns in Afghanistan and Iraq, where technological sophistication did not prevent the US from becoming mired in long, drawn-out and bloody campaigns. However, it is also argued that the RMA is not simply about the incorporation of new technologies, but also the 'transformation' of US forces and tactics in a sense that outlasts individual military interventions. Consequently the concept of the RMA is often accompanied by a range of jargon that is still used to denote various aspects of this transformation, such as the concept of 'network centric warfare' (the idea that conflict will increasingly be organised around networks and nodes of information transfer), C4I (command, control, communications, computers and military intelligence) and 'cyberwar' (attacks directed specifically against computers and communications systems that include techniques such as 'hacking' and 'jamming'). The last term – also variously referred to as 'netwar' and 'information warfare' – was identified in the 1990s as one of the key looming developments in conflict. Since the RMA is predicated on the centrality of information and information transfer, Pentagon planners quickly pinpointed the disruption of networks of information transfer as a key goal not only for US forces but also potential adversaries in the form of 'cyber-terrorism'. The prospect of a 'digital Pearl Harbour' – an unexpected attack by 'hackers' on either civilian or military infrastructure to disable the national grid, telecommunications systems or military satellites – has long been cited as a potential threat that has emerged simultaneous to the RMA. Hansen and Nissenbaum (2009) argue that the increasing focus on 'cyber-security' in political and media discourse ends up replaying many of the features of securitisation (see Chapter 6). The fear of attacks on networked computer systems now often includes non-military systems such as communication and banking infrastructures, but represents the threat of cyber attacks via militarised language and metaphors to justify exceptional measures to protect the security of states, societies and economies as referent objects.

Mediation and war

The idea of the Western way of war and the RMA are both inherently linked to the increasing *mediation* of conflict as a feature of contemporary warfare – where the term mediation can be used to denote both increasing media coverage and the growing use of forms of visual media to direct and conduct conflict. Here the Gulf War of 1991 is commonly cited as a key event. The overwhelming success of the US-led coalition against Saddam Hussein seemed to vindicate the argument that innovation in military technology would improve military effectiveness for the US, and its ability to intervene decisively (for a critique of this view see Biddle 1996). The US-led coalition deployed 795,000 troops, but suffered only 240 fatalities. During the campaign, US forces used technological superiority in the realm of air warfare to strike a decisive initial blow, using a six-week air campaign to destroy key Iraqi targets and to fatally damage the Iraqi command and control structure. In part the US success was based on the incorporation of satellite communications, targeting and reconnaissance technologies, such as GPS, leading some to dub the conflict as the 'first space war'.

Moreover, media coverage of the conflict seemed to show the decisive nature of US military systems, such as the Patriot anti-missile system, which was used to protect Kuwait from incoming Iraqi Scud missiles. Although the actual success of the Patriot in 1991 later came into question (see Postol 1992), television coverage at the time portrayed it as one of the technological successes of the conflict. Television viewers were also treated to 'real-time' recordings of smart bombs approaching their target, with images relayed from a camera mounted on the projectile itself, before the picture tuned blank as the bomb hit its target. As Martin Shaw notes, 'the idea that war could be fought *with* blanket media coverage but *without* many casualties, which were mostly not actually shown to the viewers, became mainstream with the Gulf War' (2005: 37).

Mediation of war has also become increasingly 'mainstream' in various military interventions that have followed in the wake of the 1991 Gulf War, and the growth of this trend has led some analysts to speak of the phenomenon of *spectator-sport war*:

> When Western states use force, they do so from afar, involving directly only a limited number of representatives on the field of battle. Society no longer participates; it spectates from a distance. Like sports spectators, Westerners demonstrate different levels of engagement, from those who watch unmoved and soon forget to those who follow

events, personalities, tactics, and strategies closely and empathize strongly with what is happening. But their experience is removed. They sympathise but do not suffer; they empathize but do not experience.

(McInnes 2002: 2)

Yet, with the rapid expansion of new forms of global media, the question arises as to whether we can speak of the mediation of warfare solely in terms of a straightforward (and ethno-centric) 'Western' way of representing and interpreting conflict.

Box 12.4 illustrates that the mediation of contemporary conflict is both increasingly perva-sive, ethically complex and raises challenging questions about the way images of war are produced and consumed. As Shaw argues, media management is 'essential' and both state and non-state military actors attempt to achieve this as far as possible (2005: 92). But ensuring that the 'official' line is not disrupted is growing ever more difficult given the proliferation of media outlets, most notably via satellite television and the internet (see Robinson *et al.* 2005 and Goddard *et al.* 2008). The rise of military blogging (or 'milblogging') – through which individual soldiers post their own thoughts and perspectives via blogs, online forums and social networking sites – is one example how 'perception management' in war has become even more complex and challenging. As illustrated in the recent conflicts in Afghanistan and Iraq, milbloggers frequently post personal accounts and images of conflict that challenge or even deviate from official media representations. And in the multiple uprisings of the Arab Spring of 2011, social media were employed by protestors to organise demonstrations and to

---

Box 12.4 The war of images

Television is a key facet of the technological mediation of conflict. Indeed, for some policing the way that accounts of war are taken up has itself resulted in 'a struggle over representations' (Shapiro 1990: 337). With the proliferation of media outlets globally, the invasion of Iraq in 2003 saw different styles of representation of the conflict and different assumptions of what should be broadcast. During the 1991 Gulf War, the Middle East and the rest of the world largely relied on CNN and other Western broadcasters for breaking news. Since its launch in 1996, however, the Qatar-based media outlet al-Jazeera's coverage of global events has made it one of the most watched channels in the Arab world. On 23 March 2003, al-Jazeera raised the stakes in the struggle over representation of the invasion of Iraq by broadcasting footage of captured American prisoners of war. The footage took three forms: interviews (interrogations, according to the Pentagon) with three clearly distressed soldiers – two male, one female; pictures of a fourth serviceman, badly wounded and slumped on a stretcher; and graphic images of four dead US servicemen, who appeared to have been shot in the head at close range, lying in pools of blood on the floor of a concrete room (Whitaker 2003). Television news outlets in the US and UK seemed unsure as to whether their own codes of conduct allowed broadcasting of such images. After initially withdrawing the footage, Sky News was the first British broadcaster to run the footage; BBC News 24 followed, though chose to hold off from transmitting the footage on its international service BBC World. ITN opted to manipulate the footage into still pictures. Confusion as to how to deal with or even react to the images seemed to be the order of the day. When then US Defense Secretary Donald Rumsfeld appeared on the CBS *Face the Nation* programme on 23 March, the Pentagon had been denying reports that ten US soldiers were captured or missing in Iraq. Then, presenter Bob Schieffer switched to footage from al-Jazeera showing two confused American servicemen being questioned by an Iraqi interviewer. Asked what he made of the footage, Rumsfeld replied: 'I have no idea' (Wells and Campbell 2003).

disrupt and resist the efforts of state security forces. In this context, use of and access to such visual and digital media (and the securitisation of images – see Chapter 6 and Williams 2003b) constitutes one of the most pertinent issues in contemporary security studies, as does the issue of censorship of information on the web in the name of national security (see the weblinks to CitizenLab and the Center for Democracy and Technology).

Virtual wars

The abundance of forms of mediation of warfare in the information age has led several analysts to deploy the concept of *virtual war* to characterise this trend. The term virtual war implies that the increasing technological mediation of war creates a type of war that no longer 'physically exists as such' for the user (Der Derian 2000: 75). Scholars such as James Der Derian argue that, as in the case with UAVs (see Box 12.3), certain forms of contemporary warfare create a new (virtual) reality for the operators of these hi-tech systems.

Literature on virtual wars began to expand in the late 1990s and early 2000s, particularly in the wake of the US-led NATO intervention in Kosovo, which was seen by many as the first truly virtual war (Ignatieff 2000a). US supremacy in air power and its advanced missile and targeting technologies meant that NATO could intervene in Kosovo through airstrikes alone, without actually having to put troops on the ground or engaging its Serb adversary directly. Technological supremacy seemed to achieve the fantasy of what Robert Mandel (2004) calls 'Bloodless War' (for NATO forces at least – some have argued that the nature of the intervention actually facilitated the continuation of atrocities against civilians on the ground), and Michael Ignatieff defined this form of virtual war as 'war with death removed, waged in conditions of impunity' (2000b: 1).

Although the idea of virtual war has been picked up and used by a range of scholars in security studies, it has become most notable as a concern of those working from a post-structuralist orientation. In particular the theme has been treated extensively by James Der Derian. For Der Derian the virtual 'constructs worlds – not *ex nihilio* but *ex machina* – where there were none before' (2000: 75), and the key feature of 'virtuality' is not its ability to mimic reality, but to create new realities. These virtual wars create new realities of conflict through reliance on *information*, the ability to overcome physical distance through the *speed* of information transfer allowed by new technologies, and, crucially, through the prevalence of forms of *simulation*.

As reliance on *information* is crucial to the virtual war effort, scholars such as Der Derian point out that techniques of representation and forms of mediation increase in importance and need to be critically interrogated. The capacity to enact force accurately from remote locations is central to virtual war, but it also makes it dependent on accurate information and, increasingly, on accurate interpretation of signs, images and representations of data on a computer monitor. Hence the 'security of meaning' (as discussed in Chapter 5) comes to be of key importance. If representation and interpretation of information are not seamlessly aligned in modern conflict, disaster frequently results. As Ignatieff argues in the case of Kosovo, no one questioned whether the data the NATO coalition forces relied on actually corresponded to anything real on the ground, and this arguably contributed to several high-profile 'targeting errors' (Ignatieff 2000a) most notably the bombing of civilians and of the Chinese embassy in Belgrade in 1999.

Similarly, the ability to overcome physical distance through the *speed* of new technologies of information and force transference also raises critical issues. 'The power of virtuality', Der Derian argues;

lies in its ability to collapse distance, between here and there, near and far, fact and fiction [...] the virtual effect of bringing 'there' here in near real-time and with near-verisimilitude adds a strategic as well as comparative advantage in the production of violence.

(2000: 75)

However, the ability to enact near-instantaneous force from a remote location raises a concern over whether prohibitions on the use of force become less restrictive as a result. For instance US army psychologist Lieutenant Colonel Dave Grossman has argued that for soldiers operating at long-range resistance to killing is much lower (see Grossman 1996), whilst others worry that:

As war becomes safer and easier, as soldiers are removed from the horrors of war and see the enemy not as humans but as blips on a screen, there is a very real danger of losing the deterrent that such horrors provide.

(Shurtleff 2002: 103)

In addition, it may be that the pace of information transfer can also outstrip the pace of human cognition. As more and more aspects of warfighting are delegated to technological systems there is the risk that such systems outpace the limits of human reaction times.

These themes are brought together in the discussion of the final characteristic of virtual war: *simulation*. Particularly in the form of computer-based battle simulations and war games, simulation is now a common feature of Western military training and formulation of strategy (see Der Derian 2009). Simulations are generally viewed by their users as mere preparations for or representations of worst-case scenarios; but several authors argue that they help to produce and delimit new practices of warfare through holistic training and 'hyperreal' modelling. According to Der Derian: 'Digitized, virtual wargames and peace-games, twice removed by scripted strategies and technological artifice from the bloody reality of war, take simulation into another realm [...] where distinctions between the simulated and the real begin to break down' (2000: 95). Here Der Derian draws upon the poststructuralist thinking of Jean Baudrillard, who argues that the increasing prevalence of forms of simulation 'threatens the difference between "true" and "false", between "real" and "imaginary"' (Baudrillard 1993: 344). Infamously Baudrillard took this logic to its extreme by declaring that 'The Gulf War did not take place' (1995), arguing that the heavily mediated nature of the 1991 Gulf conflict meant that for the vast majority of those not participant in the conflict (and even some of those participating on the US side) the war was experienced primarily as a series of images and representations that effectively superseded the 'reality' of the conflict (for a critique see Norris 1992).

Leaving aside the merits or otherwise of Baudrillard's provocative argument, there are instances where it might be said that simulation increasingly impacts upon both peace making and warfare in tangible ways. During the Bosnian peace talks of 1995 the negotiators for the US used state-of-the-art real-time computer simulation to bring a temporary halt to the genocide. At key points in the negotiations US officials took the Bosnian, Croatian and Serbian presidents into the 'Nintendo' room where they could see a real-time three-dimensional map of the disputed territories, and 'they reduced heated arguments over territory to a kind of computer game [...] There, Milosevic and others manipulated a joystick to zoom along electronic displays of Bosnian terrain originally developed for NATO bombing rehearsals' (Mollins *et al.* 1995).

Less positively, some commentators argue that simulated training blurs the distinction between the virtual and the actual, sometimes with tragic consequences. A case in point examined by Der Derian (1990), Gray (1997) and Michael Shapiro (1998) is the shooting down of Iranian flight 665 by the American vessel the USS *Vincennes* in 1988. The incident, which resulted in the death of 290 civilians, has received sustained attention from those interested in the theme of virtual war because of the strong possibility that the simulated training undergone by the ship's weapons operators actually facilitated the mistaken identification of the passenger plane as a 'hostile' target. Indeed it has been argued:

> The reality of the nine months of simulated battles displaced, overrode, absorbed the reality of the Airbus. The Airbus disappeared before the missile struck: it faded from an airliner full of civilians to an electronic representation on a radar screen to a simulated target. The simulation overpowered a reality which did not conform to it.
>
> (Der Derian 1990: 302)

In a similar vein other scholars have examined the occurrence of 'friendly fire' incidents involving the use of battlefield missile defence systems in the invasion of Iraq in 2003, including the shooting down of a British Tornado aircraft and the death of its two crew members. As one commander of a Partiot battalion in Iraq told a subsequent enquiry:

> when you train, you're taught to react so quickly because the Air Battles that we train on, in my opinion, are unrealistic […] there are too many things going on at one time, so all it trains you to do is just react. And that is just fine, but out here it is more complicated than that.
>
> (quoted in Peoples 2008: 26)

The merits of even the most 'hyperreal' simulation consequently come into question. As Lieutenant General William S. Wallace, one of the leading American commanders in the invasion of Iraq, admitted to reporters early on in the invasion: 'The enemy we're fighting is a bit different from the one we war-gamed against' (cited in Dwyer 2003 and Der Derian 2003: 37).

However the use of simulation in recruitment and training shows no signs of abating (see Box 12.5). The US military continues to encourage integration of both recruitment and training with battle simulations in a video game format most prominently in the development and promotion of 'America's Army Online', while the British army has recently used a series of interactive battlefield scenarios aimed at assessing the teamwork, decision making, leadership and fitness based on real missions from Iraq (entitled 'Start Thinking Soldier') as a means of attracting potential recruits (see weblinks).

Der Derian's work is frequently at pains to point out that virtual wars always have visceral, corporeal effects for those on the receiving end of modern military technologies. The grim realities of 'collateral' damage are frequently obscured or absented from slick media–military presentations of 'precision' weapons. This is why, he argues, we should pay greater attention to the incorporation of virtuality in modern military systems than to the much cited threat of 'cyberterrorism', the form of 'virtual' warfare that is more prominently referred to by military planners. Others, such as Chris Hables Gray, have also sought to reintroduce an emphasis on the corporeal, 'fleshy' humans that are the perpetrators and victims of hi-tech warfare (2003: 223). Thus, the suffering of the victims of, for example, drone attacks is obscured from the view of the general public; but, simultaneously, even for drone

---

Box 12.5 From virtual to 'virtuous war'

James Der Derian has now coined the term 'virtuous war' to describe the meshing of media and military technologies, and their virtual qualities, with a particular set of values. 'At the heart of virtuous war', he argues:

> is the technical capability and ethical imperative to threaten and, if necessary, actualize violence from a distance – *with no or minimal casualties*. Using networked information and virtual technologies to bring 'there' here in near-real time and near verisimilitude, virtuous war exercises a comparative as well as strategic advantage for the digitally advanced.
>
> (2009: xxxi, emphasis in original)

In other words, new forms of Western warfare not only emphasise virtuality, but justify and legitimate the use of violence from a distance on the virtues of allegedly greater discriminatory capability of military technology and consequent minimisation of casualties. In this sense virtuous war is 'ethically intentioned and virtually applied' (Der Derian 2003: 39). Virtuous war is thus based not only on the capacity to exert extraordinary force, but also the capacity to keep its actual consequences out of sight lest they undermine the apparent virtues of this form of warfare. Consequently management of media representations – through, for example, 'embedding' journalists and television crews within military units – are key to maintaining the efficacy of this form of violence, as are the Hollywood blockbusters and computer games that replicate and even sometimes inform military security practices. With regard to the latter, Der Derian cites the example of the Institute for Creative Technologies at the University of Southern California (see weblinks), which brings together representatives of the US military and Hollywood for 'joint modelling and simulation research […] for the army as well as for the entertainment, media, video game, film, destination theme park, and information technology industries' (2009: 162). This, Der Derian argues, is emblematic of an ever expanding 'military-industrial-media-entertainment network' that sustains virtuous war.

---

operators the use of drones may not be entirely 'risk free' (even as it avoids the risk of their own death in war), with an increasing number reporting post-traumatic stress as they struggle to 'process' the lethal effects of their actions after they enact them from a distance.

'Technostrategic' discourse and its critics

The sections above detail some of the ways in which the effects of technological innovation and the 'information revolution' have been treated within critical security studies. From a slightly different direction, however, other scholars operating within a critical framework have sought to reflect upon the seemingly unending infatuation with technology and military hardware, both within security practices and the academic study of security.

Feminist security studies

Although written during the last decade of the cold war, Carol Cohn's seminal work on 'Sex, Death and Defense Intellectuals' remains one of the most instructive and provocative studies in this regard. Operating from an avowedly feminist perspective, Cohn identified the prevalence of what she termed as 'technostrategic' discourse in the language of nuclear war planners and, by extension, the academic study of nuclear strategy in the 1980s. In a now seminal 1987 article Cohn coined the term 'technostrategic' to:

represent the intertwined, inextricable nature of technological and nuclear strategic thinking [...] strategic theory not only depends on and changes in response to technological objects, it is also based on a kind of thinking, a way of looking at problems – formal, mathematical modelling, systems analysis, game theory, linear programming – that are part of technology itself. So I use the term 'technostrategic' to indicate the degree to which nuclear strategic language and thinking are imbued with, indeed constructed out of, modes of thinking that are associated with technology.

(1987a: 690)

Written from her experiences participating at a workshop run by 'distinguished "defense intellectuals"' in 1984, Cohn's analysis focuses on one level on the highly gendered nature of the language used by American cold war nuclear planners (1987a: 687). One of the primary features of technostrategic discourse, Cohn argues, is 'the ubiquitous weight of gender' and the frequently sexualised nature of the terminology employed by military planners: 'vertical erector launchers, thrust-to-weight ratios, soft lay downs, deep penetration, and the comparative advantages of protracted versus spasm attacks' are some of the recurrent examples picked out by Cohn of terms employed by the (almost exclusively male) strategists and planners to describe the merits and disadvantages of various nuclear missile technologies (1987a: 688, 693).

At another level, though, Cohn's analysis speaks to the ways in which technostrategic language distances military planners from the visceral effects of nuclear weapons (see also Cohn *et al.* 2005), and frequently does so by rendering the weapons themselves as objects of desire or sexual anxiety. It is marked by 'elaborate use of abstraction and euphemism, of words so bland that they never forced the speaker or enabled the listener to touch the realities of nuclear holocaust that lay behind the words' (1987a: 690). Cohn picks out the example of 'clean bombs' – a term used in 1980s nuclear strategic parlance to describe bombs that use fusion rather than fission and hence have a greater destructive power. The metaphor of clean bombs, Cohn argues,

may provide the perfect metaphor for the language of defense analysts and arms controllers. This language has enormous destructive power, *but without emotional fallout*, without the emotional fallout that would result if it were clear one was talking about plans for mass murder, mangled bodies, and unspeakable human suffering.

(1987a: 691, emphasis added)

Though Cohn's analysis was developed within a discussion of cold war strategic thinking, its implications and insights can as easily be applied both to contemporary discussions of nuclear weapons, and to the prevalence of euphemisms and acronyms such as 'smart bombs', 'collateral damage' and C4I within the discourse the RMA and post-cold war military planning. It also speaks to the increasing aestheticisation of weapons and weapons systems – the processes by which the latest weapons systems are represented as the height of invention in glitzy promotional videos and simulations (see weblink to 'Lockheed Hellfire II missile' for an example) – and could in this sense overlap with at least some of the issues captured by the idea of virtual war.

In a sense, Cohn's argument takes as its concern the distancing effects that many of those concerned with virtual war discussed previously also investigate; but where it differs slightly is in locating the source of these distancing effects not necessarily in the mediating features of the technologies themselves, but in the language used to describe and domesticate these weapons and the potential consequences of their use. Hence, 'the imagery that domesticates, that humanizes insentient weapons, may also serve, paradoxically, to make it all right to ignore sentient human bodies, human lives' (Cohn 1987a: 699).

Here again, Cohn argues, the gender dimension is important to understanding in the manner in which weapons of mass destruction are rendered more familiar by use of domestic, feminised metaphors. Patterns of nuclear attack are referred to as the 'cookie cutter', weapons systems 'marry up', long-range plans for nuclear attack are termed a 'shopping list' (1987b: 18). As Cohn *et al.* have argued in a more recent discussion of the gender and proposals for eliminating WMD, the absence of emotions and human vulnerability, which are 'marked as feminine in the binary dichotomies of gender discourse', further illustrates the extent to which technostrategic discourse is gendered (2005: 5). Equally, the acronyms and abbreviations used to describe weapons systems, once learned, 'are quick, clean, light; they trip off the tongue' (Cohn 1987a: 704). All this renders technostrategic discourse all the more seductive, and potentially makes the process of forgetting the actual effects of such weapons easier. Charlotte Hooper has even gone so far as to question whether post-structuralist-oriented analysts of virtual war, such as Der Derian, are also ultimately complicit in the reproduction of technostrategic discourse by constantly quoting and imitating the jargon of military planners. Drawing on Cohn's analysis, Hooper argues that Der Derian's 'fascination with "virtual" technology resembles the earlier "toys for the boys" fascination with missile technology exhibited by more conventional contributors to strategic studies' (2001: 114).

Critical security studies

Scholars within the so-called Welsh School of CSS have also been closely concerned with the prevalence of technostrategic thinking within security discourse and practices. Although best known for its focus on the relationship between security and 'emancipation', as discussed in Chapter 2, the philosophical roots of CSS also lead it to a concern with the relationship between technology and security (see Peoples 2010). As with Cohn's work, the CSS position on technology originally grew out of a discussion of nuclear weapons and critique of the dominance of traditional approaches to strategy and security. In particular, the work of Richard Wyn Jones sought to critique the way in which strategic studies simply tended to accept the development of ever-more sophisticated and destructive technologies as a 'given'. 'Critical Theorists and concerned citizens' alike he exhorts, 'must seek to intervene in this process [weapons development] in order to try to ensure that new technologies are not developed and imposed in ways which simply re-create and reinforce present patterns of domination and injustice' (Wyn Jones 1995: 106). In tandem with its fixation with the state as the referent object of security, the traditional approach to security studies has also shown an alarming tendency to *fetishise* technology, specifically military hardware: that is, traditional approaches have a seemingly endless obsession with the development of new weapons, and assumes this development to be a 'natural' process. As a result:

> the strategists' conception of technology remains curiously underdeveloped. Though strategy texts discuss the relationship between strategy and technology, these discussions tend not to move beyond rather superficial speculation about the pace of technological change [...] The deeper issues concerning the nature of the relationship between technology and society are hardly ever addressed.
>
> (Wyn Jones 1995: 93)

By assuming that new developments in weapons technology are simply inevitable, strategic studies/traditional approaches are routinely restricted to debates over whether new technologies fundamentally alter the nature of warfare (or not). Specifically, Wyn Jones (drawing on Feenberg 1991) sees the vast part of such studies dividing into one of two camps, neither of which addresses the relationship between technology and society (and hence technology and security) beyond a superficial level. In one camp are those who adopt an 'instrumental approach'. The instrumental approach to technology 'argues that technology does not affect the social, political and cultural fundamentals in either domestic or international politics' (1995: 100). It is, as Wyn Jones characterises it, the extension of the US National Rifle Association's argument that 'it's not the gun, it's the person holding the gun' to the level of international security. Politics and strategy dictate the use of weapons, no matter how powerful or 'revolutionary' those weapons might be. The other camp Wyn Jones describes as adopting a 'substantive' approach. This approach suggests that 'technology has an autonomous logic of its own which determines a particular form of social organization' (1995: 102). In other words, far from being simply a range of neutral tools we use to achieve certain ends, technology itself has a tangible, substantive impact in shaping social relations. In short, the debate becomes one of whether new technologies simply augment existing practices of warfare, or revolutionise its very practice. One side of the debate focuses on the role that human 'users' of technology play in determining the uses to which military technologies are put to; the other emphasises the ways in which human activities and behaviours in conflict are shaped by the tools used to conduct wars.

Most contributions to the literature on nuclear weapons, Wyn Jones argues as an example, fall into one or other of these two camps. This analysis can be extended to non-nuclear weapons technologies as well. Debates on the previously discussed RMA frequently break down into one group of scholars arguing that new technologies do not alter the fundamentals of strategy and are simply tools to be used to serve existing ends, versus those who argue that new technologies are not simply 'new tools' but require a radical rethink of strategic goals and organisation. Building upon Wyn Jones' analysis, Peoples (2010) argues that this dichotomous characterisation of technological development – as either being driven by strategic goals on the one hand or determining them on the other – is present not only in academic discourse but in the practical promotion and justification of hi-tech weapons systems such as US Ballistic Missile Defence (BMD). He examines the way in which proponents of missile defence simultaneously uphold the promise of new technology as tools to be used to achieve nuclear security whilst at the same time invoking the substantivist metaphor of 'technology out of control' to characterise the spread of nuclear weapons and justify investment in BMD. Rarely are these two understandings reconciled and, Peoples suggests, in some their discursive power actually emanates from their apparent irreconcilability.

A more critical approach to technology, Wyn Jones argues, should be based in an awareness that:

> Technology *does* have a logic in that it simultaneously creates and constrains the choices available to society, yet technology *does not* predetermine which one of those particular choices is made. That decision is a social one, and as such reflects a whole series of social, cultural and power relations. The fact that these relations are contestable leads to the argument that technology is a scene of struggle.
>
> (1995: 99, emphases in original)

Rather than assuming new military technologies simply as objects for the consideration of security scholars, the CSS approach suggests that we need to look into the decisions, processes and beliefs that create the perceived need for such 'products' in the first place. Hence, in place of the traditional approach, Wyn Jones argues for 'an alternative conceptualization of strategy that embraces ends, regarding normative issues as intrinsic to the study and [that] is based on a dialectical understanding of technology' (1999: 5).

In short, where feminist scholars like Cohn point to the dehumanising effects of technostrategic discourse, those within CSS in a similar vein critique its frequently depoliticising effects. Rather than viewing (military) technology as something exogenous to society or simply as the instruments of military planners, CSS argues that one of the goals of a critical approach to security is to question the inherently social character of technology and its impacts. Although we need to acknowledge that the material aspects of technology 'create and constrain' certain security practices, CSS argues that we should also recognise the human factor in the design, development, promotion and use of particular military technologies. In doing so it seeks to guard against the technological determinism that often creeps into discussions of military technology and security.

Security, dataveillance and biopower

Often when we think of the relationship between technology and security, we tend to focus upon weaponry and battlefield technology, as if security pertains only to practices of battle as has been the case in the previous sections. With the onset of the war on terror and the growth of homeland security (see Chapter 9), however, attention has increasingly been paid to the ways in (homeland) security is also reliant on the new technologies that are now being deployed, often covertly, at a more societal, 'every day' level. Much of the scholarship in this vein has developed out of a Foucauldian-inspired concern with surveillance, biopower and the management of populations (see Chapter 5 and Box 5.1). Michel Foucault's later writing and lectures centre around an inversion of Clausewitz's famous dictum that 'war is the continuation of politics by other means'. By contrast, Foucault and the more recent work that draws upon his thinking seeks to investigate the extent to which politics is actually 'the continuation of war by other means' (Amoore 2009: 50; Dillon and Neal 2008; Dillon and Reid 2001; Foucault 2002, 2007): that is, the extent to which security practices are enmeshed into efforts to manage the movement of people and attempt to identify, monitor and contain elements of the population that might constitute a 'security risk'.

Technologies employed in such efforts include means of DNA fingerprinting and identification, electronic tagging, biometric ID cards, passports and facial recognition systems (see Box 12.6), and 'smart' CCTV systems, which in turn facilitate practices such as screening and risk-profiling. Although the phenomenon of surveillance is not particularly new (with Jeremy Bentham's idea of the panopticon dating back to 1785 – see Figure 5.1), the connection between surveillance and security has grown in tandem with the increased emphasis on international terrorism as a security threat. As Louise Amoore notes, a consensus emerged in post-9/11 US policy circles that 'had surveillance and profiling techniques been in place, the events of 9/11 "could have been predicted and averted"' and that in response 'technologies designed to classify populations according to their degree of threat – long available in the private commercial sector – should be deployed at the service of border security' (2006: 337). Indeed, border points – airports, checkpoints and border crossings – form the primary sites of deployment for such technologies of surveillance (see Chapter 11; Salter 2006, 2007).

Moreover, traditional modes of surveillance, represented emblematically by CCTV cameras, are now being supplemented by what has been identified as 'dataveillance': the monitoring and 'mining' of multiple forms of data – including financial transactions, patterns of international travel and even behavioural data (see Box 12.6) – by security professionals with the aim of identifying potentially 'risky' groups and individuals. In this sense, as with the discourse of the RMA, in dataveillance *information is key*, although this time with the focus very much on preventing the emergence of 'internal' threats rather than the 'external' application of force – as is well exemplified by the 2013 revelations of the US National Security Agency's PRISM programme.

The use of biometric technologies raises pressing questions about privacy, the storage and use of personal data and fundamental civil liberties; but, for critical scholars of security it also raises complex issues about the identification, prediction and pre-emption of security 'threats'. Amoore argues that 'The practices of this war by other means [...] are themselves productive of quite specific pre-emptive forms of war and violence' (2009: 65) that need to be critically interrogated, and others argue that given this security studies should shift its focus from geopolitics to biopolitics and its supporting infrastructures of scientific and technical knowledge (see Dillon and Reid 2001) at both the micro level of individuals and the macro level of populations.

Ultimately, Foucauldian scholars argue, these material technologies of surveillance generate what Foucault calls 'technologies of the self': 'a process of responsibilisation through which individuals are made in charge of their own behaviour, competence, improvement, security and "well being"' (Ajana 2005: 3). Amoore cites as an example the facility provided by one IT company to download the 'Most Wanted Terrorists' database to pocket PCs and mobile phones so that 'people can have the photos and descriptions at their fingertips at all times in case they spot a suspicious person, easily comparing the person to the photo without endangering themselves' (2006: 346). In this sense formal security and surveillance

---

Box 12.6 Biometric technologies and 'algorithmic war'

With the advent of biometrics, surveillance and risk-profiling have become focused on the body to a new degree in security practices. Giving tangible meaning to the connection between security and *bio*power, 'Biometric technology identifies individuals automatically by using their biological or behavioural characteristics' (POST 2001: 1). Examples of biometrics range from familiar techniques and technologies such as fingerprinting and the increasingly common biometric passports and ID cards, to retina scanners and face recognition technology. Biometric technologies are increasingly being used not only for purposes of identifying individuals, though, but also for identifying particular forms of 'suspicious behaviour'. Here biometrics relies on algorithms – essentially prefabricated mathematical models, frequently used in the commercial sector, for spotting the probability of particular actions or choices being made by individuals (Amoore 2009) – to identify security 'risks'. Such calculations may be based on the remote sensing of bodies on a railway platform, or on the monitoring of particular patterns of travel and use of a credit card. For security professionals, such technologies and techniques are justified on the basis of an enhanced ability to 'connect the dots' and predict the likelihood of, for example, terrorist attacks. Michael Chertoff, then US secretary of Homeland Security, justified the greater use of biometrics on the basis that 'After September 11 [2001], we used credit card and telephone records to identify those linked with the hijackers. But wouldn't it be better to identify such connections before a hijacker boards a plane?' (cited in Amoore 2009: 52).

technologies, such as those associated with homeland security, are seen to encourage and inculcate individual technologies of self-management (see Salter 2006, 2007), and citizens are urged to act as human supplements to formal surveillance technologies.

Conclusion

So how should the study of technology and warfare proceed from a critical perspective and what should its primary concerns be? Security professionals frequently speak of technologies that are 'over-the-horizon': that is, the next developments in technology that promise to radically change the nature of warfare. Looking to the future, some have identified space weapons and nanotechnology as potential new sources of military innovation that might provide the next 'RMA' (see Hirst 2002), while others argue that the proliferation of human–machine relationships on the battlefield portends a cultural-psychological shift towards 'post-human' soldiers (Gray 2003; Masters 2005).

Prediction, particularly in the realm of technological development, is always a dangerous pastime, and it can be argued that innovation does not in itself guarantee significance with regard to warfare. In the 2003 invasion of Iraq, for example, the US-led forces scored significant initial military success thanks to overwhelming technological superiority, which was widely characterised as 'shock and awe'; but they still found it difficult to consolidate that initial success, and only began to do so by increasing the number of actual 'boots on the ground' to fight a counterinsurgency campaign. Similarly, the adversaries faced by US forces in Iraq have proven adept at blending guerrilla tactics with their own 'asymmetric' use of technologies ranging from rocket-propelled grenades (RPGs) to car bombs to use of the internet for propaganda and recruitment.

What this might suggest is that critical approaches to the study of warfare in the information age need to take account of the potential merging of 'old' and 'new' methods of warfare and their wider social context and impacts. Indeed, Barkawi (2011) has gone so far as to argue that this warrants the development of a separate and distinct from of 'critical war studies' in its own right. Various forms of critical security studies scholarship make a contribution to the understanding of how new forms of technology affect war and security in the information age: new forms of media, weapons technology and the percolation of militarised logics into everyday practices. Scholarly opinion is divided as to the exact nature and significance of critical security scholarship in this respect, however. Barkawi argues that the field of security studies has 'widened' to such an extent, particularly in terms of its empirical foci, that its focus on the phenomenon of war has become irreversibly diluted. Conversely, Aradau (2012) makes the case that if the definition of 'war' is modified into a focus on organised political violence in its myriad forms, then the potential significance of critical approaches to the study of security becomes more apparent.

If the concept of postmodern war has any purchase, then it is in the characterisation of contemporary warfare as 'bricollage' – something that is made up of a multiplicity of divergent forms – with 'the proliferation of many different types of postmodern soldiers' (Gray 2003: 216). In the light of this, students and scholars of critical security studies might reflect upon whether a focus upon innovation in technology needs to be supplemented by greater analysis of the diffusion of 'old' technologies as well. It is worth considering whether the proliferation of small arms globally, for example, is not as important as the next development in nanotechnology, biometrics and cyber-warfare. But in thinking where critical approaches might go in future we might also reflect on whether the 'thrill of the new' constitutes its own type of fetishisation within critical security studies as well as its more traditional counterpart.

Key points

- The 1990s saw the rise of the discourse of the RMA (revolution in military affairs) in the US that focuses upon information and technological innovation as the key to military success, and of the term 'Western way of war' to characterise the emphasis placed on technological superiority and 'risk aversion' by Western militaries.
- Increasing mediation of warfare – media coverage of war and use of visual media in the conduct of war – as a result of this emphasis on technology has led to consequent discussion of the idea of 'virtual war' within critical security studies.
- Scholars drawing on feminist and critical theory critique the prevalence of 'technostrategic discourse' within discussions of military technology and security.
- Recent work drawing upon theories of biopolitics have focused upon the growth of 'everyday' security technologies that focus on monitoring the body and identifying 'risky' elements of the population.

Discussion points

- How significant are the range of technological innovations associated with the RMA?
- What does it mean to say that war is becoming increasingly 'virtual'?
- Are poststructuralist scholars right to focus upon the role of simulation in contemporary conflict?
- Do traditional approaches to security 'fetishise' military technology, as argued by feminist and critical security scholars?
- Should critical scholars be more concerned with the innovation or the diffusion of military technology?
- What, if anything, do critical approaches to the study of security have to tell us about the phenomenon of war?

Guide to further reading

Carol Cohn (1987) 'Sex and Death in the Rational World of Defense Intellectuals', *Signs: Journal of Women in Culture and Society*, 12(4): 687–718. As noted in this chapter, this remains a seminal feminist contribution to discussions of technology and war.

James Der Derian (2009) *Virtuous War: Mapping the Military–Industrial–Media–Entertainment Network* (New York: Routledge). A semi-autobiographical account of Der Derian's investigation of the use of simulations and war gaming within the US military, and is worth reading for the first-hand observations of such simulations at work as well as the theoretical content. Those looking for a more condensed version of the latter might consult Der Derian (2000) and (2003) – see Bibliography for full details.

Louise Amoore (2009) 'Algorithmic War: Everyday Geographies of the War on Terror', *Antipode*, 41(1): 49–69. An empirically rich illustration of the Foucauldian-inspired approach to biometric technologies and dataveillance as discussed in this chapter.

Richard Wyn Jones (1999) *Security, Strategy and Critical Theory* (Boulder, CO: Lynne Rienner). Provides further detail on how a critique of traditional approaches to security and strategy can be located within a broader critical theory of technology.

Robert Mandel (2004) *Security, Strategy and the Quest for Bloodless War* (Boulder, CO: Lynne Rienner). Combines an overview of several of the innovations associated with the RMA with a more substantive discussion of their potential effects in terms of the way wars are waged.

Taraq Barkawi (2009) 'From War to Security: Security Studies, the Wider Agenda, and the Fate of the Study of War', *Millennium*, 39: 701–716 makes the case, as noted in the conclusion of this chapter, for a distinct form of 'critical war studies'. Along with the ensuing response by Aradau (2012) and counter-response by Barkawi (2012) – see bibliography for full details – Barkawi's article opens up a debate about what it means to study war from a 'critical' perspective.

Weblinks

InfoTechWarPeace (The Watson Institute): www.watsoninstitute.org/infopeace/index2.cfm CitizenLab: www.citizenlab.org

Center for Democracy and Technology (on security): www.cdt.org/security Institute for Creative Technologies: http://ict.usc.edu

'America's Army Online' – US Army game/simulation site: www.americasarmy.com

'Start Thinking Soldier' – UK Army recruitment site: http://www.army.mod.uk/StartThinkingSoldier/

Lockheed Martin promotional site for the 'Hellfire II' missile: www.lockheedmartin.com/products/HellfireII.html

Bibliography

Abrahamsen, Rita (2003) 'African Studies and the Postcolonial Challenge', *African Affairs*, 102: 189–210.

—— (2005) 'Blair's Africa: The Politics of Securitization and Fear', *Alternatives*, 30: 50–80.

Abrahamsen, Rita and Michael C. Williams (2009) 'Security Beyond the State: Global Security Assemblages in International Politics', *International Political Sociology*, 3: 1–17.

Acharya, Amitav (1997) 'The Periphery as the Core: The Third World and Security Studies', in Keith Krause and Michael C. Williams (eds) *Critical Security Studies: Concepts and Cases* (London: UCL Press).

—— (2006) 'Securitization in Asia: Functional and Normative Implications', in Mely Caballero-Anthony, Ralf Emmers, and Amitav Acharya (eds) *Non-Traditional Security in Asia: Dilemmas in Securitisation* (London: Ashgate).

Acharya, Amitav and Barry Buzan (2007) 'Why is there no non-Western International Relations Theory? An Introduction', *International Relations of the Asia-Pacific*, 7: 287–312.

Adey, Peter and Anderson, Ben (2011) 'Event and Anticipation: UK Civil Contingencies and the Space Times of Decision', *Environment and Planning A*, 4: 2878–2899.

—— (2012) 'Anticipating Emergencies: Technologies of Preparedness and the Matter of Security', *Security Dialogue*, 43: 99–117.

Adler, Emanuel and Michael Barnett (1998a) 'Security Communities in Theoretical Perspective' in Emanuel Adler and Michael Barnett (eds) *Security Communities* (Cambridge: Cambridge University Press).

—— (1998b) 'A Framework for the Study of Security Communities' in Emanuel Adler and Michael Barnett (eds) *Security Communities* (Cambridge: Cambridge University Press).

Agamben, Giorgio (1998) *Homo Sacer: Sovereign Power and Bare Life* (Stanford, CA: Stanford University Press).

—— (2000) *Means Without End: Notes on Politics*, trans. V. Binetti and C. Casarino (Minneapolis, MN: University of Minnesota Press).

—— (2005) *State of Exception* (Chicago, IL, and London: University of Chicago Press).

Agnew, John (1994) 'The Territorial Trap: The Geographical Assumptions of International Relations Theory', *Review of International Political Economy*, 1: 53–80.

Åhäll, Linda (2012) 'The Writing of Heroines: Motherhood and Female Agency in Political Violence', *Security Dialogue*, 43: 287–303.

Ajana, Btihaj (2005) 'Surveillance and Biopolitics', *Electronic Journal of Sociology*, online, available at: www.sociology.org/content/2005/tier1/ajana_biopolitics.pdf (accessed 30 May 2009).

Alker, Hayward (2005) 'Emancipation in the Critical Security Studies Project', in Ken Booth (ed.) *Critical Security Studies and World Politics* (Boulder, CO: Lynne Rienner).

Althusser, Louis (1971) *Lenin and Philosophy and Other Essays* (New York: Monthly Review Press).

Amoore, Louise (2004) 'Risk, Reward and Discipline at Work', *Economy and Society*, 33: 174–196.

—— (2006) 'Biometric Borders: Governing Mobilities in the War on Terror', *Political Geography*, 25: 336–351.

—— (2007) 'Vigilant Visualities: The Watchful Politics of the War on Terror', *Security Dialogue*, 38: 315–332.

—— (2008) 'Response Before Event: On Forgetting the War on Terror', in Angharad Closs Stephens and Nick Vaughan-Williams (eds) *Terrorism and the Politics of Response* (Abingdon and New York: Routledge).

—— (2009) 'Algorithmic War: Everyday Geographies of the War on Terror', *Antipode*, 41: 49–69.

Amoore, Louise and Marieke De Goede (2005) 'Governance, Risk and Dataveillance in the War on Terror', *Crime, Law and Social Change*, 43: 149–173.

Anderson, Benedict (1991) *Imagined Communities: Reflections on the Origin and Spread of Nationalism* (London: Verso).

Andreas, Peter (2000) *Border Games: Policing the US–Mexico Divide* (Ithaca, NY, and London: Cornell University Press).

Aradau, Claudia (2004) 'Security and the Democratic Scene: Desecuritization and Emancipation', *Journal of International Relations and Development*, 7: 388–413.

—— (2008) *Rethinking Trafficking in Women: Politics Out of Security* (London and New York: Palgrave Macmillan).

—— (2010) 'Security That Matters: Critical Infrastructure and Objects of Protection', *Security Dialogue*, 41: 491–514.

—— (2012) 'Security, War, Violence – The Politics of Critique: A Reply to Barkawi', *Millennium: Journal of International Studies*, 41:112–123.

Aradau, Claudia and Rens van Münster (2007) 'Governing Terrorism through Risk: Taking Precautions, (Un)Knowing the Future', *European Journal of International Relations*, 30: 89–115.

—— (2008) 'Insuring Terrorism, Assuring Subjects, Ensuring Normality: The Politics of Risk after 9/11', *Alternatives: Global, Local, Political*, 33: 191–210.

—— (2011) *Politics of Catastrophe: Genealogies of the Unknown* (London and New York: Routledge).

Aradau, Claudia, Luis Lobo-Guerrero and Rens van Münster (2008) 'Security, Technologies of Risk, and the Political: Guest Editors' Introduction, *Security Dialogue*, 39: 147–154.

Ashcroft, Bill, Gareth Griffiths and Helen Tiffin (1989) (eds) *The Empire Writes Back: Theory and Practice in Post-Colonial Literatures* (London and New York: Routledge).

Ashley, Richard K. (1984) 'The Poverty of Neorealism', *International Organization*, 38: 225–286.

—— (1988) 'Untying the Sovereign State: A Double Reading of the Anarchy Problematique', *Millennium: Journal of International Studies*, 17: 227–262.

Austin, John L. (1962) *How to do Things with Words* (Oxford: Clarendon Press).

Ayoob, Mohammed (1983/1984) 'Security in the Third World: The Worm about to Turn?' *International Affairs*, 60: 41–51.

—— (1995) *The Third World Security Predicament: State Making, Regional Conflict and the International System* (Boulder, CO: Lynne Rienner).

—— (1997) 'Defining Security: A Subaltern Realist Perspective', in Keith Krause and Michael C. Williams (eds) *Critical Security Studies: Concepts and Cases* (London: UCL Press).

—— (2002) 'Inequality and Theorizing in International Relations: The Case for Subaltern Realism', *International Studies Review*, 4: 27–48.

Bagge Laustsen, Carsten and Ole Wæver (2000) 'In Defence of Religion: Sacred Referent Objects for Securitization', *Millennium: Journal of International Studies*, 29: 705–739.

Baldwin, David A. (1997) 'The Concept of Security', *Review of International Studies*, 23: 5–26.

Balibar, Étienne (1998) 'The Borders of Europe', trans. J. Swenson, in Pheng Cheah and Bruce Robbins (eds) *Cosmopolitics: Thinking and Feeling Beyond the Nation* (London and Minneapolis, MN: University of Minnesota Press).

Balzacq, Thierry (2005) 'The Three Faces of Securitization: Political Agency, Audience and Context', *European Journal of International Relations*, 11: 171–201.

—— (2011) (ed.) *Securitization Theory: How security problems emerge and dissolve* (London and New York: Routledge).

Barad, Karen (2003) 'Posthumanist Performativity: Toward an Understanding of How Matter Comes to Matter', *Signs: Journal of Women in Culture and Society*, 28: 801–831.

Barkawi, Tarak and Mark Laffey (2006) 'The Postcolonial Moment in Security Studies', *Review of International Studies*, 32: 329–352.

Barkawi, Taraq (2011) 'From War to Security: Security Studies, the Wider Agenda, and the Fate of the Study of War', *Millennium: Journal of International Studies*, 39: 701–716.

—— (2012) 'Of Camps and Critiques: A Reply to "Security, War, Violence"', 41: 124–130.

Barnett, Jon (2001) *The Meaning of Environmental Security: Ecological Politics and Policy in the New Security Era* (London and New York: Zed Books).

Barnett, Michael (2002) 'Radical Chic? Subaltern Realism: A Rejoinder', *International Studies Review*, 4: 49–62.

Basham, Victoria (2013) *War, Identity and the Liberal State: Everyday Experiences of the Geopolitical in the Armed Forces* (London and New York: Routledge).

Basham, Victoria and Nick Vaughan-Williams (2013) 'Gender, Race, and Border Security Practices: A Profane Reading of 'Muscular Liberalism', *British Journal of Politics and International Relations*, 15: 509–527.

Baudrillard, Jean (1993) 'The Procession of Simulacra', in Joseph P. Natoli and Linda Hutcheon (eds) *A Postmodern Reader* (Albany, NY: SUNY Press).

—— (1995) *The Gulf War Did Not Take Place*, trans. Paul Patton (Sydney: Power Publications).

—— (2002) *The Spirit of Terrorism*, trans. Chris Turner (London and New York: Verso).

Bellamy, Alex and Roland Bleiker (2008) 'Introduction', in Alex Bellamy, Roland Bleiker, Sara Davies and Richard Devetak (eds) *Security and the War on Terror* (London and New York: Routledge).

Bellamy, Alex and Matt McDonald (2002) 'The Utility of Human Security: Which Humans? What Security? A Reply to Thomas and Tow', *Security Dialogue*, 33: 373–377.

Benjamin, Walter (2003) 'The Paris of the Second Empire in Baudelaire', in Howard Eiland and Michael Jennings (eds) *Walter Benjamin: Selected Writings, Vol. 4, 1938–40* (Cambridge, MA: Belknap Press of the University of Harvard).

Bennett, Jane (2010) *Vibrant Matter: A Political Ecology of Things* (Durham and London: Duke University Press).

Bentham, Jeremy [1787] (1995) *The Panopticon Writings*, edited by Miran Bozovic (London: Verso).

Berger, Peter L. and Thomas Luckmann (1991 [1966]) *The Social Construction of Reality: A Treatise in the Sociology of Knowledge* (London: Penguin Books).

Bhabha, Homi (1994) *The Location of Culture* (London: Routledge).

Bialasiewicz, Luiza (2011) (ed.) *Europe and the World: EU Geopolitics and the Transformation of European Space* (Aldershot: Ashgate).

—— (2012) 'Off-Shoring and Out-Sourcing the Borders of Europe: Libya and EU Border-Work in the Mediterranean', *Geopolitics*, 17: 843–866.

Biddle, Stephen (1996) 'Victory Misunderstood: What the Gulf War Tells Us About the Future of Conflict', *International Security*, 21: 139–179.

Bigo, Didier (2000) 'When Two Become One: Internal and External Securitizations in Europe', in Morten Kelstrup and Michael C. Williams (eds) *International Relations Theory and the Politics of European Integration: Power, Security, and Community* (London and New York: Routledge).

—— (2002) 'Security and Immigration: Towards a Critique of the Governmentality of Unease', *Alternatives*, 27: 63–92.

—— (2007) 'Detention of Foreigners, States of Exception, and the Social Practices of Control of the Banopticon', in Prem Kumar Rajaram and Carl Grundy-Warr (eds) *Borderscapes: Hidden Geographies and Politics at Territory's Edge* (Minneapolis, MN: University of Minnesota Press).

—— (2008) 'Globalised (In)Security: The Field and the Ban-Opticon', in Didier Bigo and Anastassia Tsoukala (eds) *Terror, Insecurity and Liberty: Illiberal Practices of Liberal Regimes after 9/11* (London and New York: Routledge).

Bigo, Didier and Emmanuel-Pierre Guittet (2011) 'Northern Ireland as Metaphor: Exception, Suspicion and Radicalization in the "War on Terror"', *Security Dialogue*, 42: 483–498.

Bigo, Didier and Anastassia Tsoukala (2008) (eds) *Terror, Insecurity and Liberty: Illiberal Practices of Liberal Regimes after 9/11* (London and New York: Routledge).

Bigo, Didier, Sergio Carrera, Elspeth Guild and R.B.J. Walker (2007) 'The Changing Landscape of European Liberty and Security: Mid-Term Report on the Results of the CHALLENGE Project', Research Paper No. 4, online, available at: www.libertysecurity.org/article1357.html (accessed 10 April 2009).

Blakeley, Ruth (2007) 'Bringing the State Back into Terrorism Studies', *European Political Science*, 6: 228–235.

Booth, Ken (1991) 'Security and Emancipation', *Review of International Studies*, 17: 313–326.

—— (2005a) 'Critical Explorations', in Ken Booth (ed.) *Critical Security Studies and World Politics* (Boulder, CO: Lynne Rienner).

—— (2005b) 'Introduction to Part 3', in Ken Booth (ed.) *Critical Security Studies and World Politics* (Boulder, CO: Lynne Rienner).

—— (2007) *Theory of World Security* (Cambridge: Cambridge University Press).

Booth, Ken and Peter Vale (1997) 'Critical Security Studies and Regional Insecurity: The Case of Southern Africa', in Keith Krause and Michael C. Williams (eds) *Critical Security Studies: Concepts and Cases* (London: UCL Press).

Booth, Ken and Nicholas J. Wheeler (2007) *The Security Dilemma: Fear, Cooperation and Trust in World Politics* (Basingstoke: Palgrave Macmillan).

Brassett, James, Stuart Croft and Nick Vaughan-Williams (2013) 'An Agenda for Resilience Research in Politics and International Relations', *Politics*, 33: 221–228.

Braun, Bruce and Sarah Whatmore (2010) (eds) *Political Matter: Technoscience, Democracy and Public Life* (Minneapolis: University of Minnesota Press).

Brincat, Shannon, Laura Lima and João Nunes (2011) (eds) *Critical Theory in International Relations and Security Studies: Interviews and Reflections* (London and New York: Routledge).

Brown, Chris (1994) 'Turtles all the Way Down: Anti-Foundationalism, Critical Theory, and International Relations', *Millennium: Journal of International Studies*, 23: 213–236.

Brown, Garrett Wallace and Sophie Harman (2011) 'Risk, Perceptions of Risk and Global Health Governance', *Political Studies*, 59: 773–778.

Browning, Christopher S. and Matt McDonald (2013) 'The Future of Critical Security Studies: Ethics and the Politics of Security', *Security Dialogue*, 19: 235–255.

Bubandt, Nils (2005) 'Vernacular Security: The Politics of Feeling Safe in Global, National, and Local Worlds', *Security Dialogue*, 36: 275–296.

Bulmer, Sarah (2013) 'Patriarchal Confusion? Making Sense of Gay and Lesbian Military Identity', *International Feminist Journal of Politics*, 15: 137–156.

Burgess, J. Peter (2011) *The Ethical Subject of Security: Geopolitical Reason and the Threat Against Europe* (London and New York: Routledge).

Burke, Anthony (2007) *Beyond Security, Ethics and Violence: War Against the Other* (London and New York: Routledge).

Butler, Judith (1990) *Gender Trouble: Feminism and the Subversion of Identity* (London and New York: Routledge).

—— (1996) 'Performativity's Social Magic', in Theodore R. Schatzki and Wolfgang Natter (eds) *The Social and Political Body* (New York: Guilford Press).

—— (2004) *Precarious Life: The Powers of Mourning and Violence* (London: Verso).

Buzan, Barry (1991) *People, States and Fear: An Agenda for International Studies in the Post-Cold War Era*, 2nd edn. (Boulder, CO: Lynne Rienner).

Buzan, Barry and Lene Hansen (2009) *The Evolution of International Security Studies* (Cambridge: Cambridge University Press).

Buzan, Barry and Ole Wæver (1997) 'Slippery? Contradictory? Sociologically Untenable? The Copenhagen School Replies', *Review of International Studies*, 23: 241–250.

—— (2003) *Regions and Powers* (Cambridge: Cambridge University Press).

—— (2009) 'Macrosecuritization and Security Constellations: Reconsidering Scale in Securitization

Theory', *Review of International Studies*, 35: 253–276.

Buzan, Barry, Ole Wæver and Jaap de Wilde (1998) *Security: A New Framework for Analysis* (London: Lynne Rienner).

Caballero-Anthony, Mely, Ralf Emmers and Amitav Acharya (2006) (eds) *Non-Traditional Security in Asia: Dilemmas in Securitisation* (London: Ashgate).

Campbell, David (1992) *Writing Security: United States Foreign Policy and the Politics of Identity* (Manchester: Manchester University Press).

Campbell, David and Michael Dillon (1993) (eds) *The Political Subject of Violence* (Manchester: Manchester University Press).

Carrera, Sergio (2007) *The EU Border Management Strategy: FRONTEX and the Challenges of Irregular Immigration in the Canary Islands* (Brussels: Centre for European Studies).

CASE (2006) Collective, 'Critical Approaches to Security in Europe: A Networked Manifesto', *Security Dialogue*, 37: 443–487.

Castle, Gregory (2001) (ed.) *Post-Colonial Discourses: An Anthology* (Oxford: Blackwell).

Chandler, David (2012) 'Reslience and Human Security: The Post-interventionist Paradigm', *Security Dialogue*, 43: 213–229.

—— (2013) 'International Statebuilding and the Ideology of Resilience', *Politics*, 33: 276–286.

Chandler, David and Nik Hynek (2012) (eds) *Critical Perspectives on Human Security: Rethinking Emancipation and Power in International Relations* (London and New York: Routledge).

Chakrabarty, Dipesh (1992) 'Postcoloniality and the Artifice of History: Who Speaks for "Indian" Pasts?', *Representations*, 47: 1–26.

—— (2000) *Provincializing Europe: Postcolonial Thought and Historical Difference* (Princeton, NJ: Princeton University Press).

Chen, Ching-Chang (2011) 'The Absence of Non-Western IR Theory in Asia Reconsidered', *International Relations of the Asia-Pacific*, 11: 1–23.

Chomsky, Noam (1999) *The New Military Humanism* (London: Pluto Press).

—— (2000) *Rogue States: The Rule of Force in World Affairs* (London and New York: Pluto Press).

Christie, Ryerson (2010) 'Critical Voices and Human Security: To Endure, To Engage or To Critique?', *Security Dialogue*, 41: 169-190.

Ciută, Felix (2002) 'The End(s) of NATO: Security, Strategic Action and Narrative Transformation', *Contemporary Security Policy*, 23: 35–62.

—— (2010) 'Conceptual Notes on Energy Security: Total or Banal Security?', *Security Dialogue*, 41: 123–144.

Clausewitz, Carl von (1976) [1832] *On War*, ed. and trans. Michael Howard and Peter Paret (Princeton, NJ: Princeton University Press).

Closs Stephens, Angharad and Nick Vaughan-Williams (2008) (eds) *Terrorism and the Politics of Response* (Abingdon and New York: Routledge).

Coaffee, Jon (2010) 'Protecting Vulnerable Cities: The UK's Resilience Response to Defending Everyday Urban Infrastructure', *International Affairs*, 86: 939–954.

Coaffee, Jon, David Murakami Wood and Peter Rogers, (2008) *The Everyday Resilience of the City: How Cities Respond to Terrorism and Disaster* (Basingstoke: Palgrave Macmillan).

Cohn, Carol (1987a) 'Sex and Death in the Rational World of Defense Intellectuals', *Signs: Journal of Women in Culture and Society*, 12: 687–718.

—— (1987b) 'Slick 'Ems, Glick 'Ems, Christmas Trees, and Cookie Cutters: Nuclear Language and How We Learned to Pat the Bomb', *Bulletin of the Atomic Scientists*, 43: 17–24.

Cohn, Carol, Felicity Hill and Sara Ruddick (2005) 'The Relevance of Gender for Eliminating Weapons of Mass Destruction', paper commissioned for the Weapons of Mass Destruction Commission, online, available at: www.wmdcommission.org/files/No38.pdf (accessed 29 May 2009).

Coleman, Matthew and Kevin Grove (2009) 'Biopolitics, Biopower, and the Return of Sovereignty', *Environment and Planning D: Society and Space*, 27: 489–507.

Collins, Alan (2010) (ed.) *Contemporary Security Studies*, 2nd edn. (Oxford: Oxford University Press).

Commoner, Barry (1971) *The Closing Circle* (New York: Knopf).

Connolly, William E. (1974) *The Terms of Political Discourse* (Lexington: D.C. Heath and Co.).

Coole, Diana and Samantha Frost (2010) (eds) *New Materialisms: Ontology, Agency and Politics* (Durham and London: Duke University Press).

Coward, Martin (2009) *Urbicide: The Politics of Urban Destruction* (London and New York: Routledge).

—— (2012) 'Between Us in the City: Materiality, Subjectivity and Community in the Era of Global Urbanization', *Environment and Planning D: Society and Space*, 30: 468–481.

Cox, Robert W. (1981) 'Social Forces, States and World Orders: Beyond International Relations Theory', *Millennium: Journal of International Studies*, 10: 126–155.

—— (1983) 'Gramsci, Hegemony and International Relations: An Essay in Method', *Millennium: Journal of International Studies*, 12: 162–175.

Croft, Stuart (2006) *Culture, Crisis and America's War on Terror* (Cambridge: Cambridge University Press).

—— (2012) *Securitizing Islam: Identity and the Search for Security* (Cambridge: Cambridge University Press).

Curley, Melissa G. and Jonathan Herington (2011) 'The Securitisation of Avian Influenza: International Discourses and Domestic Politics in Asia', *Review of International Studies*, 37: 141–166.

Dalby, Simon (2002) *Environmental Security* (Minneapolis, MN, and London: University of Minnesota Press).

—— (2007) 'Ecology, Security and Change in the Anthropocene', *Brown Journal of World Affairs*, 13: 155–164.

Dauphinee, Elizabeth and Cristina Masters (2007) (eds) *The Logics of Biopower and the War on Terror: Living, Dying, Surviving* (Basingstoke and New York: Palgrave Macmillan).

Davies, Sara E. (2008) 'Securitizing Infectious Disease', *International Affairs*, 84: 295–313.

de Beauvoir, Simone (1997 [1949]) *The Second Sex*, trans. H.M. Parshley (London: Vintage Books).

Debrix, François (2008) *Tabloid Terror: War, Culture and Geopolitics* (London and New York: Routledge).

De Genova, Nicholas and Natalie Puetz (eds.) (2010) *The Deportation Regime: Sovereignty, Space, and the Freedom of Movement* (Durham and London: Duke University Press).

De Goede, Marieke (2007) 'Underground Money', *Cultural Critique*, 65: 140–163.

De Larrinaga, Miguel and Mark G. Doucet (2008) 'Sovereign Power and the Biopolitics of Human Security', *Security Dialogue*, 39: 517–537.

Der Derian, James (1990) 'The (S)pace of International Relations: Simulation, Surveillance and Speed', *International Studies Quarterly*, 34: 295–310.

—— (1992) *Antidiplomacy: Spies, Terror, Speed, and War* (Oxford: Blackwell).

—— (2000) 'The Art of War and the Construction of Peace: Toward a Virtual Theory of International Relations', in Morton Kelstrup and Michael C. Williams (eds) *International Relations Theory and the Politics of European Integration* (London and New York: Routledge).

—— (2003) 'War as Game', *Brown Journal of World Affairs*, 10: 37–48.

—— (2009) *Virtuous War: Mapping the Military–Industrial–Media–Entertainment Network* (London and New York: Routledge).

Der Derian, James and Michael Shapiro (1989) (eds) *International/Intertextual Relations: Postmodern Readings of World Politics* (New York: Lexington).

Derrida, Jacques (2003) 'Autoimmunity: Real and Symbolic Suicides – A Dialogue with Jacques Derrida', in Giovanni Borradori (ed.) *Philosophy in a Time of Terror: Dialogues with Jürgen Habermas and Jacques Derrida* (Chicago, IL, and London: University of Chicago Press).

Deudney, Daniel (1990) 'The Case Against Linking Environmental Degradation and National Security', *Millennium: Journal of International Studies*, 19: 461–476.

—— (1999) 'Environmental Security: A Critique', in Daniel Deudney and Richard Matthews (eds) *Contested Grounds: Security and Conflict in the New Environmental Politics* (Albany, NY: SUNY Press).

Dijstelbloem, Huub and Albert Ameijer (eds) (2011) *Migration and the New Technological Borders of Europe*. (Basingstoke: Palgrave Macmillan).

Diken, Bülent (2004) 'From Refugee Camps to Gated Communities: Biopolitics and the End of the City', *Citizenship Studies*, 8: 83–106.

Dillon, Michael (1996) *Politics of Security: Towards a Political Philosophy of Continental Thought* (London and New York: Routledge).

Dillon, Michael and Andrew Neal (2008) *The Liberal Way of War: Killing to Make Life Live* (London and New York: Routledge).

Dillon, Michael and Julian Reid (2001) 'Global Liberal Governance: Biopolitics, Security and War', *Millennium: Journal of International Studies*, 30: 41–66.

Dirlik, Arif (1994) 'The Postcolonial Aura: Third World Criticism in the Age of Global Capitalism', *Critical Inquiry*, 20: 328–356.

Doty, Roxanne (1993) 'Foreign Policy as Social Construction: A Post-Postivist Analysis of US Counterinsurgency Policy in the Philippines', *International Studies Quarterly*, 37: 297–320.

—— (1996) *Imperial Encounters* (Minneapolis, MN: University of Minnesota Press).

—— (1998) 'Immigration and the Politics of Security', *Security Studies*, 8: 79–93.

—— (2007) 'States of Exception on the Mexico–US Border: Security, "Decisions", and Civilian Border Patrols', *International Political Sociology*, 1: 113–127.

—— (2009) 'Why is People's Movement Restricted?' in Jenny Edkins and Maja Zehfuss (eds) *Global Politics: A New Introduction* (London and New York: Routledge).

Duffield, Mark (2001) *Global Governance and the New Wars: The Merging of Development and Security* (London: Zed 2001).

—— (2005) 'Getting Savages to Fight Barbarians: Development, Security and the Colonial Present', *Conflict, Security and Development*, 5: 141–159.

—— (2007) *Development, Security and Unending War: Governing the World of Peoples* (London: Polity).

—— (2010) 'Risk Management and the Fortified Aid Compound: Every-day life in Post-Interventionary Society', *Journal of Intervention and Statebuilding*, 4: 453–474.

—— (2012) 'Challenging Environments: Danger, Resilience, and the Aid Industry', *Security Dialogue*, 43: 475–492.

Dunn Cavelty, Miriam and Kristian Søby Kristensen (2008) (eds) *Securing 'The Homeland': Critical Infrastructure, Risk and (In)security* (London and New York: Routledge).

Dwyer, Jim (2003) 'A Gulf Commander sees a Longer Road', *New York Times*, 28 March, online, available at: www.nytimes.com/2003/03/28/international/worldspecial/28GENE.html (accessed 9 June 2009).

Edkins, Jenny (2007) 'Missing Persons: Manhattan September 2001', in Elizabeth Dauphinee and Cristina Masters (eds) *The Logics of Biopower and the War on Terror: Living, Dying, and Surviving* (Basingstoke and New York: Palgrave Macmillan).

Elbe, Stefan (2005) 'AIDS, Security, Biopolitics', *International Relations*, 19: 403–419.

—— (2006) 'Should HIV/AIDS be Securitized?' The Ethical Dilemmas of Linking HIV/AIDS and Security', *International Studies Quarterly*, 50: 119–144.

—— (2008) 'Risking Lives: AIDS, Security and Three Concepts of Risk', *Security Dialogue*, 39: 177–198.

—— (2009) *Virus Alert: Security, Governmentality and the AIDS Pandemic* (New York: Columbia University Press.

—— (2010) *Security and Global Health: Toward the Medicalization of Insecurity* (Cambridge: Polity Press).

Elliott, Lorraine (2004) *The Global Politics of the Environment* (Basingstoke and New York: Palgrave Macmillan).

Enloe, Cynthia (2000) [1989] *Bananas, Beaches and Bases: Making Feminist Sense of International Politics*, 2nd edn. (Berkeley, CA, and London: University of California Press).

Eriksson, Johann (1999) 'Observers or Advocates? On the Political Role of Security Analysts',

Cooperation and Conflict, 34: 311–330.

Fagan, Madeleine (2013) *Ethics and Politics After Poststructuralism: Levinas, Derrida and Nancy* (Edinburgh: Edinburgh University Press).

Falk, Richard (1971) *This Endangered Planet: Prospects and Proposals for Human Survival* (New York: Random House).

—— (1975) *A Study of Future Worlds* (New York: The Free Press).

Fanon, Frantz (2001) [1961] *The Wretched of the Earth* (London: Penguin).

Feenberg, Andrew (1991) *Critical Theory of Technology* (Oxford: Oxford University Press).

Fidler, David P. (2005) 'From International Sanitary Conventions to Global Health Security: The New International Health Regulations', *Chinese Journal of International Law*, 4: 325–392.

Fierke, Karin M. (1997) 'Changing Worlds of Security', in Keith Krause and Michael Williams (eds) *Critical Security Studies: Concepts and Cases* (London: UCL Press).

—— (1998) *Changing Games, Changing Strategies: Critical Investigations in Security* (Manchester: Manchester University Press).

—— (2007) *Critical Approaches to International Security* (Cambridge: Polity).

Floyd, Rita (2007) 'Towards a Consequentialist Evaluation of Security: Bringing Together the Copenhagen and Welsh Schools of Security Studies', *Review of International Studies*, 33: 327–350.

—— (2011) 'Can Securitization Theory be used in Normative Analysis? Towards a Just Securitization Theory', *Security Dialogue*, 42: 427–439.

Foong Khong, Yuen (2001) 'Human Security: A Shotgun Approach to Alleviating Human Misery?', *Global Governance*, 7: 231–236.

Foucault, Michel (1980) *Power/knowledge* (Padstow: Harvester Press).

—— (1991) 'Polemics, Politics, and Problematisations: An Interview', in Paul Rabinow (ed.) *The Foucault Reader* (New York: Penguin).

—— (1998) *The Will to Knowledge: The History of Sexuality Volume 1*, trans. R. Hurley (London: Penguin).

—— (2002) *'Society Must Be Defended': Lectures at the Collège de France, 1975–76*, trans. David Macey (New York: Picador).

—— (2007) *Security, Territory, Population: Lectures at the Collège de France* (Basingstoke: Macmillan).

Galtung, Johan (1996) *Peace by Peaceful Means: Peace and Conflict, Development and Civilization* (London: Sage).

Geddes, Andrew (2000) *Immigration and European Integration: Towards Fortress Europe?* (Manchester: Manchester University Press).

Gheciu, Alexandra I. (2005) *NATO in the 'New Europe': International Socialization After the Cold War* (Stanford, CA: Stanford University Press).

Givens, Terri, Gary Freeman and David Neal (2009) (eds) *Immigration Policy and Security: US, European, and Commonwealth Perspectives* (London and New York: Routledge).

GlobalSecurity.Org (2009) 'MQ-1B Predator', online, available at: www.globalsecurity.org/military/ systems/aircraft/mq-1b.htm (accessed 26 May 2009).

Goddard, Peter, Piers Robinson and Katy Parry (2008) 'Patriotism Meets Plurality: Reporting the 2003 Iraq War in the British Press', *Media, War and Conflict*, 1: 9–30.

Gramsci, Antonio (1971) *Selections from the Prison Notebooks* (London: Lawrence and Wishart).

Gray, Chris Hables (1997) *Postmodern War: The New Politics of Conflict* (London: Routledge).

—— (2003) 'Posthuman Soldiers in Postmodern War', *Body and Society*, 9: 215–226.

Gray, Colin S. (1999) 'Clausewitz Rules, OK? The Future is the Past – with GPS', *Review of International Studies*, 25: 161–182.

—— (2004) *Strategy for Chaos: Revolutions in Military Affairs and the Evidence of History* (London: Routledge).

Grayson, Kyle (2003) 'Securitization and the Boomerang Debate: A Rejoinder to Liotta and Smith-Windsor', *Security Dialogue*, 34: 337–343.

—— (2004) 'A Challenge to the Power over Knowledge of Traditional Security Studies', *Security*

Dialogue, 43: 357.

—— (2012) 'The Ambivalence of Assassination: Biopolitics, Culture and Political Violence', *Security Dialogue*, 43: 25–41.

Grayson, Kyle, Matt Davies and Simon Philpott (2009) 'Pop goes IR? Researching the Popular Culture-World Politics Continuum', *Politics*, 29: 155–163.

Groenendijk, Kees, Elspeth Guild and Paul Minderhoud (2003) (eds) *In Search of Europe's Borders* (The Hague, London, and New York: Kluwer Law International).

Grossman, David (1996) *On Killing: The Psychological Cost of Learning to Kill in War and Society* (Boston, MA: Little, Brown and Company).

Guha, Ranajit and Gayatri Chakravorty Spivak (1988) (eds) *Selected Subaltern Studies* (New York: Oxford University Press).

Guild, Elspeth (2009) *Security and Migration in the 21st Century* (Cambridge: Polity).

Gunning, Jeroen (2007) 'Babies and Bathwaters: Reflecting on the Pitfalls of Critical Terrorism Studies', *European Political Science*, 6: 236–243.

Gusterson, Hugh (2004) *People of the Bomb: Portraits of America's Nuclear Complex* (Minnesota, MN: University of Minnesota Press).

Hall, Stuart (1985) 'Signification, representation, ideology: Althusser and the post-structuralist debates', *Critical Studies in Mass Communication*, 2: 91–114.

Hansen, Lene (2000) 'The Little Mermaid's Silent Security Dilemma and the Absence of Gender in the Copenhagen School', *Millennium: Journal of International Studies*, 29: 285–306.

—— (2011) 'Theorising the image for Security Studies: Visual securitization and the Muhammad Cartoon Crisis', *European Journal of International Relations*, 17: 51–74.

Hansen, Lena and Helen Nissenbaum (2009) 'Digital Disaster, Cyber Security and the Copenhagen School', *International Studies Quarterly*, 53: 1155–1175.

Hayes, Jarrod (2013) *Constructing National Security: US Relations with India and China* (Cambridge: Cambridge University Press).

Heath-Kelly, Charlotte (2013) 'Counter-Terrorism and the Counterfactual: Producing the 'Radicalisation' Discourse and the UK PREVENT Strategy', *British Journal of Politics and International Studies*, 15: 394–415.

Held, David (2004) *Introduction to Critical Theory* (Cambridge: Polity).

Herring, Eric (2013) 'Historical Materialism' in Alan Collins (ed.) *Contemporary Security Studies*, 3rd edn. (Oxford: Oxford University Press).

Herz, John H. (1950) 'Idealist internationalism and the security dilemma', *World Politics*, 2: 157–180.

Higate, Paul and Marsha Henry (2004) 'Engendering (In)security in Peace Support Operations', *Security Dialogue*, 35: 481–498.

Hirst, Paul Q. (2002) 'Another Century of Conflict? War and the International System in the 21st Century', *International Relations*, 16: 327–342.

Hobson, John M. (2007) 'Is Critical Theory always for the White West and for Western Imperialism? Beyond Westphalia towards a Post-racist Critical IR', *Review of International Studies*, 33: 91–116.

Home Office (2009) *Pursue, Prevent, Protect, Prepare: The United Kingdom's Strategy for Countering International Terrorism* (London: HMSO).

Home Office (2011) *CONTEST: The United Kingdom's Strategy for Countering Terrorism* (London: HM Government).

Homer-Dixon, Thomas (1999) *Environment, Scarcity, and Violence* (Princeton, NJ, and Oxford: Princeton University Press).

Hoogensen, Gunhild and Kirsti Stuvøy (2006) 'Gender, Resistance and Human Security', *Security Dialogue*, 37: 207–228.

Hooper, Charlotte (2001) *Manly States: Masculinities, International Relations and Gender Politics* (New York: Columbia University Press).

Hopf, Ted (1998) 'The Promise of Constructivism in International Relations Theory', *International Security*, 23: 171–200.

Howarth, David and Yannis Stavrakakis (2000) 'Introducing Discourse Theory and Political Analysis', in David Howarth, Aletta Norval and Yannis Stavrakakis (eds) *Discourse Theory and Political Analysis: Identities, Hegemonies, and Social Change* (Manchester: Manchester University Press).

Howell, Alison (2011) *Madness in International Relations: Psychology, Security, and the Global Governance of Mental Health* (London and New York: Routledge).

Human Security Centre (2005) *Human Security Report 2005: War and Peace in the 21st Century* (Oxford: Oxford University Press).

Hutchings, Kimberley (2009) 'Simone de Beauvoir', in Jenny Edkins and Nick Vaughan-Williams (eds) *Critical Theorists and International Relations* (London and New York: Routledge).

Huysmans, Jef (1995) 'Migrants as a Security Problem: Dangers of "Securitizing" Societal Issues', in Robert Miles and Dietrich Thranhardt (eds) *Migration and European Integration: The Dynamics of Inclusion and Exclusion* (London: Pinter).

—— (1998a) 'Security! What do you Mean?', *European Journal of International Relations*, 4: 226–255.

—— (1998b) 'The Question of the Limit: Desecuritization and the Aesthetics of Horror in Political Realism', *Millennium: Journal of International Studies*, 27: 569–589.

—— (2000) 'The EU and the Securitization of Migration', *Journal of Common Market Studies*, 38: 751–777.

—— (2006) *The Politics of Insecurity: Fear. Migration and Asylum in the EU* (London and New York: Routledge).

Hyndman, Jennifer (2012) 'Introduction: The Geopolitics of Migration and Mobility', *Geopolitics*, 17: 243–255.

Hynek, Nik and David Chandler (2013) 'No emancipatory alternative, no critical security studies', *Critical Studies on Security*, 1: 43–63.

ICISS (International Commission on Intervention and State Sovereignty) (2001) *The Responsibility to Protect: Report of the International Commission on Intervention and State Sovereignty*, online, available at: www.iciss.ca/report2-en.asp (accessed 2 November 2009).

Ignatieff, Michael (2000a) *Virtual War: Kosovo and Beyond* (London: Chatto & Windus).

—— (2000b) 'Virtual War', *Prospect Magazine*, 51, online, available at: www.prospectmagazine. co.uk/2000/04/virtualwar/ (accessed 31 December 2009).

Jabri, Vivienne (2011) *The Postcolonial Subject: Claiming Politics/Governing Others in Late Modernity* (London and New York: Routledge).

Jackson, Richard (2005) *Writing the War on Terrorism: Language, Politics and Counter-Terrorism* (Manchester: Manchester University Press).

—— (2007) 'The Core Commitments of Critical Terrorism Studies', *European Political Science*, 6: 244–251.

—— (2008) 'The Ghosts of State Terror: Knowledge, Politics and Terrorism Studies', *Critical Studies on Terrorism*, 1: 377–392.

Jackson, Richard, Marie Breen Smyth and Jeroen Gunning (2009) (eds) *Critical Terrorism Studies: A New Research Agenda* (London and New York: Routledge).

Jackson, Richard, Marie Breen Smyth, Jeroen Gunning and Lee Jarvis (2011) *Terrorism: A Critical Introduction* (Hampshire and New York: Palgrave MacMillan).

Jackson, Robert (1990) *Quasi-States: Sovereignty, International Relations and the Third World* (Cambridge: Cambridge University Press).

Jarvis, Lee and Michael Lister (2013a) 'Vernacular Securities and Their Study: A Qualitative Analysis and Research Agenda', *International Relations*, 27: 158–179.

—— (2013b) 'Disconnected Citizenship? The Impacts of Anti-Terrorism Policy on Citizenship in the UK', *Political Studies*, 61: 656–675.

Jervis, Robert (1978) 'Cooperation under the security dilemma', *World Politics*, 30: 167–214.

Johns, Fleur (2005) 'Guantánamo Bay and the Annihilation of the Exception', *European Journal of International Law*, 16: 613–635.

Johnson, Corey, Jones, Reece, Paasi, Anssi, Amoore, Louise, Mountz, Alison, Salter, Mark and

Rumford, Chris (2011) 'Intervention: Rethinking the Border in Border Studies', *Political Geography*, 30: 61–69.

Johnson, Heather (2013) 'The Other Side of the Fence: Reconceptualizing the "Camp" and Migration Zones at the Borders of Spain', *International Political Sociology*, 7: 75–91.

Jones, Adam (2004) (ed.) *Gendercide and Genocide* (Nashville, TN: Vanderbilt University Press).

Kaldor, Mary (1999) *New and Old Wars: Organized Violence in a Global Era* (Cambridge: Polity).

Kamradt-Scott, Adam and Simon Rushton (2012) 'The Revised International Health Regulations: Socialization, Compliance and Changing Norms of Global Health Security', *Global Change, Peace and Security*, 24: 57–70.

Kaplan, Robert (1994) 'The Coming Anarchy', *Atlantic Monthly*, February: 44–76.

Katzenstein, Peter (1996) (ed.) *The Culture of National Security: Norms and Identity in World Politics* (New York: Columbia University Press).

Katzenstein, Peter J. (1996a) 'Introduction: Alternative Perspectives on National Security' in Peter J. Katzenstein (ed.) *The Culture of National Security: Norms and Identity in World Politics* (New York: Columbia University Press).

Katzenstein, Peter J. (1996b) 'National Security in a Changing World' in Peter J. Katzenstein (ed.) *The Culture of National Security: Norms and Identity in World Politics* (New York: Columbia University Press).

Keohane, Robert (1988) 'International Institutions: Two Approaches', *International Studies Quarterly*, 44: 83–105.

Khong, Yuen Foong (2001) 'Human Security: A Shotgun Approach to Alleviating Human Misery?' *Global Governance*, 7: 231–236.

Khosravi, Shahram (2010) *Illegal Traveller: An Auto-Ethnography of Borders* (Basingstoke and New York: Palgrave Macmillan).

King, Gary and Christopher J.L. Murray (2001) 'Rethinking Human Security', *Political Science Quarterly*, 116: 585–610.

Klare, Michael T. (2002) *Resource Wars: The New Landscape of Global Conflict* (New York: Henry Holt and Company).

Klein, Bradley S. (1994) *Strategic Studies and World Order: The Global Politics of Deterrence* (Cambridge: Cambridge University Press).

Kolossov, Vladimir (2005) 'Border Studies: Changing Perspectives and Theoretical Approaches', *Geopolitics*, 10: 155–179.

Krasner, Stephen D. (1981) 'Transforming International Regimes: What the Third World Wants and Why', *International Studies Quarterly*, 25: 119–148.

Krause, Keith (1998) 'Theorizing Security, State Formation and the "Third World" in the Post-Cold War World', *Review of International Studies*, 24: 125–136.

Krause, Keith and Michael C. Williams (1997) (eds) *Critical Security Studies: Concepts and Cases* (London: UCL Press).

Krishna, Sankaran (1999) *Postcolonial Insecurities: India, Sri Lanka, and the Question of Nationhood* (Minnesota, MN: University of Minnesota Press).

—— (2008) *Globalisation and Postcolonialism: Hegemony and Resistance in the Twenty-First Century* (Lanham, MD: Rowman and Littlefield).

Leander, Anna (2005) 'The Power to Construct International Security: On the Significance of Private Military Companies', *Millennium: Journal of International Studies*, 33: 803–825.

Lemanski, Charlotte (2012) 'Everyday human (in)security: Rescaling for the Southern City', *Security Dialogue*, 43: 61–78.

Lewis, Martin and Kären Wigen (1997) *The Myth of Continents: A Critique of Metageography* (Berkeley, CA: University of California Press).

Lippmann, Walter (1943) *US Foreign Policy: Shield of the Republic* (Boston: Little and Brown).

Lisle, Debbie (2007) 'Defending Voyeurism: Dark Tourism and the Problem of Global Security', in Peter M. Burns and Marina Novelli (eds) *Tourism and Politics: Global Frameworks and Local Realities* (Oxford: Elsevier).

Litfin, Karen T. (1999) 'Constructing Environmental Security and Ecological Interdependence', *Global Governance*, 5: 355–397.

Lobasz, Jennifer and Laura Sjoberg (2011) (eds) 'The State of Feminist Security Studies: A Conversation', *Politics and Gender*, 7: 573–604.

Lobo-Guerrero, Luis (2012) *Insuring Security: Biopolitics, Security and Risk* (London and New York: Routledge).

Loomba, Ania (1996) *Colonialism/Postcolonialism* (London and New York: Routledge).

Lundborg, Tom and Nick Vaughan-Williams (2011) 'Resilience, Critical Infrastructure, and Molecular Security: The Excess of "Life" in Biopolitics', *International Political Sociology*, 5: 367–383.

Lyotard, Jean François (1984) *The Postmodern Condition: A Report on Knowledge* (Minneapolis, MN: University of Minnesota Press).

McDonald, Matt (2003) 'Environment and Security: Global Eco-politics and Brazilian Deforestation', *Contemporary Security Policy*, 24: 69–94.

—— (2007) 'Emancipation and Critical Terrorism Studies', *European Political Science*, 6: 252–259.

—— (2008) 'Securitization and the Construction of Security', *European Journal of International Relations*, 14: 563–587.

McInnes, Colin (2002) *Spectator-Sport War: The West and Contemporary Conflict* (Boulder, CO: Lynne Rienner).

McInnes, Colin and Kelley Lee (2006) 'Health, Security and Foreign Policy', *Review of International Studies*, 32: 5–23.

—— (2012) *Global Health and International Relations* (Cambridge: Polity Press).

McKay, Susan (2004) 'Women, Human Security, and Peace-Building: A Feminist Analysis', online, available at: http://pdf2.hegoa.efaber.net/entry/content/511/women_human_security_peacebuilding_feminist_analysis.pdf (accessed 2 November 2009).

McNevin, Anne (2013) 'Ambivalence and Citizenship: Theorising the Political Claims of Irregular Migrants', *Millennium: Journal of International Studies*, 41: 182–200.

McSweeney, Bill (1996) 'Identity and Security: Buzan and the Copenhagen School', *Review of International Studies*, 22: 81–94.

—— (1999) *Security, Identity and Interests: A Sociology of International Relations* (Cambridge: Cambridge University Press).

Mack, Andrew (2002) *The Human Security Report Project: Background Paper* (Vancouver: Human Security Centre).

Malcolm, James (2013) 'Project Argus and the Resilient Citizen', *Politics*, 33: 311–321.

Mandel, Robert (2004) *Security, Strategy and the Quest for Bloodless War* (Boulder, CO: Lynne Rienner).

Marx, Karl (1971) [1859] *A Contribution to the Critique of Political Economy* (London: Lawrence and Wishart).

Masco, Joseph (1999) 'States of Insecurity: Plutonium and Post-Cold War Anxiety in New Mexico', in Jutta Weldes, Mark Laffey, Hugh Gusterson and Raymond Duvall (eds) *Cultures of Insecurity: States, Communities and the Production of Danger* (Minnesota, MN: University of Minnesota Press).

Massumi, Brian (2005) 'The Future Birth of the Affective Fact', proceedings of the 'Genealogies of Biopolitics' conference, online, available at: http://radicalempiricism.org (accessed 28 June 2009).

Masters, Cristina (2005) 'Bodies of Technology: Cyborg Soldiers and Militarized Masculinities', *International Feminist Journal of Politics*, 7: 112–132.

—— (2009) 'Femina Sacra: The "War on/of Terror", Women and the Feminine', *Security Dialogue*, 40: 29–49.

Matthew, Richard A., Jon Barnett, Bryan McDonald and Karen L. O'Brien (2010) (eds) *Global Environmental Changes and Human Security* (Cambridge MA: MIT Press).

Mbembe, Achille (2003) 'Necropolitics', trans. Libby Meintjes, *Public Culture*, 15: 11–40.

Mollins, Carl, Luke Fisher and Louise Branson (1995) 'Dayton Accord Signed', *Maclean's Magazine*, online, available at: www.thecanadianencyclopedia.com/index.cfm?PgNm=TCE&Params=M1ARTM0010523 (accessed 5 June 2009).

Moore-Gilbert, Bart (1997) *Postcolonial Theory: Contexts, Practices, Politics* (London: Verso).
Morgan, Patrick M. (2000) 'Liberalist and Realist Security Studies at 2000: Two Decades of Progress?', in Stuart Croft and Terry Terriff (eds) *Critical Reflections on Security and Change* (London: Frank Cass).
Mountz, Alison (2010) *Seeking Asylum* (Minneapolis: University of Minnesota Press).
Muller, Benjamin (2010) *Security, Risk and the Biometric State: Governing Borders and Bodies* (London and New York: Routledge).
Mutimer, David (1999) *The Weapons State: Proliferation and Visions of Security* (Boulder, CO: Lynne Rienner).
—— (2010) 'Critical Security Studies: A Schismatic History' in Alan Collins (ed.) *Contemporary Security Studies* (Oxford: Oxford University Press).
Mutlu, Can and Mark B. Salter (2013) *Research Methods in Critical Security Studies: An Introduction* (London and New York: Routledge)
Myers, Norman (1986) 'The Environmental Dimension to Security Issues', *Environmentalist*, 6: 251–257. Nancy, Jean-Luc (1993) 'Abandoned Being', trans. B. Holmes, in Jean-Luc Nancy (ed.) *The Birth to Presence* (Stanford, CA: Stanford University Press).
National Commission on Terrorist Attacks upon the United States (2004) *The 9/11 Commission Report: Final Report of the National Commission on Terrorist Attacks upon the United States* (New York and London: W.W. Norton and Company).
Nayak, Meghana and Eric Selbin (2010) *Decentring International Relations* (London and New York: Zed Books).
Neal, Andrew (2009) *Exceptionalism and the Politics of Counter-Terrorism: Liberty, Security and the War on Terror* (London and New York: Routledge).
Nederveen Pieterse, Jan (1992) 'Emancipations, Modern and Postmodern', *Development and Change*, 23: 5–41.
Neocleous, Mark (2008) *Critique of Security* (Edinburgh: Edinburgh University Press).
Neufeld, Mark (2004) 'Pitfalls of Emancipation and Discourse of Security', *International Relations*, 18: 109–123.
Nevins, Joseph (2010) *Operation Gatekeeper and Beyond: The War on "Illegals" and the Remaking of the U.S.-Mexico Boundary*, 2nd edn. (London and New York: Routledge).
Newman, Edward (2010) 'Critical Human Security Studies', *Review of International Studies*, 36: 77–94.
Nordstrom, Carolyn (1999) 'Visible Wars and Invisible Girls, Shadow Industries and the Politics of Not-Knowing', *International Feminist Journal of Politics*, 1: 14–33.
Norris, Christopher (1992) *Uncritical Theory: Postmodernism, Intellectuals and the Gulf War* (London: Lawrence and Wishart).
Nunes, João (2012) 'Reclaiming the political: Emancipation and critique in security studies', *Security Dialogue*, 43: 345–361.
—— (2013) *Security, Emancipation and the Politics of Health: A New Theoretical Perspective* (London and New York: Routledge).
Nussbaum, Martha C. (2000) *Women and Human Development: The Capabilities Approach* (Cambridge: Cambridge University Press).
O'Neill, Kate (2009) *The Environment and International Relations* (Cambridge: Cambridge University Press).
Ostergard, Robert L (2002) 'Politics in the Hot Zone: AIDS and National Security in Africa', *Third World Quarterly*, 23: 333–350.
Ó Tuathail, Gearóid (1996) *Critical Geopolitics* (London and New York: Routledge).
Parashar, Swati (2013) 'Feminist (In)Securities and Camp Politics', *International Studies Perspectives*, 14: 440–443.
Paris, Roland (2001) 'Human Security: Paradigm Shift or Hot Air?' *International Security*, 26: 87–102.
Parker, Noel and Nick Vaughan-Williams (2009) 'Lines in the Sand? Towards an Agenda for Critical Border Studies', *Geopolitics*, 14: 1–6.

—— (2013) *Critical Border Studies: Broadening and Deepening the 'Lines in the Sand' Agenda* (London and New York: Routledge).

Parport, Jane and Marysia Zalewski (1998) (eds) *The 'Man' Question in International Relations* (Boulder, CO: Westview Press).

—— (2008) (eds) *Rethinking the Man Question: Sex, Gender and Violence in International Relations* (London and New York: Zed Books).

Patel, Rajeev and Philip McMichael (2004) 'Third Worldism and the Lineages of Global Fascism: The Regrouping of the Global South in the Neoliberal Era', *Third World Quarterly*, 25: 231–254.

Peoples, Columba (2008) 'Decoding Ballistic Missile Defense: Semiotics and the Power of the Image in American Ballistic Missile Defense', *Social Semiotics*, 18: 17–32.

—— (2010) *Justifying Ballistic Missile Defence: Technology, Security and Culture* (Cambridge: Cambridge University Press).

—— (2011) 'Security After Emancipation? Critical Theory, Violence and Resistance', *Review of International Studies*, 37: 1113–1135.

Petersen, Karen Lund (2011) 'Risk Analysis – A Field Within Security Studies?', *European Journal of International Relations*, 23: 1–25.

Peterson, Jenny H. (2013) 'Creating Space for Emancipatory Human Security: Liberal Obstructions and the Potentials of Agonism', *International Studies Quarterly*, 57: 318–328.

Peterson, V. Spike (1992) (ed.) *Gendered States: Feminist (Re)Visions of International Relations Theory* (Boulder, CO, and London: Lynne Rienner).

Pettiford, Lloyd (1996) 'Changing Conceptions of Security in the Third World', *Third World Quarterly*, 17: 289–306.

PICUM (2010) 'Main concerns about the fundamental rights of undocumented migrants in Europe', online, available at: http://picum.org/picum.org/uploads/publication/Annual%20Concerns%20 2010%20EN.pdf (accessed 5 January 2012).

Poku, Nana K. and Jacqueline Therkelsen (2013) 'Globalization, Development and Security' in Alan Collins (ed.) *Contemporary Security Studies*, 3rd edn. (Oxford: Oxford University Press).

POST (2001) *Biometrics and Security* (UK Parliamentary Office of Science and Technology) online, available at: http://www.parliament.uk/post/pn165.pdf (accessed 30 May 2009).

Postol, Theodore A. (1992) 'Lessons of the Gulf War Experience with Patriot', *International Security*, 16: 119–171.

Prakash, Gyan (1990) 'Writing Post-Orientalist Histories of the Third World: Perspectives from Indian Historiography', *Comparative Studies in Society and History*, 32: 383–408.

—— (1992) 'Postcolonial Criticism and Indian Historiography', *Social Text*, 31/32: 8–19.

Pratt, Nicola and Sophie Richter-Devroe (2011) (eds) 'Critically Examining UNSCR 1325', Special Issue, *International Feminist Journal of Politics*, 13: 489–611.

Pugliese, Joseph (2006) 'Asymmetries of Terror: Visual Regimes of Racial Profiling and the Shooting of Jean Charles de Menezes in the Context of the War in Iraq', *borderlands e-journal*, 5.

Rajaram, Prem Kumar and Grundy-Warr, Carl (2004) 'The Irregular Migrant as Homo Sacer: Migration and Detention in Australia, Malaysia, and Thailand', *International Migration*, 42: 33–64.

Razack, Sherene (2008) *Casting Out: The Eviction of Muslims from Western Law and Politics* (Toronto: University of Toronto Press).

Rees, Wyn and Richard J. Aldrich (2005) 'Contending Cultures of Counterterrorism: Transatlantic Divergence or Convergence?' *International Affairs*, 81: 905–923.

Reid, Julian (2012) 'The Disastrous and Politically Debased Subject of Resilience', *Development Dialogue*, 58: 67–81.

Risse-Kappen, Thomas (1996) 'Collective Identity in a Democratic Community: The Case of NATO', in Peter J. Katzenstein (ed.) *The Culture of National Security: Norms and Identity in World Politics* (New York: Columbia University Press).

Robinson, Piers, Robin Brown, Peter Goddard and Katy Parry (2005) 'War and Media', *Media, Culture & Society*, 27: 951–959.

Roe, Paul (2004) 'Securitization and Minority Rights: Conditions of Desecuritization', *Security*

Dialogue, 35: 279–294.

Rowley, Christina and Jutta Weldes (2012) 'The Evolution of International Security Studies and the Everyday: Suggestions from the Buffyverse', *Security Dialogue*, 43: 513–530.

Rumford, Chris (2008) (ed.) *Citizens and Borderwork in Contemporary Europe* (London and New York: Routledge).

—— (2012) 'Toward a Multiperspectival Study of Borders', *Geopolitics*, 17: 887–902.

Rushton, Simon (2011) 'Global Health Security: Security for Whom? Security from What?', *Political Studies*, 59: 779–796.

Said, Edward W. (2003) [1978] *Orientalism* (London: Penguin).

Salter, Mark B. (2006) 'The Global Visa Regime and the Political Technologies of the International Self: Borders, Bodies, Biopolitics', *Alternatives*, 31: 167–189.

—— (2007) 'Governmentalities of an Airport: Heterotopia and Confession', *International Political Sociology*, 1: 49–66.

—— (2011) 'The Geographical Imagination of Video Games: Diplomacy, Civilization, America's Army and Grand Theft Auto IV', *Geopolitics*, 16: 359–388.

Salter, Mark B. and Can E. Mutlu (2013) (eds) *Research Methods in Critical Security Studies: An Introduction* (London and New York: Routledge).

Saussure, Ferdinand de (1986) [1916] *Course in General Linguistics*, ed. and trans. Charles Bally (Paris: Open Court).

Schlosser, Eric (2013) *Command and Control* (London: Allen Lane).

Schmitt, Carl (2005) [1922] *Political Theology: Four Chapters on the Concept of Sovereignty*, trans. George Schwab, 3rd edn. (Chicago, IL, and London: University of Chicago Press).

Sen, Amartya K. (2000) 'Why Human Security?', online, available at: http://indh.pnud.org.co/files/rec/SenWhyHS.pdf (accessed 5 October 2009).

Shactman, Noah (2009) 'Drone "Surge": Predator Flights Up 94% in 2008', online, available at: www.wired.com/dangerroom/2009/02/drone-surge-pre/ (accessed 26 May 2009).

Shani, Giorgio (2008) 'Toward a Post-Western IR: The *Umma, Khalsa Panth*, and Critical International Relations Theory', *International Studies Review*, 10: 722–734.

Shapiro, Michael J. (1981) *Language and Political Understanding: The Politics of Discursive Practices* (New Haven: Yale University Press).

—— (1990) 'Strategic Discourse/Discursive Strategy: The Representation of "Security Policy" in the Video Age', *International Studies Quarterly*, 34: 327–340.

—— (1998) 'That Obscure Object of Violence: Logistics and Desire in the Gulf War', in David Campbell and Michael Dillon (eds) *The Political Subject of Violence* (Manchester: Manchester University Press).

Shaw, Martin (2005) *The New Western Way of War: Risk-Transfer War and its Crisis in Iraq* (Cambridge: Polity).

Sheehan, Michael (2005) *International Security: An Analytical Survey* (Boulder, CO: Lynne Rienner).

Shepherd, Laura J. (2007) '"Victims, Perpetrators and Actors" Revisited: Exploring the Potential for a Feminist Reconceptualisation of (International) Security and (Gender) Violence', *British Journal of Politics and International Relations*, 9: 239–256.

—— (2008) *Gender, Violence and Security: Discourse as Practice* (London and New York: Zed Books).

—— (2013a) (ed.) 'The State of the Discipline: A Security Studies Forum', *International Studies Perspectives*, 14: 439–462.

—— (2013b) (ed.) *Critical Approaches to Security: An Introduction to Theories and Methods* (London and New York: Routledge)

Shewly, Hosna (2013) 'Abandoned Spaces and Bare Life in the Enclaves of the India–Bangladesh Border', *Political Geography*, 32: 23–31.

Shurtleff, D. Keith (2002) 'The Effects of Technology on our Humanity', *Parameters*, Summer: 100–112.

Singer, Peter W. (2001) 'Corporate Warriors: The Rise of the Privatized Military Industry and its Ramifications for International Security', *International Security*, 26: 186–220.

Slater, David (2004) *Geopolitics and the Post-Colonial: Rethinking North–South Relations* (Oxford: Blackwell).

Slemon, Stephen (2001) 'Post-Colonial Critical Theories', in Gregory Castle (ed.), *Post-Colonial Discourses: An Anthology* (Oxford: Blackwell).

Smith, Steve (2000) 'The Increasing Insecurity of Security Studies: Conceptualizing Security in the Last Twenty Years', in Stuart Croft and Terry Terrif (eds) *Critical Reflections on Security and Change* (London: Frank Cass).

Spearin, Christopher (2003) 'American hegemony incorporated: the importance and implications of military contractors in Iraq', *Contemporary Security Policy*, 24: 26–47.

Spivak, Gayatri Chakravorty (1988) 'Can the Subaltern Speak?' in Cary Nelson and Lawrence Grossberg (eds) *Marxism and the Interpretation of Culture* (Urbana, IL: University of Illinois Press).

Steans, Jill (1998) *Gender and International Relations* (Oxford: Polity Press).

—— (2009) *Gender and International Relations: Issues, Debates, and Future Directions* (Cambridge: Polity Press).

Steele, Brent (2008) *Ontological Security in International Relations: Self-Identity and the IR State* (London and New York: Routledge).

Squire, Vicki (2011) (ed.) *The Contested Politics of Mobility: Borderzones and Irregularity* (London and New York: Routledge).

Stierl, Maurice (2012) '"No One Is Illegal!" Resistance and the Politics of Discomfort', *Globalizations*, 9: 425–438.

Stritzel, Holger (2007) 'Towards a Theory of Securitization: Copenhagen and Beyond', *European Journal of International Relations*, 13: 357–383.

Sylvester, Christine (2006) 'Bare Life as a Development/Postcolonial Problematic', *Geographical Journal*, 172: 66–77.

—— (2007) 'Anatomy of a Footnote', *Security Dialogue*, 38: 547–558.

Taureck, Rita (2006) 'Securitization Theory and Securitization Studies', *Journal of International Relations and Development*, 9: 53–61.

Thomas, Caroline (1999) 'Where is the Third World Now?' *Review of International Studies*, 25: 225–244.

—— (2000) *Global Governance, Development and Human Security* (London: Pluto Press).

—— (2002) 'Global Governance and Human Security', in Rorden Wilkinson and Steve Hughes (eds) *Global Governance: Critical Perspectives* (London: Routledge).

Thomas, Nicholas and William T. Tow (2002) 'The Utility of Human Security: Sovereignty and Humanitarian Intervention', *Security Dialogue*, 33: 177–192.

Tickner, J. Ann (1992) *Gender in International Relations: Feminist Perspectives on Achieving Global Security* (New York: Columbia University Press).

Tickner, Arelene B. and Ole Wæver (2009) *International Relations Scholarship from Around the World* (London and New York: Routledge).

Tuchman Matthews, Jessica (1989) 'Redefining Security', *Foreign Affairs*, 68: 162–177.

UN (United Nations) (1987) *Our Common Future: Report of the World Commission on Environment and Development* (New York: UN Publications).

—— (2000) *The World's Women 2000: Trends and Statistics* (New York: UN Publications).

—— (2006) *Trends in Total Migrant Stock* (New York: UN Publications).

—— (2013) *Trends in International Migration: The 2013 Revision* (New York: UN Publications).

UNDP (United Nations Development Programme) (1990) *Human Development Report* (Oxford: Oxford University Press).

—— (1994) *New Dimensions of Human Security* (New York: Oxford University Press).

van Houtum, Henk (2005) 'The Geopolitics of Borders and Boundaries', *Geopolitics*, 10: 672–679.

van Munster, Rens (2008) 'Review of Ken Booth, *Theory of World Security*', *Cambridge Review of International Affairs*, 21: 437–450.

Vasilaki, Rosa (2012) 'Provincialising IR? Deadlocks and Prospects in Post-Western IR Theory', *Review of International Studies*, 41: 3–22.

Vaughan-Williams, Nick (2007) 'The Shooting of Jean Charles de Menezes: New Border Politics?' *Alternatives: Global, Local, Political*, 32: 177–195.

—— (2009) *Border Politics: The Limits of Sovereign Power* (Edinburgh: Edinburgh University Press).

Voelkner, Nadine (2011) 'Managing Pathogenic Circulation: Human Security and the Migrant Health Assemblage in Thailand', *Security Dialogue*, 42: 239–259.

Walker, Jeremy and Cooper, Melinda (2011) 'Genealogies of Resilience: From Systems Ecology to the Political Economy of Crisis Adaptation', *Security Dialogue* 42: 143–160.

Walker, R.B.J. (1993) *Inside/Outside: International Relations as Political Theory* (Cambridge: Cambridge University Press).

Walt, Stephen (1991) 'The Renaissance of Security Studies', *International Studies Quarterly*, 35: 211–239.

Walters, William (2002) 'Mapping Schengenland: Denaturalising the Border', *Environment and Planning D*, 20: 564–580.

Waltz, Kenneth N. (1979) *Theory of International Politics* (Reading, MA: Addison-Wesley).

Watson, Scott (2012) '"Framing" the Copenhagen School: Integrating the Literature on Threat Construction', *Millennium: Journal of International Studies*, 40: 279–301.

Wæver, Ole (1995) 'Securitization and Desecuritization', in Ronnie D. Lipschutz (ed.) *On Security* (New York: Columbia University Press).

—— (1998) 'Insecurity, Security and Asecurity in the West European Non-War Community', in Emanuel Adler and Michael Barnett (eds) *Security Communities* (Cambridge: Cambridge University Press).

—— (2000) 'The EU as a Security Actor: Reflections from a Pessimistic Constructivist on Post Sovereign Security Orders', in Morton Kelstrup and Michael C. Williams (eds) *International Relations Theory and the Politics of European Integration* (London and New York: Routledge).

—— (2004) 'Aberystwyth, Paris, Copenhagen: New "Schools" in Security Theory and their Origins between Core and Periphery', paper presented at the 45th Annual Convention of the International Studies Association, Montreal, Canada, 17–20 March.

—— (2008) 'Foreword', in Miriam Dunn Cavelty and Kristian Søby Kristensen (eds) *Securing 'the Homeland': Critical Infrastructure, Risk and (In)security* (London and New York: Routledge).

Wæver, Ole, Barry Buzan, Morton Kelstrup and Pierre Lemaitre (1993) *Identity, Migration and the New Security Agenda in Europe* (London: Pinter).

Weiss, Thomas G. (1995) 'Foreword', in Mohammed Ayoob, *The Third World Security Predicament: State Making, Regional Conflict and the International System* (Boulder, CO: Lynne Rienner).

Weldes, Jutta (1999) *Constructing National Interests: The United States and the Cuban Missile Crisis* (Minnesota, MN: University of Minnesota Press).

Weldes, Jutta, Mark Laffey, Hugh Gusterson and Raymond Duvall (1999) 'Introduction: Constructing Insecurity', in Jutta Weldes, Mark Laffey, Hugh Gusterson and Raymond Duvall (eds) *Cultures of Insecurity* (Minnesota, MN: University of Minnesota Press).

Wells, Matt and Duncan Campbell (2003) 'Footage of Captives puts New Channels under Pressure from Pentagon', *Guardian*, 25 March, online, available at: www.guardian.co.uk/media/2003/mar/25/tvnews.iraqandthemedia1 (accessed 29 May 2009).

Wendt, Alexander (1992) 'Anarchy is What States Make of It: The Social Construction of Power Politics', *International Organization*, 46: 391–425.

—— (1995) 'Constructing International Politics', *International Security*, 20: 71–81.

—— (1999) *Social Theory of International Politics* (Cambridge: Cambridge University Press).

Whitaker, Brian (2003) 'Al-Jazeera Screens Gruesome Footage of Battle Casualties', *Guardian*, 24 March, online, available at: www.guardian.co.uk/Archive/Article/0,4273,4632004,00.html (accessed 29 May 2009).

WHO (World Health Organization) (2007) *A Safer Future: Global Public Health Security in the 21st Century*, Geneva: WHO.

—— (2013) *World Health Statistics 2013* (Geneva: WHO Press).

Wibben, Annick (2011) *Feminist Security Studies: A Narrative Approach* (London and New York: Routledge).

Wilkinson, Paul (2000) *Terrorism Versus Democracy: The Liberal State Response* (London: Frank Cass).

—— (2007a) 'Introduction', in Paul Wilkinson (ed.) *Homeland Security in the UK: Future Preparedness for Terrorist Attack since 9/11* (London and New York: Routledge).

—— (2007b) (ed.) *Homeland Security in the UK: Future Preparedness for Terrorist Attack since 9/11* (London and New York: Routledge).

Williams, John (2003a) 'Territorial Borders, International Ethics, and Geography: Do Good Fences still make Good Neighbours?', *Geopolitics*, 8: 25–46.

Williams, Michael C. (2003b) 'Words, Images, Enemies: Securitization and International Politics', *International Studies Quarterly*, 47: 511–531.

—— (2013) 'In the Beginning: The International Relations Enlightenment and the Ends of International Relations Theory', *European Journal of International Relations*, 19: 647–665.

Williams, Michael C. and Iver B. Neumann (2002) 'From Alliance to Security Community: NATO, Russia, and the Power of Identity', *Millennium: Journal of International Studies*, 29: 357–387.

Williams, Paul (2008) 'Security Studies, 9/11 and the Long War', in Alex Bellamy, Roland Bleiker, Sara Davies and Richard Devetak (eds) *Security and the War on Terror* (London and New York: Routledge).

Williams, Raymond (1976) *Keywords: A Vocabulary of Culture and Society* (London: Croom Helm).

Winch, Donald (1992) (ed.) *Malthus: An Essay on the Principle of Population* (Cambridge: Cambridge University Press).

Wolfers, Arnold (1952) '"National Security" as an Ambiguous Symbol', *Political Science Quarterly*, 75: 481–502.

World Resources Institute (2007) *Earth Trends: Environmental Information* (Washington, DC: World Resources Institute), online, available at: http://earthtrends.wri.org (accessed 1 May 2009).

Wyn Jones, Richard (1995) 'The Nuclear Revolution', in Alex Danchev (ed.) *Fin De Siècle: The Meaning of the Twentieth Century* (London: Taurus).

—— (1996) 'Travelling without Maps: Thinking about Security after the Cold War', in Jane Davis (ed.) *Security Issues in the Post-Cold War World* (Brookfield, VT: Edward Elgar).

—— (1999) *Security, Strategy, and Critical Theory* (Boulder, CO: Lynne Rienner).

—— (2005) 'On Emancipation, Necessity, Capacity and Concrete Utopias', in Ken Booth (ed.) *Critical Security Studies and World Politics* (Boulder, CO: Lynne Rienner).

Young, Robert J.C. (2001) *Postcolonialism: An Historical Introduction* (Oxford: Blackwell).

Zalewski, Marysia (2013) *Feminist International Relations: Exquisite Corpse* (London and New York: Routledge).

Zebrowski, Christopher (2009) 'Governing the Network Society: A Biopolitical Critique of Resilience', *Political Perspectives*, 3: 1–38.

Zehfuss, Maja (2001) 'Constructivism and Identity: A dangerous liaison', *European Journal of International Relations*, 7: 315–348.

Index